Learning for Sustainable Living

Psychology of Ecological Transformation

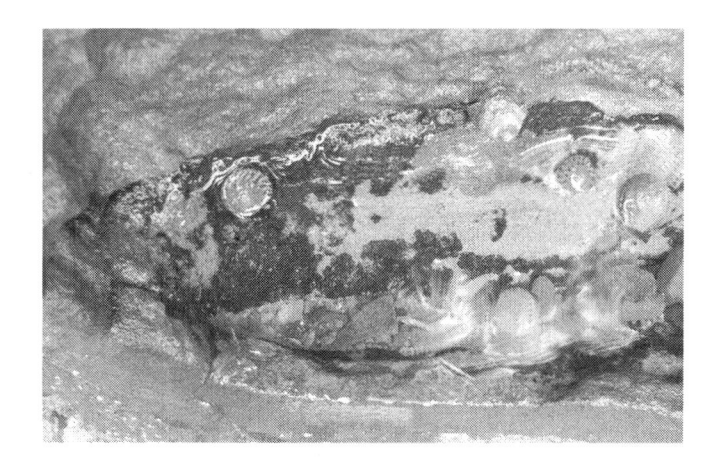

Werner J. Sattmann-Frese

Stuart B. Hill

Lulu

Lulu.com - Morrisville

Printed and bound by Lulu Enterprises, 3131, RDU Center Drive, Suite 210, Morrisville, NC 27560, USA

Sattmann-Frese, Werner J & Hill, Stuart B: Learning for *Sustainable Living: Psychology of Ecological Transformation*, Morrisville: Lulu.com, 2008

© Werner Sattmann-Frese and Stuart Hill, 2008

All rights reserved. No part of this book may be reproduced, in any form or by any means, without permission in writing from the authors.

Printed in the USA

ISBN 978 – 1 – 4092 – 5102 – 6

An online learning program associated with this book is available at www.lfsl.com.au

Book Description

With the election of Barack Obama to become the 44th president of the United States of America, billions of people worldwide are now holding out hope that the new Administration will be committed to creating a saner and more sustainable society. Yet, he will only be able to institute the promised changes if he can forge a "Coalition of the Willing" of millions of people ready to further develop their abilities to lead emotionally, psychosocially, and environmentally sustainable lives.

Acknowledging that the consumption-driven economic boom of recent years, and growing debt crisis, have prevented us from orchestrating the urgently needed economic downshift, the current economic downturn – brought on mainly by greed and the resulting disproportionate distribution of income and wealth within and between nations – now challenges us to clarify our values concerning what it means to have a meaningful, satisfying, and sustainable life.

What we must resist is imagining that we can revert back to the kind of boom economy that we are just leaving behind. Rather it will be a sign of positive progress if we can emotionally conceptualize the emerging recession (or depression) not just as an ecologically necessary economic downturn, but more hopefully as an opportunity to pave the way for a more sustainable society, one in which we can ALL be enabled to have a much smaller and sustainable ecological footprint.

Considering that the current downturn is not the result of orchestrated political and social efforts, but rather of unsustainable economic and other societal structures, bringing about this shift in consciousness is likely to be a complex and challenging process. Despite this, we believe that our willingness to re-examine our values and habits can enable us to gain in consciousness and wellbeing what we may loose in monetary wealth.

This book has been written to provide a theoretical framework and practical tools to enable all of us to play effective roles in this transformation process. Together with an associated learning program – available at www.lfsl.com.au – it explores the complex psychological underpinnings of our ecological crises and outlines the steps involved in changing from the currently dominating growth and consumption-driven ego-self consciousness towards a wellness, maintenance, and relationship-oriented eco-self consciousness. Integrating the work of many well-known psychologically aware ecologists and educators, we outline the key features of an interdisciplinary, holistic, and ecopsychologically aware approach to the kind of sustainability education that can help us achieve personal wellbeing and sustainable ecological change.

Werner J. Sattmann-Frese, MAppSc, PhD

Werner Sattmann-Frese studied conventional medicine and body-oriented psychotherapy from 1977 until 1984. Since then he has been working as a psychotherapist mainly in private practice. Since 1992 he has also been supervising psychotherapists and training students in psychotherapy, psychosomatic medicine, and holistic bodywork.

Werner attained his PhD in Social Ecology in 2006 at the University of Western Sydney for a research project on the interrelationships between personal, social, and environmental sustainability. In private practice as a psychotherapist and supervisor, he also presents workshops on holistic perspectives of ecological crises for environmentalists and health professionals, and works as a sessional lecturer and tutor at the School of Biomedical and Health Sciences and the School of Management at the University of Western Sydney.

Stuart B. Hill

Professor Stuart B. Hill is Foundation Chair of Social Ecology at the University of Western Sydney.

Prior to 1996 he was at McGill University, in Montreal, where he was responsible for the zoology degree and where in 1974 he established Ecological Agriculture Projects, Canada's leading resource centre for sustainable agriculture (www.eap.mcgill.ca).

He has published over 350 papers and reports. His latest book (with Martin Mulligan) is *Ecological Pioneers: A Social History of Australian Ecological Thought and Action*, Cambridge UP, 2001.

In Canada he was a member of over 30 regional, national and international boards and committees. He is currently on the editorial board of five international refereed journals, and until 2004 he represented professional environmental educators on the NSW Council on Environmental Education.

Stuart has worked in agricultural and development projects in the West Indies, French West Africa, Indonesia, The Philippines, China, and the Seychelles, as well as in the UK, Canada, New Zealand, and Australia.

His background in chemical engineering, ecology, soil biology, entomology, agriculture, psychotherapy, education, policy development and international development, and his experience of working with transformative change, have enabled him to be an effective facilitator in complex situations that demand both collaboration across difference and a long-term co-evolutionary approach to situation improvement.

Dr Werner Sattmann-Frese
Sustainable Living for a Sustainable Earth (SLSE)
PO Box 4051
Wagstaffe, NSW 2257, Australia
E-mail: slse@bigpond.net.au
www.slse.edu.au

Professor Stuart Hill
University of Western Sydney
Locked Bag 1797
South Penrith DC
NSW 1797, Australia
E-Mail: s.hill@uws.edu.au

Contents

Contents vi

List of Tables ix

List of Figures x

Foreword xi

Preface xiii

Acknowledgments xvii

Introduction 1

1   The Project 13

   Aims and limitations of this study 16
   Methodology 18
   Towards an alternative approach 29
   Philosophical background 34
   Psychological background 43

2   Notions on Consciousness and Self 50

   Notions on Consciousness 50
   Notions of 'self' 57
   Aspects of ego-self consciousness 62

3   Manipulated Eco-self Consciousness (Stage One) 66

   Problems with distinguishing between behaviourist and cognitive psychology 66
   The nature of manipulated eco-self consciousness 67
   Behavioural technologies used to foster sustainable behaviours 68
   Benefits of behaviourist interventions 70

4   Learned Eco-self Consciousness (Stage Two) 72

   Cognitive psychology 72
   Learning eco-self consciousness 72
   Benefits of an approach based on cognition and learning 74

5   Participatory Eco-self Consciousness (Stage 3) 76

   Education for Sustainability (EFS) 76
   The notion of participatory eco-self consciousness 76

Benefits of education for sustainability 77
Education for Sustainable Development 80
Education for Sustainable Development 80
Comparing education for sustainable development and education for sustainability 81

6 **Deep Eco-Consciousness (Stage 4) 83**

Key concepts of depth psychology 83
Our search for emotional identity, happiness, freedom, and belonging 89
A defence mechanism perspective of ecological crises 92
An object relations and character structure approach to ecological psychology 103
Ecological crises and the oral-exploiting condition 109
Ecological crises and the narcissistic-shaming condition 114

7 **Holistic Eco-self Consciousness (Stage 5) 126**

Epistemology 127
Metaphors of unsustainable living 132
The separation metaphor 133
The pollution/waste metaphor 140
The growth/excess metaphor 144
The exhaustion metaphor 148

8 **Person-planet Unity Consciousness (Stage 6) 155**

Six person-planet unity experiences 156
Issues of transpersonal psychology 158
Traumas and loss of person-planet unity 161
Cosmic consciousness 163
Person-planet unity and energy 165
Redefining object-relations theory 167
The schizoid-rejecting condition and the natural environment 169
The schizoid condition and terrorism 175

9 **Placing the Six-stage Model in Larger Frameworks 185**

Linear and Circular Models of Consciousness Transformation 185
From education towards change towards an enabling of sustainable living 188
Deep and shallow change 193

Limitations of approaches to change based on behaviourist psychology 198
Limitations of a cognitive approach to environmental change 203
Depth psychology and postmodern environmental education 207
Critique of aspects of constructive postmodernism 215
Ecological psychotherapies 220

10 **From Sustainable Development to Sustainable Living 225**

Sustainability and sustainable development 225
Aspects of sustainable living 230
Sustainability indicators 234
Sustainable living through downshifting 244

11 **Learning for Sustainable Living (LfSL) 251**

Ecological approaches underpinning LfSL 251
Objectives of Learning for Sustainable Living 259
Features of LfSL 262
Sustainability policies and 'sustainology' 264

12 **Summary and Conclusion 270**

Appendix A – Summary of Research Findings 279

Appendix B – Learning for Sustainable Living Programme 286

References 292

Index 318

List of Tables

Table 1.1	Topics relating to a holistic versus a mechanistic worldview 30
Table 2.1	Aspects of ego-self and eco-self 62
Table 3.1	Behaviourist approaches to change 68
Table 5.1	Modern versus deconstructionist postmodern psychology 78
Table 5.2	Cognitive modern versus cognitive postmodern education foci 79
Table 5.3	Assumed causes of ecological deterioration (modern versus deconstructionist postmodern) 80
Table 5.4	Emphasised aspects of change (modern versus deconstructionist) 81
Table 6.1	Psychological comparison between coloniser and colonised 124
Table 7.1	Exoteric and esoteric/holistic principles 131
Table 7.2	Aspects of the separation metaphor 140
Table 7.3	Aspects of the wastefulness/pollution metaphor 144
Table 7.4	Aspects of the growth/excess metaphor 148
Table 7.5	Aspects of the exhaustion metaphor 152
Table 7.6	Body-mind and person-planet synergies and compensatory structures 153
Table 8.1	Comparison between the disconnected and the integrated child 173
Table 9.1	Comparison of deconstructionist and depth psychology values 210
Table 9.2	Comparing environmental education based on a mechanistic, postmodern, ecological, and depth psychology worldview 211
Table 9.3	Theoretical framework, schools of thought, and aims of postmodern, cognitive psychology and depth psychology 212
Table 9.4	Assumptions concerning causes of environmental degradation 213
Table 9.5	Strategies for supporting behavioural change 213
Table 9.6	Comparison of deconstructionist, Spretnak's ecological postmodernism and an ecology based on depth psychology and transpersonal psychology 215
Table 10.1	Issues relating to health (added features appear in italics) 241
Table 10.2	Issues relating to education 241
Table 10.3	Issues relating to births and childrearing (Added features appear in italics) 242
Table 10.4	Issues relating to relationships (added features appear in italics) 242
Table 10.6	Physio-emotional sustainability testing questions 243
Table 10.7	Environmental sustainability testing questions 243

Table 11.1 Examples of sustainable and unsustainable structures 267
Table 11.2 Knowledges underpinning ESD and LfSL 268
Table 11.3 Objectives of ESD and LfSL 268
Table 11.4 Means to achieve ESD and LfSL 268
Table 11.5 Foci of ESD and LfSL 268
Table 11.6 Issues facilitated by ESD and LfSL 269
Table 11.7 Issues promoted by ESD and LfSL 269

List of Figures

Figure 1.1 The unconscious is really unconscious 24
Figure 1.2 Happiness and spending money 26
Figure 9.1 System on different levels of sustainability 189
Figure 9.2 System surrounded by resistance walls 189
Figure 9.3 System on three of the possible six stages 190
Figure 9.4 Forces acting at a point of crisis 193
Figure 9.5 Schematic distribution of consciousness among modern people 195
Figure 9.6 Schematic distribution of consciousness achieved through Education for Sustainable Development 195
Figure 9.7 Schematic distribution of consciousness achieved through Education for Sustainable Living 196
Figure 11.1 Sustainability Mapping Process 261

Foreword

The social sciences in general have been noted for their failure to acknowledge the human body as significant in their desire to master the arts of cognition and behaviour.

Even more outside the scope of most social science approaches to counselling and psychology has been an acknowledgment of the role played by ecology both in shaping and as result of the pain and suffering of the disordered mind.

It would seem that body focused and eco-aware approaches in this field remain in the alternative stream of unacknowledged or to be avoided ways of offering help in human pain and disorganization. I suspect in this we are confronted by a deep-seated fear, particularly by those who hold power, of the turbulent forces that rage beneath the cognitive covering of the Cartesian split.

Werner Sattmann-Frese's and Stuart Hill's work challenges these limiting protocols of our age by bringing a multi-leveled eco-awareness to our current Global dilemma. Our physical environment becomes a profound expression of the conflicts raging in the depths of our psychosomatic being.

The exciting part of this book for me is the careful hierarchical layering from the simplistic assumptions of behavioural psychology through the cognitive to the deeper realisations that have come with the postmodern and the somatic awarenesses that shape our ecological frameworks.

The authors demonstrate how "key aspects of our ecological crises are predictable outcomes of stalled self development with its associated body-mind splits" and point to the prevailing character structures that need the most attention if global action is to bring true change.

Drawing on the resource of many disciplines, Werner and Stuart bring some unique gifts and history to this task. Werner's training in medicine, body-focused psychotherapy, and social ecology, and Stuart's training and experience as an ecologist and psychotherapist and his long academic career culminating in his appointment as the Foundation Chair in Social Ecology at the University of Western Sydney, bring a deep ecological awareness to their teachings and practices. Their depth of experience across three continents brings a challenge to traditional therapeutic thinking, whereas their research highlights the value but severe limitation of most of the current pathways to healing of modern society.

Werner and Stuart provide a developmental framework that will add greatly to the work of counsellors and therapists from all schools as well as to professionals in the fields of community work and environmental and sustainability education.

I will be using this work to reflect and influence my therapeutic practice over the coming years and trust it will gain a wide and readership.

Rev. Doug Sotheren

Body Focused Relationship Therapist

Preface

The year 2007 might become known in future as the year in which even leading neoliberal politicians had to acknowledge the harmful effects of global warming on the natural environment and the living conditions of human and other-than-human beings. It might also become known as the year in which many of us, including environmental scientists suspicious of the concept of global warming, finally had to acknowledge how little we really know about the ecological processes taking place in nature. In their article *Race Against the Clock,* Wendy Frew and Stephanie Peatling write:

> Last year a series of lakes formed on the vast body of ice that covers most of Greenland. Acting like a lubricant, the water quickly made its way to the base of the ice sheet, forcing giant slabs of ice to rise, then slide into the ocean. The speed at which the ice broke off shocked many scientists. "We used to think that it would take 10,000 years for melting at the surface of an ice sheet to penetrate down to the bottom. Now we know it doesn't take 10,000 years; it takes 10 seconds", says Richard Alley, a professor of geosciences at Pennsylvania State University (SMH, 3-4 February, 2007, p. 25).

Much of the scientific evidence discussed at the recent Intergovernmental Panel on Climate Change shows that the effects of climate change are far more severe than previously expected. Mountain glaziers are currently shrinking three times faster than they did in the 1980s, sea levels are rising faster than predicted, the world's major fisheries are threatened due to changes in ocean currents, and more heat waves, wild storms, and water scarcity in many areas of this planet will make the lives of an increasing number of people more difficult in the decades to come.

These latest findings are indeed alarming, and alarmed we should be. Yet, according to Clive Hamilton of the Australia Institute, even these facts are already outdated, and some important research has not even been included because it is too controversial. In other words, the psychological defence mechanism of denial that keeps preventing us, both as individuals and as a society, from facing the true magnitude of our ecological predicament is alive and well. As Doctor Graeme Pearman put it recently in his response to ABC's Kerry O'Brien who asked: *"As one of the leading scientists in this field over a long period of time, what are the words that come closest to your mood now, as a result of reading the report? Alarm? Depression? Hope"?*

I think it's probably a degree of depression and I think it comes out of the fact that this report, all of us who have been in this field have worked in this field hoping that someone would find that we were wrong and that isn't the case, it's just simply confirming what we have thought was the issue and what was the problem over a long period of time and as I say, secondly, it's the issue of whether human societies - not any one government, not any one country but human societies in general - have the capacity to respond to a major threat of this kind in a timely fashion and at the moment, I am not clear we are going to have that. (www.abc. net.au/ 7.30/ content/ 2007/ s1839403.htm)

His hunch is likely to be correct. If the results of climate change research mentioned above are bad news, the results of psychological research on our capacity to deal with our ecological predicament are probably worse. In this book, Sattmann-Frese and Hill will show that currently the majority of people living in so-called civilised societies lack the emotional maturity to adequately address our pressing ecological problems. Whereas a minority of us is trying hard to lead ecologically sustainable lives and to contribute towards creating a more sustainable society, the majority of us still continue to behave like gambling addicts sitting mesmerised in front of gaming machines. Pushing away any nagging thoughts about the destructive effects of their addictive habit, we are fascinated by the excitement of the possibility of 'winning a free lunch'. Of course, as gamblers usually destroy their lives, and often the lives of their next of kin, our addictive need to shore up self-support through the unsustainable consumption of non-essential goods and services is now threatening our home, the Earth.

This book addresses the pressing issues of psychosocial and ecological deterioration by examining their background from the perspectives of depth psychology, holistic thinking, and transpersonal psychology. Based on a doctoral research project, it argues for the necessity for an accelerated transition from our current state of consciousness—here called egocentred consciousness—towards advanced levels of eco-self consciousness. We believe that this radical transformation of consciousness will be dependent on our willingness to:

- overcome the view that the health of the natural environment can be separated from the health and wellbeing of humans and other living beings;

- conceptualise the meaningful interdependencies between personal, social, and environmental issues; and
- embed ecopsychological theories and practices in our community work and health provision practices.

Believing that humans have a built-in capacity and desire to heal and that deep change is possible, in this book we make a case for developing a holistic understanding of the interdependencies between manifestations of unsustainable living, such as AIDS, cancer, exploitation, terrorism, ecological deterioration, and others. We also emphasise that the transition from our current dominant ego-consciousness towards an advanced level of eco-consciousness has to address these manifestations by embedding them in the educational aspects of community development. Jim Ife (2002) writes about this topic:

> Despite the formidable achievements of modern, Western, industrialized society, it has become clear that the current social, economic and political order has been unable to meet two of the most basic prerequisites of human civilisation: the need for people to be able to live in harmony with their environment, and the need for them to be able to live in harmony with each other. If these two needs cannot be met, in the long term, the achievements and benefits of modern society will be transitory (2002, p. xi).

Yet, the ongoing efforts of millions of us demonstrate that change is possible, in particular when we accept that we have to change at a personal level. If we fail to achieve these deep social and environmental changes in the foreseeable future, our fate would indeed not to be determined by our conscious actions but by:

- wars over resources perceived as scarce, such as oil, water and a shrinking land surface;
- the psychological effects of emotional and social exploitation of increasing numbers of people both in developing and developed nations;
- food insecurities resulting from loss of topsoil, lack of water for irrigation, and control over seeds;
- infectious illnesses afflicting the ones among us who have not learned to lead psychosocially and physio-emotionally sustainable lives;

- the effects of environmental health hazards, such as air, water, soil and electromagnetic pollution, including the effects of the unfettered use of mobile phones; and
- an increasing number of environmental catastrophes, such as severe draughts, floods, landslides, and violent storms.

We consequently argue that the achievement of a healthy and sustainable social and natural environment will be dependent on the efforts of large numbers of individuals to achieve advanced levels of ecological consciousness as well as on our willingness as communities to protect the environment through legislation, information, manipulated behaviour change, and technological innovation. Filling a niche in the emerging body of ecopsychology publications, we believe that this book will make a significant contribution to the mutually influencing factors and complex interdependencies between emotional, social, and ecological aspects of sustainable living.

Acknowledgments

The creation of this book would not have been possible without the qualified and passionate support of other people.

We feel indebted to Dr John Cameron for his unwavering dedication to Social Ecology at the University of Western Sydney, to Kathy Adams, and to staff and students at Social Ecology for maintaining a stimulating and sane environment within an unsustainable modern culture.

We would also like to express our gratefulness to the research participants for sharing their insights into their struggles with becoming more sustainable people, and to Associate Professor Daniella Tilbury at Macquarie University, Sydney, for her suggestion to integrate the depth psychology perspectives on ecological deterioration with the change strategies employed in the various approaches to environmental education. Doug Sotheren, Judith McCreath, Roy Garner, Anny James, and Barbara Hasslacher deserve recognition for their assistance in editing this manuscript and associated brochures and conference material, whereas Claus Bargmann, Tony Carrigan, Alan Isherwood, and Norbert Schrauth deserve our appreciation for their support and challenging questions.

We would like to express our gratefulness to Professor Deborah DuNann Winter, Dr Sarah A. Conn, and Dr Allen D. Kanner for examining the doctoral thesis on which this book is based and for their generous, scholarly, and supportive comments.

Last, but not least, we are grateful to our partners Lisa Frese and Judy Pinn for putting up with our obsession with facilitating deep social and ecological change.

Introduction

After more than forty years of caring for the natural environment – if we define the publication of Rachel Carson's book, *Silent Spring*, as the beginning of environmentalism – humankind is more than ever facing a scenario of "confusing, paralysing complexity" (Hill, 2003a). On the one hand, there has undoubtedly been great progress in some parts of the world in areas such as fuel-efficiency of cars, waste control, pollution reduction, water quality, and biodiversity. Many countries are now enforcing environmental protection laws, many contaminated areas have been cleaned up, and the level of knowledge in the public on ecological issues has risen dramatically. All these improvements have led many environmentalists to believe and argue that the ecological state of the world is improving, and that all we have to do is to more vigorously enforce the change practices that are already in place.

Acid rain on increase in China
More of China's cities are suffering from acid rain and its big rivers and lakes are heavily polluted, the government said in a report that highlighted the environmental costs of surging economic growth. It said acid rain – blamed on smoke from coal-burning factories and power plants – is spreading, with 218 cities suffering from severe levels (*The Guardian Weekly*, Volume 172, No 25, p. 2).

Yet, social ecologists, deep ecologists, and other radical environmentalists are not so sure about this progress. Many argue that such a positive assessment relies on a narrow range of sustainability indicators, and that our positive outlook changes drastically if we include in our equation social factors such as community health, drug addiction, alcohol consumption, suicide statistics, and issues relating to social equity. In other words, these people suggest that the improvements in some areas are being outweighed by a concurrent deterioration of sustainability in many other areas of our lives. The continuing deterioration of the natural environment, marked, for example, by the sharp increase in electromagnetic pollution ('electrosmog') and the worsening political, ecological, and psychosocial effects caused by the re-emergence of imperial enterprises, suggest that the overall quality of living may in fact be declining.

Considering that it is easy to include certain sustainability indicators in statistics, and to exclude others, it appears that few people acknowledge the vastness and complexity of the predicament our planet and its inhabitants are currently facing, and fewer still seem to show an interest in identifying the underlying causes that have led to the continuing deterioration of our living conditions. With the exception of the radical ecologists, most environmentalists continue to either monitor our extinction (Hill, 2000) or work on projects that, although they might improve local sustainability, often fail to address the deep emotional and psychosocial dysfunctions that underpin our ecological crises.

The continuing ecological deterioration has been marked by a general trend of conservative governments taking office in many countries. This trend continues to result in significant rollbacks of recent environmental achievements. In relation to the USA, Pope and Rauber (2004, p. 22) remark:

> History and opportunity thus combined to strip American conservatism of the sunny optimism of Goldwater and Reagan, and led it to abandon even George H. W. Bush's promise of a "kinder, gentler America." The harsh new ethos that came to dominate the Bush administration was a modern variant of social Darwinism, the ideology of the nineteenth-century robber barons.

In their book, these authors provide examples of the achievements that are now being rolled back, such as the decline of smog in Los Angeles and the decline of the emission of toxic chemicals by nearly 50 per cent between 1988 and 1996. A list of the present rollback of achievements fills several pages of Pope's and Rauber's (2004, pp. 241–242) book, and includes issues such as the following:

- Bush seeks to open Arctic National Wildlife Refuge to oil development (01/20/01);
- Bush appoints industry apologist John Graham as regulatory gatekeeper (03/06/01);
- Bush Administration seeks to roll back Roadless Area Conservation Plan (03/16/01);
- Bush Administration rejects Kyoto Protocol on global warming (03/28/01); and
- Bush seeks to relax requirements of Endangered Species Act (04/09/01).

These five political manoeuvres, which took place between January and April 2001, are just representative of hundreds of manoeuvres by the USA

Administration aimed at undermining and rolling back past efforts to make the USA a healthier and more sustainable place to live and work. The beneficiaries of these rollbacks are in most cases corporations and property developers, which have been enabled to increase their profits at the expense of the wellbeing of humans and the other-than-human[1] environment.

Such examples suggest that environmentalism is sliding into a deeper crisis. The efforts of millions of people to improve sustainability are being sabotaged by such large-scale rollbacks at the highest levels of government. The result is that the living conditions for most people on this planet are still deteriorating. Furthermore, some have argued that after the events on 9/11, because of a shift in focus from the environment to the so-called 'war on terrorism', our relationship with the natural environment has dramatically worsened. It is now generally acknowledged that:

- glaciers are melting because of global warming;
- sea levels are rising, leading to increasing devastation of low-lying areas, particularly coralline islands, with all its psychosocial and economic consequences;
- deforestation and desertification are continuing on a large scale;
- access to fertile soil is being further reduced; and
- in many regions, potable water is becoming scarcer.

An inclusive list of sustainability indicators would also acknowledge issues of ecological deterioration, such as:

- a sharply increasing inequality between poor and wealthy people in many parts of the world;
- the increasing control over seed production by petrochemical and biotechnology multinationals, with the effect that the diversity of vegetable varieties has been dramatically reduced (cf. O'Sullivan 1999, p. 114);
- the increasing transnational globalisation continues to create a growing underclass of the working poor, of dispossessed and disfranchised people (cf. O'Sullivan, 1999; Nozick, 1992);
- an increasing decline in job security leading to growing chronic fear and a rise in the number of suicides, particularly of middle-aged men (SMH 23/11/2004);

---

[1] Although the term 'more-than-human' is used in the literature, we have used what we believe to be a more neutral term, 'other-than-human'.

- an increase in religious fundamentalism;
- a continuing shift from a society of citizens to a society of consumers (O'Sullivan, 2003); and
- a downward trend in civic engagement and volunteerism (cf. Cox, 2000; Putnam, 2000).

Between 1992 and 2002, that is, between the World Summits on Sustainable Development in Rio de Janeiro and Johannesburg:

- in the USA, the discrepancy in salaries between chief executive officers of large corporate companies and average wages rose from 40 times the average wage to 531 times the average wage;
- the world lost another 10 per cent of its forests;
- the extinction of mammals continued to rise such that now 24 per cent of all known mammals are extinct; and
- the number of people needing food aid further increased.

Kals (1996), for example, notes that in Germany some minor impairments of the ecological environment have been reduced through protective measures, but that major and more long-lasting damage to the environment is still increasing. The situation is likely to be very similar in many other parts of the world. In Australia, and many other First-World countries, politicians are increasingly unable to withstand the pressures by industry and other stakeholders, and are making decisions that prioritise job creation, increased dividends for shareholders, and expansion of our economy over more fundamental environmental and psychosocial concerns. If governments regard sustainability as an important issue at all, they prefer to adopt what has been called a 'weak sustainability' as their preferred *modus operandi* (cf. Naess, 1973; Sessions, 1985).

Degradation of the natural environment is continuing, despite the fact we now have ample knowledge of ecological problems. We know that we must:

- not take more from nature than we can give back;
- buy local products to minimise the use of resources for transportation;
- use public transport whenever possible;
- move from a consumer to a conserver society (Trainer, 1995);
- first repair goods before we replace them; and
- constantly be aware of our impact on the natural environment.

Knowing what we must do leaves us with the problem of finding out how we can ensure that we change our actual behaviour to match this knowledge. Although we have attained a deep understanding of many key environmental issues, we still are not able to answer the three questions posed by Kanner and Gomes (1995, pp. 78-79), who ask:

> [...] Why is [the] fantasy of effortless consuming so attractive? Why is it that when environmentalists speak of the need to reduce consumption they arouse such intense anxiety, depression, rage, and even panic? Why is the consumer way of life nonnegotiable?

The response to these questions by most conventional environmental educators has been to disseminate even more knowledge on environmental degradation. Yet, just disseminating such knowledge on the ecological functioning of our planet and its deterioration will not enable us to achieve deep sustainability. Theorists such as Finger (1994) and Lubell (2002) hold that there is only scant evidence of a causal link between environmental knowledge and appropriate action.

In this present study, the continuing degradation of our overall living conditions, briefly outlined in this introduction, is addressed by making meaning of our ecological crises from the perspectives of depth psychology, holism, psychosomatics, and transpersonal psychology. A number of people have already published important work on many aspects of these fields. These include Roszak (1973, 1975, 1981, 2001), Shepard (1982), Winter, (1996), Metzner (1986, 1999), Kanner and Gomes (1995), Hill (1992, 1999b, 1999c), Conn (1995), Wilber (1983, 1996, 1997, 2000a, 2000b), Fox (1990), Kidner (2001), Fisher (2002) and other scholars who have moved in their thinking beyond the currently dominant behaviourist and cognitive paradigms. In diverse yet complimentary ways, these scholars have described what is commonly referred to as a crisis of the ego-self. They also have highlighted the need to replace our currently limited self-perception with a wider and more integrated and transpersonal perception of self, and some of these scholars have suggested that our ecological predicament is to a high degree the result of four key metaphors. These metaphors, according to Metzner (1995, p. 59), relate to arrested development, autism, addiction, and collective amnesia. They will be explored in more detail within a character-analytical context in Chapters 6, 7 and 8.

The research initially undertaken for this study builds on the work of the abovementioned scholars by integrating it with the notions of sustainability and sustainable development currently used by most environmentalists and environmental educators. These insights gained from an extensive literature review complement the findings obtained from a survey with a small number of research participants, the majority of which are leaders in the fields of body-oriented and process-oriented psychotherapy who have an interest in ecological concerns. The analysis of these views on ecological concerns suggested that it may be helpful to conceive of the transformation from an ego-self to a fully realised eco-self as a six-stage process.

It is expected that this integration will not only enhance our understanding of the complex emotional, psychosocial, and political scenarios that are still causing psychosocial and environmental deterioration, but also enable environmentalists to develop new educational and social-change tools for their work towards ecological sustainability.

The understanding of the world promoted by the abovementioned scholars, which is placed here in the wider context of environmental education, represents a radical departure from the current dominant practice of seeking to solve problems by mainly addressing their symptoms. It suggests that our ecological crises need to be made redundant by healing the underlying conditions, and by achieving a high level of eco-self consciousness among the population. This understanding also suggests that our ecological crises are not problems to be solved and managed, but rather challenges to heal ourselves for the benefit of humans and the other-than-human environment.

Note on Writing Style

This book comprises 12 chapters, a reference list, and an index. The chapters are divided into segments, which, in turn, are logically subdivided into headings and topics. Unlike books on technical subjects that are usually constructed by using passive voice and by refraining from using the 'We', we have chosen in this study to use the We-form where it improves readability. This will be mainly at the beginning and conclusion of each chapter and segment.

We also wish to justify our decision to take a 'bird's eye' approach to research by focusing on the synergies and analogies between the various manifestations of our ecological crises, rather than on extensive elaborations on the manifestations themselves. Although the study is broad, in that it embraces a large part of the field of ecological crises, we also believe that it achieves depth by embracing the subject with an epistemology designed to deliver deep insights into many of the root causes of our ecological degradation.

It should also be noted that the focus of this book has not been on examining and discussing the distinctions between the various approaches to environmental and social change, and by doing so fostering discord rather than integration. Rather, our aim of has been to make a significant contribution towards a deeper understanding of our world's ecological crises, and to place the positive aspects of the existing theories and practices within this extended framework, thereby enabling genuine progress to be made.

Overview

Synopses of the 12 chapters are provided below:

Chapter 1: The Project

In this chapter, we explore ways of making sense of our ecological crises, outline underlying assumptions, and outline the parameters of this study. We also define the scientific framework, highlight the need to employ a transpersonal research approach, and describe the research methodology and the philosophical and psychological epistemology employed in this study. The particular philosophical disciplines that will be applied to deepen our understanding of the complex nature of our ecological crises and of sustainable living include social ecology, phenomenology, perspectivism, hermeneutics, ecological philosophy, and relational and esoteric thinking.

The key psychological disciplines used by various authors to deepen our understanding of environmental concerns include:

- behaviourist psychology
- cognitive psychology
- environmental psychology
- postmodern psychology
- depth psychology
- transpersonal psychology
- psychosomatic/holistic psychology

Chapter 2: Notions of Consciousness and Self

In this chapter, we provide an outline of some important models of consciousness, views on the notion 'self' relevant to this study, and a brief synopsis of key aspects of our Western hegemonic experience of ego-self consciousness.

Chapter 3: Manipulated Eco-Self Consciousness (Stage 1)

At this point of the discussion, we present a comprehensive description of what is conceptualised in this study as the first stage of an eco-self consciousness transformation. This level of consciousness, called here 'manipulated eco-self consciousness', is based on the application of behaviourist technologies now used by behaviourally informed environmentalists to influence people to adopt more environmentally sustainable behaviours. In the chapter we also briefly describe these technologies and examine their usefulness when viewed from within the behaviourist paradigm.

Chapter 4: Learned Eco-Self Consciousness (Stage 2)

Here we describe a form of consciousness based on the notions of learning, perception, and knowledge, and the processing, storage, and retrieval of information. Environmental education and education for sustainable development – disciplines based largely on cognitive psychology – assume that sustainable development and sustainability can be achieved by:

- changing our behaviour through provision of knowledge and insights into ecological issues;
- teaching people to use practices such as recycling, the wise use of resources, etc.
- applying a social-reformist approach to ecological change
- continuing to work within the paradigm of economic growth
- applying a technological approach to ecology that promises quick fixes;
- teaching students about ecological issues without questioning the values of modernity;
- applying an approach to environmental education based on cognition and conventional science
- using an approach to education that is discipline-based, that works with abstract and theoretical problems, and that stays within the paradigm of conventional modern schooling;
- teaching environmental education in schools and by using teachers primarily as dispensers of factual knowledge, and by
- using predefined curricula based on the work of professionals committed to research that employs the conventional scientific paradigm.

Chapter 5: Participatory Eco-Self Consciousness (Stage 3)

Here we conceptualise a postmodern approach to environmental education (education for sustainability) as the third stage of my proposed framework for self-transformation. Education for sustainability goes beyond other approaches to environmental education by:

- addressing our general crisis of modernity;
- focusing on a critique of the notion of right or wrong information;
- emphasising the economic, social, political and cultural underpinnings of our ecological crises; and by
- proposing process-oriented, interdisciplinary, and empowering attitudes and practices in environmental and sustainability education.

This deconstructionist, postmodern approach to environmental education has produced a learning environment that enables students to focus on local agendas and learn about the natural environment in an experiential and self-empowering manner.

Chapter 6: Deep Eco-Consciousness (Stage 4)

In this chapter, we describe stage four of the model of self-transformation. The focus at this stage of consciousness transformation is on broadening and deepening our understanding of our ecological crises from a number of depth psychology perspectives. At this level of consciousness, we conceptualise that many key aspects of our ecological crises are predictable outcomes of stalled self-development, with its associated body-mind splits, typically experienced by people living in both modern and deconstructionist postmodern societies. This lack of self-development is commonly encountered in cultural environments that neglect the essential needs for emotional safety, adequate nurturing, body contact, and mirroring.

Chapter 7: Holistic Eco-Self Consciousness (Stage 5)

Here we describe stage five of the proposed six-stage system of self-transformation. Key aspects of ecological degradation are perceived as manifestations of the dominant egocentric consciousness experienced in Western societies. Whereas conventional environmentalism focuses mainly on issues such as air and water pollution, waste control, greenhouse emissions, loss of biodiversity, salinisation, and population control, a holistic and perspectivist view of our ecological crises suggests that ecological issues such as psychosomatic illnesses, new colonialist adventures, and terrorism are predictable manifestations of the currently dominant level of egocentric consciousness. The metaphors of separation, pollution/waste, growth/excess, and exhaustion are used to examine the synergies between these aspects of our ecological crises, and as a logical continuation of this undertaking. The notion of sustainability is explored in its physio-emotional, psychosocial, environmental, and institutional aspects.

Chapter 8: Person-Planet Unity Consciousness (Stage 6)

In this chapter we describe the 'last' stage in my proposed system of self-transformation, which we call person-planet unity consciousness. In this stage we expand our consciousness by moving beyond intellectual meaning-making and construct worldviews based on a felt sense and direct experience of person-planet unity.

In this chapter, we also present the last of three distressed character structures that we believe need to be recognised when constructing a holistic understanding of our ecological crises. This structure, called here the schizoid-terrorising condition, is at the heart of our difficulty in experiencing a felt sense of person-planet unity, and prevents us from experiencing a simultaneousness of personal and transpersonal, self-experiences. The chapter concludes with a depth psychology interpretation of the phenomenon of terrorism, a phenomenon that, together with imperial state terrorism, is currently a major source of ecological degradation and unsustainable living for many people worldwide.

Chapter 9: Placing the Six-Stage Model in Larger Frameworks

In this chapter, we explore the relevance of the six-stage model of consciousness transformation in relation to some existing systems of cultural development. We also examine the limitations of approaches to change based on behaviourism, cognitive, and postmodern psychologies, and present a critical examination of some of the concepts held by deep ecologists, ecofeminists and postmodern environmentalists.

Chapter 10: From Sustainable Development to Sustainable Living

Here we examine a number of important limitations of the currently dominant concept of sustainable development, and formulate key issues of the more inclusive notion of sustainable living. The triple-bottom-line (economic, social, and environmental) approach to sustainability is modified by emphasising physio-emotional, psychosocial, environmental, and institutional sustainability. Sustainability indicators and objectives are critically reviewed, and the currently used ESD indicator framework is significantly enhanced by proposing that new sets of indicators be included in its social sustainability section.

This chapter concludes with my proposal to conceptualise an epistemology and approach to the kind of research needed for a 'science of sustainable living', which we are calling 'Sustainology'. We compare this approach with our current epistemology and dominant ways of doing research based on conventional Western science.

Chapter 11: Learning for Sustainable Living

In this chapter, we focus on practical applications needed to enable people to experience both a strong personal self and a transpersonal self, and to enhance their ability to live sustainably. we provide a brief overview of existing ecopsychology and ecotherapy practices, outline important approaches to transformative learning, and present courses that we have developed in conjunction with this study to facilitate physio-emotional, psychosocial, and environmental sustainability. These courses focus on key issues of sustainable living, such as the psychological background of ecological crises, on the synergies of cancer and what has been called 'earth cancer', and on attention deficit disorder (ADD) and attention deficit hyperactivity disorder (ADHD). They provide processes designed to identify the areas in which people lack physio-emotional, psychosocial and environmental sustainability, and assist participants in deepening a felt sense of body-mind and person-planet unity.

Chapter 12: Summary and Conclusions

Here we summarise our key conclusions from existing knowledge, from the hermeneutic reinterpretation of relevant texts, from clinical observations, and from the knowledge held by research participants. We provide suggestions for remedial action, and offer some thoughts on possible future developments.

Before proceeding to Chapter 1, we wish to comment on an issue that could easily lead to the misunderstanding that we hold anti-American views. The gestation of this project has taken place during a time of dramatic developments. These started with the much debated first election of the present US government, continued with the events of 9/11, proceeded with the short (or ongoing) war in Afghanistan, and continues with the war in Iraq. Having followed these events through reading many publications, we have become aware of what many people observing USA politics have come to regard as a new wave of imperialism. The views on empire held by members of the US administration were succinctly outlined by an unnamed Bush official - probably Karl Rove - in his remarks to Ron Suskind in summer 2002. There the official declared:

> That's not the way the world really works anymore. We're an empire now, and when we act, we *create our own reality*. And while you're studying that reality – judiciously, as you will - we'll act again, creating other new realities, which you can study too, and that's how things will sort out. We're history's actors ... and you, all of you, will be left to study what we do (Alterman, Bush's War on the Press).

We wish to state here that our criticism is exclusively directed against the policies and actions of the current government of the USA, not against the American people, who, like millions of other people have, in our opinion, been deceived by manipulative strategies designed to enable the government to take their country to war.

We are aware that the governments of dozens of other nations – among them Great Britain and Australia, Werner's home country – support these wars and have become occupying forces for their own economic and/or strategic reasons. When we write in this text more about the USA than about other occupying countries, this is because we believe that the USA:

- is the main driving force behind these wars;
- is the main beneficiary of these wars; and
- is using the economic dependency of some small states for their own economic and strategic purposes.

Whereas we believe that many other Western countries – and in particular their wealthy elites – benefit from this new US imperialism, we do not regard the economic or moral downfall of any of these occupying countries, or their governments, as the solution to the problem; rather we will argue consistently throughout the text that the solution to our present crises will have to be achieved through major changes in consciousness of large numbers of people.

1   The Project

More than four decades after the beginning of modern environmentalism, an event usually associated with the publication of Rachel Carson's book *Silent Spring* (1962), new ways of thinking about the natural environment are emerging to make meaning of our environmental crises. In recent years, numerous, and sometimes conflicting, remedial actions have been proposed by scientists and grassroots activists concerned with the continuing degradation of the environment to solve our pressing ecological problems. Issues commonly regarded as features of our environmental crises include the following:

- Global warming
- Rising sea levels
- Excessive consumption of natural resources
- Soil erosion
- Concentration of greenhouse gases
- Air pollution
- Water pollution
- Desertification of dry lands
- Increasing lack of drinking water
- Loss of biodiversity
- Deforestation and shortage of fuel wood

Features commonly regarded as underlying contributors to environmental deterioration include, but are not limited to, the following:

- Modernism
- Capitalism
- Lack of political will
- Consumerism (over-consumption) in the wealthy Western countries
- Unsupportable population growth
- Lack of institutional arrangements and supports
- Extensive waste production
- Excessive burning of and dependence on fossil fuels

Remedies that have been suggested to solve our ecological crises include the following:

- Environmental education
- Using mainly renewable resources
- Proper management and prioritisation of non-renewable resources
- Developing ecologically sustainable technologies
- Strengthening the World Bank, and other key environmental organisations, such as the United Nations Environment Program (UNEP) and the United Nations Development Program (UNDP)
- Better coordination of environmental management
- Community networking
- Integrating ecological and economic concerns
- Global cooperation
- Selecting sustainable patterns of growth
- Giving women a greater role in society
- Recycling of materials
- Enhancing our caring for the environment
- Inclusion of environmental costs in the pricing of goods
- Abolishing poverty
- Charging taxes on carbon emissions
- Solving the conflicts of interest between nations
- Adopting energy-efficient technologies
- Deepening our understanding of the gender aspects of environmental problems
- Restraining energy use
- Facilitating a North/South consensus

Although the above-suggested remedies seem important, a growing number of environmentalists and ecologists hold the view that many of these approaches to environmental change are likely to result only in superficial behavioural change and crisis management, and are thus insufficient to significantly prevent further ecological degradation. These people, who include social ecologists, ecofeminists, deep ecologists, and many ecological psychologists, propose that nothing less than a total change in cultural values and a redefinition of what it means, and how it feels, to be human, is needed to avert an impending ecological and psychosocial catastrophe (Hill, 1999a; Berry, 1988). Almost thirty years ago, in his book *Small is Beautiful*, Fritz Schumacher (1974, p. 28) pointed out that "the establishment of a sane equilibrium can only come through a deeper understanding of the individual human being, that the problems lie deep within human nature." These radical ecologists charge that, although the present Western hegemonic approaches to sustainable thinking may have slowed ecological deterioration, they have so far failed to both halt deterioration and to enable a healing process capable of leading to a reversal of environmental deterioration and planetary recovery.

Recent concepts on what constitutes ecological crises have become increasingly inclusive and holistic. The *UNESCO Draft International Implementation Scheme*, which outlines a vision for the Decade of Education for Sustainable Development (DESD), now includes 22 key action themes. These include, among others, poverty, gender equality, HIV/AIDS, climate change, biodiversity, indigenous knowledge, and corporate responsibility. Whereas the visions and beliefs outlined in the document are broad and holistic in scope, and undoubtedly represent a major step forward, they still lack a deep understanding of the underlying psychological causes of our ecological crises, of the deep motivations, life experiences, feelings, and conflicts underlying modern people's unsustainable behaviours.

In this study, an attempt is made to address this lack by employing the perspectives of depth psychology, holistic/psychosomatic and social ecology thinking, and transpersonal psychology. Viewed from these perspectives, a new and more comprehensive vision of environmental sustainability and new remedial strategies for change emerges. These ways of thinking about the environment and change, employed by a small but growing number of ecologically-minded depth psychologists and transpersonal psychologists, are different from those produced by Western science, which, to date, have mainly involved change strategies based on the application of technology and of cognitive and behaviourist psychology.

The view that we are advocating acknowledges that many aspects of these ecological crises are predictable manifestations of our currently dominant limited ego-consciousness (Watts, 1961, 1962; Macy 1991), with its inherent atomism and individualism. It also recognises that, regardless of gains that may be made through technological progress, many of us (largely unknowingly) still behave in ways that inflict incalculable suffering on fellow human beings and the other-than-human environment in our pursuit of comfort, power and money.

As will be shown in this study, the examination of our environmental crises from these psychological perspectives suggests that even the tendency to focus on the environment and on environmental crises is a problem, because it prevents us from relating these issues with the many other indicators of unsustainable living, including:

- domestic violence;
- psychosomatic illness;

- the need to consume drugs;
- social and economic inequality;
- gender inequality;
- a lack of fairness in the workplace;
- a lack of freedom from emotional, sexual, and economic exploitation;
- a right to lead a meaningful and creative life;
- an abuse of animal rights; and
- a lack of opportunities to live healthy, physically and psychologically sustainable lives.

Rapid growth in the number of 4WD vehicles on city roads has focused attention on the increased danger to other motorists and pedestrians, while studies have identified 4WDs as more 'aggressive' vehicles. It may be that this aggressiveness attracts some people to purchase large 4WDs for city use. The people who market these vehicles know that primarily they are bought to reflect a certain self-image associated with the outback. They are promoted as 'rugged', 'muscular', 'bold', 'tough', 'powerful' and 'supremely capable'. Yet, aware that they are mostly driven between school, work and shops in the city, the creature comforts are also emphasised with ads suggesting that such vehicles can be 'thought-provoking', 'elegant', 'stylish', 'refined' and 'cosmopolitan' (Hamilton and Barbato, 2005, p. 1).

As shown in this list, an exclusive focus on the degradation of the natural environment neglects the psychological forces that underpin the degradation of both the natural environment and the social fabric of our societies. It also neglects the high level of physio-emotional and psychosocial illiteracy that are manifest in the varied pathological symptoms typical for modern and postmodern societies. Acknowledging these shortcomings, this study reframes the issues to be examined by using the term *ecological* rather than *environmental* crises. This more inclusive term stands for the complex and interrelated scenarios in which humans waste precious natural resources, human capital, and time and energy as so many unconsciously act out unhealed traumatic experiences.

Aims and limitations of this study

We are pursuing this study at a time of continuing degradation of our natural environment. As indicated above, this time is also beset with a rollback of the progress that has been achieved, and by a subsequent increase in frustration and burnout among many environmentalists

(Shields, 1993). The aim of this study is to deepen our understanding of the psychological factors leading to these phenomena by employing the psychological perspectives mentioned earlier.

The complexity of this project demands that many important discussions on environmental topics be taken as a given. Although we will justify my conviction that many aspects of "the world are getting worse", and that sustainable living continues to decline, we will not further engage in the continuing debate on the validity of ecological issues such as climate change. An enormous body of scientific evidence that supports the proposition that environmental degradation is continuing can be found in data published, for example, by the Worldwatch Institute and a multitude of other respected agencies. We support Reason's (2002, p. 8) view that "humanity is having an impact on the biosphere of macroscopic proportions, while our consciousness remains relatively small scale." A key aim of this study is to deepen and broaden this "small scale consciousness".

Limitations also emerge in relation to my claim that this project is interdisciplinary. This study is obviously fraught with the contradiction between its claim to describe unsustainability (unsustainable living) from an interdisciplinary and perspectivist position, and the necessity to keep it within the bounds of a workable postgraduate research project. To keep the project manageable, important works of scholars such as Lamarck (1914), Pollmann (1977), Margulis (1998), Steele et al. (1998) had to be excluded. The work of these scholars, which may be conceptualised as the genetic side of sustainability and change, is, however, highly important, and will be discussed in a future publication.

We also not examine here the effects of technological progress on sustainable development. This may come as a surprise to those among us who believe that technological progress is playing a major role in the creation of a more sustainable world. Have we not, for example, made enormous progress in developing more fuel-efficient cars, and have we not built a huge array of devices that help conserve energy in our homes and workplace? Yes, we have, but at the same time, an increasing number of people drive their bigger and more powerful sports utility vehicles often for longer distances, and by doing so significantly compromise this technological progress (see for example, Hamilton and Barbato, 2005).

Rather than focusing on establishing the infrastructure and consciousness that would foster the need to use public transport, the focus on building more fuel-efficient cars allows larger numbers of people to take their cars to the cities where consequently more green spaces have to be converted into streets and parking facilities. In other words, technological progress does not have an effect independent of people's consciousness. To the extent that humans are engaged in unconscious compensatory behaviour, we will predictably continue to sabotage the energy and resource-saving effects of any new technological possibilities. Within the context of the psychological considerations employed in this study, true technological progress will require us to focus on the design of goods that are not only biodegradable, but also sustain their value and functionality over a long time. Most current designs, however, employ built-in obsolescence to maintain an ever-expanding economy.

Methodology

In this segment, we critically examine the scientific framework currently used to make sense of our environmental crises. This examination suggests that the natural science paradigm used to underpin our efforts to improve sustainability is currently too limited to allow for a profound understanding of our ecological crises, and needs to be extended by including concepts of social ecology, holism, depth psychology, psychosomatics, and transpersonal psychology. The segment proceeds by outlining the philosophical and psychological knowledge needed to support my arguments, and to justify the choice of methodology employed to access the data.

Defining a scientific framework

Kirkman (2002, p. 17) writes about current efforts made to achieve change in our behaviour towards the natural environment:

> Environmentalism will succeed only if its advocates can bring about a change in the way people behave. How can environmentalists do this? Answers come from all sides: regulate, legislate, litigate, negotiate, innovate, and educate; restructure the market place to create new incentives; restructure the schools to create a new kind of citizen, restructure civilization itself.

As Kirkman indicates, there has been no lack of approaches for influencing people to change their behaviour towards the natural environment. Yet, most of these efforts have employed interventions associated with a technocentric, behaviourist, and cognitive paradigm. Considering the failure of these attempts to curb environmental degradation, it is suggested in this study that we will require a different and more inclusive scientific framework, one that can serve as a container for the complex issues relating to sustainable living, with all its psychosomatic, psychodynamic, and psychosocial aspects and implications. Schumacher (1978) points out that the knower has to possess adequate capabilities to make sense of what is to be known; or as Skolimowski (1996) puts it: "The universe reveals nothing to the unprepared mind." Such statements support Goethe's (1749–1832) belief that for the eye to be able to see, it has to be sun-like, thereby pointing at a way of thinking that has existed in esotericism for a long time. Applied to this study, Schumacher's and Skolimowski's statements highlight the necessity to create a container that is appropriate to this inquiry. It is also argued in this study that such a container has to make sense of the complex psychological background of people's destructive behaviour towards the natural environment.

A critique of modern science

Most current studies of our ecological crises are conducted within the limitations imposed by the modern research paradigm. The so-called classical or positivist paradigm is associated with the notion of linear progress and a technocentric view of the world. According to Pepper (1996, p. 124), this paradigm holds that "environmental problems must be approached and managed scientifically, objectively and rationally", and progress will ensue. Pepper's (ibid.) point highlights that the modern understanding of the world has "a conception of nature as machine-like and fundamentally separate from humans, and open to control and manipulation once it is understood". Modern beliefs about nature assume:

- linear reasoning and progress;
- that science and technology are able to solve our ecological problems;
- that technological progress and the consumption of goods and services will improve living conditions;
- that the world is ultimately knowable, and that our materialistic scientific methodologies will finally lead to a full understanding of the functioning of the cosmos;
- that human beings are the masters of the universe, as formulated by Francis Bacon, and that they should have power over nature; and
- that scientists are politically independent, neither subject to fashion nor to fad.

Echoing the writings of people such as Bertalanffy (1960, 1966, 1976), Whitehead (1997), and Mumford (1934, 1938), many ecocentrics such as deep ecologists, social ecologists, and ecofeminists are critical of many of the tenets of classical science. They voice, for example, objection to the discontinuation of studies whose findings clash with the scientific *status quo* and the interests of powerful stakeholders. Many ecocentrics also contend that modern science contributes to ecological crises because it has enabled technology and industrialism to become the most influential forces in Western society. Failing to live up to its own Baconian ideals, classical science has failed to act as a container for the complexity of human living.

There is also a growing awareness that science is not, and cannot be, an objective and value-free way of discovering and making sense of events. Diamond (1986, p. 7) writes:

> In fundamental ways they [the concepts and theories in science] are manifestations of the larger society in which they are produced and adopted. And they embody social premises at their very core.

Diamond uses a striking example to make his point, by describing the so-called discovery of Neanderthal Man in 1956. The bones of this ancient person had, in fact, been discovered many centuries earlier, but they could be officially discovered only after the adoption of Darwin's notion of evolution, since pre-Darwinian beliefs did not allow the view that species could have been extinct. Such a belief would have implied that God was a poor designer – a thought impossible for medieval human beings to contemplate.

Another key shortcoming of the natural science paradigm is its lack of interest in meaning. With its insistence on explaining nature exclusively in terms of the cause-and-effect mode, it limits itself to the statistically verifiable truths emerging from macrophysical quantities (cf. Jung, 1972, p. 7). Yet, unlike statistically verifiable causes, meaning relates to the sphere of the individual person, to her or his life experience, which is influenced by a complex web of emotional, psychosocial, and ecological factors.

In contrast to the classical scientific approach towards environmental issues and the human condition, a depth-psychology perspective holds that humans are widely influenced by their unconscious feelings and motivations, many of which are the result of trauma experienced in childhood. The holistic approach to depth psychology employed in this study recognises the mutually influencing effects of internalised traumas on the creation of the social and natural environment and of the external natural and social environments on our bodies, minds, and souls. Perceived from this perspective, we can argue that the limitations of classical science occur because it is based on a Cartesian understanding of reality as one, knowable truth produced by the mind. Jones (1993, p. 8) puts it this way:

> Unfortunately it was assumed that this particular Cartesian understanding of reality, instead of being no more than one serviceable representation within the limitations of the culture in which it originated.

With the emergence of quantum theory, Heisenberg's theory of indeterminacy, evolutionary thinking, non-linear thermodynamics, and complexity theory, our exclusive adherence to linear thinking has taken a sharp decline. Although this turn to "postmodern" science acknowledges the subjective viewpoints of the observer, it has so far failed to deconstruct the present valorisation of mind over body. Neither has it led to a significant interest in the role of traumatic experiences in the formation of worldviews or a shift in our perception of the world from cause-and-effect thinking to an emphasis on the notion of meaning.

We will know that we have reached this goal when we are able to ask questions such as the following:

> We know that the bubonic plague is *caused* by the bacterium *Pasteurella pestis*, but what is the *meaning* of the fact that Nostradamus, although he was as a medical doctor more exposed to the microorganism than most of his fellow humans, never contracted the disease?

We know that AIDS is caused by the HIV virus, but what is the meaning of the fact that it is possible that a gay man has died of AIDS, whereas his partner has not contracted the virus even after years of engaging in unprotected sex?

We know that symptoms of Multiple Sclerosis are caused by a hardening of the myelin sheaths surrounding certain nerves, but what is the meaning of the fact that a woman, who had been bound to a wheelchair for many years, could jump out of the wheelchair and run to the garden gate when she was overjoyed to see an old friend approaching the gate?

Committed almost exclusively to cause-and-effect thinking, present conventional medicine views such events as unexpected and unexplainable blips in a system that is regarded as essentially coherent and profoundly capable of explaining things. Yet, Jung (1972, p. 8) is not so sure when he writes that:

> The experimental method of inquiry aims at establishing regular events which can be repeated. Consequently, unique or rare events are ruled out of account. Moreover, the experiment imposes limiting conditions on nature, for its aim is to force her to give answers to questions devised by man.

And he concludes that "[t]he so-called 'scientific view of the world' based on this can hardly be anything more than a psychologically biased partial view, which misses out all those by no means unimportant aspects that cannot be grasped statistically" (1972, p. 8). To keep the natural science paradigm intact, conventional medicine, and in a wider sense natural science as a whole, frequently ignore the results achieved by people engaging in profound healing journeys, accuse people of inventing stories, and often ridicule practitioners who use alternative and more holistic healing methods.

Whereas the limitations of the natural science paradigm have been described so far in relation to health and ill health – an important aspect of sustainability still ignored by most ecologists – they also relate directly to environmental sustainability. One of the key results of this study is the conclusion that significant further improvements of environmental sustainability will be widely dependent on the willingness of large numbers of people to improve their emotional and psychosocial sustainability. Both the data obtained from research participants, and from the study of literature on ecological psychology suggest that emotional, psychosocial, and environmental sustainability are highly interrelated, and that one cannot improve sustainability in one field significantly without the others. A question that environmentalists and ecologists have yet to ask is, "What is getting worse if the natural environment is finally improving, if this improvement is not informed by a general planetary healing process?"

Postmodern ways of knowing

As briefly indicated earlier, the postmodern worldview holds that knowledge is socially constructed. Thus, Oelschlaeger (1995, p. 4) holds that "[A] scientific account of the world is no more and no less than an explanation proffered at a particular place and time that is judged by a particular community of researchers to be true".

A psychohistorical exploration of the development of science suggests that our present ways of knowing the world is, while we live in ignorance of ourselves, in itself a manifestation of our egocentric consciousness. Classical science, like conventional (non-psychosomatic) medicine, and our present systems of law, based on guilt and punishment, are all based on the same premise, that is, on a splitting of the experience of unity between "object" and "subject", and the subsequent denial and externalisation (projection) of the disowned reality.

Since the systems of research employed by conventional science form the dominant paradigm, social scientists often struggle to justify ways of researching based on a holistic worldview. This should not be necessary, since conventional science has failed to prove that the mechanistic modern worldview can be successfully applied to the complexities of human living. Scientific approaches based on mathematics, physics, and mechanics are now increasingly regarded as inappropriate, since they operate with linear functions, whereas the psychological world of human beings needs an approach that allows for paradoxes and ambiguity.

A view of being human based on depth psychology proposes that human beings often do not operate exclusively according to linear and rational processes, but are motivated by unconscious feelings and motivations. In other words, if we were rational beings, we would hardly destroy the natural environment upon which we rely for our existence. Similarly, the human needs for relationship, love, contact, and meaning, as well as associated experiences of frustration, rage, fear and disappointment, cannot be measured by the methodologies employed in the natural sciences. The realms of emotional and spiritual life are rather guided by "laws" based on emotional physiology, ambiguity, complexity, paradox, change, and creativity. The following segment will outline some of these paradoxical phenomena.

Example 1: Illustrating that the unconscious is really unconscious

A hypothetical survey of people's conscious recollection of emotional trauma is presented in Figure 1.1 on the following page. In such a survey, we would ask people to quantify the level of trauma that they experienced in childhood. The clinical experience of psychotherapists frequently shows that most people would report they experienced a happy childhood.

The figure shows a person's reported subjective experience of trauma on the y-axis, and the sum of the actually experienced level of trauma on the x-axis. In this schematic diagram, the hypothetical person A has not experienced any significant traumatic experiences during his or her childhood, and consequently reports a level of zero.

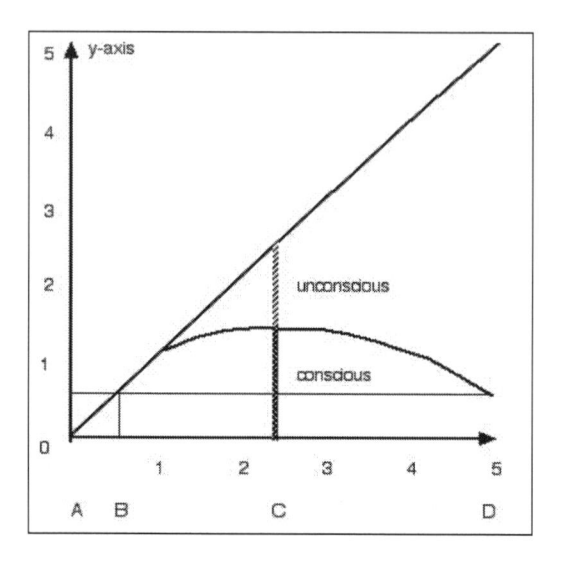

Figure 1.1 The unconscious is really unconscious

Person B, in contrast, has experienced a small amount of developmental trauma, leading to a reading of 0.7 on this arbitrary scale. Person C has experienced a moderate level of trauma. His or her ability to hold the trauma in conscious memory (1.5 on this arbitrary scale) has been marked with the word 'conscious'. This demonstrates the buffer capacity of what he or she can tolerate without having to resort to emotional defence mechanisms. The portion of the person's experience that he or she had to repress is marked with the word 'unconscious' in the graphic. It illustrates the difference between consciously remembered trauma and the trauma actually experienced.

Person D, on the other hand, has experienced a high level of trauma (5 on this arbitrary scale), but only reports a low level of remembered trauma (0.7 on this arbitrary scale). Person D's high level of trauma has resulted in the repression of a large part of his or her traumatic experience in order to stay free of anxiety and to maintain a sense of emotional stability. Interestingly, the graph shows that the highly traumatised subject D reports the same level of subjectively experienced trauma as person B, who actually has experienced a very low level of trauma.

This example serves to illustrate that a scientific inquiry that only considers what is subjectively reported by research participants has no way of differentiating between people who have experienced a very high or low level of trauma. Such surveys would consequently be misleading and thus of limited value. And most conventional psychologists, by being unaware of the role of muscular armouring (Reich 1972; Lowen 1958, 1972, 1980, 1985; Dychtwald, 1986) and tissue armouring (G. Boyesen 1976, 1985), and the psychosomatic role of physical illness (Alexander, 1950; Dethlefsen, 1984; Dethlefsen and Dahlke 1990; Zander 1989; Porsch 1997; von Uexkuell 1963, 1976) are not able to fully conceptualise people's degree of emotional disturbance and emotional defence structures.

Psychologists and psychotherapists with an awareness of the complex psychological and psychosomatic manifestations of our unconscious feelings and motivations are, however, more likely able to establish a coherent understanding of the psychosocial and psychosomatic manifestations of their clients' unconscious traumas by considering the defence mechanisms that typically include:

- projection
- denial
- conversion
- reaction formation
- tissue armour
- muscular armour
- low-level psychosomatic symptoms such as chronic cold feet
- psychosomatic illness

Example 2: A rationale of happiness

Researchers have for some time now considered the links between consumption and happiness by acknowledging that advertising and other marketing techniques, which produce a desire for industrial products, continue to reinforce the belief held by many of us that spending money will enhance people's sense of happiness and fulfillment. The views employed by the advertising industry suggest the existence of a linear relationship between the ability to spend money and the level of wellbeing, as indicated by the straight line in Figure 1.2 on the following page.

However, as Durning (1995) has pointed out, many indicators suggest that increased consumption does not necessarily fill emotional voids. Although health, wellbeing, and happiness increase with spending power up to a certain point (A), the increase in happiness soon reaches a peak (B). After this point, additional spending money might even reduce the overall wellbeing, since there is evidence to suggest that excessive wealth:

- often increases the levels of conflict and guilt;
- inadvertently strengthens the formation of a pseudo self-esteem (false self) based on money and power;
- increases people's superficial attitude towards life, other people, and the natural environment;
- focuses people's lives on keeping and increasing their wealth and power; and
- fosters a tendency to make people cold-hearted and careless.

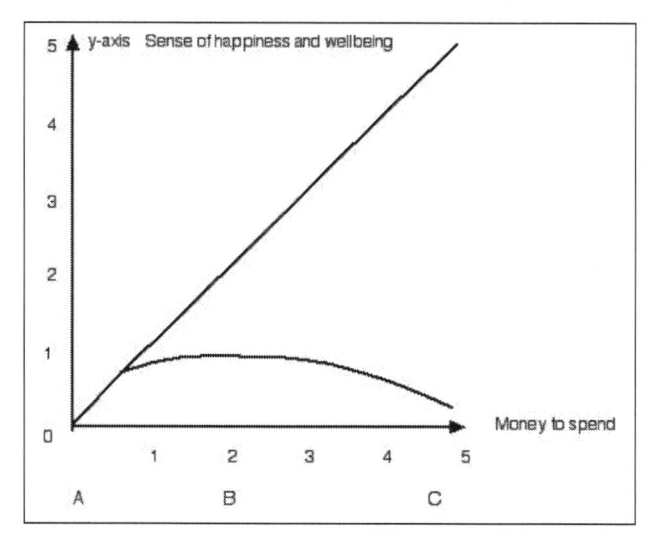

Figure 1.2   Happiness and spending money

Example 3: Disease as metaphor

Modern science demands that experimental findings must be reproducible in order to produce a scientific truth. Therefore, in conventional medicine the emergence of repetitive and identical clusters of symptoms (a syndrome) warrant the formulation and nomination of a particular illness. Once this illness is diagnosed, medical doctors usually prescribe drugs (created and produced by pharmaceutical companies, who frequently fund the research) deemed to work as a cure for this illness. Psychosomatic medicine, in contrast, tries to understand symptoms as symbolic expressions of hidden stories of emotional suffering and struggles with self-experience.

Although psychosomaticists consistently describe such stories on 'dis-ease', conventional medicine still shows little interest in them if it can be shown that factors such as genetic defects, microorganisms, or pathophysiological processes are involved. True to conventional scientific belief, such stories are not regarded as important because, as personal stories, they are anecdotal and can often not be generalised. Conventional medical science, being exclusively concerned with generalisable principles, and to keep its scientific paradigm intact, has to dismiss anecdotal evidence and people's life stories.

In 1986 Werner facilitated an awareness-raising group with people suffering from Multiple Sclerosis for the MS Society of Hessen, Germany. Sitting in a wheelchair in front of me was a young man of about 17 years of age, diagnosed with Multiple Sclerosis. As he was permanently pressing his knees together with considerable force, he needed a rubber wedge between his knees to protect his knees from being damaged. When it was his turn to talk, he told the group that he was able to lie in bed with relaxed knees when his body was covered with a blanket. On hearing this, I walked over to his room, fetched his blanket, and covered his legs. After some minutes the wedge dropped to the floor, and the young man spent the remainder of the time with his legs apart in relaxation.

Postmodern science

Considering that views on our ecological crises based on social ecology, holism, depth psychology, psychosomatics, and transpersonal psychology share some of the critique offered by many postmodern ecocentrics, it would make sense to adopt a postmodern worldview and its associated scientific paradigm as the *modus operandi* for this study. Listed below are some key beliefs of this worldview. Deconstructionist postmodern thinking is widely based on the belief that:

- reality is socially constructed, and mirrors the larger societal context with its power relations, economic and political decisions;
- there is no truth that can be ascertained, because facts and truths exclusively reflect the cultural values held in a society;
- we cannot know nature's objective properties because our perception will always work as a filter;
- the culture-nature dichotomy has to be overcome (Frodeman, 1995)
- modern rationality has truncated our understanding of, and our relationship towards nature;

- we have to reject modernism's belief in quantification as the defining character of the real;
- we have to overcome the modern habits of giving higher values to men over women, and logic over emotion and intuition; and
- the world is exclusively experienced within the framework of language.

Although some of the above notions are compatible with the perspectives applied in this study, others are clearly incompatible. A depth psychology approach to ecological thinking questions, for example, whether this variety of postmodernism will be able to make lasting theoretical and practical contributions to psychosocial and environmental sustainability, because of:

- the lack of awareness of its own shortcomings;
- the rejection of the concept of (deep) healing;
- the rejection of the importance of a stable sense of self;
- the exclusive reliance on languaged meaning; and
- the lack of consideration of the importance of deep feelings and lasting relationships.

The philosopher, Ludwig Wittgenstein, once remarked that the limits of language mean the limits of his world. We understand this to mean he is talking about spoken or written language. Deconstructionist postmodern thinking shares these limitations because it is widely based on language and the activity of thinking, at the expense of feelings and intuitions. By being exclusively concerned with words and images, which postmodernism regards as being exclusively shaped by social discourses and developments, it dismisses the importance of important somatic channels of communication such as facial expression, posture, gesture, energetic presence, and the sharing of genetic codes between living organisms (Pollmann, 1977).

By insisting that an understanding and experience of, and communication about and within, the world can only take place through language, postmodernists continue to deaden the senses that would enable them to extend their experience of the world through the experience of its complex nonverbal dimensions. By failing to recognise that human beings communicate on many different channels at the same time, postmodernists believe that they live in a world of superficial appearances. As Kvale (1992, p. 37) puts it:

Postmodern thought focuses on the surface, with a refined sensibility to what appears, a differentiation of what is perceived. The relation of sign and signified is breaking down; the reference to a reality beyond the sign recedes.

This postmodern argument can easily be misused to establish new tyrannies behind the smokescreen of the commitment to pastiche and contradiction (Hillman and Ventura, 1993).

Towards an alternative approach

Having argued that neither modern nor deconstructionist postmodern scientific systems of science are appropriate to function as the framework for this study, it will be necessary to turn towards alternative ways of making sense of people's feelings, behaviour, and motivations towards the natural environment. The following sections outline a number of key topics that are intended to provide an alternative scientific background for this study.

Worldviews as symptoms

A scientific system adequate to serve as a framework for this project needs to be able to critically reflect on the psychological underpinnings of worldviews. In a sense, it has to go beyond Kuhn's (1970) belief that science goes through phases of stability during which scientists adhere to a commonly supported paradigm, phases that are at times disturbed by scientific revolutions. Reason (2002, pp. 3, 4) writes the following about worldviews:

> Our worldviews are not simply rational things, they are about the mood of the times, the metaphors we use without knowing we are using them, the spirit of the times. A worldview encompasses our total sense of who we are, what the world is, how we know it. It encompasses our sense of what is worthwhile and important, what are the moral goods to pursue. It guides our sense of the aesthetic and the spiritual. And it is the basis of our social organization and political, personal, professional and craft practices.

The holistic view on our ecological crises employed in this study suggests that our present hegemonic modern and postmodern worldviews are as much manifestations of our ego-self consciousness as many other aspects of our ecological crises. Suggesting that worldviews change over time, Reason points at the shifts from the Middle Ages era to the Renaissance and to the modern world. He thus supports the widely held view that societies are indeed progressing, and that deep changes have occurred and continue to take place. A depth psychology perspective, in contrast, suggests that these changes are superficial. Although progress in technology and other factors have changed the lives of many people on the surface, we continue to express and embody the same egocentric consciousness that has been the dominant self experience, at least since the scientific revolution. Phenomena such as social equality, love-power conflicts, and body-mind unity issues have changed little and have possibly even deepened. Increased greed, hatred and ignorance – three emotions often referred to by Buddhists – continue to dominate human experience, and can now be found at the core of our ecological crises (Jones, 1993).

In this study, it is consequently argued that an examination of history reveals an intricate dance of two major consciousness paradigms, rather than a linear development. These paradigms can be framed as a holistic-feminine and a mechanistic-masculine way of making sense of the world (Spretnak 1991, 1997). In such a view, observable changes in worldviews relate to alternating phases of a mechanistic-masculine perception of nature, social life and culture, and a holistic-feminine interpretation of these entities. Some of the issues associated with these two fundamental perceptions of the world are highlighted below in Table 1.1:

Table 1.1 Topics relating to a holistic versus a mechanistic worldview

Holistic-feminine Worldview	*Mechanistic-masculine Worldview*
Orientation towards love	Orientation towards power
Trust in nurturing	Fear of death
Sharing	Competition
Owning of feelings	Projection (externalisation) of feelings
Notion of healing (transgressing duality consciousness)	Notion of change and progress
Romantic sentiment	Aggressive sentiment
Perspectivist, inclusive, democratic transcending worldviews	Monocausal, exclusive, autocratic worldviews
Complexity, convergence, grey-shades	Polarising, black and white, good and bad, right and wrong
As well as; x is expression of y	The either/or mode of thinking

Ecocentric science

One of the results of this study is the conclusion that environmental deterioration can be conceptualised as a manifestation of egocentric (neurotic) functioning, which has been the normal state of being for many hundreds of years, and is still the dominant self-experience for most in our modern society. The ecocentric approach to science employed here acknowledges that in our modern world we are caught in an egocentric trap that only allows us to identify feelings and behaviour as neurotic when we also have a felt sense of body-mind and person-planet unity. Yet, as will be argued in subsequent chapters, many people living in our modern society have significant difficulties with transgressing their egocentric consciousness and observing our society from a relatively integrated perspective. From this realisation has arisen the necessity to find research participants who are substantially less emotionally disconnected from their bodies, from nature, and from other humans. These would have to be people who either have survived childhood with relatively little emotional deprivation, who have worked with their traumatic experiences in psychotherapy, or other healing journeys, and who hold alternative ways of thinking about the environment and issues relating to sustainability.

Transpersonal research approaches

As described above, a particular emphasis has been on the creation of an inclusive research paradigm. To select a methodology for this study that is both wide enough and appropriate in content, it was necessary to choose a research approach that validates direct experience. This approach has to be able to validate knowledge attained by means of meditation, direct knowing (intuition) through spiritual and energetic experiences, and the knowing that emerges as a result of catharsis. Transpersonal research methods meet the criteria needed to provide the extended framework that is necessary to validate the experiences referred to in this study. The methods reviewed and summarised by Braud, Anderson and their collaborators (1998) are based on concepts of transpersonal psychology, a branch of psychology that emerged in the 1960s in the USA. Following is a brief description of integral and intuitive inquiry, two modalities that we considered relevant to this study.

Integral inquiry

Braud and Anderson (1998, p. 256) write:

Examples [of integral inquiry] include accessing and honoring one's tacit knowledge, bodily wisdom, emotions and feelings, intuitions and direct knowing or paranormal access to otherwise inaccessible information; working with findings not only through the rational processing of ordinary waking consciousness but also through other representations and modes (e.g., imagery, proprioception, and direct apprehensions) that may occur more readily in nonordinary states of consciousness (e.g., meditative states and hypnoidal states)...

Integral inquiry thus provides the framework for studies that make meaning of topics from a number of perspectives, and that validate experiences that are often referred to as transpersonal or peak experiences.

Intuitive inquiry

Intuitive inquiry, another transpersonal approach to research suggested by Braud and Anderson, is based on heuristic, phenomenological, and feminist research methods. It uses transpersonal skills such as meditation and alternative states of consciousness as its main methods of inquiry. Our reason for choosing this approach is the conviction that, unlike indigenous people, many of whom have retained their ability to access deep perceptions of reality, most Western people can only access these deeper levels by means of meditation, deep breathing and other techniques that decentre the rational mind. It is hoped that some of the people selected as research participants will have previously engaged in processes that have deepened their psychosocial and physio-emotional sustainability. Anderson and Braud (1998, p. 259) advocate the use of intuitive inquiry because its strength lies in its "support for incorporating the full dimensionality of human knowing into the conduct of research".

Academic rigour

All methods of inquiry have their advantages and disadvantages, and their strengths and weaknesses. Both the natural science and the transpersonal research approaches have devised systems aimed at preventing researchers from doing 'sloppy' research. Whereas in quantitative research data are statistically checked for equivalence and difference, for degrees of relationship and covariations, in intuitive inquiry we employ persistent observation, referential adequacy, negative case analysis, and thick description to verify research data. In this study, we balance the re-interpretation of texts, many years experience as psychotherapists and educators, and experiences in becoming more sustainable persons with the sustainability stories of research participants.

An important feature of academic rigour in intuitive inquiry is consistency. There is an intuitive feeling that bad research is being done when findings are badly documented, but even more so when they contradict other findings and the similar research of other people. In other words, the weakness of the transpersonal research approach, which is the researchers' tendency to be biased and prejudiced, can be counter-weighted by bringing in independent researchers for verification, and by checking the findings for inconsistency. An example of such inconsistency would be the emergence of sexist or racist attitudes in a study that claims to be informed by holism and depth psychology.

Consistency is achieved when an exploration makes sense from within its own inherent rules. A good example here is the psychosomatic and environmental-ecological exploration of a person's physical illness. Consistency demands that a psychosomaticist has to be able to skilfully interpret a person's physical symptoms as predictable outcomes of the client's complex set of unique life circumstances. These include his or her traumatic experiences, any available antigens and environmental health hazards, the roles of available resources and emotional coping strategies, the role of the natural environment in the person's life, and the supportive and limiting effects of available institutions. It is this consistency and the empathic ability of the psychosomaticist to create a disease story that the client can identify as his or her life story that will form the foundation for his or her healing process.

One of the cornerstones of the natural science approach to research is its demand to be able to reproduce the findings. If, for example, enough laboratory animals injected with a virus produce the same symptoms, a causal link between the antigen and the symptoms can be established. Because the experiment can be reproduced at other laboratories and will lead to the same result, the demand for reproducibility can be satisfied.

Similarly, psychosomatic inquiries can be reproduced. However, what is reproducible is not the connection between cause and effect of the illness, but the process of psychosomatic and ecological interpretation. Although a particular conflict can lead to different symptoms in different people, and different conflicts can emerge in different people and at different times as the same symptom, the process of interpretation and understanding generations of clients' symptoms within the context of their life experiences can be shared and verified by professionals with the same training background.

Grounded Theory

The research approach used in the study has similarities to Grounded Theory. This impression emerges when one conceptualises the process over the years. Having started with the simple assumption that health workers hold important knowledge on the links between body-mind integration and sustainability, the study branched out into many interrelated fields, such as social ecology, holism, psychosomatics, transformative education, environmental education, radical ecopsychology, and community development, and arrived at the final concept of the six-stage process of eco-self development. In this sense, the theory is grounded in the data, as was described by Glaser, Strauss, Corbin, and their co-workers (Glaser and Strauss, 1967; Strauss and Corbin, 1990).

Literature review

The desktop research for this study uses relevant literature in disciplines such as social ecology, holism, depth psychology, transpersonal psychology, biology, somatic (body-oriented) psychotherapy, ecological psychotherapy, and various approaches to environmental education. Views of relevant authors in these fields are considered and compared with my own thoughts, and the views of radical environmentalists such as ecofeminists, social ecologists, deep ecologists, and ecological psychologists.

Philosophical background

The philosophical foundations for this study are provided in this section. The primary philosophical disciplines being applied here to deepen our understanding of our ecological crises and sustainable living are perspectivism, hermeneutics, phenomenology, ecological philosophy, and relational and esoteric thinking.

Perspectivism

Perspectivism is a way of knowing the world that regards behaviour, relationships, objects, and events from many different perspectives. In a perspectivist view of the world, we replace the black-and-white perspective employed in many worldviews with a complex web of grey shades. We acknowledge that events have meaning on various levels of depth, which means that, depending on our point of view, things can simultaneously be of both a symbolic and concrete nature. The notion of perspectivism is used here also to conceptualise circular processes and the belief that rather than "leaving worldviews behind", as suggested for example by Gergen (1991), we are instead losing conscious sight of them.

Perspectivism suggests that many true assumptions can be produced from diverse perspectives. The assumption of a perspectivist position allows the conceptualisation of:

- a physiological-energetic perspective;
- a political and social perspective;
- a cognitive-behaviourist perspective;
- a depth-psychological/esoteric perspective;
- a spiritual or religious perspective; and
- an anthropological perspective.

Although a choice was made by the use of social ecology, holism, depth psychology, psychosomatics, and transpersonal psychology as the epistemological background for this inquiry, many other perspectives are acknowledged as being useful in our quest for sustainability. The following statements demonstrate the notion of perspectivism by briefly outlining a number of distinct views on the issue of smoking:

- After a certain critical point, an increased presence of nicotine in the synaptic gaps between nerves leads to a reduced transmission of nervous impulses.
- Smokers are more likely to die of lung cancer than non-smokers.
- Smoking has the tendency to make people addicted.
- The tobacco industry makes profits from the consumers' addiction to its products.
- Many smokers show little concern about the effects of their smoking on people around them.
- Smoking is used to assist in the repression of anxiety and other feelings by taking over the role of a variety of other possible emotional defence mechanisms.
- In an esoteric (vertical) worldview, the habit of smoking resides in the vertical chain together with other drugs, lies, fog, steam saunas, the planet Neptune, the blurring of boundaries, the need to merge, and many others.
- Smoking is a symbolic way of creating connectedness, and is often used by people who feel otherwise disconnected from others. Activities related to smoking provide a good reason to make contact with others.

- Conversely, and paradoxically, smoking can also be used to create distance by producing the proverbial smokescreen.

Although many readers may disagree with some of these "truths" about smoking, a perspectivist stance posits that each and all of them may be regarded as true, because perspectivism allows the validity of many different aspects of a theme, and attempts to establish possible analogies between them.

Applying such a perspectivist view enables us to look at the world through a variety of different lenses. Using perspectivism might enable us, for example, to conceptualise the development of humans as influenced by:

- an inherited genetic code;
- the emotional behaviour of parents and other providers of care;
- the social and spiritual values on which family life and education are based;
- the understanding of the medical, psychiatric, and psychosomatic system;
- language-mediated social and formal learning;
- knowing based on intuition;
- gene-mediated "learning" through "infection" with viruses (Pollmann, 1977);
- spiritual practices;
- society's beliefs and practices on sustainability and physio-emotional self-regulation;
- society's beliefs about embodiment and the body-mind connection;
- society's system of production, reproduction, and power-sharing;
- the available foods and other physical commodities; and
- responses to changes in the natural environment, such as the effects of electromagnetic fields.

This list highlights a reality that being human is a phenomenon that cannot sufficiently be embraced by an exclusive worldview such as the epistemological frameworks of modernism or deconstructionist postmodernism. If we were to define the above list as the landscape of being human, we might see the limitations of modernism and postmodernism perspectives, which focus on the specific at the expense of the whole, much as a microscope focuses on the cell but not the entire body. We can also see that deconstructive postmodernism constitutes a shift in focus, rather than an extension of the horizon. In contrast, by applying perspectivism, we are able to utilise many different worldviews, and thus become able to see the larger picture.

Hermeneutics

Hermeneutics is a philosophical discipline that was initially concerned with interpretations and meanings of religious texts, but is now used in many areas of scholarship. One of its important concepts is *verstehen* (German: to understand). Hermeneutics appears relevant to this study because, like depth psychology, it asks *why* something is happening. In doing so, it differs from philosophies that underpin the natural sciences, which are predominantly interested in questions concerned with 'what', 'how' and 'how much'. As a philosophical discipline, hermeneutics mainly relies on the use of language. As Crotty (1998, p. 67) notes:

> Language is pivotal to, and shapes, the situations in which we find ourselves enmeshed, the events that befall us, the practices we carry out and, in and through all this, the understandings we are able to reach.

The literature reviewed for this study continuously requires the reinterpretation of texts to produce new meanings from the psychological perspectives of depth psychology and other modalities. Hermeneutics allows for the possibility that readers can bring meaning to texts that the author may not even have considered. At the same time, we have to be mindful not to overemphasise the importance of language at the expense of other forms of communication. Holistic thinking suggests that contemporary academic culture has an overemphasis on spoken (and written) language, and on cognition and verbal communication, at the expense of intuition, body sensations, feelings, facial expression, and posture. Spretnak (1991, pp. 234-235) explains:

> Its supporters [the supporters of deconstructionism] seem to overlook the fact that there is no room in this rigidly language-based theory of human existence for all kinds of experiences that are not "repressed" into total denial simply because they do not fit well into our interior monologue of language when we attempt to label them or reflect on them – a child's quirky, magical perception of the world, spiritual experience, the orgasmic state, substance-induced altered states of consciousness, the artist's process, and *feelings*.

Here Spretnak is referring to forms of experience, expression, and communication that the wisdom traditions have been operating with for a long time. It is the phenomenon that certain experiences cannot be communicated verbally, and that trying to explain them would be futile since many insights can only be felt and experienced by the individual.

Holistic thinking

Holistic thinking has a long history in the wisdom traditions of many cultures. In its modern manifestation, it is often associated with the views of Smuts (1926) and 'General Systems Theory', developed mainly by the Austrian antireductionist and organicist, Bertalanffy. Initially researching topics on biology, comparative physiology, biophysics, and the physiology of cancer, Bertalanffy formulated his theory in the late 1940s, and extended his work from the 1950s onwards towards the areas of cognitive psychology and the philosophy of science (1955). Adhering to the humanist philosophy, he developed a holistic epistemology (1960, 1966) that criticised neobehaviourism, which was then the dominant paradigm in psychology. By critiquing this paradigm, he proposed a holistic way of perceiving the world. This worldview proposes that:

- any kind of system – biological, psychological, and social – operates in accordance with the same fundamental principles;
- the lives of living organisms cannot be explained exclusively by physics and chemistry;
- we have to attend to causes and not just symptoms of a problem, and analyse the whole system, not just its individual components;
- there are interrelationships (isomorphisms) between many levels of appearance, such as body, mind, spirit, and society; and
- the view that the whole is bigger than the sum of its parts.

In the same vein, Clayton and Ratcliffe (1996, p. 18) remark that:

> [a] systems approach involves placing as much emphasis on identifying and describing the connections between objects and events as on identifying and describing the objects and events themselves.

General Systems Theory and systems thinking found applications in areas as varied as family dynamics, chaos theory, cybernetics and computer science. An application of holistic thinking that is highly relevant for our ecological crises is Meadow's (http://

www.sustainer.org/pubs/Leverage_ Points.pdf) concept of twelve leverage points of intervening in complex systems. These leverage points consider factors such as constants, goals of systems, time delays, buffering capacities, the structure of information flow, positive feedback loops, and others.

Holistic thinking also informs Gestalt philosophy (Ehrenfels and Smith, 1988) and Lovelock's (1989) Gaia theory. Gestalt thinking recognises that the whole is more than its parts, and that the relationship between elements is often more important than the actual elements. Like systems thinking, Gestalt philosophy and later Gestalt psychology (Perls 1973, 1992) "emphasise the holistic nature of perception, the importance of studying the relationship between elements, and the human proclivity for creating meaning through seeing the form or pattern that exists between separate elements" (Winter, 1996, p. 283).

The application of holistic thinking is important for this project because it questions the modern view that regards people, animals, and things as separate entities in a largely fragmented and meaningless world. As Winter (1996, p. 283) points out, "our environmental problems are in part a product of focusing on the autonomy of the individual without seeing the relationship of individuals to each other and to the larger ecosystem in which they are embedded", or as Gomes and Kanner (1995, p. 113) suggest, "[r]adical autonomy is a cultural ideal that does not allow for other forms of growth, especially those based on relationship and connection".

Phenomenology

Many radical ecologists, such as Winter (1996), Evernden (1992, 1993), Livingston (1981), and Fisher (2002), to mention but a few, regard our difficulty in experiencing the world in its unity as one of the root causes of our ecological crises. Whether Livingston claims that reasoning is not a motivation deep enough to save the wetlands, or whether Evernden accuses environmentalists who adopt a technocratic language and an anthropocentric attitude of betraying their own cause, both view the common denominator as our culturally produced difficulty in treasuring the experience of living.

The philosophical discipline concerned with such experiences is phenomenology, a form of philosophical inquiry that is concerned with lived experience prior to reflection and meaning-making. In trying to achieve a "direct and primitive contact with the world" (Merleau-Ponty and Smith, 2002), phenomenologists try to "bracket out" our encultured conceptual thinking. Phenomenology is thus concerned 'with the things by themselves' (German: *an den Dingen an sich*).

Phenomenology is also the term for historical inquiries into the development of self-consciousness. Yet, whereas Hegel, for example, regarded self-development as a process moving from sense experience to "fully rational, free thought processes capable of yielding knowledge (see Blackburn 1994, p. 284), Husserl, one of leading phenomenologists of the twentieth century, shifted the focus to the experiencing body. Husserl (1970), as well as Merleau-Ponty and Smith (2002), emphasised the importance of the perceiving body in relationships to others. This study follows Husserl's and Merleau-Ponty's path by emphasising the importance of both sensual and intuitive experiences and by suggesting that an eco-self experience has to be based on our ability to have a deep and consistent experience of body-mind and person-planet unity.

Both phenomenology and depth psychology attempt to make the unconscious conscious. Whereas depth psychology focuses on traumatic experiences and difficulties with self-development to heal the split between human beings and the non-human world, and tries to assist people in getting a fresh view of the world, phenomenology aims to enhance people's consciousness of 'the things by themselves' by using reflection on our cultural belief systems. Both operate from the assumption that the unconscious is by its very nature unconscious, and that we have to detach ourselves from our encultured ways of thinking and feeling in order to gain access to an unmediated understanding of the world.

Social Ecology

Social Ecology is a field of inquiry developed most extensively in the 1960s by the American anarchist Murray Bookchin, who holds that the domination of nature has its roots in the domination of humans by humans (Bookchin, 1980; Hill, 2000). Bookchin emphasises the importance of spontaneity, complementarity, and mutualistic rather than hierarchical relationships. He, along with other social ecologists, holds the view that a sustainable society will have to be built on bioregionalism and active participatory democracy (Hill, http://www.zulenet.com/see/chair.html), rather than on the current propaganda-managed democracies (Pilger, 2005; Carey, 1987).

Although Bookchin undoubtedly opened up an important new field of inquiry, many social ecologists have come to distance themselves from Bookchin's approach because of its narrow focus on a political and social analysis of society. In contrast, social ecologists, such as Hill and his colleagues at the University of Western Sydney, acknowledge the importance of psychological and spiritual issues in relation to sustainability. For these scholars, who have greatly informed our thinking and feeling about society and environment, Social Ecology:

- integrates the personal, social, environmental and 'spiritual';
- emphasises issues of equity and social justice;
- recognises the importance of context and diverse ways of knowing, and the need to collaborate across difference;
- addresses issues of power, gender, and race;
- fosters experiential, whole-person learning;
- highlights the need to redesign our complex managed systems;
- emphasises the importance of a holistic perception of societal and ecological phenomena (big-picture views), but also acknowledges the importance of small, meaningful steps towards achieving social change (Hill, 2000);
- promotes a commitment to being fully alive as members of our species and our communities;
- fosters an acceptance of responsibility and respect in our relationships with others; and
- has a strong interest in the workings of body and mind (Hill, 2000).

Informed by fields of inquiry such as ecology, psychology, health studies, ecofeminism, sociology, and spirituality, to mention but a few, Social Ecology integrates many of the other systems of knowledge briefly outlined in this section.

In this study, the strong focus on depth psychology, holism, psychosomatics, and transpersonal psychology suggests a terminology that is slightly different from the one used by Hill and his colleagues. Rather than considering personal, spiritual, social, and environmental aspects of sustainability, it considers particularly physio-emotional, psychosocial, environmental, and institutional aspects of sustainable living.

Deep Ecology

Deep Ecology is an approach to environmentalism that questions many of the beliefs underpinning the functioning of modern societies. Deep ecologists are marked by their vital concern for the health and survival of the environment, and by the message that people can become more mature, and therefore abandon their uncaring and destructive behaviour towards the Earth. Deep Ecology aims to cultivate ecological consciousness, and supports "a process of learning to appreciate silence and solitude and rediscovering how to listen" (Devall and Sessions, 1985, p. 8). It asks people to become more receptive, and more trusting in the flow of life. It is also concerned with the establishment of a non-exploitative science and technology.

Deep Ecology's concerns for the environment are conceptually incorporated in a social movement that has become known under the term 'Deep Ecology Platform' (DEP). The ecological approach explored in this study shares many of the beliefs held by this ecological movement. These include:

- a commitment to diversity;
- a cultural and intellectual pluralism;
- a rejection of anthropocentrism;
- a rejection of the belief in economic growth;
- a rejection of the practice of exploitation;
- a flowing-with rather than forcing nature attitude;
- a view that the Earth is first of all our life space;
- a love for nature as it is and the willingness to live with it rather than dominate it;
- the possibility to be in harmony with nature; and
- a consciousness of place (bio-region) and the necessity to be rooted in communities.

Ecofeminism

Historically, the primary goal of feminism has been the establishment of equal rights between the genders on the different levels of society. In pursuing this goal, feminism has been one of the major driving forces of social progress over the last decades. Ecofeminism, the branch of feminism of particular interest for this study, holds "that the ideology which authorizes oppressions such as those based on race, class, gender, sexuality, physical abilities, and species is the same ideology which sanctions the oppression of nature" (Gaard, 1993, p. 1). In the same vein, Gomes and Kanner (1995, p. 112) note that:

> [i]t is not a coincidence that when women are raped, the land becomes parched and desolate, and when "feminine" qualities are oppressed, the human mind is cut off from participation in mystery and left with a disenchanted world.

Consequently, ecofeminism argues that the process of liberation of women will not be complete without the liberation of nature. Integrating feminism, ecology, and socialism, ecofeminism is concerned with "the struggles on behalf of women, animals, and the earth" (Gaard, 1993, p. vii).

Ecological philosophy

Ecological philosophy is concerned with our ways of perceiving the relationships between humans and the other-than-human environment. It is particularly concerned with definitions of the notion of environment and the question as to whether it is justified to allocate an elevated position to humans. To make sense of destructive behaviour towards the natural environment, we need to achieve a deep understanding of the phenomenon environment, not only as a cultural phenomenon (Evernden, 1992), but also as the external manifestation of our internal unhealed reality.

Ecophilosophers presently distinguish between relationships of human beings and the other-than-human world based on what they call instrumental value and intrinsic value theories. In contrast, supporters of the instrumental value theory believe that the other-than-human world essentially exists to be used by humans. If they entertain any hesitations, then these relate to the question whether it is permissible to exploit the other-than-human world without restraint or with the view in mind that we have to preserve resources for our children.

Supporters of the intrinsic value theory, in contrast, argue that it is important to recognise the intrinsic value of at least some members of the nonhuman world. The intrinsic value theory may be subdivided into ethical sentientism, biological and autopoetic ethics, ecosystem ethics, and cosmic purpose ethics. These ethical beliefs differ with reference to the egocentredness of the relationships between humans and the other-than-human environment.

Psychological background

We will now provide a brief overview of the psychological disciplines that in recent decades have contributed significantly to our understanding of environmental concerns and a brief introduction to key concepts of the psychological disciplines underpinning this study. These include:

(1) behaviourist psychology
(2) cognitive psychology
(3) environmental psychology

(4) social psychology
(5) postmodern psychology

Disciplines that are still being neglected in public discussions on ecological crises, and that consequently require more detailed attention, include:

(6) depth psychology
(7) transpersonal psychology
(8) Gestalt psychology/holistic psychology
(9) ecological psychology

(1) Behaviourist psychology

Behaviourist psychology, often also referred to as behaviourism, is the study of human behaviour. According to Winter (1996, p. 154), "it focuses on the ways in which our outward behaviour is controlled by the environment, especially by the rewards and punishments that follow what we do." Believing that what ultimately counts is that people replace inappropriate behaviour towards the natural environment with more appropriate and sustainable behaviour, behaviourists have developed an array of strategies and techniques that can be used to foster or enforce environmentally sustainable behaviour.

One of the key distinctions of behaviourism is the distinction between classical conditioning (Pavlov, 1927; Watson, 1925, 1928) and operant conditioning (Skinner, 1948, 1953, 1971). Whereas classical conditioning describes changes in behaviour resulting from stimuli designed to change this behaviour, operant conditioning describes how the consequences of initial behaviour influence future behaviour. In other words, operant conditioning conceptualizes how an action leads to a response in the environment (e.g., praise for a particular behaviour) and the positive reinforcement is likely, in turn, to lead to a strengthening and repetition of the initial behaviour.

Believing that what really counts is that people adopt certain behaviours, this field of inquiry is not concerned with why people behave in certain ways, but with ensuring that people change their behaviour in accordance with defined standards. As regards our ecological crises, behaviourism is mainly concerned with developing manipulation strategies that can be used to foster or enforce environmentally sustainable behaviour.

(2) Cognitive psychology

Cognitive psychology is the study of thinking. It focuses on the processes that take place when people make decisions, identify problems, formulate solutions, and in a more general sense, try to make meaning of their experiences. Using a computer-related terminology, we could say that cognitive psychology, also called cognitivism, is concerned with the ways we perceive, store, process, and disseminate information. As regards our environmental crises, cognitivism is predominantly concerned with the ways in which we process information on the environment, and with ensuring that this information leads to desired behaviour change.

(3) Environmental psychology

Environmental psychology examines the interrelationships between natural environments and human behaviour. As De Young (1999) points out, the field of environmental psychology defines the term 'environment' very broadly by including all that is natural on the planet, as well as social settings, built environments, learning environments, and informational environments. Scull (1999), on the other hand, holds that environmental psychology has traditionally focused on human-made environments, and could be characterised as 'architectural psychology'. According to Davis (1999), environmental psychology is the field of inquiry dealing with:

- the effects of environmental stimuli, such as noise, temperature, and weather, on emotions, cognitive processes, performance, and social interactions;
- the effects of the social environment, crowding, personal space;
- psychological effects of environmental disasters;
- psychological effects of pollution and environmental toxins;
- psychological effects of low-level background environmental destruction and habitat loss;
- environmental design issues, architectural psychology;
- psychology of home, and psychological antecedents and effects of homelessness; and
- ways in which contact with nature enhances health.

(4) Social psychology

Social psychology is the scientific study of social influence (Winter 1996, p. 63). Dealing with the ways in which our interactions with people affect our thoughts, attitudes, beliefs, and behaviour, it is concerned with the dynamics of people's social interactions, such as the strategies we might use to gain people's trust. Social psychology is also concerned with emotional states such as happiness, and in phenomena such as overconsumption. As a socially critical discipline, it is concerned with phenomena such as androcentrism and sexism (male dominance), colonialism, and other unsustainable societal phenomena.

(5) Postmodern psychology

Postmodern psychology is concerned with the ways in which we construct our experiences and sense of self in response to cultural and environmental changes. It assumes that we cannot understand ourselves directly, but have to "infer our self-concepts from the imagined perceptions of others" (Winter, 1996, p. 287). Winter also points out that our sense of self is not stable, but often dependent on our ability to perform in various environments and on our place in social hierarchies. Yet, the view that our selves are mainly defined by the perceptions of others also poses a problem often overlooked by deconstructive postmodernists. This is because a self that is not also supported by internal self-supporting structures leaves us highly vulnerable to being manipulated by people who have access to mass media and are willing to use these media to strengthen their power base.

(6) Depth psychology

Depth psychology focuses on the unconscious feelings and motivations that underpin our perceptions and behaviours. Unlike other psychological disciplines that assume humans are conscious agents of their fate, depth psychology regards many aspects of our behaviour and perception as manifestations of a distorted and fragmented sense of self that usually emerges as a result of traumatic childhood experiences. As regards ecological crises, this approach to psychology assumes that our ecological degradation may be regarded as proof of our unconscious functioning, since conscious beings are unlikely to destroy the very environment on which they depend for their wellbeing and survival.

(7) Transpersonal psychology

Transpersonal psychology is the field of inquiry concerned with "transcendent experiences, those that illuminate the parts of our being that lie beyond our individual, unique, or separate sense of self" (Winter, 1996, p. 242). Proponents of this approach to psychology hold that most people living in our Western culture have a limited ability to experience altered states of consciousness – an ability that humans gradually lost as part of our cultural shift towards rationality, logic, and mechanistic thinking.

Transpersonalists often support their views by pointing to traditional cultures in which many people have retained a transpersonal awareness by maintaining and nurturing this awareness through meditation and other consciousness-altering practices.

(8) Gestalt psychology/holistic psychology

Gestalt psychology is a field of inquiry concerned with 'wholes' and the holistic nature of perception. Based on the work of von Ehrenfels (1988), Kohler (1975), and others, this approach to psychology emphasises the importance of studying the relationships between elements rather than of studying the element in all its details. As regards our ecological concerns, this means, as Winter (1996, p. 233) points out, that "[c]hanging our environmentally problematic behaviour will require a perceptual shift of seeing ourselves as embedded in a group, as well as in a complex ecosystem". Holistic psychology, to my knowledge, has not established itself as an approach to psychology in its own right. Based on a holistic worldview and on the holistic thinking briefly outlined in the previous segment, it is an eclectic discipline mainly concerned with the unity of body and mind, psychosomatics, stress-related physical disorders, substance abuse, and trauma recovery.

(9) Ecological psychology

A particular focus in this thesis is on ecological psychology, a field of inquiry "that integrates psychology and environmentalism, addresses the ways the Earth suffers as a result of people's behaviour, and how people in turn suffer from a degraded Earth" (Harms, 2005). Ecological psychology is concerned with the interrelationships between humans and the other-than-human environment, with a humbling of the self, and with the integration of the ill-conceived culture-nature dichotomy (Fisher, 2002, p. 119). It is, in Suzuki's (1997, p. 179) words, "an attempt to reconnect us with our natural home and to remedy some of the harm caused by our exile in the modern city". The term 'ecological psychology' appears to have been first formulated by Theodore Roszak (1973, 1975, 1981, 1995), who reworded the term 'psychoecology', which Robert Greenway had been using since the late 1960s in his courses at Sonoma State University (cf. Schroll, 2005). The history of ecological psychology can also be traced to the scholars working at the Center for Psychology and Social Change, which the late John E. Mack founded at the Harvard Medical School. According to Mack (1995, p. 282), an ecological psychology:

would have to be dynamic psychology - in the sense that it would need to explore profound, largely ignored conscious and unconscious feelings, impulses, and desires in relation to the physical world - rather than one of the variations on neurophysiology or biochemistry that now dominate the American psychiatric establishment.

In addition to the aforementioned scholars, the field now comprises the work of people such as Macy (1991), Metzner, (1999), Clinebell (1996), Kanner and Gomes (1995) Winter (1996), Hill (1999a, 1999c, 2001, 2003a), Abram (1995, 1997), Conn (1995), Fisher (2002), Scull (1999), Sewall (1995), Shapiro (1995), Anthony (1995), Fox (1990), Schroll (2000), and others. Ecological psychology differs from environmental psychology, which is, as indicated earlier, mainly concerned with issues such as the effects of the built environment and noise on human beings (Bechtel and Churchman, 2002).

It has to be emphasised that all approaches briefly described here deserve acknowledgment for their various contributions to our present understanding of our ecological crises. As will be pointed out in various places in this study, the recovery of this planet and its human and nonhuman dwellers, and its ecosystems as a whole, will be dependent on changes emerging from many different psychological and educational approaches, and many social institutions. At the same time, there is still an imbalance regarding the application of these approaches and institutions in research and educational practice. Because of their compatibility with the modern worldview, the technological, cognitive, and behaviourist approaches to environmental change are still dominating our societal enterprises, academic research, and educational practice. Recently, postmodern psychology has contributed to the emergence of education for sustainability, whereas the holistic, body-oriented, and transpersonal approaches have so far gained only limited attention from both government and non-government institutions concerned with environmental education and sustainability.

In this chapter we have outlined the methodology and epistemology for this study. We have described some of the limitations of a conventional natural science approach to ecological concerns, and have suggested that the achievement of a deep understanding of the complex psychosocial factors of our ecological crises will depend on our willingness to shift from a natural scientific to a transpersonal and holistic research paradigm. The chapter has also provided a brief outline of a transpersonal research framework, explained the methodology used to obtain relevant data both from research participants and existing sources, and described the psychological and philosophical underpinnings for this study.

Readers interested in the findings generated by the practical research project that underpins this study are referred to a summary of the findings in the appendix.

2 Notions on Consciousness and Self

The research on which this book is based suggests that many key aspects of our ecological crises may be expressions of a disrupted emotional and spiritual self-development of people in modern Western societies. This disruption emerges as lack of self-experience of unity consciousness or coherence with the creation. Laszlo writes about this topic:

> An amazing form and level of coherence characterizes nearly everything in the universe, from the largest structures of the cosmos to the smallest particles of the microworld. It characterizes the human body as well [...] Coherence, after all, is a precondition of life itself (2996, p. 7).

This emphasis on coherence, or on what we refer to here as eco-self consciousness, requires a vastly difference perception of and behaviour towards many aspects of nature and culture. It will in particular force us to abandon the modern notion of fighting against what we perceive as causing us harm, e.g., illness, terrorism, viruses, and poverty. It teaches us, as Dethlefsen (1984) and Dethlefsen and Dahlke (1990) put it, that these phenomena are expressions of deeper ecological and psychological problems and can only be made redundant, not fought.

To lay the foundation for a deep understanding of the issues relating to the kind of self-development and self-transformation that can lead to the felt sense of coherence we provide in this chapter an outline of relevant notions on consciousness and self. These include Gebser's (1986) 'Integral System of Consciousness', Beck and Cowan's (1996) 'Spiral Dynamics', and Wilber's (1997) 'Four Quadrant Model' of self-development. Following the description of key notions of 'self', we also provide a brief synopsis of key aspects of experiences of ego-self-consciousness that dominate in modern societies.

Notions on Consciousness

It has to be said at the outset that the field of consciousness studies is too complex to attempt a comprehensive treatment in this study. Along with such concepts as mind, soul, and freedom, consciousness eludes a clear definition, and can only be explored from within the worldview of a particular paradigm. Jordan (2000, p.32) notes:

All such attempts [to describe various dimensions of consciousness] are inevitably formulated within some type of discourse. I believe that it is too much to expect of any discourse that it should be able to integrate all other discourses about consciousness development to produce a superior framework.

Although acknowledging this difficulty, an attempt will be made in Chapters 3 to 8 to construct a model of consciousness transformation that will reach across and integrate psychological and ecological disciplines. Although this model is nomothetic (law-seeking), it still allows for idiographic (self-writing) processes by considering that individuals are often challenged by fate to make quantum leaps across several realms of consciousness. This will be described in more detail in Chapter 9. Our aim at this point is to present a brief overview of three important systems of consciousness transformation and three notions of consciousness that are particularly relevant to this study.

1 - Wilber's Four-Quadrant System

The transpersonal psychologist Ken Wilber (1995, 1996, 1997) has developed a complex system that he represents as the following four 'choice' quadrants:

- interior-individual, emphasising phenomena such as sensations, impulses, and emotions;
- exterior-individual, concerned with matter, from molecules to anatomical structures;
- interior-collective, emphasising developmental stages of consciousness such as the archaic, magic and mythic; and
- exterior-collective, concerned with ecosystems, families and tribes.

Numbered from the center to the periphery, Wilber's system features along its axes the development of consciousness and its associated anatomical and psychosocial structures. Higher structures include all the possibilities of the preceding structures, and the items with the same number in each quadrant are interrelated.

2 - Spiral Dynamics

Another important model of consciousness development has been formulated by Beck and Cowan (1996). Based on the work of Graves (1974), a psychologist who explored human thinking and value systems in the 1970s, these authors further developed the system known as Spiral Dynamics (SD). It describes the organising principles behind thinking and perceiving, and focuses on the 'containers' that shape our worldviews. Approaching these issues mainly from a cognitive perspective, Spiral Dynamics describes a double helix system, which displays, on one side, various life conditions, and, on the other side, their matching coping mechanisms. Beck and Cowan also developed a system of colour coding that serves to distinguish between their eight progressive stages:

- Beige stands for archaic-instinctual principles, and relates to issues such as survival, food, warmth, sex, and safety.
- Purple indicates a magical-animistic consciousness, characterised by the importance of kin spirit, the living in tribes, and the engagement of rituals to appease the spirits.
- Red represents the impulsive and egotistical quality. Thinking on this level is egocentric, the world is perceived as dangerous and tough, and there is a driving force to dominate others.
- Blue symbolises a mythic and purposeful quality. People at this level of consciousness focus on outcomes. The world is perceived as hierarchical and dualistic, and there is a perceived necessity to obey authorities.
- Orange stands for a rationalist and achievist mindset. People at this level of consciousness usually act from self-interest, and have a desire to achieve. The world is perceived as a place of opportunities for exploration, competition, and material success.
- Green symbolises pluralistic and communitarian consciousness, the striving for inner peace, the sharing of resources, and the achievement of fairness and social equality. People at this level of consciousness usually strive for growth and the experience of mutual support.
- Yellow symbolises the systemic-integrative, the principle of the "flowing with", and the acceptance of life as an existential and unpredictable enterprise. At this level of consciousness, thinking is systemic and integrative, and conflict is perceived as a challenge to heal and grow.
- Turquoise represents a global-holistic sensibility, an experience of wholeness, and a unity of body, mind, and spirit. At this level of consciousness the world is perceived as a single, dynamic organism, and the self is perceived as both personal and as an integral part of the whole.

Further levels are yet to be recognised, named, and described.

3 – Gebser's system of unfolding consciousness

Gebser (1986), a German cultural philosopher, who spent most of his life in Spain, France, and Switzerland, where he also taught for Jung, developed a system of five stages of consciousness development, which he labelled the archaic, magic, mythical, mental, and integral. These stages describe consciousness development as a process moving from what he calls zero dimensionality to a holistic way of perceiving the world based on an awareness of four dimensions, whereby the fourth dimension is both time and timelessness.

The archaic stage of consciousness is characterised by:

- a perception of the world devoid of any perspectivity and differentiation;
- a minimum awareness of self and relationships to the world;
- a lack of past experience, which he calls 'maximum latency' as opposed to 'maximum transparency' (see stage five);
- a complete lack of individuation; and
- a sense of complete immersion with creation.

The magic stage of consciousness is characterised by:

- its egolessness;
- a rudimentary sense of self;
- timelessness;
- spacelessness;
- the slow emergence of language;
- a strong association and lack of distinction with nature; and
- the belief that plants, animals, and inanimate objects share the same fate as humans.

The mythical stage of consciousness is characterised by:

- the emergence of shamanism and symbolism;
- the emergence of sophisticated tools and larger social structures;
- the emergence of an interest in time and calendric reckoning;
- the emergence of polarity (two-dimensionality);
- the emergence of a self-experience in opposition to the surrounding world;
- the initial concretization of the 'I' of man (Mahood, 1996);

- the emergence of mythical stories as the primary expression of this period; and
- the emergence of the notion of an afterlife.

The mental stage of the unfolding of consciousness is characterised by:

- the shift from a two-dimensional to a three-dimensional view of the world;
- the attempts of human beings to break free from the past and its confusing mythical and symbolic images;
- the shift to the worldviews advocated by Pythagoras, Socrates, and Aristotle;
- the discovery of causality;
- the emergence of the belief that time unfolds in a linear fashion;
- the emergence of abstraction;
- the emergence of philosophy as the primary form of expression;
- the emergence of monotheism in the Western world;
- the final accomplishment of separation from nature; and
- full development of the 'I'.

The fifth and last stage, called 'integral consciousness', is characterised by:

- the shift to a four-dimensional space-time continuum;
- diaphaneity, that is, the recognition of the whole beyond its parts;
- transparency, which stands for the ability to perceive the true nature of things; and
- the replacing of philosophy with 'eteology', the study of the state of being-in-truth.

Whereas Gebser's model is predominantly concerned with an historical perspective of consciousness development, Wilber's, and Beck and Cowan's models focus on consciousness transformation, in that they describe progressive stages in the development of consciousness among people alive today.

1 – *From coma to samadhi*

Another possible distinction of consciousness states includes:

- the reduced states of consciousness, such as coma;
- our normal everyday consciousness; and

- the expanded state of consciousness that is called *nirvana* in Buddhism, *unio mystica* in Catholicism, or *samadhi* in Yoga (cf. Dean, 1974).

It is remarkable, as Dean (1974) points out, that whereas humankind has embarked on an ambitious exploration of the frontiers of space, it has relatively neglected the exploration of consciousness. Addressing this will likely to improve our ability to lead personally and ecologically sustainable lives.

2 – From automatism to emotional integration

The following simple model of consciousness transformation confirms Freud's (1910, 1920, 1923, 1926, 1935, 1940, 1964) notion that the unconscious is 'really unconscious'. This may be illustrated by considering smoking.

Many smokers light up with little awareness of their act of smoking. For those, the motions of getting a cigarette out of a packet, of finding a lighter, of lighting up and of inhaling the smoke are essentially automatic and ritualised. They display a behaviour that Ralph Metzner (2005a) has referred to as 'unconscious or automated knowing'. Such people might become aware of the number of cigarettes they have smoked only when they notice that their packet is almost empty. In terms of consciousness, these people function in 'automatic mode' in the same way as we might drive a car or walk up stairs. Most smokers use smoking unconsciously as a form of 'medication' to keep anxiety in check.

A second category of smokers may be viewed as smoking consciously in that they have a higher level of awareness of their act of smoking. Such smokers take their time to get their smoking apparatus organised and to experience the effects of the inhalation upon their bodies. Especially those who smoke pipes and cigars rather than cigarettes, seem to consciously enjoy the ritual of lighting up, frequently changing the flavour of their tobacco, and taking ample time to keep their equipment clean and in good repair. As regards consciousness, we would say that these people are highly conscious of their actions and their sensual experiences. They have a here-and-now awareness of their activity, and possibly have a conscious self-image of being connoisseurs, proud of their sophistication and style.

This form of smoking is contrasted with a third category of smokers, who are conscious of the fact that their habit is addictive and will at some stage probably lead to serious health problems. Being conscious of their addiction, they often smoke with a sense of guilt, self-defeat and shame about being out of control. They may seek "healthier" cigarettes, yet such smokers accept that they will ultimately have to quit smoking – and often attempt to do so by using hypnosis or other behaviour-modification techniques – or they will have to accept the consequences.

The fourth and last category of 'smokers' have managed to stop smoking by using counselling, psychotherapy, or similar processes to work with the feelings that underpin their addictive and self-destructive habit. Consciousness here relates to their conscious awareness of the past and present conflicts and feelings that have led them (and others) to medicate their feelings through smoking. Having faced the anxiety and disowned feelings about their past traumatic experiences, they are enabled to meet the world without this unsustainable habit.

These four expressions of consciousness frequently overlap, and do not necessarily form a logical continuum. Consciousness does not appear to be a stable state, but is often subject to external influences such as stress and manipulation. Connoisseurs under emotional pressure may become automatic smokers, 'automatists' may become connoisseurs, and people with a conflict consciousness may abandon their struggle and slip into the self-destructive mode.

The purpose of these descriptions is mainly to illustrate that different people can experience the same phenomenon (in this case smoking) from very different states of consciousness, and that consciousness is in a state of flux. Perhaps the most interesting state of consciousness within this categorisation is the second one, for, when viewed from a depth psychology perspective, it represents a 'conscious way of staying unconscious'. In other words, it is possible to sense a fundamental difference between a conscious awareness of being in the present (stream of consciousness) and a state of consciousness that involves the integration of thinking, feeling and past (traumatic) experience. It is this distinction that forms the foundation for the three advanced stages of eco-self consciousness (depth psychology, holistic, and what we call person-planet unity consciousness), described later in this study.

The paradoxical phenomenon of using quasi-conscious behaviour and experiences as defences against unconscious feelings and conflicts is highly institutionalised in Western societies, and constitutes one of the driving forces of unsustainability (Winter, 1996). As explained in more detail in a later chapter, advertising that skillfully uses people's struggle with their sense of self advocates the pleasures of conscious consumption of non-essential goods and services, and thereby contributes to the continuing degradation of our natural environment and of social relationships (Kanner and Gomes, 1995). Such advertising uses our culturally created need to be intellectually conscious and to be informed consumers to sell products that enable us to stay unconscious at deeper levels.

3 – *Consciousness and transformation*

Consciousness, as mentioned above, is often associated with the notion of transformation. Metzner (1986, p. 37), for example, relates a transformation of consciousness with ideas and experiences relating to:

- discovery, that is, an uncovering;
- disillusionment, an abandonment of illusions;
- revelation, the pulling back of a veil;
- awakening; and
- insight, that is, looking below surface appearances.

These notions of transformation are associated with a discovery of what is already present, which is, in psychoanalytic terms, an undoing of neurosis rather than a development of psychological capabilities, as described, for example, in Gebser's model of phylogenetic consciousness development. These notions can be associated with the Mahayana tradition in Buddhism, which assumes an inherent completion. As Aitken writes:

> The attitude that all is complete from the very beginning fulfils the ideals of the Arhat [one who is free from craving] and the Bodhisattva [one who forgets the self in working with others]... Counting our breaths [in Zazen meditation], we practice the inherent completion of all things (1982, p. 63).

Notions of 'self'

Defining 'self'

The argument held by radical ecologists that a possible reversal of environmental degradation is likely to be dependent on our ability to shift from an ego-self to an eco-self requires a brief outline of our present understanding of the notion self. According to Blackburn (1994, p. 344), the self is "the elusive 'I' that shows an alarming tendency to disappear when we try to introspect it". In contrast, Chaplin (1985) defines the 'self' as the individual, and as a conscious being. He consequently equates it with the ego. Flew (1979), on the other hand, regards the term 'self' as an obsolescent technical term for an incorporeal and essentially conscious person.

In contrast to the Freudian terms 'ego', 'super-ego', and 'id' (Freud, 1923), the term 'self' is widely used in general language, mostly in compound words such as 'myself', and when we want to express that we reflect on our own thoughts, feelings, and actions. In this respect, the term seems thus to be associated with our ability to regard ourselves as objects.

In clinical practice as psychotherapists we tend to present the terms 'id', 'self', 'ego', and 'super-ego' in the form of a spectrum. At one end we may locate the body with its inherent functions and instincts (id). Next to the id, we may place the self, which acts in this view as the psychological lobby of the body reality. In this construction, the self is not able to turn against and compromise the body and its inherent needs and instincts. It is this self that 'contains' one's psychological 'self-healing' mechanisms. After the self, we may place the ego as a psychological structure that tries to mediate between outer demands and the body-self. As part of this mediation, the ego often works in the interest of the super-ego, which 'wants' us to perceive the world and to act in accordance with outside demands. Thus, the super-ego is positioned next to the ego at the other end of the spectrum.

Fox (1990) has proposed the following three notions of self: the desiring-impulsive self, the rationalising-deciding self, and the normative-judgmental self. Suggesting parallels of this tripartite structure with the Freudian notions of id, ego, and super-ego, Fox describes a compelling correspondence between the above notions of self and our behaviour and attitudes towards the other-than-human environment. He associates the desiring-impulsive self with our unrestrained exploitation and expansionist approach towards the natural environment, the rationalising-deciding self with the attitude of resource conservation and preservation, and the normative-judgmental self with attitudes favouring the intrinsic value theory approach to environmentalism (1990, p. 206).

No-self and all-self

The views on the phenomenon 'self' described so far conceptualise a personal self that is somewhat located within our personal boundaries. An expanded view of the self, however, suggests that our self is not limited by our skin or aura, but extends beyond our personal self-boundaries. In such a view, we exist as much outside of ourselves as the outside world exists inside of us. Indeed, humans and other living organisms are not isolated entities, but are permeated by subtle energy and inhabited by bacteria, viruses, and other microorganisms. Such a view helps us to be aware that our inner organism is surrounded by semi-permeable membranes, and that we maintain homeostasis not through isolation, but through active adaptive metabolic processes.

The notion of 'no-self' was described by the Buddha more than 2500 years ago. Macy (1985, 1991), for example, describes this notion as a characterising feature of the whole universe. The associated notion of dependent co-origination (or co-arising) stands in strong contrast to the notion of 'independent wellbeing', which is favoured in modern Western societies. People operating from this Buddhist notion of consciousness regard the notion of independence as an unsustainable fiction that needs to be replaced with the notion of inter-dependency. They acknowledge that we are dependent on others, as much as others are dependent on us. From this viewpoint, all attempts to be independent must eventually end in a crisis and in final emotional and physical disintegration. In a similar vein, Kohut (1971, 1977) believes that we need constant validation and mirroring from others in meaningful relationships to develop and maintain our sense of self and emotional homeostasis.

At the same time, it is important to consider that, as psychotherapists, we cannot encourage people to go beyond their personal self (ego) before they have had a chance to establish a strong sense of personal self, a phenomenon that Wilber (1983, 1995) has called the pre-post fallacy. Boadella and Waal (1987, p. 125) acknowledge that it "[is] necessary to do 'ego-building' before proceeding with deep vegeto-therapy if one [wants] to avoid the risk of psychotic breakdown". In other words, the development of a coherent personal self is a necessary precondition for the development of a more transpersonal consciousness.

The observing self

An important concept of self, which is still widely neglected in environmentalism and environmental education, is what Deikman (1982) calls the observing self. This notion of self characterises the ability to transgress the identification with our feelings without having to separate from them. From such an emotional position, we can experience ourselves, and the people we are with, with a sense of empathy, even in the face of conflicting interests. This concept of the observing self has so far been used mainly in the various mystical schools, although some forms of somatic psychotherapy, such as Hakomi (Kurtz, 1990), seem to support the development of this kind of self-consciousness.

From an ethics-based to an experience-based sense of self

Present environmental thinking tends to view our relationships with the other-than-human world mainly with reference to preferred values and ethics. This ethics-based environmentalism still widely neglects the perception of the relationships between humans and the more-than-human as an experience of person-planet unity. Value and ethics-based concepts of the relationships between humans and the rest of nature are prone to fluctuation, since they are frequently influenced by changes in the political landscape, by new developments in technology, and by manipulation through the media. Experience-based concepts of our relationships with nature, in contrast, tend to be more stable because they are not only based on external factors, but also on embodied human self-experience. Watts has particularly informed my thinking about our being in the world. The following quotation was one of the starting points for my interest in working with our energetic connection to the world:

> This feeling of being lonely and very temporary visitors in the universe is in flat contradiction to everything known about man (and all other living organisms) in the sciences. We do not "come into" this world; we come *out* of it, as leaves from a tree. As the ocean "waves", the universe "peoples". Every individual is an expression of the whole realm of nature, a unique action of the total universe. This fact is rarely, if ever, experienced by most individuals. Even those who know it to be true in theory do not sense or feel it, but continue to be aware of themselves as isolated "egos" inside bags of skin (1966, p. 8).

This statement is intended to make us aware that our common ideas of self, as much as our felt egocentric self-experience, produce a belief that we are individuals among other individuals, in much the same way as we regard islands as being isolated from other islands. By attaining an ecological consciousness, we realise that we are deeply connected with the biosphere in the same way that islands are connected to each other under the ocean's surface. Feeling isolated, we often fail to make meaningful contact with others, and forget that we all are made from the same fabric, suffer the same pain about our difficulty with experiencing love, and need the same basic 'cures' on this deep level of existence.

Conn (1995, p. 157) emphasises that all human beings have the in-built capacity for the awareness of person-planet unity when she writes:

Each of us has, with or without awareness, the ability to connect to the whole interdependent web of life on Earth at any moment and in any activity in our daily lives. [....] But most of us still seem to act as if the Earth and its nonhuman aspects were separate from us, something "out there" with no life of its own, and therefore unrelated to our "merely personal" concerns.

Yet, awareness appears to be an important factor because, because most non-indigenous modern people, who have lost their sense of connectedness in the process of their upbringing, acknowledging their lack of ability to experience person-planet unity is an important motivating factor for the commencement of a personal healing journey, a journey that, according to Conn (1995, p. 160), "requires an exploration of ways to remember our wholeness, to reconnect with other humans and with the natural world".

The currently dominant self-experience of disconnectedness has created the myth of independent wellbeing, which is often emphasised by wealthy elites in modern societies. Although these people usually do have access to cleaner air and water, to healthier and more diverse foods, and to more time to care for their body-minds, this does not enable them to remain immune from the rest of society. As Diamond (2005) comments in his book *Collapse*, even rich and powerful people suffer the same fate as common people—they simply starve last.

Ego-self and eco-self

Recently, an increasing number of environmentalists and ecological psychologists (Matthews, 1994; Winter, 1996) have used the notions of ego-self and eco-self, to which we refer extensively in this study. Although commonly accepted definitions of these terms do not appear to exist, present usage suggests that the term 'ego-self' stands for a mindset centred on the awareness of individuality, a sense of separation from nature, and the predominant satisfaction of personal needs. In contrast, the term 'eco-self' denotes a sensibility of connectedness to other human beings, to the wider biosphere, and to a lifestyle concerned with preservation of resources and the satisfaction of communal needs. An overview and comparison of these two notions is provided in Table 2.1 on the next page.

Table 2.1 Aspects of ego-self and eco-self

Ego-self	*Eco-self*
Satisfaction of personal needs	Satisfaction of communal needs
Separateness	Connectedness
Expansion and economic growth	Conservation and personal growth
Sense of self based on consuming and owning of goods and the attainment of power	Sense of self based on belonging and embodiment (energetic connection)
Focus on using people	Focus on being with people (relating)
Projection of disowned feelings	Reclaiming of disowned feelings

Aspects of ego-self consciousness

An increasing number of scholars characterise Western societies as being made up mainly of people who operate from an ego-self consciousness. Since 'belief' in this paradigm has become normalised, it has become difficult to observe our behaviour objectively in order to understand the pathology of our present consciousness. Since this form of consciousness, with its widespread web of perceptions and behaviour is all-encompassing, it will only be possible to outline a small selection of its aspects.

1 – Egocentrism

When operating from a state of ego-self consciousness, people are usually more interested in their personal wellbeing than in the wellbeing of both other humans and the other-than-human environment. Although they might extend their caring to family members and friends, they are usually more interested in having a good life and easy access to cheap resources than in the fate and living conditions of other people. At this level of consciousness, people usually do not question why most people in Western societies have relatively easy access to inexpensive goods and services, whereas, most in developing countries continue to live in poverty and squalor. The term 'squalor' is used here to denote the physical results of poverty, not moral degradation, since moral degradation is not limited to people living in poverty. Conversely, it is probably fair to say that the moral degradation of rich and powerful people both in Western and Third World countries contributes to many of the causes of poverty in the Third World.

2 – *Outward orientation*

A typical manifestation of ego-consciousness is an orientation towards external stimuli, stimuli that fail to provide lasting satisfaction (cf. Hill, 2003a). In such an orientation, many people experience faith by worshipping religious idols (cf. Fromm, 1979), by favouring external 'objective truths' over their intuitive gut feelings, and by trusting the skills and expertise of so-called specialists. With such an orientation, they also exclusively expect healing to come from external sources, such as remedies or surgery, rather than from a psychosomatic exploration and healing of disowned feelings and conflicts.

3 – *Sense of freedom*

Ego-self consciousness often produces an aggressive approach to life. This approach can be characterised variously by an active and bullying – and also a passive and manipulative – approach to people and the other-than-human environment. Typical ego-self consciousness behaviour may be observed on freeways, where many people put their own life, and the lives of others, at risk by engaging in tailgating and risky overtaking maneuvers. For these people, limitations and rules seem to exist only to be challenged without consideration about whether or not many of these limitations and rules enable us to coexist harmoniously on this small planet. When operating from an ego-self consciousness, many will tend to bend rules that they experience as impinging on their sense of freedom. Freedom, in this context, is not a mutualistic but an individualised experience (Hill, 2000). It is not perceived as freedom *from* our neurotic or egocentric condition and its associated compulsions, but as the freedom *to* use, destroy and exploit, often unknowingly, but often also knowingly.

4 – *Denial of environmental crises*

People operating from an ego-self consciousness rarely give a thought to the natural environment. They tend to view many aspects of our ecological crises as nothing but the morbid inventions of people who worry too much, and who would be better off lightening up and having a good time. They might feel that after all, there are still many species of animals left on this planet, and what's the point of feeling guilt and gloom anyway.

When confronted with undeniable data on our ecological crises, these people often tend to justify their lifestyle by referring to environmentalists who hold the belief that modern science and technology will be able to fix the ecological problems as they arise. They also tend to regard social injustice as mainly self-inflicted, and often blame people in developing countries for unwisely using the generous monetary and other support offered by institutions such as the World Bank; and they also tend to focus on their need to practice birth control.

5 – *Having versus being*

People operating from an ego-self consciousness tend to focus on having rather than on being. Fromm (1979) points out that many aspects of human living can be experienced in both a having and a being mode. Faith, he writes, is experienced in the having mode if we lay claim to our faith as being the right one, that is, if we are "the happy owners of the right faith" (1979, p. 49). In terms of loving, Fromm (1979, p. 52) holds that living in the having mode makes us become "strangling, deadening, suffocating, killing, not life-giving". Fromm (1979, p. 52) also suggests that, during the last two millennia, only a small minority of parents have been able to love their children in the being mode. He describes "cruelty against children, ranging from physical to psychic torture, carelessness, sheer possessiveness, and sadism, so shocking that one must believe that loving parents are the exception rather than the rule".

6 – *Loss of enchantment*

A salient feature of egocentric living is the loss of enchantment. Moore (1996, p. xvii) writes about this topic:

> Some psychological theories equate childhood with paradise and conclude that to live as mature adults we should separate heroically from childhood and enter this vale of tears called maturity. They're afraid that if we don't overcome childhood, we'll become stuck in infantile illusions. Some experts believe that life is essentially disenchanted and that those who think otherwise are naïve or psychotic.

In this quotation, Moore, similar to Watts (1961), and Walker (1979), aptly describes how people living in modern societies have normalised the self-experience of numbness and fragmentation, and have marginalised experiences of deep meaning, purpose, and person-planet unity. Having also constructed psychological views and educational and philosophical systems around this self-experience, we are now embedded in a society whose worldviews, values, policies, and practices perpetuate egocentric living.

In Chapter 2 we have described a number of key notions on consciousness and self, notions that place our predicament in a larger context of self-development. We have also provided a brief outline of egocentric consciousness, a form of self-experience that is presently dominant in Western society. In Chapter 3, we proceed to describe the fist stage of eco-self transformation, a shift in consciousness that we associate with the application of behaviourist psychology to our ecological crises.

3 Manipulated Eco-self Consciousness (Stage One)

In this chapter we describe what we regard as the first stage of eco-self consciousness development: manipulated eco-self consciousness. At this level, behaviour technologies – developed by behaviourists such as Skinner (1948, 1953, 1971), Geller et al. (1982), and Eagly and Kulesa (1997) – are used to persuade and influence people to adopt environmentally sustainable behaviours. Here, we briefly describe these technologies and examine their usefulness when viewed from within a behaviourist paradigm. Possible limitations of this approach to consciousness are discussed in Chapter 9.

Problems with distinguishing between behaviourist and cognitive psychology

In our attempt to distinguish between manipulated eco-self consciousness in this chapter and learned eco-self consciousness (discussed in the next chapter) we encountered an epistemological problem arising from the difficulty to distinguish between these two systems. In an ideal world the term behaviourist psychology would exclusively be used to describe the external stimuli that can be employed to guide or reinforce particular behaviour. An example here is the possible increase of the price of fuel to a level at which large numbers of people switch to the more ecologically sustainable public transportation system (Kals, 1996).

However, behaviourist psychology often describes an integration of behaviourist and cognitive processes, as outlined in the following citation:

> To illustrate, consider a food-deprived rat in an experimental chamber. If a particular movement, such as pressing a lever when a light is on, is followed by the presentation of food, then the likelihood of the rat's pressing the lever when hungry, again, and the light is on, is increased. Such presentations are reinforcements, such lights are (discriminative) stimuli, such lever pressings are responses, and such trials or associations are learning histories (Stanford Encyclopedia of Philosophy, 2005 p. 2).

In fact, psychological behaviourism has its roots in Locke's associationism, which holds that human beings are born without any innate capabilities and which regards intelligent behaviour as the product of associative learning.

The second issue that makes it difficult to clearly distinguish between behaviourist and cognitive constructs is the contentious issue of persuasive communication (Eagly and Kulesa, 1997). We regard this issue as contentious because we believe that repetitive exposure of people to information designed to achieve a particular outcome has more in common with behaviourist manipulation than with providing information to foster learning. This is, we believe, particularly true when fear-inducing appeals are used to make persuasion more effective (Eagly and Kulesa, 1997, p. 124).

Acknowledging that a comprehensive clarification of this issue is beyond the scope of this study, we resolved the issue for the purpose of this study by making the following distinction: We shall describe under the term manipulative eco-self consciousness the strategies that use persuasion, other influencing skills, and the provision of biased information to achieve predefined goals. In contrast, we shall employ the term learned eco-self consciousness where learners are widely free to form their own judgments on the basis of new information. To this purpose, information should be designed to provide a complex picture of issues, including their pros and cons and causes and effects.

The nature of manipulated eco-self consciousness

We regard this first of the six levels of eco-consciousness that we will be describing as emerging from manipulation by social forces. At this level, people respond positively to the interventions of people and institutions that base their behaviour change strategies on behaviourist psychology. This approach to change is based on the assumption that the behaviour of many of us is maladapted to the requirements of the environment in which we live. People at this level of eco-consciousness are likely to:

- accept the authority of specialists who claim to have identified certain behaviours as inappropriate and unsustainable;
- agree to being persuaded or coerced into adopting more sustainable behaviour;
- respond positively to behaviourist interventions such as incentives and disincentives.

A brief overview of this behaviourist approach to change is provided in Table 3.1 on page 68.

Behavioural technologies used to foster sustainable behaviours

Behaviourists have developed an impressive array of technologies aimed at changing people's behaviour. These include stimulus control, contingency management, provision of feedback, legislation, and pricing. Stimulus control is an antecedent strategy focusing on stimuli that have the capacity to facilitate ecologically sustainable behaviour. It includes devices such as the optimal placement of signs to remind us to switch off lights when we leave a room or to dispose of waste in the appropriate garbage bins.

Table 3.1 Behaviourist approaches to change

	Behaviourism
Focus	*Scientifically observable behaviour*
Theoretical framework	Stimulus-Response Psychology (Watson, 1914, 1925, 1928) Theory of operant conditioning (Skinner, 1948, 1953, 1971) Behaviour/environment relationships (Skinner, 1971) Reinforcement Schedules (Ferster & Skinner 1957)
Aims	Controlling unsustainable behaviour
Assumed causes of our ecological crises	Inappropriate human behaviour Short-term satisfaction is being chosen over concern for long-term consequences
Assumptions underlying strategies for change	Our culture needs to be redesigned to achieve environmentally appropriate behaviour (Skinner, 1971) Behaviour is not right or wrong – it simply reflects the contextual environment in which we behave
Central approach to change	We will change our behaviour in response to changes in the preceding stimuli Change occurs by modifying people's behaviour
Dominant change strategies	Persuasion by emphasising the benefits (e.g., momentary) of change
Basis for change	Based on the notion of motivation
Expected emotional outcomes	Feelings, emotions, and behaviour can be manipulated by means of stimulus control

Stimulus control

Another stimulus control device is the modelling of environmentally appropriate behaviour. This approach has achieved high levels of compliance, for example, in promoting energy-conserving shower heads (Aronson and O'Leary, 1982, 1983).

Contingency management

Contingency management focuses on activities that can act to reinforce a particular desired behaviour. Such reinforcement strategies include:

- rewarding people for using public transport with tokens;
- providing incentives for buying more fuel-efficient cars;
- paying people money for collecting aluminum cans;
- providing consumer rebates for bottles returned to outlets; and
- providing fast lanes for cars occupied by three passengers or more.

Feedback

Research on the effects of providing feedback (cf. Geller et al., 1982; VanHouten et al., 1980) has shown that it can be as effective as providing rewards. This strategy has been used, for example by publishing achievements in newspapers, to provide people with feedback on their efforts to reduce energy consumption and waste production. The idea behind feedback is that people are more likely to conserve energy if they can see in figures or graphs the results of their efforts.

Legislation

In our modern society, much of our behaviour is being enforced by legislation. Acts established by law-making institutions try to enforce particular behaviours by discriminating between permissible and punishable behaviour. An increasing number of countries have formulated environmental Acts that determine which kinds of behaviour manifest punishable offences against the other-than-human environment. Such offences include:

- polluting waterways;
- pollution of the soil with non-biodegradable substances;
- dumping garbage in forests and other public places; and
- killing certain kinds of animals during particular times of the year.

Pricing

The pricing of commodities represents a powerful way to manipulate behaviour. By subsidising sustainable behaviour and placing disincentives on unsustainable behaviour, legislators are potentially able to manipulate the ways in which we spend our money and behave. Legislators could, for example:

- make the prevention of illness more accessible by subsidising massage, Yoga, working out at the gym, etc.;
- make the use of public transport more attractive by subsidising it and by making individual transport much more costly; and
- subsidise basic food items by placing higher taxes on non-essential and ecologically damaging goods and services.

The emphasis here is on 'could', since legislators in many countries have so far shied away from using such powerful mechanisms. In fact, people who try to live healthily and sustainably are often punished by having to pay extra, for example, for unsubsidised illness-prevention routines on top of compulsory government levies for health insurance.

Skinner (1948, 1953), acknowledged that a key problem with such approaches is that short-term consequences differ from long-term consequences, and that our behaviour is mainly controlled by short-term reinforcers. This suggests that people tend to satisfy short-term needs even if they lead to adverse effects in the long term, a phenomenon that has been called a 'social trap' (Hardin, 1968; Platt, 1973). As a solution to this problem, Skinner suggests bringing the short-term consequences in line with the long-term consequences. In relation to the other-than-human environment, this might mean charging people for the real environmental costs of the goods and services they consume (Winter, 1996). This would then make it more attractive to use public transportation, or to repair rather than replace defective goods.

Benefits of behaviourist interventions

There is no doubt that some change strategies based on behaviour control and manipulation are useful and will continue to play an important role in our attempts to create a more sustainable society. These strategies have the advantage that they:

- may produce relatively quick results;
- can be enforced by legislation;
- may produce behaviour that can be controlled and measured; and
- do not challenge existing economic and philosophical paradigms.

Yet, the behaviourist approach to changing people's behaviour is also limited because it fails to address the deeper roots of our ecological crises. The arguments supporting this claim will be presented in Chapter 9.

In Chapter 3, we have focused on the first step towards eco-self transformation. This step is marked by societal attempts to influence and manipulate people into changing their behaviour towards the natural environment. Whereas scientists committed to behaviourism and manipulated change seem to believe that the implementation of these strategies is all that is needed to make their efforts work, many ecologists have recognised the limitations of manipulation, and place their hopes on enabling learning and understanding. This educational approach is described in the following chapter.

4 Learned Eco-self Consciousness (Stage Two)

In this chapter we describe a form of consciousness-raising based on the notions of learning, changing perceptions, the creation of knowledge, and the processing, storing and retrieval of information. Environmental educators favouring this cognitive approach to environmental change hold that manipulative practices alone are not sufficient to lead to lasting changes in people's attitudes, values, and behaviour, and that they need to be augmented by an approach based on learning and cognition. Key limitations of this form of consciousness-raising are discussed in Chapter 9.

Cognitive psychology

This second stage of eco-self transformation can be framed in terms of cognitive psychology. Based on the work of Chomsky (1957, 1959), Piaget (1959), Anderson (1983), Feigenbaum (1970), and many others, cognitive psychology assumes the existence of a mind and of higher mental processes.

According to cognitive psychology, learning is the process of acquiring, encoding, and storing information. Data from sensory experiences stored in our brains and nervous systems represent an internal representation of the outer world, and becomes knowledge that can be retrieved and used for complex thinking processes. Knowledge can exist either as a representation of images, sounds and smells, or in the form of abstract concepts. Either way, it is usually processed in our minds in language form, in particular, if it is to be shared with other people.

In its early formulations, the explicit aims of environmental education were often concerned with stimulating a sense of individual responsibility for the physical and aesthetic quality of the total environment based on a knowledge of general ecological principles, an understanding of the impact of human society on the biosphere, and an awareness of the problems inherent in the environmental change (Gough, 2002, p. 1201).

Learning eco-self consciousness

The discipline that has embraced the task of teaching people eco-self consciousness is environmental education. Having become diversified over time to accommodate diverging views on the causes of our ecological crises, environmental education has developed into streams called environmental education (EE), education for sustainable development (ESD), and education for sustainability (EFS). The first approach will be covered under the heading *Learned Eco-self Consciousness* in this chapter, whereas education for sustainable development (ESD) and education for sustainability (EFS) will be part of stage three of this system of eco-self-development.

The term 'environmental education' (EE) was first used internationally in 1977 at the International Union for the Conservation of Nature and Natural Resources (IUCN) Conference, in Tbilisi. At this conference, delegates agreed on the following three goals of environmental education:

- To foster clear awareness of, and concern about, economic, social, political, and ecological interdependence in urban and rural areas.
- To provide every person with opportunities to acquire the knowledge, values, attitudes, commitment, and skills needed to protect and improve the environment.
- To create new patterns of behaviour of individuals, groups, and society as a whole towards the environment (UNESCO, 1977).

To put more life into these goals, environmentalists in the UK formulated a set of statements that suggested environmental education should, according to Palmer (1998, pp. 10 - 11):

- be a life-long process;
- be holistic and interdisciplinary in nature and application;
- emphasise active responsibility; and
- encourage the development of sensitivity, awareness, understanding, critical thinking, and problem-solving skills.

Environmental education and education for sustainable development are based on the assumption that sustainable development and sustainability can be achieved by:

- changing people's behaviour through providing knowledge and insight into ecological issues;
- teaching people to use practices such as recycling and the wise use of resources;
- applying a socially reformist approach to ecological change (see O'Riordan, 1981);
- continuing to work within the paradigm of economic growth;

- mainly applying a technological approach to ecology;
- teaching students ecological issues without questioning the values of modernity;
- applying an approach to environmental education based on cognition and conventional science;
- applying an approach to education that is discipline-based, that works with abstract and theoretical problems, and that stays within the paradigm of conventional modern schooling;
- doing environmental education in the classroom, and by utilising teachers as dispensers of factual knowledge (Stevenson, 1987; Goodlad, 1984; Young, 1980); and
- using predefined curricula based on the work of professionals committed to research that employs the conventional science paradigm.

The approach to environmental education briefly outlined above is based on cognitive and educational psychology, and on the assumption that people can change their behaviour when they understand (have the insight) that changing their behaviour will make the Earth a better place to live. This view is also the cornerstone of the 1991 World Conservation Strategy, entitled *Caring for the Earth: A Strategy for Sustainable Living* (IUCN/UNEP/WWF, 1991).

Benefits of an approach based on cognition and learning

Learning is fundamental to being alive. As part of our ontogenetic development, we learn to crawl, to walk, to speak one or more languages, to adapt to the demands made on us, and to persuade people to respond favourably to our needs. Considering that learning is essential to being alive, it is reasonable that environmentalists hold out great hope that people can be taught to behave sustainably towards the natural environment.

Learning about the nature of human-nature relationships and about the ecological workings of nature provides for many of us sufficient motivation to care for the natural environment. The ecological knowledge provided at school and in the media has provided an understanding of the importance of issues such as kerbside recycling, of using hessian (rather than plastic) bags for shopping, of saving energy at home and work, of properly disposing of items such as batteries (still only possible in a few countries), and of composting food scraps.

There can be little doubt that millions of people have adopted such sustainability practices in response to their learning, and have consequently contributed to the slowing down of the ecological deterioration of our Earth. Since learning, probably more than being manipulated into certain behaviours, provides the foundation for being proud of our achievements, many of us continue to increase our sense of pride and self through inventing and refining new ways of contributing towards what Trainer (1995) has called a conserver society.

Environmental education and education for sustainable development are, at present, probably the most widely employed modalities used to teach students in the primary and secondary education sector about the deterioration of our natural environment, and about ways of caring for the environment. More holistically inclined environmental educators, however, argue that this way of educating students fails to address the larger context of modernity, and avoids questioning the validity of the meta-narratives of modernity. Since such reflection and discourse analysis constitute a paradigm shift, we will describe this expanded consciousness in the next chapter, under the title Participatory Eco-self Consciousness.

5 Participatory Eco-self Consciousness (Stage 3)

In this chapter we describe two approaches to change that share important aspects, but are also in many respects distinct. These approaches are Education for Sustainability (EFS) and Education for Sustainable Development (ESD).

Education for Sustainability (EFS)

The shift in consciousness associated with a political critique of modernity by mainly deconstructionist postmodern scholars is education for sustainability (EFS). Proponents of this educational approach suggest that conventional environmental education is limited in its effectiveness and scope because:

- it fails to address our general crisis of modernity;
- it is technocentric rather than ecocentric (O'Riordan, 1988);
- it applies a technological approach to ecology that promises quick fixes (Enzensberger, 1974);
- it teaches students ecological issues without encouraging structural transformation and democratisation (Huckle, 1990);
- it applies an approach to environmental education based on conventional natural science (not including post-normal science); and
- it applies an approach to education that is exclusively discipline-based, that works with abstract and theoretical problems, and that stays within the paradigm of conventional modern schooling.

This transformation in consciousness is expressed in the shift from an adherence to the tenets of cognitive psychology towards a commitment to those of deconstructive postmodern psychology. The consequently emerging deconstructionist postmodern approach to environmental education is based on the notion of social constructionism, as, for example, described by Gergen (1991, 1997). A critical examination of the limitations of this approach to ecological thinking and environmental education is provided in Chapter 9.

The notion of participatory eco-self consciousness

The third stage of the development of eco-self consciousness leaves behind what has been called the modern worldview. People at this level of consciousness have learnt to focus on the complex relationships between different entities, have left behind the mechanistic and atomistic modern paradigm, and have adopted a more holistic understanding of the cosmos. Environmental educators such as Tilbury (1993, 1995), Tilbury and Stevenson (2002), Tanner (1974), Emery (1981), Stevenson (1987), Huckle (1983), Robottom (1982, 1983), Gough (1987) Volk et al. (1984), and Robottom and Hart (1993) have focused on the shift from an education based strictly on cognition and scientific materialism, towards an education also based on human perception, awareness of local agendas, and direct action. They also charge that conventional environmental education is predominantly concerned with educating young people rather than the adults who actually harm the natural environment, and that it fails to question important power relations.

I argue that both science educators and environmental educators need to rethink the relationships between science education and environmental education. If we are to achieve sustainable development then science education must have a role in encouraging ecological thinking (instead of being kept at a distance) and environmental education must move on from the insecure relationships that accompany the abstract arguments for it to adopt a holistic approach, rooted in a broad interdisciplinary base' [UNESCO 1978:24] (Gough, 2002, p. 1203).

Benefits of education for sustainability

There is no doubt that education for sustainability is the most inclusive approach to environmental education so far. With its emphasis on extending "the boundary of care and concern beyond the immediate and personal to a participative sense of solidarity with others, distant people, environments, species and future generations" (Sterling, 1996, pp. 23-24), education for sustainability has integrated and balanced correlated pairs that were dissociated and distorted in the dominant dualistic paradigm.

The benefits of the participatory consciousness arise from a critique of the metanarratives of modernity and of our dominant psychological views (Kvale, 1992; Gergen, 1997). Some key aspects of this critique of our dominant paradigm are outlined in Table 5.1 on the following page.

The British Environment, Development, Education and Training (EDET) report described EFS as a process rather than a goal. It is a process that, according to Sterling (1992, p. 2):

- enables people to understand the interdependence of all life on this planet, and the repercussions that their actions and decisions

may have both now and in future, on resources, and on the global community as well as their local one, and on the total environment;
- increases people's awareness of the economic, political, social, cultural, technological and environmental sources which foster, or impede, sustainable development; and
- develops people's awareness, competence, attitudes and values, enabling them to be effectively involved in sustainable development at local, national and global level, and helps them to work towards a more equitable and sustainable future.

Table 5.1 Modern versus deconstructionist postmodern psychology

Modern Psychology:	*Postmodern Psychology:*
focus: individuals	relationships and communities
research: done in laboratories	done in real-life situations
approach: predominantly pure science	predominantly applied science
interest: observable facts and behaviour	values and motivations
nature: viewed as a machine	as a complex, living organism
aims to exclude subjectivity	includes subjectivity
single discipline as container for knowledge	interdisciplinary approach to knowing
works within existing political and cultural paradigm	critical of dominant modern paradigm; seeking radical social change

Orr (1994) claims that conventional education continues to educate people as if there were no planetary emergency; and suggests that the public needs to learn about the state of the environment as well as to embrace the necessity to take more responsibility.

Fien and Gough (1996), on the other hand, describe environmental education as an approach to learning that individuals and groups can use to attain a better understanding of the interrelationships between individuals and environments. To address the perceived shortcomings of conventional approaches to environmental education, Sterling (1996, pp. 22–24) suggests that education for sustainability:

- has to be contextual and address the crises of modernity;
- should be applied and grounded in the local economic, social and ecological context and community, followed by regional, national, international and global contexts;

- has to be integrative, interdisciplinary and transdisciplinary, process-oriented and empowering rather than product-oriented;
- has to revise and re-evaluate education and learning as intrinsic to life;
- has to be engaged and participative rather than passive;
- has to have an emphasis on learning rather than teaching, and use action research with an emphasis on critical reflection, experiential learning cycles and democratic ownership of change;
- has to be critical, ideologically aware, and recognise that no educational values are politically neutral; and
- should draw on the body of critical theory associated with deep green and red-green orientations.

Key issues relating to shifts from the modern-cognitive to the postmodern cognitive worldview are highlighted in Tables 5.2, 5.3, and 5.4 below and on the following pages.

Table 5.2 Cognitive modern versus cognitive postmodern education foci

Cognitive (modern)	Cognitive (postmodern)
The workings of the mind, the quality of information available to people, and the ways in which the information is processed	Education as an agent of change supporting improved 'constructions'
Cognitive Psychology (Neisser, 1967); Theory of cognitive development, understanding of rules and structures (Piaget, 1959); Information processing in computers and man (Simon and Newell, 1964); Learning by understanding and applying rules (Chomsky, 1957); Knowledge Construction (Winn and Snyder, 1996)	Deconstructionism (Derrida, 1978); New environmental paradigm (Milbrath, 1989); Critique of the dominant scientific paradigm (N. Gough, 1987; Elliott, 1991; Fien, 1992; Robottom and Hart, 1993); Postmodern education (Huckle and Sterling, 1996); Education in the senses (Emery, 1981)
The functioning of nature can be understood through structured learning processes (conventional ecology)	Nature is socially constructed and its causal powers and objective properties are mediated by social processes (Huckle, 1996)
Understanding unsustainable behaviour and replacing it with ecologically sustainable behaviour	Social and cultural change; Overcoming unsustainable practices through an integrative, contextually sensitive, process-oriented and reflective critical process of learning sustainability

Education for Sustainable Development

The second approach, situated between environmental education and the depth psychology approach described in the following chapter, is education for sustainable development (ESD). Like EFS, it:

- is interdisciplinary and holistic in nature;
- is values-driven;
- insists on participatory decision-making;
- focuses on locally relevant as well as global issues;
- is based on critical thinking and problem solving; and
- insists that teachers and learners work together to acquire knowledge and skills.

Table 5.3 Assumed causes of ecological deterioration (modern versus deconstructionist postmodern)

Modern	*Deconstructionist postmodern*
Lack of appropriate information and biased/distorted information processing	Logical result of capitalism's "in-built tendency to discount present and future environmental costs" (Huckle, 1996, p. 3); Focus on capital accumulation, destruction of common property; Private ownership of land, the means of production and reproduction; Focus on atomistic and materialistic Western science
Achievement of 'sense of self' based on learning and cognition	"There is no stable self: identity is continuously emergent, re-formed, and redirected as one moves through a sea of ever-changing relationships" (Gergen, 1991, p. 155)
The symptoms of suffering from: quantitative illiteracy, visual dependency, having a confirmation bias; responding to irrelevant information, selective attention, etc.	Lack of holistic thinking, replacement of intrinsic values with instrumental values, and exclusive reliance on positivistic and empiricist science

Education for Sustainable Development

The second approach, situated between environmental education and the depth psychology approach described in the following chapter, is education for sustainable development (ESD). Like EFS, it:

- is interdisciplinary and holistic in nature;
- is values-driven;
- insists on participatory decision-making;
- focuses on locally relevant as well as global issues;
- is based on critical thinking and problem solving; and
- insists that teachers and learners work together to acquire knowledge and skills.

Comparing education for sustainable development and education for sustainability

Although there is a significant overlap between the two approaches to social and environmental change, there are also significant differences. In general, ESD shows a greater reluctance to critique the tenets of modernity. In comparison with EFS, it appears less critical and confrontationist, less willing to name the destructive effects of capitalism and globalisation. Although ESD mentions corporate responsibility as a key action theme, a discourse analysis of the language used and a critical view of its underlying beliefs suggests that ESD is less radical in its demands on powerful stakeholders to fundamentally change their modes of operating. Unlike proponents of EFS, proponents of ESD consciously, or unconsciously, avoid any reference to a distinction between modern and postmodern mindsets. A second point of difference is ESD's acceptance of science and technology.

Table 5.4 Emphasised aspects of change (modern versus deconstructionist)

Modern	*Deconstructionist*
A strong ethical code is needed to tell us, with certainty (right information), what is sustainable and what is unsustainable behaviour	The natural environment suffers from our modern ways of perceiving the world and of producing goods and services
We will change our behaviour if we clearly understand the need to do so; change occurs by having access to the right information, by eliminating irrelevant information, and by improving our processing skills	We will change our behaviour if we adopt and embrace ecological issues by means of problem-solving, action-based activities that deal with real-life and local issues
Convincing by improving our understanding of the need to	Achieving change through participating in direct action aimed at improving

behave differently; subject-based curriculum in environmental education	ecological conditions
Access to, and understanding of, correct and relevant information	Empowerment, development of a contextual worldview, critical and reflective thinking; changing values
We have to learn to love the natural environment	Sense of empowerment; increased interest in processes rather than in goals; sense of participation and belonging; increased valuing of intuition

With the emancipatory approach described in this chapter, environmental education has reached the present boundaries of formal environmentalism and environmental education. Although it has moved a long way towards holistic and systemic thinking, EFS and ESD, like its modern counterpart, EE, have so far shown little interest in the emotional and psychological underpinnings of our ecological crises. Focusing mainly on a political analysis, and being committed to the surface appearances typical for deconstructionist thinking, they have remained committed to the view that humans are conscious agents of their fates, a view questioned in the following chapters.

Education for sustainability provides a tool to assist and engage us in negotiating this future and deciding the consequences of our decisions. This means that education is more than the traditional practice of environmental Education, which focuses on teaching and learning about, in and 'for' the environment. Instead, education for sustainability seeks a transformative role for education in which people are engaged in a new way of seeing, thinking, learning and working (Tilbury and Wortman, 2004, p. 9).

6 Deep Eco-Consciousness (Stage 4)

In Chapter 6, we will describe stage four of our six-stage model of eco-self transformation. The focus at this stage of consciousness is on broadening and deepening our understanding of our ecological crises from a depth psychology perspective. At this level of consciousness, we have come to acknowledge that:

- human beings are far less conscious of their feelings and motivations than is commonly assumed;
- we have to replace the limited notion of social change with the deeper notions of personal and planetary healing;
- many key aspects of our ecological crises are predictable outcomes of the stalled self-development typical for our modern society; and
- this stalled self-development results from an upbringing in families and a wider society that significantly compromises the natural human needs for emotional safety, adequate nurturing, body-contact, and mirroring.

In this chapter, the findings summarised in Appendix 1 are used as tools for a deepened understanding of our ecological crises. The views expressed by some of the research participants are reframed as defence mechanisms and character structures (Winter, 1996; Johnson, 1985, 1994; Reich, 1933, 1942; Lowen, 1958, 1972, 1980, 1985) to interpret ecologically unsustainable perceptions of, and behaviour towards, the other-than-human environment. Key aspects of our ecological crises are also conceptualised as predictable outcomes of the oral and narcissistic character structures. Together with the schizoid structure that will feature predominantly in Chapter 10, these two emotional conditions can be regarded as the dominant psychological conditions in Western societies.

Key concepts of depth psychology

The unconscious

Freud's notion of the unconscious and his distinction of ego, superego, and id challenged the belief held by Descartes and Locke that human beings are conscious agents of their lives. His views on humans' psychological functioning imply that people's unconscious feelings and motivations are significant contributing factors of our ecological crises, and that these factors have become normalised and institutionalised as integrated parts of our social, political, and educational systems.

The concept of neurosis

An important concept of depth psychology is neurosis. In conventional depth psychology, the term is used for a way of being in the world marked by the experience of conflict and the automatic suppression (repression) of feelings. In a state of conflict, we are usually pulled in one direction by our need to lead pleasurable and psychosocially sustainable lives, and in another direction by the demands of a society that is widely out of touch with our basic needs for emotional integrity, happiness, and belongingness. Although as adults we usually have a greater variety of liberties and choices of behaviour, many of us nevertheless continue to respond to the internalised demands of our early caregivers rather than to the needs and necessities of our core selves (Hill, 2003a).

The view held by depth psychologists, that the neurotic way of being has become the norm in modern societies, has caused much confusion in a psychology and philosophy that would rather view humans as conscious agents of their fates. Fromm (1955, p. 15) notes:

> The fact that millions of people share the same vices does not make these vices virtues, the fact that they share so many errors does not make the errors to be truths, and the fact that so many people share the same forms of mental pathology does not make these people sane.

Because the unconscious is really unconscious, an emotional situation is unlikely to be recognised as pathological and problematic if most members of a society share it. Fromm concludes that an unhealthy state of being might even be elevated to virtue status by a culture, and thus may give people a sense of achievement (1955, p. 15). In other words, as we have become neurotic as a culture, many of us in Western societies tend to marginalise and pathologise people who refuse to, or cannot manage to, organise a working emotional defence structure, or whose emotional defences are eroded by stress or a lack of self-stabilising resources.

The notion of culture seems to act like a smokescreen, and even lures scholars engaged in attempts to formulate a vision of ecologically sustainable living into believing that "the quality of human-ness is as much if not more a function of such symbolic [cultural] representation as it is of direct physical, ecological pressures" (Matthews, 1991, p. 136). In many ways, this tendency to valorise culture over nature stems from our fascination with the symbolic, abstract, and language, and is a manifestation of the prevalent loss of body-mind and person-planet unity experiences that are described in this and the following chapters.

When we expand our consciousness by including a depth psychology perspective of our ecological crises, as many of the research participants have done, we learn to conceptualise many of our perceptions, feelings, and behaviour towards the natural environment as:

- predictable manifestations of unconscious feelings, emotions, motivations, and values;
- defence mechanisms against the conscious awareness of developmental traumas or shock traumas experienced in childhood and in later life;
- byproducts of our attempts to stabilise our incoherent and deficient sense of self;
- compulsive acts of repeating earlier traumatic experiences as unconscious attempts to reconnect to the trauma and to find healing and acknowledgment for these traumatic experiences;
- associated with our striving for emotional integrity, happiness, freedom, and security; and
- manifestations of typical emotional patterns, such as the systems of defence mechanisms and character structures.

Such views on the background of our environmental deterioration are disconcerting to many, which is perhaps one of the reasons why few psychiatrists and psychotherapists have so far acknowledged the links between depth psychology and ecological concerns. Such views are indeed radical and dangerous (Fisher, 2002). However, as Fisher points out, a small number of people, such as Kovel (1976, 1981, 1984), Lasch (1980), Breggin (1991), and Cushman (1990), have politicised conventional psychology and psychiatry – disciplines that are still widely colluding with many of our neurotic societal structures rather than questioning them.

Possibly even more disconcerting may be the view that neurosis represents an adaptive survival process, not only at the ontogenetic but also at the phylogenetic level, meaning that adaptive processes taking place in an individual lead to adaptive mutations that may be passed on to the person's offspring. The work of Shapiro on selection-induced mutation, the work of Cairns et al. on the environmental induction of genetic variation in Escheria coli, the work of Pollmann on the role of viruses and gene-fragments in the transfer of information, and the work of

Steele et al. on soma-to-germline feedback loops in the immune system, could all be interpreted in a way that suggests that consciousness and lived experiences may also be encoded and passed on to future generations.[2]

Whether or not geneticists will finally discard the Darwinian concept of random mutation and selection of the fittest in favour of the Lamarckian view of an inheritance of acquired characteristics may be in fact more a political than a scientific issue, one of the preservation of status and influence rather than one of scientific inquiry. As Steele et al. (1998, p. 209) put it:

> The Darwinian revolution was a resounding success, but the problem with intellectual revolutions is that they often harden into suffocating dogma – and at their apogee tend to be guarded by the holders almost as a sacred mantra. For a while the dogma is useful, but then an 'establishment' inevitably forms, the individuals of which find it almost impossible to break ranks, because if they do their careers and financial livelihood are put at great risk.

The question as to whether neurosis, or egocentric consciousness, as it is also called here, has become a part of our egocentric make-up is important because it would confirm the view proposed in this study, that achieving deep sustainability will be dependent on our willingness to engage in ways of working that also has the potential of altering our genetic make-up and consequently of creating a deep conscious evolution.

From a Freudian to a Reichian Self-concept

In this study, the Reichian and object-relations perspectives to make meaning of our ecological crises will be employed because classic Freudian theory can be applied to our ecological crises in only a limited way. This is because, as pointed out above, Freud supported a view that suggests that nature, both external and internal, needs to be tamed, and that, emotionally, health has to be achieved by the use of a well-managed emotional defence system. Prochaska (1984, p. 22), for example, wrote the following about classic Freudian psychoanalytic thinking:

> The individual is forced to develop defense mechanisms or inner controls that can keep sex and aggression from being expressed in

---

[2] Otto Warburg, a German physiologist, is said to have suggested in the 1920s that human experiences are genetically encoded and passed on to their offspring.

uncontrollable outbursts. Without such defenses, civilization would be reduced to a jungle of raping, ravaging beasts.

By regarding the natural needs of babies as a 'cauldron of seething excitation', he concluded that "the infant is totally maladapted by obeying the pleasure principle without reference to external reality" (Rycroft 1972, p. 138), and that the natural way of raising children must be to adapt them to what he called the reality principle. Consequently, Freudian theory regards affect renunciation and sublimation as the logical elements of ego-development, and Freud regarded the taming process as successful when human beings have become able to function in our modern society without developing major psychosomatic illnesses or psychological pathologies.

This taming of children, then, is still regarded as a primary task of our present child-rearing practices and modern education. Both these practices are thus more interested in adapting children to the egocentric values and behaviour dominant in modern society than in assisting children to become self-regulating and sustainable human beings. By referring to DeMause (1982), Hill (2003a) points out that Western society holds the belief that children must be socialised, molded, and guided, rather than supported in pursuing their internally derived (yet externally informed) assumptions and agendas. Stuart Hill continues by suggesting that most child-rearing has the effect that most people relinquish their power, lose their awareness of their deep selves (and of the world around them), and become distanced from their internal agendas, visions, and values.

Wilhelm Reich, one of Freud's students and later co-workers, developed a model of self that is based on a tripartite structure of self. This model posits a positive view of children's needs for nurturing and support at the core of their psyche. Reich acknowledged the high dependency of babies and infants as a necessary and natural feature of being human, instead of accusing babies of being selfish, irrational, and maladapted. He also recognised the difficulties with emotional living and embodiment caused by the neurotic (egocentric) values of modern society, values that made it both then, and still now, difficult for parents to attend to children's natural developmental needs. Whereas Freud regarded babies as greedy monsters in need to be tamed, Reich emphasised their tremendous ability to share love and curiosity with people who have retained the emotional ability to respond, and who care to make the time to do so.

Reich is often regarded as the originator of body-psychotherapy, a field of theoretical inquiry and practice that assists people in getting access to their unconscious and repressed traumatic experiences by working with the vital functions of the body-mind, which are breathing, sensing, moving, and expressing feelings and emotions. Reich's work has informed, both directly and indirectly, the work of many bodyoriented psychotherapists, including Lowen (1958, 1972, 1975, 1980, 1985), G. Boyesen (1976, 1985), Pierrakos (1974), Boadella (1976, 1987), Johnson (1994), Goerlitz (1998), Schrauth (2001), Staunton (2002), Heisterkamp (1993), and many others. Unlike conventional psychiatrists, bodyoriented psychotherapists and other practitioners engaged in transformative therapeutic practices have been under continuous pressure to reflect on their theory and practice, and have identified many of their 'failures' and problems (Murphy, 1992).[3]

The secondary level in this model takes seriously, according to Reich, the feelings that predictably emerge when children's core needs for nurturing, body contact, and other emotional support are not fully met. Boadella (1987, p. 152) writes about this secondary layer, that it "was the repressed unconscious with its forbidden drives, frequently destructive or confused".

Pierrakos (1974) puts it succinctly when he describes this secondary layer as the part of the self that contains the blockages and frustrations that children experience as result of parents' failure to adequately attend to their core needs. Besides feelings of frustration, this layer also holds the pain, despair, shame, and loneliness that emerge as a result of poor parenting in a society that does not give a high priority to proper emotional and spiritual development.

Since the expression of many of the feelings relating to the secondary layer are also rejected by society, Reich conceptualised that we are forced to develop a third layer of self, which, in Boadella's (1987, p. 152) words, is "the level of character defences, substitute contacts, and the conformist social veneer, well-adapted to the culture pattern". Yet, psychosomatically literate people acknowledge that this third layer does not disguise the primary and secondary layer completely. The feelings and emotions contained in both of these layers continually break through to the relational world, where they manifest in scenarios such as psychosomatic illness, addictions, aggressive and destructive or uncaring behaviour towards humans and the other-than-human environment.

---

[3] Critical psychiatry (antipsychiatry) is an expanding field. See, for example, Breggin's (1994) publication entitled *Toxic Psychiatry*. The only training manual of psychiatry we know of that is self-reflective and socially critical is Doerner, Plog, Teller, and Wendt's book, *Irren ist menschlich: Lehrbuch der Psychiatrie und Psychotherapie* (1984), now in its fourth edition.

Whereas classic Freudian theory regards neurosis as the result of a failure of the emotional defences, the Reichian theory of self-development regards neurosis as the emotional distortion that leads to the emergence of adaptive processes. Neurosis is thus a term for the emotional deficit itself, a deficit that leads to the necessity to employ defence and other adaptive mechanisms to maintain at least a superficial emotional stability. As will be demonstrated in this study, the Reichian view of self enables us to envisage an emotionally and ecologically sustainable life without having to resort to distractions and emotional defence mechanisms.

Although the term 'neurosis' is still widely used in psychiatry, psychology, and psychotherapy, in this study we will employ the term 'ego-centredness' because it more succinctly describes the relational aspects of this condition. In this sense, ego-centredness is the result of trauma-related emotional fixation that has prevented most of us from developing a mature, relational sense of self.

Our search for emotional identity, happiness, freedom, and belonging

We believe that depth psychology is concerned with four profound human needs: the needs for emotional integrity, happiness, freedom, and belonging. The views on our ecological crises based on depth psychology and other holistic approaches explored here suggest that we need to satisfy these needs to a high degree to live personally and environmentally sustainable lives. Depth psychology recognises that many people living in industrialised countries experience severe frustrations when these core needs are unmet during childhood. These frustrations, and the associated need to compensate for them, then dominate many of our perceptions, feelings, and behaviour as adults. In other words, a substantial lack in the fulfillment of these basic needs determines much of our journey through life, which, when viewed from such a holistic perspective, can consequently be regarded as a healing journey. Yet, instead of finding deep healing through turning our suffering into spiritual and emotional journeys, most of us continue to settle for the compensatory mechanisms offered by modern society (Hill, 2003a, in press b), mechanisms that not only prevent us from finding healing and inner peace, but also keep our unsustainable economies going and continue to harm the natural environment. The solution here is to turn inwards to re-examine our deep feelings and motivations (cf. Jones, 1993), rather than to continue to harm the world through our compensatory self-support scenarios.

Emotional integrity

Emotional integrity is used here for the need to be in touch with one's core self (Hill, 2003a). Viewed in the context of a Reichian approach to depth psychology, this need requires us to integrate the feelings held on the second layer and thus facilitate access to the emotional qualities associated with our core selves. Doing so will help us reclaim the aspects of our personality that we had to relinquish as children in order to survive in a world that is widely out of touch with children's needs for love, nurturing, mirroring, and belonging (Kohut, 1971, 1977, 1984; Basch, 1980, 1988).

Emotional integrity, the natural ability to feel what we think, and think what we feel, is based on a high level of body-mind integration. Most bodyoriented psychotherapists believe that most human beings living in modern society have largely lost this integrity, and thus unconsciously engage in activities that provide opportunities to compensate for this loss of integrity.

Happiness

Our striving for happiness as an important goal of life has been acknowledged by people as diverse as Buddha and Marx. This suggests that many of the things we try to achieve serve to expand our experience of happiness and emotional ease. However, the clinical experience of counsellors and psychotherapists consistently shows that many of us unconsciously recreate misery and hardship, often unnecessarily, and that we permit being exploited or engage in activities that lead to the re-experience of shame and guilt. It seems that our striving for happiness is a double-edged sword, in the sense that we all want more of it, and yet many of us continue, in diverse ways and often involving postponement, to avoid it.

Freedom

Freedom, the third notion essential to a depth psychology perspective of living, can be defined as our ability to choose our own fate and to express our feelings in relation to others. According to this commonly accepted meaning of freedom, we are free when:

- we are not dominated by other people and can rule ourselves according to our own needs and interests;
- we are able to choose between meaningful alternatives;
- we can voice our opinions without being punished;

- we can exercise free will without interference from external forces; and
- there are no restrictions placed on our movements]

Yet, freedom always has to be a relative freedom, an aspect often overlooked in the so-called developed countries. This is because personal freedom is always limited by the need for freedom of other living organisms. If we do not want others to interfere with our freedom, then we also have no permission to interfere in the affairs of others. In other words, we have to negotiate freedom on a level playing field. Such *freedom from* interference and exploitation has been transformed into the notion of *freedom to* exploit, intervene, and manipulate, by egocentric people who feel that they have the right to exercise an absolute freedom to exploit other human beings, animals, and natural resources. Whereas many people in the 'developed' countries have been exercising their economic power and technological superiority, and have operated from this perception of freedom for some time, the USA Administration has now taken the abuse of personal freedom to a new level by deciding that it has the right to dominate the world. This freedom to dominate the world is expressed in the fact that the USA now has military bases in more than one hundred countries (Ali, 2003), and in its perceived right to wage pre-emptive wars against sovereign countries. It is also expressed in the belief in its right to possess weapons of mass destruction, a right it denies to many other sovereign states, such as Iraq, Iran, and North Korea.

Belonging

Like most developed animals, humans are social beings, meaning that they have a strong need to belong and to be in meaningful relationships. We belong to an original birth family and often join another family through marriage or by living in *de facto* relationships. Most of us also 'belong to' a group of friends, to clubs, to a work environment, to a professional organisation, and to a spiritual association. Having the psychosocial skills to nurture these meaningful relationships is vital for our emotional and physical health and wellbeing, and for our ability to contribute to an ecologically sustainable society. Yet, many living in 'developed' countries significantly lack these psychosocial skills, with the result that they frequently suffer from isolation and alienation. As a result, they often engage in unsustainable compensatory behaviour to achieve at least a short-term sense of belonging.

A defence mechanism perspective of ecological crises

In this segment, we examine, as Winter (1996) has done, our ecological crises by using emotional defence mechanisms as a frame of reference. Many of the views presented here are metaphors of individual psychopathology applied to the relationships between humans and the other-than-human natural world. This transposition of thinking from one area of inquiry to another has been used, for example, by Reich (1946) in his work on the mass psychology of fascism, and by DeMause (1982) in his psychoanalytic interpretations of historic events. Bertalanffy's (1976) General Systems Theory, and the ancient Hermetic concept 'as above, so below', are other useful theoretical foundations for this transposition of personal to societal psychopathology.

Ecological crises as result of conflict

According to Rycroft (1972, p. 22), conflict is an:

> [o]pposition between apparently or actually incompatible forces. Internal or psychological conflict may be between instinctual impulses, (e.g. libidinal and aggressive, [...] or between structures (e.g. ego and id). The idea that all psychological conflict is neurotic is not part of psychoanalytical theory; conflicts are only neurotic if one party is unconscious and/or if they are resolved by the use of defences other than sublimation.

Or, as Kovel (1976, p. 35–36) puts it:

> In other words, a person in the grip of neurotic experience is embroiled in an emotional conflict seems set against understanding, because at least one of its sides would lead to *anxiety* if it were allowed expression.

These citations suggest that we experience conflict when essential motives are turned into an either-or situation. A child's need to be loved unconditionally and his or her parents' difficulty with providing this unconditional love may force the child to make an either-or choice between emotional and physiological self-regulation. He or she then faces the necessity to adapt to his or her parents' and society's demands and emotional limitations. The emerging conflict predictably leads to emotional (and possibly physical) pain, frustration, rage, and finally to the creation of the egocentric condition. In severe cases, such conflicts can lead to severe emotional distortion and disintegration beyond the level of neurotic functioning. Since conflict is at the heart of the egocentric experience and the fabric of our daily struggles, it is suggested that our attempts to deal with the psychological underpinnings of our ecological crises will have to address people's conflicts and assist them in finding solutions that foster the ability to live sustainably.

Defence mechanisms

Anna Freud (1937) suggested that we develop psychological mechanisms in association with our attempts to avoid the experience of anxiety. Regarding most of these mechanisms as pathological, she viewed a defence mechanism that she and Sigmund Freud called sublimation as necessary to desexualise and deaggressify people's unsocial drives. According to Manfield (1992, p. 32):

> defences are patterns of behaviour or thought that people use to protect themselves from emotional pain or discomfort arising from present life situations usually linked to painful childhood memories.

People develop defences against feelings and emotions because their ability to hold strong conflicts in their consciousness is limited. Painful feelings resulting from shock trauma and developmental trauma create an unmanageable emotional pressure that forces people to unconsciously develop ways of suppressing these feelings and emotions through physiological and psychological mechanisms. When the initial suppression becomes an unconscious and automatic response, it turns into what is called repression, a state of consciousness in which we have 'forgotten' the troubling feelings and associated conflicts.

Defence mechanisms thus represent compromises between our inner demands for psychosocial and physio-emotional self-regulation, and the demands made on us by parents, teachers, and those who have power over us in a society that is widely out of touch with children's developmental needs. These demands, in turn, reflect the cultural values held by society at that time. In other words, our present socio-economic system relies on a number of emotional defence systems for its functioning. These defence mechanisms include phenomena such as:

- the ten psychological defences (e.g., compensation, projection, reaction-formation) outlined by Anna Freud (1937);
- muscular tensions that serve to repress feelings (Reich, 1942);

- tissue armouring that prevents biological energy from flowing and creating consciousness (G. Boyesen, 1976, 1985); and
- shallow or disconnected breathing that prevents feelings from reaching consciousness (Reich, 1933; Lowen, 1958; Dychtwald, 1986).

Winter (1996) suggests that defence mechanisms play a significant role in creating the phenomena that we associate with our ecological crises. In this framework, the contributing factors of harmful and destructive behaviour towards the environment can be regarded as a complex network of processes that include people's feelings and internal conflicts, economic forces, and ethical considerations. Looking at environmental and psychosocial degradation from the perspective of defence mechanisms thus provides a useful way of understanding people's deep motivations for their actions.

Compensation

Blakiston (1980, p. 186) describes compensation as "[t]he process of counterbalancing a lack or a defect of a bodily or physiological function." A typical form of compensation is the emphasis on mental functioning by people who have a very low level of embodied self-esteem. Behaviour in which compensation emerges includes:

- the consumption of goods and services that compensates us for the lack of inner (psychosomatic) or outer (societal) freedom;
- the compensation for the difficulty with experiencing love through the attainment of personal power and control; and
- the psychological mechanism underpinning anthropocentrism, androcentrism, racism, and the belief in the superiority of particular religious systems or worldviews.

Many advertisements used by corporations to sell their goods and services are designed to create links between our need for freedom, independence, and aggressive behaviour towards the outside world. Such advertisements associate freedom with off-road motoring, fast cars (e.g., in Germany), smoking (e.g., in France and Japan), carrying handguns (e.g., in the USA), and the use of a multitude of gadgets that promise more freedom and more available leisure time. Yet, as many critics of our modern worldview have pointed out, these promises have remained unfulfilled and have even deepened our dependency on goods and services for the momentary stabilisation of our increasingly fragile selves.

Sublimation

In Freudian theory, sublimation is the term for an emotional 'tool' that is meant to help human beings to move from an adherence to the 'pleasure principle' to an acceptance of what Freud called the 'reality principle'. According to Rycroft (1972, p. 159), sublimation is the "developmental process by which instinctual energies [...] are discharged [...] in non-instinctual forms of behaviour". The aim of sublimation is thus to desexualise and subdue instinctual impulses, and to transform our libido into impulses that are more acceptable to the values held in Western societies. Sublimation thus involves a process of the displacement of energies from activities and objects of primary biological interest, to ones of a lesser instinctual interest. In this view, sublimation has been successful if we have managed to channel our sexual and emotional energies into creative and societally useful projects.

Although confusing in theory, the concept makes sense when we observe it in action. Sublimation uses many channels of expression, of which some, such as creating works of art, have no or very little negative impact on the natural environment. Yet, many people, being too tired and exhausted from the grind of their daily chores, seem to channel their libidinal needs into consuming non-essential goods and services. Advertising companies have been using sublimation successfully for many decades to sell non-essential (symbolic) goods and services to the public. In channeling people's libido away from primary needs such as love, freedom, belongingness, body contact, and the need for an enchanted life (Moore, 1992, 1996), towards 'wants' for industrial products, they have become addicted to the superficial and fleeting pleasures of consumerism. Yet, it is increasingly acknowledged that the purchase of non-essential goods and services leads to addiction, because, although it provides our craving soul with some 'peace of mind' for a limited time, it cannot sustainably satisfy our underlying needs.

Freudian classic theory, in lacking an understanding of a positive core at the heart of the person, regards sublimation as a benign mechanism aimed at helping develop a civilised society. Although Freud certainly had good intentions in developing the concept, it appears that he seriously underestimated the addictive nature of the sublimated (repressed) impulses. Freud could not foresee that the disowned core needs would one day contribute towards global ecological crises.

Displacement

Displacement is the term for defence mechanism with which people disown their feelings and displace them onto other people or onto the other-than-human world. At a time when the proverbial kicking of the cat and aggressive expressions against people are for good reasons sanctioned by society, displacing aggressive feelings onto the natural environment is becoming a feasible option.

Clinical experience of psychotherapists shows that many people displace feelings such as frustration and anger onto the environment by being uncaring, and through destructive behaviour. Experience shows that they direct their emotional charge against the natural environment by destroying trees, disposing of garbage in natural habitats, attacking animals, or by vandalising objects and places that instill feelings of peace and harmony.

A depth psychology view of such aggressive activities suggests that destructive acts against the natural environment can be regarded as a way of discharging emotional pressure that would either lead to anxiety or, when expressed towards humans, would cause severe disruptions in relationships. It also suggests that people who act in such destructive ways experience a sense of, at least temporary, relief from this emotional pressure. Assuming that we have a deep need for emotional continuity, it makes sense to consider that harming the world around us provides many people a sense of relief when they see the external environment come to match their inner unhealed self-experience. Holding unhealed frustration, anger, and hate in our body-minds, many of us seem paradoxically to experience a sense of being in 'harmony' with their inner unhealed world when they see the external environment in a state of destruction and disorder.

It should be noted here, however, that many of us do exactly the opposite by compulsively compensating their sense of inner turmoil through a compulsive need to create order in the external environment. Scholars such as Spretnak (1991, 1997) also have suggested that such aggressive acts directed at 'Mother Earth' might represent displaced anger and frustration against mothers.

Projection

Projection occurs when we unknowingly hate and reject in others our disowned feelings and emotions. We are probably projecting unconscious feelings when we view ourselves as peace-loving people, but feel that we are continuously confronted with anger and hate from people around us. Having unconsciously banned the emotion anger from our consciousness because it does not fit our self-image as loving people, this disowned emotional quality is mirrored back to us through the behaviour of others.

Projection of disowned feelings in relation to ecological concerns can take place in a variety of forms. DeMause (2002) has described in *The Emotional Life of Nations* how whole groups of people develop what he calls group-fantasies against women, who are perceived as dangerous, or against blood, which is perceived as poisonous. Using Adolf Hitler's projection of violent childhood experiences and fears onto Jews as an example, he points out how shared childhood traumas can lead to social catastrophes.

In relation to the natural environment we might, for example, experience this environment as violent and dangerous, and feel that it needs to be tamed and controlled. Projection is also at work when we accuse others of harming the natural environment without being aware of our own destructive attitudes and actions. We might, for example, point with scorn at the harmful output of factories, while ignoring the fact that the sum total of household waste and emissions from privately owned cars form a large part of our waste and air pollution problem.

Projection differs from denial, another defence mechanism, in that with projection we accept the existence of the problem, but project our own involvement onto others. In this view, projection is also at work if we accuse industry of failing to produce goods in cleaner ways, but are not prepared to pay higher prices for cleaner and locally produced 'green' goods.

Reaction Formation

Reaction formation is the term for an emotional defence pattern with which we avoid the pain of frustration by exaggerating the opposite quality or by emphasising the positive value of a compromise. Freud formulated this defence mechanism in relation to experiences around what he called the anal stage of ego-development, the stage during which the child enjoys playing with faeces, but is often forced to adapt to the parents' need to control his or her bowels (toilet training). Reaction formation in this original sense refers to the child's identification with the parents' needs and the rejection of its anal desires to be messy. By developing reaction formation as an emotional defence, the child has turned its desire into the opposite and, in the management of this conflict, has lost a fundamental aspect of his or her self-regulation.

Reaction formation works by reducing the emotional investment in an object or need and by redirecting this emotional charge. When, for example, as children we experience a lack of emotional support, we learn to deny our need for support, and develop the belief that it is both an essential and a positive quality to be independent and self-reliant.

Reaction formation can be regarded as a form of denial (see below) in which the conflict is not simply ignored, but is solved by exaggerating the opposite, or by the favouring of a compromise position. In contrast, people in denial avoid the experience of conflict, often by disowning their own feelings and actions and attacking the offending messenger.

At first glance, reaction formation appears elusive in relation to environmental concerns. An in-depth exploration, however, reveals two major mechanisms that most of us know very well. We can observe that people attempt to escape the experience of conflict by joining the perpetrators. In relation to the environment, this means that we might join the people harming the environment when we cannot stop them in their destructive behaviour. When we experience our caring for the environment as painful and disempowering because we see many others committing destructive acts towards the environment, we can avoid this conflict by simply joining the "winning team".

Reaction formation is at work when people insist that the world is a beautiful place and full of opportunities. Although this is to a certain extent true, the ones among us who describe the world in such glowing terms deny the existence of environmental degradation because acknowledging it and its ramification for our lives would be a conflict-creating experience. Similarly, we can regard as a reaction formation the current emphasis on positive aspects of our modern life, which often includes the cornucopian idea that our problems will be solved by simply expanding our economic output. This emotional defence saves us from the experience of conflict, pain, despair, and powerlessness, feelings that may indeed overwhelm the ones among us who already struggle with sustainable living in many areas of their lives. Another aspect of reaction formation is proposed by Winter (1996, p. 130), who suggests that some environmentalists who "proclaim self-denying holier-than-though attitudes about American comforts" might secretly still find these comforts desirable.

Denial

Denial is a defence mechanism with which we deny or ignore the existence of a conflict, problem, or threat. Although similar to reaction formation, it lacks reaction formation's exaggeration, but attempts to prevent the experience of conflict by doubting and attacking instead the credentials of people providing discomforting information.

We are in the grip of denial if we unconsciously filter out troubling ecological problems before they reach our consciousness. When being in denial, and being confronted about it, we often respond with strong emotional resistance, for example, when we accuse environmentalists of scaremongering, doubt their qualifications, or blame them for having hidden agendas, or for simply being not like us.

Denying the existence of environmental crises is relatively easy if people are not closely connected to the immediate locations of environmental damage. In contrast, it takes a lot of denial to refuse to acknowledge environmental destruction if they live in landscapes damaged by deforestation, rising sea levels, or the smog of big cities. If the degradation of the environment is obvious to the point that it cannot be denied, many people change the argument and deny that the damage is caused by human activities. After all, dinosaurs suffered from rheumatism and were made extinct not by greenhouse gasses, but by a large comet that hit the Earth.

Denial as a defence pattern is frequently used by scientists who continue to publish articles questioning the existence of environmental deterioration or associated health problems, despite strong statistical evidence of a continuing deterioration. Such scientists, many of whom adhere to the biased and narrow natural science paradigm, have denied the dangers of smoking for many decades until the evidence became so incontrovertible that they were forced to relent. Similarly, a significant body of evidence has been amassed in many countries in relation to the health problems caused by mobile phones and the towers built to relay their signals. Yet, it will probably take many years before scientists can be forced to fully acknowledge the destructive effects of these convenient gadgets.

A good example of the occurrence of denial is the well-known debate on greenhouse gas emissions, in which people with an interest in preserving the *status quo* continue to argue that we do not know for sure that cutting down on emissions will actually affect the increase of global warming. Denial here protects the industry by putting the onus of proving that products have destructive effects onto the people who want to preserve the environment. If we were not in denial, we would demand proof from industry that their products are safe for general use and do not contribute to ecological degradation.

Compartmentalisation (isolation)

A special form of denial that we believe has so far not yet received adequate acknowledgment is what could be called compartmentalisation, the emotional defence of experiencing the world as a series of isolated entities. People affected by this emotional condition lack the awareness that everything is interrelated, interconnected, and purposeful, and that there is no chance occurrence.

We are affected by this defence mechanism when we believe that a problem is occurring somewhere else (spatial disconnection), not connected to our behaviour (causal disconnection), and not relevant in terms of time (temporal disconnection), or when we uncritically accept the validity of certain terms and phrases (linguistic compartmentalisation).

Spatial compartmentalisation takes place, then, when we believe that the problem is 'out there' rather than 'in here'. Diesendorf (1997) points out that many people plug their electric devices into the wall outlet often without being aware that somewhere, possibly not even far away, electricity is produced in ways that cause damage to the natural environment.

Just as the Korean War, Pearl Harbour and the sinking of the *Lusitania* taught us that we can't immunize ourselves against the world's problems, Sept. 11 must spur us to launch a new era of American internationalism. Let's not squander this opportunity (Kagan and Asmus, *The Washington Post*, January 29, 2002, cited in Yirmemahu, SCAM.COM, 15 June 2005).

In contrast, causal compartmentalisation is at work when we can watch starving children in the news without realising that the poverty in their countries is mainly caused by exploitation by the developed countries. We might then also use this defence to make ourselves believe that people in the developing world are poor because they are lazy or because they have refused to embrace our Western way of living (see also rationalisation).

The notion of temporal compartmentalisation, on the other hand, could be used to describe our 'habit' to forget what has caused or contributed to certain events. A good example here is the debate in the media about North Korea's nuclear ambitions, which conveniently overlooks that North Korea restarted its nuclear programme only *after* it was included by the USA Administration in its list of countries belonging to the so-called 'Axis of Evil'. Similarly, this kind of convenient amnesia is experienced at present by people who have forgotten, or do not want to know, that many of the so-called enemies of the so-called free world have been for many years on the USA payroll.

The notion of compartmentalisation could also be used for a phenomenon that is increasingly used by the media to conceal the real meaning of present world events. Euphemisms such as collateral damage (death of civilians), insurgents and terrorists (people trying to defend their sovereign country), friendly fire, and the 'war on terrorism', allow us to decontextualise and disconnect from the disconcerting real meaning of these notions (linguistic compartmentalisation).

Another possible occurrence of compartmentalisation is the endless rounds of 'yes-buts' that have become another hallmark of shallow approaches to sustainability (Naess, 1973; Neass and Rothenberg, 1990; Sessions, 1985). We might say that we want to create a more sustainable natural environment, but we cannot economically afford the increase of unemployment seemingly related to it. Likewise, we might agree that it makes sense to save the spotted owl (Winter, 1996), but we might be concerned that hundreds of forestry workers will lose their jobs. After all, it is only an owl, and there are still thousands of animal species left.

Compartmentalisation produces difficulties in understanding the bigger picture; for example, that people might not lose their jobs because of the need to preserve a certain species of owls, but because of an economic system based on exclusive reliance on market forces. It also fails to acknowledge that the natural environment will probably not be destroyed through a grand catastrophe but the death of a thousand cuts, of which the deliberate extinction of the spotted owl is just one cut, the burning of our rainforests another.

Rationalisation

According to Rycroft (1972, p. 136), rationalisation is "the process by which a course of action is given *ex post facto* reasons that not only justify it but also conceal its true motivation." Winter (1996, p. 127), on the other hand, suggests that, "rationalisation occurs when we create an attractive but untrue explanation for our behaviour".

Rationalisation is one of the defence mechanisms frequently employed by proponents of shallow sustainability who seek to improve the natural environment through technology and clever management (Naess, 1973, 1990). The standard argument used by people adhering to this approach to sustainability is that our technological advances will always be able to deal with the ecological problems as they arise. They dismiss the possibility that:

- it is highly possible that we will create a disastrous environmental situation that is far too big for the human race to tackle;
- because nuclear power plants are not exempt from our capitalistic ways of producing goods and services, they pose a high risk of creating ecological and social disasters; and

- systems often develop their own dynamic processes, and by doing so can get out of human control.

A good example of such optimistic thinking is the present occupation of Iraq by the USA and the so-called 'Coalition of the willing', a number of nations that actively support the invasion of Iraq. Shortsighted optimism, the ignoring of warnings, and the belief that problems can be tackled as they emerge has led to a quagmire for the occupying forces in Iraq. In particular, the recent pictures showing systemic abuse of Iraqi prisoners at Abu Ghraib prison has the potential to lead to a significant loss of reputation and the ensuing decline of the 'American Way of Life'.

Another example is provided by Winter (1996), who regards as a rationalisation the argument that it makes sense to purchase non-essential goods that are 'on special' – that special opportunities are rare and need to be taken.

Intellectualisation

According to Winter (1996, p. 128), "intellectualisation occurs when we distance ourselves emotionally from the problem by describing it in abstract, intellectual terms". Many somatic psychotherapists view intellectualisation as connected with what they call the head-body split (Dychtwald, 1986), an energetic phenomenon in which people split energetically off from their bodies to avoid the strong anxiety resulting from repressed feelings and conflicts. By living mainly in their heads and minds, these people often lose access to the gut feelings and intuitions that would enable them to feel deep empathy for other people and the other-than-human environment.

By using intellectualisation, we acknowledge the existence of our ecological deterioration, but talk about it without experiencing our anxiety about its impact. By detaching our emotions from the visible problem, we can think and talk about ecological crises without having to feel the guilt and shame that we would experience if we allowed ourselves to be emotionally affected. Without sensing the urgency emotionally, we can then view ecological problems as intellectual exercises, and deny the necessity to look for ways of taking personal action.

Some thoughts on the dissolution of emotional defences

The logical consequence of the above-described scenarios is that, to solve our ecological crises we need to identify and dissolve many of our ego-defences. This means that those in denial will have to learn to acknowledge, and be affected by, ecological problems, and people who project their disowned feelings onto the natural environment will have to learn to own these feelings and to deepen their perception of self. Those using intellectualisation as an emotional defence will need to make friends with their embodied reality and learn to feel what they think, and think what they feel. The ones among us who use rationalisations to defend against acknowledging the full extent of our ecological problems will need to acknowledge that technological fixes alone will not lead to planetary recovery. Ecopsychologists such as Winter (1996), Macy (1991, 1995), Clinebell (1996), Conn (1995), Fisher (2002), and many others, have addressed many of these issues. Some aspects of this thinking will be briefly described and compared with a depth psychology approach to ecological crises in Chapter 9.

An object relations and character structure approach to ecological psychology

Object Relations Theory

Object relations theory (ORT) is a discipline of thought that describes the development of people's selves in relation to the interactions with their early caregivers. This theory is important for this study because it underpins the views expressed by some research participants that many aspects of environmental destruction result from the difficulties that modern people experience in developing emotional maturity, and with experiencing body-mind and person-planet unity.

Observing the interactions between mother and child during the crucial time of children's emotional development, object relations theorists established that these early interactions form templates along which children, and later adults, interpret and validate their own impulses and the feelings, and actions of other people. Mahler (1975) and her co-workers divided the process of emotional maturation into four phases, which they called (1) autism, (2) symbiosis, (3) separation/individuation, and (4) object constancy.

The phase of autism denotes a state of being in which infants experience undifferentiated sensations that are mainly focused on gratifying their needs for nurturing and body contact. Mahler suggests that at this stage of self-development infants do not experience themselves as separate entities, and maintain only little contact with the external environment.

During the following phase of symbiosis, which, according to Mahler and her coworkers, lasts approximately from the second to the eighth month, infants realise that their mothers are independent persons, but experience themselves in symbiotic unity with them. Being successfully attached (bonded) to their mothers, and sharing a boundary with them, they are able to participate in mother's omnipotence.

At around the fifth month of a child's life, the long phase of separation/individuation commences, during which infants increasingly move away from their mothers, while reassuring themselves that their mothers are still available for support, nurturing and soothing.

In the fourth, and final, phase of self-maturation, infants achieve what object theorists call a sense of object constancy. Having internalised the caring and soothing of their mothers, they become adequate self-objects. At this stage of development, infants are able now to trust that people, and the world at large, will provide consistent nurturing and mirroring.

Problems with self-development

According to object relations theory, problems with self-development occur if:

- infants are confronted with demands that are beyond their developmental capabilities;
- parents are not sufficiently able to parent their infants, or even expect their children to satisfy their adult needs;
- parents interfere with their infants' self-regulation;
- parents fail to provide appropriate empathic attunement and mirroring (Kohut, 1971); and
- emotional support is withdrawn too early.

These shortcomings in adequate parenting force children to create compensatory mechanisms (Hill, 2003a), and what many have referred to as a 'false self' (Winnicott, 1969). When acting from this emotional position, children fight for their emotional survival by limiting and hiding their aliveness, and by trying to become what the environment wants them to be. In doing so, they disrupt their natural energetic flow and consequently lose trust in people, and the world, as providers of nurturing and support. No longer able to trust their inner resources and nurturing, they learn to fill the void by reaching for the symbolic fulfilment offered by modern society.

Possibilities of object relations theory for an ecological psychology

Object relations theory, as much as self psychology, an approach to psychotherapy based on it (Kohut 1971, 1977, 1984), potentially enables social scientists to understand ecological crises as the consequences of modern peoples' struggle with their sense of self. This struggle with self-esteem is not limited to direct consequences, such as people's attempts to define their identity and to find nurturing through the purchasing of non-essential goods and services. It also finds expression in our human-centred (anthropocentric) attitudes, in our discrimination against other races, in the repression of women, and in other consequences that arise from our struggles with our sense of self. Many of these struggles have also found expression in philosophical constructs and ideologies that promote atomism, individualism, and superficiality. In contrast to deconstructionism, which views the notion of a stable self as a superfluous relic of modernism, object relations theory and self psychology regard a coherent sense of self as the foundation for healthy functioning, which in turn enables us to care for others and the other-than-human environment.

Some critical remarks on object relations theory

Although object relations theory represents a useful system for our understanding of child development and its associated difficulties, in its present form it is also a limited system because of its exclusion of intra-uterine and environmental influences. Hill (2003a) describes the role of nature in the development of sense of place and emotional and psychosocial autonomy in children. He refers to the work of Josselson (1996), who proposes a system of eight, overlapping, and mutually supportive processes. These include four sensory-grounded ones (holding, attachment, passionate experience, eye-to-eye validation), and four cognitive ones (identification, idealisation, mutuality and resonance, tending and caring). By suggesting that Josselson's system can be extended to serve as a basis for an understanding of our relationships with nature and place, Hill expands Josselson's structure by including the experiences of nature that he believes refer to the eight different stages. He thus describes experiences such as lying on the grass and looking at the clouds while being with a caregiver nearby (holding), or our caring for nature through recycling and the willingness to redesign our lifestyles and ways of interacting with nature and others (tending and caring).

Hill's (2003a) views represent an important extension of object relations theory by making us aware of the importance of the other-than-human world in the process of child rearing. He also extends Miller's (1997) view that not only primary caregivers, but often also other people and the child's living environment, are influential in children's development of self. With these views, Josselson and Hill have made an important contribution to our understanding of the complex relationships between human beings and nature, an understanding that Orr has called our ecological, biological and cultural literacy (Orr, 1992, 1994).

Overview of Character Structures

The system of character structures has the capacity to enable us to achieve an even deeper understanding of the depth psychological scenarios underpinning many key aspects of our ecological crises. According to Lowen (1958), character is defined as a fixed pattern of behaviour and a typical way in which an individual handles, physiologically and psychologically, his or her striving for pleasure. The system of character structures integrates an understanding of:

- a child's traumatic experiences;
- the emotional defence mechanisms that people instinctively develop to cope with these experiences; and
- postures and tissue consistencies in adults resulting from emotional and physical armouring processes.

This system of character structures does not evaluate or categorise characters as either good or bad, but has been developed to provide psychotherapists with an understanding of the complex links between their clients' conflicts, behaviour, self-experiences, and physical and physiological structures. Although not being without flaws, the system has proved to be useful in the work with clients, and can be used as a tool for researching people's harmful behaviour towards the environment.

First formulated by Reich (1933), and later refined by psychotherapists such as Lowen (1958, 1985), Keleman (1975), Boadella (1976, 1987) and Johnson (1985, 1994), the five character structures form a spectrum along the development of object relations, beginning with the schizoid structure, followed by the oral, the symbiotic, the psychopathic, the masochistic, and ending with the rigid structure. In this study, a more recent version of the system is employed, in which the psychopathic structure has been replaced with the formulation of the symbiotic and narcissistic structures (Johnston, 1994).

Departing from conventional terminology, in this study we will call the oral character structure the 'oral-exploiting condition' to highlight the important links between personal psychology and its effects on the social world and the natural environment. Similarly, we will call the schizoid structure the schizoid-terrorising condition' (see Chapter 8), and the narcissistic structure the 'narcissistic-shaming condition'. The reasons for altering these terms will become more apparent during the following discussion.

Character formation

Johnson (1985) considers the formation of character as a five-stage process that includes (1) self-affirmation, (2) the negative environmental response, (3) the organismic reaction, (4) self-negation, and (5) the adjustment process.

Self-affirmation

A person has the right to exist, the right to have needs, the right to separate and become independent, the right to be assertive, and the right to love and love sexually. All these basic rights are emotional qualities built into our organisms. In our Western culture, however, many people experience developmental trauma when one or more of these basic rights are negated or severely compromised.

Negative environmental response

Due to their own upbringing, many parents struggle with responding positively to these basic rights. By responding from belief systems and values that reflect their own traumatic upbringing and our dominant modern values, parents frequently fail to adequately acknowledge their children's basic needs and rights. In terms of the five basic rights, many parents often:

- meet the infant's existence with coldness or even hostility;
- struggle with adequately nurturing their infants through breast-feeding and body contact;
- have difficulties with allowing the child to separate and establish their personal self-regulation;
- feel threatened by the child's assertiveness, and thus struggle with supporting the child in becoming assertive and in following his or her own agenda; and
- have difficulties relating to the child's emerging sexuality.

Organismic reaction

If parents negate the basic rights of their children, children will react with all aspects of their personality. Johnson (1985, p. 26) writes:

Essentially, these negative organismic reactions may be boiled down to the three essential negative affective states with their behavioural expressions: rage, terror, and grief. These organismic reactions are extremely powerful and provide the "good enough" parent a clear sign to modify her response to her offspring.

Parents confronted with their children's reactions have two ways of responding: they may learn to attune to their emotional reality and thus respond in an affirming way, or they may continue to negate the organismic reaction, thereby pushing the child into despair and pain. The child then has to live with what Johnson (1985, p. 26) calls "unrelenting internal turmoil".

Self-negation

If parents fail to learn from their children's organismic reactions, the children's emotional frustration and despair become a permanent self-experience. Having been overwhelmed by painful feelings over an extended time, they have no choice but to join the environment in negating their self-expression. In this state of emotional turmoil, the children are threatened both by the unsupportive or hostile outside and by the emotional pressure inside. They will stop being themselves and strive to adopt the values of their environment (adaptation becomes maladaptation). On the physical level, reduced breathing and muscular tensions will help them keep the pain and frustration manageable.

Adjustment process

The last stage of character structure formation in Johnson's model is the process of adjustment. It represents the children's attempts to find compromises by modifying their behaviour. These compromises provide them with the minimum of love and nurturing they need to make life emotionally and physically manageable. Relegating their true selves, their body-mind unity, and their spontaneous life force to an existence in the shadow, they create the complex web of emotional defences, psychosomatic symptoms, addictions, dreams, and uncontrolled behaviour that will shape their later adult lives. Liedloff (1976, p. 94) reframes this adjustment process by suggesting that

> [t]he search for in-arms experience, as the years pass and we grow up, takes on a great many forms. Loss of the essential condition of well-being which should have grown out of one's time in arms [the arms of mother and other important caregivers] leads to searches

and substitutions for it. Happiness ceases to be a normal condition of being alive, and becomes a goal.

Finally, it is important to note that the system of character structures is a classification of coping mechanisms and defensive positions, not of the people themselves. It is also recognised that no individual is a pure type, but that every person combines to different degrees, within his or her personality, some, or all, of these coping mechanisms.

Ecological crises and the oral-exploiting condition

The oral-exploiting scenario: a violation of the right to have needs

Many of us have developed an oral-exploiting condition in response to traumatic experiences relating to our needs for adequate nurturing and body contact. As babies and infants between birth and eighteen months of age, we reach out for closeness, body-contact, and mother's warm and nourishing breast. If mothers have emotional difficulties with emotional bonding and breastfeeding, or if social or environmental circumstances prevent such a nurturing bonding, our clearly expressed needs are likely to be chronically frustrated. This lack of physical touch and oral gratification from the beginning of life leads to what character analysts call the orally repressed character structure, whereas a sudden premature interruption (sickness of mother, etc.) often leads to the so-called orally unsatisfied structure.

The adult with the oral-exploiting condition

In this emotional landscape, mothers (and often fathers as well) are usually in conflict with their own neediness, and the emotional environment in the family is usually one of competition around the right of having needs. Character analysts hold that the core belief of people afflicted with the oral-exploiting condition is the belief that the world owes them a living.

Adults affected by the oral-exploiting condition have two principal ways of dealing with their internalised frustration: (1) to expect satisfaction of their needs through the efforts of other people or institutions, or (2) to initially deny their needs, and hope that their needs will be satisfied through serving others. In the first scenario, adults with the oral-exploiting condition tend to exploit other humans and/or the natural environment, whereas those belonging to the second category usually adopt the role of caregivers in our society. They hope to get satisfaction through caring for the needs of others, and that the initial investment will finally lead to the satisfaction of their own needs. The predictable drawback of the compensated-oral condition is that many people end up feeling shortchanged when their original investment fails to lead to the satisfaction of their own needs. The emerging feelings of betrayal, bitterness, and resentment are predictable results of this condition, and often lead to the belief that the world is not a nurturing place – a belief that when projected onto the natural environment can serve as justification for its exploitation.

The death of more than 20,000 people [of extreme poverty] on a single day would be one of the most momentous stories of the year – full of heartbreak and horror, particularly as so many of the victims were children. [...] But because this event happens every day of the year, for complex reasons that are hard to solve, it makes little news (Fairfax Digital, 1 July, 2005).

Effects of the oral-exploiting condition on the environment

Consumerism

A character structure perspective that focuses on the oral-exploiting scenario, as well as on the narcissistic-shaming condition examined in the following segment, identifies consumerism as one of the key issues of our ecological crises. Ecologically aware psychologists such as Winter (1996) suggests that consumerism (retail therapy) is the predictable result of internalised traumas of deprivation that unconsciously urges many of us to consume non-essential goods and services as a way of coping with what is called here the oral-exploiting dilemma. Yet excessive consumerism is really retail compensation, since consuming non-essential (symbolic) goods and services neither fulfils basic emotional needs, nor facilitates a deep understanding of the underlying emotional conditions that prompts us to consume, 'to shop till we drop'. It simply serves "to alleviate the anguish of an empty life" (Kanner and Gomes, 1995, p. 79). In the absence of deep learning and emotional integration, consuming non-essential goods is an addictive enterprise, and has to be regarded as an emotional defence mechanism. In fact, as Wachtel (1989, p. 71, cited in Kanner and Gomes, 1995, p. 78) notes, "having more and newer things each year has become not just something we want but something we need". In other words, an increasing number of people have lost the ability to distinguish between wanting and needing.

Chasing the nipples

Arising from the core belief that the world owes them a living, people affected by this condition often fail to take full responsibility for their self-support and for becoming economically and emotionally independent. When considering who these people in our Western society are, we often think of the unemployed, of alcoholics, and of other drug-addicts. Yet, although many of these people do indeed struggle with the oral-exploiting condition, they only form the tip of the proverbial iceberg because the oral-exploiting condition is to a large degree embedded in modern culture.

A depth psychology perspective of the effects of the oral-exploiting condition recognises that a large number of people in the developed countries avoid becoming conscious of their oral deprivation by symbolically chasing their mothers' nipples. Besides addictive drinking and smoking, people with this condition compulsively try to either get something for nothing, or, at least, for very little investment on their own part. To this end, modern societies have created and sanctioned numerous ways of exploiting other people and the natural environment. As Durning puts it, "Consumption [...] is almost universally seen as a good – indeed, increasingly it is the primary goal of national economic policy" (1992, p. 21, cited in Kanner and Gomes, 1995, p. 80). Unconscious oral pain prevents many of us from asking why someone else should pay for their self-support, or why they should be entitled to have a good life at the same time as billions of people on this planet struggle to make ends meet or die of starvation. Since exploitation has become an integral part of our dominant modern Western paradigm, those who suffer from the oral-exploiting condition experience very few challenges to their exploiting perceptions and behaviour.

The two pre-eminent social institutions in which the oral-exploiting condition is at work are our capitalistic way of producing and trading goods and services, and the stock exchange. Capitalism works on the unthinking assumption that it is ethically acceptable that people who own money and hold power are entitled to use these assets to further increase their wealth and power. Since the oral-exploiting condition is unconscious and addictive, however, most rich and powerful people lack a sense of when enough is enough. Supported by institutions that sanction exploitation and create suitable corporate myths (Hamilton, 2003), they can use manipulation, repression, and even military force to take exploitation to levels that presently threaten the very fabric of community life, both nationally and internationally. At present, humanity is going through such a stage of heightened exploitation, one marked by globalisation and the willingness of corporate companies to pay their CEOs ridiculously generous remuneration packages.

The stock exchange is the second social institution that sanctions and normalises exploitation. It is a meeting-place for people who wish to benefit from the commodification of goods, services, and money, and who believe that it is morally justified to use their money – or the money of others – to accumulate wealth and power for personal gain. Early deprivation leads people to believe that it is acceptable to accumulate wealth at the expense of others by 'taking money out of the market' for personal profit. It also makes them blind to the fact that somewhere on this planet people have to work hard and consume very little to enable them to achieve a high return on their investment.

The idea of using money to make more money, of earning interest, and of making profit is so entrenched and sanctioned in Western societies that it has become difficult for most people to understand its underlying psychopathology. Having become one of the most fundamental features of industrialised countries, we have only a few alternatives with which to compare our values. To get an idea of other perceptions on wealth, we have to resort to values held by indigenous cultures, or by eastern philosophies such as Taoism or Zen Buddhism. The following Zen-related story, taken from Reps's (1971) book *Zen Flesh, Zen Bones*, serves to illustrate a possible antithesis to our oral-exploiting mindset:

Real Prosperity

A rich man asked Sengai to write something for the continued prosperity of his family so that it might be treasured from generation to generation.

Sengai obtained a large sheet of paper and wrote: 'Father dies, son dies, grandson dies.'

The rich man became angry. 'I asked you to write something for the happiness of my family! Why do you make such a joke as this?'

'No joke is intended,' explained Sengai. 'If before you yourself die your son should die, this would grieve you greatly. If your grandson should pass away before your son, both of you would be broken-hearted. If your family, generation after generation, passes away in the order I have named, it will be the natural course of life. I call this real prosperity.'

The wisdom expressed in this Zen story refers to a sense of wealth and happiness that has become widely meaningless for modern people whose sense of what is valuable is almost completely reduced to the things money can buy. This attitude was perversely expressed in the USA Administration's recent offer to reimburse with money Iraqi victims of American abuse at the Abu Ghraib prison for their suffering and shaming (McGeary, 2004).

Having become a key constituent of many aspects of our ecological crises, greed resulting from psychophysical deprivation not only continues to deplete the planet's non-renewable resources, but also continues to contribute to psychosocial problems, such as:

- the creation of a new social class of the working poor, that is a class of people who do not manage to move beyond poverty despite being employed;
- the increasing social inequality between the rich and poor and the associated erosion of the middle class;
- a continuing shift from democracies to plutocracies, which are political systems in which wealthy people form the governments and use their political power to increase their personal wealth; and
- the present destruction of civil rights under the pretext of a perceived necessity to fight terrorism.

This shift from democracies towards plutocracies, societies ruled by the wealthiest people, has emerged in countries such as Thailand, Italy, and the USA, where the present Administration, by supporting the profit interests of companies such as Bechtel and Halliburton at the expense of social cohesion and equity, is now threatening our fragile global stability. The neo-colonial war presently being fought in Iraq is reminiscent of the situation during and after the Second World War, when German companies such as Krupp first achieved enormous profits from producing weapons, and later from producing artificial limbs for amputees, and steel products for the rebuilding of Germany (Engelmann & Wallraff, 1976). The enormous greed that informed decisions at Krupp even allowed the company officials to sell fuses for bombs to Great Britain, which, as we remember, was Germany's enemy at the time.

These examples of corporate greed are used here to illustrate the point that the oral-exploiting condition constitutes a mental illness that makes people blind in respect to ethics, to the feelings and needs of others, and to the dangers that it creates for humanity and the rest of the biosphere. Whereas psychiatrists have invented suitable labels for people who compulsively wash their hands (obsessive compulsive disorder), and who suffer from severe mood swings (bipolar disease), greed, even when it contributes to the degradation of the natural environment and to the death of thousands of people, is still not regarded as a pathological condition in need of therapeutic treatment, and as such remains unlabelled.

It is increasingly becoming obvious that this situation needs to be rectified, since building a complex world economy on an addictive and pathological structure can only lead to catastrophic long-term effects on humanity and the rest of the biosphere. To achieve this, however, we need to address the oral wounds described above. Without addressing these, we might not be able to fully appreciate the emotionally nurturing effects of the inexpensive and fully sustainable pursuits such as "religious practice, conversation, family and community gatherings, theatre, music, dance, literature, sports, poetry, artistic and creative pursuits, education and appreciation of nature" (Durning, 1995, p. 75).

Ecological crises and the narcissistic-shaming condition

The second of three character structures associated with our ecological crises is what character analysts have termed the 'narcissistic character structure' (Kernberg, 1985). Whereas the effects of the oral-exploiting condition on the natural environment have been widely neglected, the effects of narcissism have been explored by Lasch (1980), Lowen (1985), Winter (1996), Fisher (2002), and others. The task here is thus to summarise and deepen some of the issues explored by these authors.

Narcissism – developing a false self

Narcissism is the term for a psychological condition that is characterised by a lack of a real sense of self. Almaas (1994, p. 3) writes:

> As human beings we want to be real, authentic, and truly ourselves. [...] We want the sense of who we are to be stable, and we want this stability to be firmly established beyond the need for it to be shored up by external factors.

The narcissistic condition, called here the 'narcissistic-shaming condition', is the result of an upbringing in which, according to Johnson (1994, p. 156), the message to the emerging person is:

Don't be who you are, be who I need you to be. Who you are disappoints me, threatens me, angers me, overstimulates me. Be what I want and I will love you.

The narcissistic-shaming condition emerges as a predictable response to continued shaming and humiliation for self-expression, or to humiliation arising from a child's failure to meet his or her parents' exaggerated and untimely expectations. In the first instance, a child experiences narcissistic injuries and learns to feel bad, ashamed, wrong, and inadequate for being who he or she is, whereas, in the second instance, the child feels ashamed and unworthy for being unable to meet his or her parents' expectations.

American consumer habits reflect both the grandiose and the empty side of narcissism. In terms of the arrogant false self, Americans feel entitled to an endless stream of new consumer goods and services. Material abundance is not only an assumed privilege and a right of the middle and upper classes but proof of the cultural and political superiority of the United States (Kanner and Gomes, 1995, p. 79.

In a broad sense, all traumatic experiences are ultimately an affront to a person's development of a coherent self. In a more narrow sense, this is true for the development of the narcissistic-shaming condition, which leads to an emerging polarity of grandiosity and worthlessness. Whereas the oral-exploiting condition is formed as a result of insufficient nurturing, bonding, and body-contact, the narcissistic-shaming condition emerges as the logical consequence of continued interference with the child's emerging sense of self and self-regulation. To develop a coherent self, small children need to feel for an adequate amount of time, and enough, that they are the centre of the world. This enables them to develop the "healthy narcissism" that they later need to be able to establish relationships as adults based on mature love (Kohut, 1971, 1977, 1984). For this natural narcissism to develop, however, they need parents who are warm, empathic, responsive, and supportive, and who validate their uniqueness. Children who experience this love and caring are then enabled through a psychological mechanism, which Kohut called 'transmuting internalisation', to compensate for the minor failures of their parents. Receiving sufficient mirroring and validation (Kohut, 1971, 1977) from parents able to employ 'helping mode parenting' (DeMause, 1982, 2002) can develop a healthy sense of self. Experiences of continuous empathic disappointments, in contrast, are beyond the buffer capacity of this transmuting internalisation, and can lead such children to feeling unacceptable in their uniqueness, and to feeling worthless and ashamed of themselves.

The narcissistic adult

The struggle with the narcissistic-shaming condition in later life ranges from a mild form to what is called a narcissistic disorder. This disorder is characterised by people's expectations to be "loved in the form of agreement and adulation" (Manfield 1992, p. 135). Disagreement is experienced as severe criticism, because people struggling with narcissism are convinced that they are without fault. Challenges to this belief are usually experienced as deep hurt. If people cannot maintain a sense of superiority in the face of the challenge, they often threaten to, or indeed abandon the relationship with the person who challenges their fragmented self.

People struggling with milder forms of this condition usually turn their ability to love inward to stabilise their own sense of self. Holding themselves together in this way, they have little love left to provide caring and support to others or to the natural environment. Even at this level of experience, the narcissistic-shaming condition makes people oblivious to the realities, needs, and uniqueness of others.

Effects of narcissism on social and the natural environment

Lasch (1980), Winter (1996), and others point out that the narcissistic condition has to be regarded as a principal driving force of our continuing ecological deterioration. They suggest that people influenced by this condition behave to the Earth in the same way as they behave towards other people and their own bodies. The narcissistic condition affects people and the biosphere through:

- the creation of an image-related culture;
- relating to the body as an object;
- the craving for stimulation;
- the need for compensation arising from the adoption of superficiality as motivating principle;
- the denial of limitations;
- the need for power and control;
- an anthropocentric attitude;
- manifestations of racism and sexism; and
- the manifestation of a colonial attitude.

Narcissism and image

Lowen (1985, p. 137) writes about narcissism:

> On the individual level, it [narcissism] denotes a personality disturbance characterised by an exaggerated investment in one's image at the expense of the self. Narcissists are more concerned with how they appear than how they feel. Indeed, they deny feelings that contradict the image they seek.

He continues by noting that narcissists lack the true values of the self, which he recognises in self-expression, self-possession, dignity, and integrity. Lowen (1985, p. 25) also points out that in our culture narcissism has become so much part of our way of life that people who show little interest in their appearance are often regarded as emotionally disturbed. The point here is not that people should neglect their physical appearance, but that the narcissistic over-identify with images and symbols, and have set benchmarks for style and quality that may not be ecologically sustainable.

As Winter (1996) points out, the interference with people's developing self creates a false self that leads to the compulsion to use external objects to stabilise the false or fragmented self. Unable to find a sense of selfhood within their beingness, people with well-developed false selves tend to create symbolic relationships with other people, and rely for their emotional stability on the short-term satisfaction attained from the purchase of goods and services. Having become the surrogate for a healthy embodied self-experience, expensive houses and cars, designer clothes, expensive holidays, and the like, have become so much part of their self definition that losing these articles would be experienced by many such people as a loss of self-esteem. In other words, they have become addicted to these articles.

Adapting to a crazy world

Narcissists fit well into the modern Western world because this world is in many ways created by narcissists for narcissists. It is thus no wonder that narcissists are often successful and know how to "work the system", generally better than people affected by the other character conditions. Lowen (1985, p. 196) holds that:

> If the world we live in, that is, the world of culture, is unreal, then an inability to adapt would not be regarded as crazy. As I see it, narcissists are perfectly adapted to the world we live in; they

subscribe to its values, they flow with its constantly changing patterns, and they feel at home in its superficiality.

Relating to the body as an object

People affected by the narcissistic-shaming condition not only have difficulty in caring for others, but are also widely insensitive to their own embodied needs. This may sound paradoxical, considering that narcissists are usually depicted as being very concerned with, and aware of, their bodies. The point, however, is that narcissists love their self-image, rather than their real, embodied self. Getting access to their embodied feelings would require of them to embrace the deep sense of inadequacy that they continue to repress. If people struggling with the narcissistic condition engage in bodywork, they usually do so to improve their body image or to slow down their ageing process, not to feel their feelings and body sensations, sense their limitations, or to harmonise with their needs. Consequently, they spend considerable amounts of money on products designed to either slow down or to avert the ageing process. The production of goods used for this purpose is an unnecessary burden on the environment, and often relies on research during which animals are killed or hurt. The narcissists' emphasis on the prevention of ageing prevents them from gracefully growing old as wise people, matured by the vicissitudes of a conscious and embodied life.

Craving for stimulation

Having become dissociated from their bodies as containers of their feelings and painful memories, many people struggling with this condition crave for external stimuli to provide them with a sense of being alive. As Lowen (1985, p. 177) puts it:

> The ego's safety lies in a deadened body, with little emotion. Yet this very deadness creates a hunger for sensation, leading to the hedonism typical of a narcissistic culture.

Besides using the short-term buzz of retail therapy/compensation to bolster their fragmented sense of self, those struggling with this condition often feel drawn to drugs such as caffeine and alcohol, and to the pseudo vibrations that these substances provide. For the same purpose, many also seek the thrill of dangerous sports or the excitement provided by activities such as gambling.

> For Aborigines who have lived in their 'country' for countless generations, each place has a set of stories that relate to its natural and human history. They see white people as having shallow and transitory relationships with such places (Mulligan and Hill, 2001, p. 233).

Denial of limitations

The narcissistic-shaming condition leads many to abuse their bodies by denying their limitations, and by placing inappropriate demands on them to function well and impress others. In many ways, we do the same with the planet, which some ecologists with a spiritual orientation such as deep ecologists (Naess, 1973; Naess and Rothenberg, 1990; Sessions, 1985) regard as our 'outer body'. Having lived in a narcissistic-shaming culture for a long time, we have come to believe that both the human potential and the potential of our 'outer body' are unlimited, and that we might even be able to avoid the final insult to narcissists, which is the ultimate limitation imposed on us by our own death.

If people with this condition experience limits, they tend to challenge them by using drugs as limit busters, or by attending so-called breakthrough workshops to achieve miraculous changes in the space of a weekend. Lowen (1985, p. 10) writes:

> There is an absence of self-restraint in their responses to people and situations. Nor do they feel bound by custom or fashion. They see themselves as free to create their own life-styles without societal rules.

Relating this attitude to the biosphere, we continue to disregard the natural limitations imposed by the planet's carrying capacity, and continue to pretend that our energy resources, such as fossil fuel, are unlimited. Monbiot (*Guardian Weekly*, Vol. 170/No 2) puts it aptly when he writes:

> Every generation has its taboo, and ours is this: that the resource upon which our lives have been built is running out. We don't talk about it because we cannot imagine it. This is a civilisation in denial.

Monbiot concludes that we have to redesign our cities, our farming and our lives (ibid), and he takes our psychological conditions into account by suggesting that political pressure will not be enough to change people's minds, since people take to the streets not to fight for austerity but to fight for easier access to cheap goods and services.

The craving for power and control

Lowen (1985, p. 75) writes about narcissism:

> A striving for power and control characterizes all narcissistic individuals. Not every narcissist gains power and not every person with power is a narcissist, but a need for power is part of the narcissistic disorder.

Lowen's citation aptly summarises the intimate relationship between the narcissistic-shaming condition and power. This need for power emerges as a predictable result of the infliction of direct humiliation of the child's emotional expression, and the humiliation children experience when they fail to meet their parents' untimely demands. In the first scenario, adults try to attain power in order to ensure that they themselves will never ever be humiliated again; in the second scenario, they continue to use the power they have been hiding since childhood to avoid re-experiencing their earlier failures and humiliations. This latter scenario has been described as the psychopathic character structure (Lowen, 1985). Distinguishing between five different subsets of the narcissistic condition, Lowen (1985, p. 22) writes about psychopathy:

> All psychopathic personalities consider themselves superior to other people and show a degree of arrogance that verges on contempt for common humanity. Like other narcissists they deny their feelings.

The need for power is addictive for the psychopath because it provides an assurance against the dreaded re-experience of humiliation. Power is also addictive because it provides people who have widely lost their sense of beingness through the experience of subtle streamings, and other pleasurable body sensations (see Chapter 9) with the experience of pseudo aliveness described above.

The narcissistic-shaming condition and anthropocentrism

Anthropocentrism is the term used for the inflated ego of humankind, a worldview held by most people living in developed countries. This worldview provides compensatory emotional stability by making them believe that humans are at the pinnacle of creation. This unsustainable worldview is, however, not generally shared by many indigenous people living in so-called premodern cultures. Those have retained an embodied sense of self and sense of place (Cameron, 2003) and are thus far less dependent on the external self-support to which the Western world has become accustomed.

A closer look at our modern anthropocentric values and attitudes reveals that there is little to be proud about. Human beings are the only species on this planet that:

- struggle with their embodiment and self-esteem;
- raise their offspring in a way that creates a deep split between body and mind;
- continue to destroy the environment on which they depend for their sustenance;
- have built social systems based on egocentric features such as greed, power, control, competition, and personal success; and
- use drugs to medicate feelings experienced by many of us as unmanageable, or to attain an experience of feeling alive and connected.

Recently, a number of scholars have linked anthropocentrism with our upbringing under the influence of Christianity. In his classic paper entitled *The Historic Roots of Our Ecologic Crisis*, White (1967) argues that Christianity has evolved into the most anthropocentric religion the world has ever seen. He distinguishes between the Christian tradition that developed in the Latin West and the one that developed in the Greek East. Whereas the latter maintained a contemplative-intellectualist approach, the Western version developed into a tradition that seeks to understand God's mind by discovering how his (sic) creation works. White also concludes that Christianity has come to bear a great amount of guilt because of its notion that 'good' Christian humans are the rightful masters of this planet. This arrogant view has enabled Christians to kill millions of indigenous people who refused to be converted to Christianity in large parts of the world.

Metzner (1999, p. 103) remarks that, starting with the emergence of renaissance humanism, Europeans have gained "a much-needed boost to human self-esteem, burdened as it was with a thousand years of indoctrination about original sin". He proceeds by noting that the early Italian humanists could not foresee that this increase in self-esteem would develop into the human superiority that has become the hallmark of the twentieth century (ibid.). This human-centeredness is a powerful belief and hard to eradicate, because it provides people who have widely lost their embodied sense of self with a pseudo self-definition. The Christian faith provides people who have to a large degree lost their felt sense of body-mind and person-planet unity (see also Chapter 9) with a compensation for this loss. Yet, unlike other religious systems that encourage people to seek liberation and unity in this life, Christianity relocates these unity experiences to the life after death, and continues to support unsustainable living by:

- associating the meaning of sin with guilt rather than with the state of separateness (lack of person-planet unity);
- continuing to instill guilt in people for having sexual needs;
- by maintaining an androcentric stance by defining God as a male, and by supporting the myth that Eve was created by cutting a rib from Adam's body and giving this rib a soul; and
- by emphasising the dualistic principle of good and bad, right and wrong, subject and object, and body and mind.

In this sense, many aspects of unsustainable living, deriving from compensations for natural needs and perceptions, can be traced back to the Christian worldview. Christians have for a long time viewed the natural world of earth and water, animals and plants, flesh and blood, feelings and pleasures of the senses, as the corrupted world of the Fall, and associated these earthly qualities with the notion of sin and the handiwork of the devil (Metzner, 1999, p. 105). Although modern people may have stopped talking about the Fall, many of the fundamental separations persist. Our hesitation to feel our bodies and their associated stories can be witnessed when visiting a modern gymnasium. There, many 'weapons of mass *distraction*', such as television sets and magazines, ensure that body and mind stay well separated.

In a similar vein, Spretnak (1991, p. 119) explains how the distortions emerging in Christian belief have forced humans to "transcend nature and the flesh (which meant primarily man's escaping the 'lure" of women's flesh)". It deserves to be acknowledged, however, that an increasing number of Christians are highly critical of many of the 'body-denying' and anthropocentric aspects of their faith, and are seeking ways to ecologise their religious system (Bradley, 1990; Berry, 1988).

Narcissism and racism

In the *Encyclopedia Britannica* (2002), racism is described as "the theory or idea that there is a causal link between inherited physical traits and certain traits of personality, intellect, or culture, and, combined with it, the notion that some races are inherently superior to others." According to this source, racist views have been put forward by de Gobineau (1986), the

British Prime Minister Sir Chamberlain, Woltmann (1936), and the American eugenicist Stoddard – people who claimed and justified superiority of the white race above others. De Gobineau and Chamberlain, in particular, tried to establish scientific evidence for the superiority of the Nordic, Teutonic race, thereby supporting Hitler in justifying the detention and murder of millions of Jews, Gypsies, and other people belonging to marginalised groups.

Far from being a relic of the past, racism is presently evident in the propaganda of the USA Administration, which bombards the American public and the Western world with images of the USA as a democratic country dedicated to peace and democracy. At the same time, it denounces countries that do not agree with USA policies and values as uncivilized, as economic backwaters, and as nations that support terrorism against innocent Western nations.

A sense of place, as an imaginative event, is experienced in the body for everything happens in the body, including our most fanciful imagination and our deepest reverie. A sense of place is not being used as a mystifying abstraction; rather, it is a part of our day-to-day relationships with one another, with our broader environment and ourselves (Russell, 2003, p. 152).

The narcissism-shaming condition and colonialism

Imperialism, with its complex relationships between coloniser and colonised, has frequently been described as "narcissistic" (Simmons, 2002). Jan Mohamed (1986), for instance, writes that European colonisers produced a narcissistic self-recognition by the subjugation of the natives of other lands. He also notes that natives usually receive the disowned negative elements of the colonisers' selves. Struggling with a deficient sense of self due to a lack of internalised love by important love objects, the colonised were, and still are, forced to stabilise the narcissist's false self.

Simmons (2002) describes how colonised people are usually forced to admire and confirm the grandeur of the imperialist. Colonisers achieve this through military force and the withholding of essential goods, permissions, and education. Simmons continues by suggesting that colonisers ward off their own feelings of shame and self-contempt by treating colonised people with contempt, and by shaming or sadistically punishing them. Likewise, the narcissistic element in the relationship between coloniser and colonised is evident in the exploitative and sometimes parasitic quality of this particular kind of relationship. In this context, Hyam's (1992) claim that imperialistic rulers, as a group, display a high degree of emotional deprivation supports this argument.

The relationship between coloniser and colonised can also be explained by using Meyer's (1986) concept on parent-role and child-role interaction. Meyer suggests that such relationships usually revolve around a shared trauma experience, wherein one of the partners manages to stay unconscious of the original developmental trauma by adopting the role of the parent, whereas the other partner remains unconsciously locked in the role of the child. Relationships between people struggling with the oral-exploiting and the compensated oral-exploiting condition, and between sadists and masochists, and between coloniser and colonised are good examples of such matching pairs. Table 6.1 highlights some of the complementary structures in the relationship between coloniser and colonised.

Table 6.1   Psychological comparison between coloniser and colonised

Coloniser	Colonised
Belief that one is entitled to rule others	Belief that one deserves to be ruled
Feeling of self-contempt compensated through projection	Feelings of self-contempt due to upbringing under narcissistic-shaming conditions
Claim to be in possession of sophistication and superior values	Feeling of shame about a perceived lack of sophistication
Arrogance masks underlying struggle with self-esteem	Struggle with self-esteem paralyses the will to defend one's values

Colonisers often justify the supposed necessity for conquering a sovereign country by believing that they are entitled to:

- bring natives into contact with the values of their superior political, economic or ethical system;
- liberate a country from an evil dictator;
- maintain a dominance of power;
- establish a forward base to attain a strategic influence in the region; and
- maintain a high living standard in one's own country (regarded as a birthright, even if this necessitates exploiting and enslaving other people).

A character-structure view of these beliefs suggests that imperialism is based both on the oral-exploiting and narcissistic-shaming conditions. If we associate imperialism with terrorism, we can also assume a strong involvement of the schizoid-rejecting condition that will be described in detail in Chapter 7. The effects of colonisation on the natural environment are varied and widespread. Space permits only a brief list of effects. These include:

- the wasting of natural resources and the creation of pollution from transporting goods over large distances that could also be produced locally;
- the well-documented effects of poverty and the exploitation of the natural environment; and
- ecological destruction associated with the resistance against colonisation (e.g., the present destruction of Iraq's infrastructure, dwellings, and pipelines).

In Chapter 6, we have described some of the salient features of our ecological crises as predictable outcomes of modern people's attempts to come to terms with developmental traumas. Although the depth psychology perspective employed in this examination offers profound insights into the emotional and psychosocial background of our ecological crises, it nevertheless still has a limited focus on people's perception of, and attitudes towards, the natural environment and fellow human beings. It still lacks an awareness of the synergies between our egocentric consciousness, unsustainable societal structures, illnesses, addictions, and harmful behaviour towards the other-than-human environment. In recognition that a deeper understanding of such a "human ecology" requires a further shift in our level of consciousness, we attempt to formulate such a human ecology in the next chapter.

7 Holistic Eco-self Consciousness (Stage 5)

In this chapter we describe stage 5 of the system of eco-self transformation. By expanding on the previous stage, we conceptualise relevant aspects of environmental deterioration as manifestations of the egocentric consciousness. Whereas conventional environmentalism focuses predominantly on issues such as resource preservation, air and water pollution, waste control, and greenhouse emissions, and whereas the depth psychology perspective mainly focuses on environmental deterioration and the exploitation of human beings, a holistic perception of ecological crises regards many other phenomena of unsustainable living as arising from the same underlying psychosocial and emotional dilemmas. Such an holistic view of our ecological crises thus includes a description of:

- the analogies between internal (body-mind) and external (psychosocial and environmental) pollution;
- the phenomena of cancer (and other degenerative dis-eases) as expressions of conflicts with freedom and self-expression, and its analogy with what has been called Earth-cancer (Weigel, 1995); and
- the synergies and circular processes between physio-emotional, psychosocial, ecological, and institutionalised unsustainability.

The notion of holism refers here to the conscious perception of a meaningful construction of the universe based on meaningful coincidences rather than chance occurrences (Dethlefsen, 1984; Dethlefsen and Dahlke, 1990). The arguments presented in this chapter are underpinned by a commitment to synchronicity of events and structures (Peat, 1987; Jung, 1971), by an esoteric and psychological worldview (Dethlefsen 1984, 1990), by psychosomatics (Alexander, 1950; von Uexkuell [MISSING from Reference list!], 1963, 1979; Overbeck, 1984), and by systems thinking (Bertalanffy, 1960, 1966, 1976). By referring to key metaphors such as separation, pollution, growth/excess, and exhaustion, we outline how humans unconsciously shape their natural and social environment as complex and interrelated mirror images of their egocentric self-experience.

Here, we also describe key aspects relating to a shift from the Western hegemonic notion of sustainable development to the more inclusive notion of sustainable living. We present this notion in a manner that both acknowledges the importance of our external efforts to create a more sustainable environment, and emphasises the importance of an inclusion of consciousness-related issues. The importance of our ability to be sustainably embodied, of being able to lead creative and fulfilling long-term relationships with others, and of our ability to experience a deep sense of connectedness to creation as a whole, is highlighted.

Epistemology

The following segment contains a brief outline of the epistemology needed for a structured understanding of our ecological crises from a holistic perspective.

Psychosomatic thinking

The term 'psychosomatics' integrates the Greek words *psyche* (soul, breath) and *soma* (body), and conceptualises the varied interrelationships and synergies between the two. Psychosomatic medicine, a discipline that employs psychosomatic thinking, regards psychological processes as causative factors of somatic illness. It suggests that people fall ill because they are unconscious of strong conflicts and/or struggles with handling and expressing certain feelings and emotions.

A second view of psychosomatics holds that various events can start with what Overbeck (1984) calls the 'somato-psychosomatic circle'. An accident with a physical wound, for example, may lead to a feeling that is beyond the buffer capacity of the person, and is consequently disowned. This split, then, can manifest as another physical symptom. The concept of cause and effect is still extant, but has been converted into a circular process of intermittent psychological and somatic events. In this view of psychosomatics, although we may still fall ill, we can usually restore our health through appropriate therapeutic support.

A third way of making meaning of illness suggests that we do not *fall* ill, but that we *are* ill (Dethlefsen, 1984, 1990). In this view, physical illness is only one of many expressions of our lack of all-consciousness and wholeness, and our task as embodied beings is to become conscious of ourselves, and to find our roots and purpose for living.

In this project, the terms 'psychosomatics' and 'psychosomatic thinking' are employed in relation to complex interactions and analogies between soul and body, psyche and soma, as, for example, described by Alexander (1950). He suggested that psychological and somatic phenomena take place in the same organism, and are merely two aspects of the same process. If body and mind are two aspects of the same phenomenon, then the mind and soul obviously express themselves through the body. Somatic psychotherapists and psychosomaticists are trained to read this "language of the body" and integrate the knowledge gained about people's condition into their therapeutic undertaking. In this sense, the soul may express its condition through:

- a person's behaviour;
- a person's attitudes, values, and worldviews;
- the shape and consistency of a person's body;
- facial expression; and
- the way a person moves and stands.

Beyond these physical expressions, we also reveal to psychosomatically literate people our unhealed wounds through our choices of partners and physical and social environments, and through the nature of our relationships.

Whereas conventional psychosomatics is predominantly concerned with the conversion of unconscious feelings into psychosomatic symptoms (Freud's notion of conversion neurosis), a spiritually oriented approach to psychosomatic thinking expands this sensibility by including issues of person-planet unity. The latter is particularly concerned with the ways in which emotional traumas diminish people's ability to experience a felt sense of person-planet-unity. This complex process is briefly described in the following section.

To cope with traumatic experiences, children unconsciously reduce the depth of their breathing and/or develop other energy-disrupting breathing patterns. They also develop muscular contractions in specific parts of their bodies (Dychtwald, 1986). The subsequently reduced physio-emotional charge and the muscular armouring lead to the fragmentation of the energetic flow, which then renders emotions more manageable. The emerging chronic energetic blocks, combined with the reduced emotional charge resulting from shallow and/or disconnected breathing, diminish children's self-experience as streaming beings. With the gradual loss of the internal streamings, children also loose their energetic connection to a sense of creation and oneness, because the connection of animals and humans to the world is mainly experienced through the flow of subtle energy.

Holistic and esoteric thinking

Like depth psychology, holism questions why things are as they are. It involves a belief in the individual path that everyone must follow in order to gain knowledge. A person following a holistic and esoteric path accepts the challenges produced by life as opportunities that can enable them to make profound and beneficial changes. Dethlefsen (1984, p. 12) holds that "[i]n taking this path we are aiming at completeness, wisdom, the joining of polarities, union with God, the *unio mystica*, the chymical marriage, cosmic consciousness".

The law of analogy

The ingenious formulation 'as above, so below' allows us to apply the structures and laws that we can perceive and understand with our body-mind to the levels not immediately accessible to our senses. Yet, to make use of the law of analogy, we have to accept that this universe is a 'cosmos', meaning that it is structured in an orderly way, and that there is no room for chance occurrence in this system (Dethlefsen, 1984).

According to Metzner (1999, p. 25), the "hermetic axiom 'As above, so below' encapsulates the ancient idea that there is an analogy, a pattern correspondence, between the macrocosm and the human microcosm". Metzner continues by pointing out that analogical thinking is not absent from natural science, and has been used for example by Bohr to describe the analogy between the structure of the atom and our solar system. Likewise, it also applies to Haeckel's (1999) observation that ontogeny recapitulates phylogeny. The law of analogy may also be regarded as the basis for vertical thinking, the intuitive way of placing analogical items of different horizontal categories in vertical chains (Dahlke and Klein, 1986). Such analogical thinking can also be associated with the notion of creativity, which is often regarded as "the ability to associate divergent ideas and thoughts" (Gosselink, 1999). Yet, from a vertical thinking perspective we may consider that these creative ideas and thoughts may only appear to be diverse when viewed from within a horizontal worldview, and we may not need to regress to primitive levels of the mental hierarchy, as Koestler (1990) suggests, but switch to the alternative vertical mode of perceiving the world. The law of analogy may also be regarded as the basis for vertical thinking, the intuitive way of placing analogical items of different horizontal categories in vertical chains (Dahlke and Klein, 1986).[4]

---

[4] For an excellent exploration of creativity from the perspectives of psychoanalysis, behaviourism, and humanistic psychology refer to Carlisle Bergquist, *A Comparative View of Creative Theories: Psychoanalytic, Behaviourist, and Humanistic*, http://www. vantagequest.org/trees/ comparative.htm

The environment as mirror of our unconscious

Dethlefsen (1984) points out that our environment serves as a mirror for us in order to gain access to the unconscious elements of our personalities. This view implies that we often unconsciously structure the world as a mirror image of our own unconscious reality. It is then up to us whether we make efforts to understand what we perceive "out there" as our externalised reality (projection), or whether we continue to fight the mirror image in order to remain unconscious. Dethlefsen (1984, p. 60) writes:

> The external world is the most reliable source of information for the personal situation in which we find ourselves at any given time. When a person learns to take everything that happens to him and looks for its real meaning, he will not only come to understand himself and his problems better but also discover the possibilities for changing things.

The notion of healing

For esoteric psychologists, illness is, as Dethlefsen (1984, p. 105) puts it, "the most common way of discharging fate". This view suggests that healing is about making whole. It is the process of creating unity by transgressing the dualistic 'view' of the world through learning that all feelings are good and important, and that they represent important guides on the journey towards wholeness (Mindell, 1984).

Form and content (fact and meaning)

The esoteric notion of form and content integrates the objective and the subjective, and highlights the double existence of fact and meaning – a position increasingly supported by quantum physics. Arguing that both positions are relevant and should not be viewed in an either-or mode, this view is explained here by using trees as an example.

Trees have existed for millions of years before the emergence of human beings on this planet, and they did then what they still do today, which is represent the physiological "antithesis" to organisms that only use, but do not produce, oxygen. Together with other green plants, trees are important elements within the symbiotic web of life on this planet.

Besides regenerating the air as part of this symbiotic exchange with the oxygen-producing organisms, trees "do" other things as well. They may kill or wound people when they fall on them; they may save somebody from drowning in a flood; they may be cut in pieces to build furniture; and they may be sold overseas as woodchips to bolster a country's GDP. Many people love trees for their beauty and strength, and hug them to increase their sense of grounding. Others may feel threatened by ones that stand too close to their house and remove them.

People's needs, feelings, and perceptions of trees often change over time. Whereas many of us still widely ignore the metabolic and symbiotic functions of trees, and emphasise their monetary value, an increasing number of ecologically aware people have come to appreciate them again as living partners in our complex eco-system. Regardless of our changing ideas about trees, however, trees themselves have their own lives, and will continue to be rooted both in the soil and in their physiology.

Exoteric versus holistic and esoteric notions

When we argue in this study that our ecological crises are expressions of a wider crisis of our dominant ego-consciousness, we also suggest that this ego-consciousness is associated with a grave imbalance between inner and outer-oriented living (Hill, 2003a). The current dominance of outward orientation finds expression in a form of thinking, and a way of perceiving the world that almost exclusively focuses on external phenomena.

Those familiar with Taoism would probably prefer to describe the phenomena in question as an imbalance between Yin and Yang, and would probably suggest that we have become too Yang-oriented. Although agreeing with this Taoist way of dividing the world into two categories, we prefer to use the Western notion of esoteric (inward- or consciousness-oriented) versus exoteric (outward-oriented) thinking and living. The following table provides a collection of phenomena relating to the distinction between inward and outward orientation:

Table 7.1 Exoteric and esoteric/holistic principles

Exoteric principles	*Esoteric and holistic principles*
Active - assertive	Passive - receptive
Yang	Yin
External environment (natural environment)	Internal environment (soul and body)
Masculine	Feminine
Culture	Nature
Superficial	Deep
Thinking and doing	Feeling and intuiting

Both the exoteric and esoteric principles shown in the above table need to be integrated to enable sustainable living. The domination of any one principle is likely to produce conflict and contribute to ecological crises. An expression of the predominance of the exoteric way of making meaning of the world is the currently dominant assumption that humans are almost exclusively shaped by cultural influences. Such a view does not take into consideration that many of the values and ethical constructs that shape our behaviour are informed by the influence of nature, by our unconscious expectations, and by our projections of unresolved conflicts onto other people and the natural environment.

Metaphors of unsustainable living

Unlike ecological catastrophes, such as the recent tsunami in Asia, ecological degradation usually emerges slowly, and thus attracts little attention. Yet, it is probably in the long term even more destructive than the ecological catastrophes that we have experienced. The numerous occurrences of environmental deterioration, such as deforestation, desertification, rising sea levels, salinisation, and waste accumulation, cause increasing problems for the living conditions of human beings, animals and plants, yet they represent only some of the environmental aspects of a much larger spectrum of our ecological (and social and personal) crises. As disastrous as these ecological disasters and forms of deterioration are, a holistic perspective suggests that they are no more than multiple tips of the proverbial iceberg, an ecological iceberg with far more tips than many environmentalists presently acknowledge. In other words, unsustainability has many facets that are still widely neglected.

The data obtained from the research participants, my clinical experience as psychotherapist, and the views held by many radical ecologists, suggest that most people in Western societies struggle with a whole plethora of issues relating to personal sustainability, issues that impair their ability to care for others and to make meaningful contributions to the ecological sustainability of this planet. Under the influence of permanent emotional distress, the idea and the practice of caring for the world is often experienced by people as overwhelming, and is then readily delegated to specialists. As Jones (1993, p. 167) has noted:

> A large part of our inability to deal effectively with the eco-social crisis we have created lies in our persistent refusal to recognise that our political and economic remedies must be grounded in transformative strategies that go to the heart of the human condition.

Although the manifestations of unsustainability and insanity are omnipresent in large parts of the world, many of them usually go unrecognised because they have become an almost invisible part of the fabric of our modern lifestyles. Harmful, destructive, and antisocial behaviour and addictions, often regarded as normal or tolerable in Western societies, include items such as:

- the addictive smoking of tobacco;
- the excessive consuming of alcohol;
- the dependence on prescription drugs;
- the consuming of expensive designer goods;
- the excessive need for individuality;
- the excessive need for power and control;
- the attacking of non-standard social values;
- the leading of an exhausting (so-called dynamic) lifestyle;
- the occurrence of stress-related symptoms;
- the seeking of facelifts and other expressions of narcissism;
- the rampant competitiveness; and the
- spin-doctoring (as is currently used to justify the wars in Iraq and Afghanistan).

To date, few environmentalists and ecologists have attempted to examine the intimate interrelationships and analogies between these manifestations of our ego-self consciousness, a task that is indeed complex and daunting. In the following section, we examine possible analogies and synergies between different aspects of unsustainable living and by describing them metaphorically. The aim of this examination is to describe the emotional background of unsustainable behaviour and the interrelationships and analogies between their various occurrences. The metaphors focus on:

- separation
- pollution
- growth/excess
- exhaustion

The separation metaphor

Keywords:

- Body-mind split
- Mind over matter
- Person-planet split

- Loss of roots
- Energetic disruptions in the human body
- Disconnected language systems
- The notion of chance occurrence
- Dualism
- Atomistic worldview
- Mechanism
- Spin-doctoring

Physio-emotional separation

Body-mind splits

A central feature of ego-consciousness is the well-described split between body and mind (Dychtwald, 1986). This split emerges in all areas of our lives, such as in our perception of self, in the management of our psycho-physiological energies, in our language, and in our ways of making sense of the world. The split between body and mind, which also manifests as discontinuity between feeling and thinking, has led us to develop the concepts of self and ego, and made many of us believe that the mind should rule the body. By believing in the notion of 'mind over matter', most of us are unaware that, by subscribing to the dualistic view of the world, our self is 'forced' to create symptoms as a way of re-establishing unity or 'power sharing' between body and mind (Dethlefsen, 1984, 1990).

A far-reaching consequence of the loss of body-mind unity is the common loss of purpose and direction. Deikman (1982) suggests that the sense and purpose of our existence seems to lie outside our conscious awareness. He points out that much of our suffering stems from the loss of an awareness of our deeper roots and destiny, and he holds that physical and emotional health require the expansion of consciousness and the discovery of meaning and purpose in our lives. As a consequence of this loss, we have adopted ways of living oriented towards wealth, sex, power and control. This orientation continues to maintain many key aspects of our ecological crises.

Taboos about the body

The most 'real' thing about us from the beginning is our embodiedness. Siegelman (1990, p. 25) writes of the body:

> Our first perceptions in utero are of visceral sensations, and we are constantly getting feedback of our boundedness – the kinesthetic

knowledge that we have limbs that move, stretch, cramp, and reach. Something in our chest races, slows, pounds, skips beats; something up there clenches when danger approaches. Something "down there" roils when we are afraid. And we can feel real products streaming out of our openings – saliva, urine, sweat, faeces – that are objects first of wonder, later often of distaste.

In this quotation, Siegelman draws attention to the basic features of embodiment that we all share with one another. We do not have a body, but we *are* our bodies, and the shapes of these bodies reflect who we are and what we struggle with. Whereas many of us keep our bodies socially acceptable by taking 'them' to gymnasiums to keep them fit, move them to reduce them in size and weight, and take them to the beautician to keep them smooth, we still do not quite admit that we are these bodies. Although we may seem to have given up some old taboos about our bodies, we tend to compensate by creating new ones in other areas of human existence. Watts (1962, p. 3) contends that most people seem to need taboos. He writes:

There is always something taboo, something repressed, unadmitted, or just glimpsed quickly out of the corner of one's eye because a direct look is too unsettling. Taboos lie within taboos, like the skins of an onion.

These new taboos may include:

- the repressing of natural functions of our bodies, such as burping and farting;
- the lack of awareness that yawning is not only an indicator of tiredness, but also an expression of the movement of biological and emotional energy in the body-mind;
- the controlling of our natural impulse to sneeze by turning the sneezing inside rather than enjoying this powerful mechanism of organismic self-regulation;
- a lack of awareness that repeated sneezing can discharge accumulated biological energies to the extent that we feel bliss and a strong sense of inner harmony;
- being ashamed of the noises of our guts (borborygmi), noises that indicate that energy is flowing freely, and that we are in a state of relaxation (G. Boyesen, 1976, 1985);

- the wasting of much of our physiological energy through the unconscious maintenance of a muscular armour that prevents disowned feelings from reaching our consciousness (Reich 1933, 1942; Lowen, 1958, 1980);
- a lack of awareness that itching and the need to scratch represent an unconscious self-regulation system that contributes to the maintenance of our physio-emotional homeostasis;
- a struggle with experiencing emotionally and physiologically satisfying full-body orgasms; and
- an adoption of a manipulative-demanding rather than a nurturing attitude towards our bodies.

Psychosocial separation

Many radical environmentalists, including ecological psychologists, deep ecologists, ecofeminists, and social ecologists (e.g., Fromm et al., 1971; Winter, 1996; Fisher 2002) argue that Western societies are experiencing a deep crisis. They describe the depersonalisation, automation, and separation of humans from themselves, from their peers, and from nature. With the separation of body and mind and the neglect of the phenomenon of soul, we continue to inhabit an egocentred world in which everybody feels like, and acts, as an isolated individual. Watts (1968, p. 8) writes:

> We suffer from an hallucination, from a false and distorted sense of our own existence as living organisms. Most of us have the sensation that "I myself" is a separate centre of feeling and action, living inside and bounded by the physical body - a centre which "confronts" an "external" world of people and things, making contact through the senses with a universe both alien and strange.

Having lost a deep sense of connectedness with the biosphere, many of us then project our deep need to belong onto our relationships, which in increasing numbers crumble under the expectation that such needs will be met mainly from outside of ourselves.

Relationship break-ups

Statistics indicate that, in most developed countries, the number of divorces has been steadily on the rise, and has now reached a level at which approximately one in two marriages end in divorce or annulment. This not only leaves children and the separated partners, often for many years, in great emotional and social distress, but it has also led to a large increase in the number of single-person households, with all their additional pressures on the environment. These consist of the necessity to run two households, to transport children from one partner to the other, and to soothe emotional distress by means of the increased consumption of non-essential goods and services.

Heart diseases

Medical research has revealed that 40 per cent of the 15-year-olds in Australia suffer from arteriosclerosis (Heart Foundation advertisements in *Time Magazines*). One in 400 people in Australia will die from a heart-related disease in the coming year, which means that in Sydney alone 10,000 people will die from a heart-related disease. Considering that these figures are very similar in most developed countries, approximately 25 million people of the billion people living in these countries will die of heart-related illnesses in the next year. Many of them will be only in their forties and fifties.

According to Roderick (www.thirdage.com/news/archive/ALT02010206-01.html), diseases of the heart have been associated with:

- difficulties relating to the experience of love and sexuality and with frigidity and sexual dissatisfaction;
- difficulties with expressing hurt and emotional pain through sobbing and crying;
- people's lack of social contact and failure to join social institutions; and
- a lack of drawing sustenance from religious and spiritual practices.

According to the Journal 'Psychosomatic Medicine', heart diseases also have been associated with a lack of optimism, depression, and the suppression and expression of high levels of anger (Kubzansky et al., 2001).

Environmental separation

At the level of the environment, our egocentric consciousness emerges as our sense of disconnection from the other-than-human environment, in the rupture of the relationships between human beings and nature (Roszak, 1981), and in the loss of our sense of place and belonging (Cameron, 2003). Emerging in the context of our anthropocentric attitudes towards the other-than-human environment, these attitudes allow us to dominate and exploit plants, animals, and natural resources with little ethical consideration. Our experiences of separation from other humans and the other-than-human environment are, when viewed from the character structure perspectives explored in the previous chapter, a direct and logical consequence of our current egocentric consciousness. Embodying physio-emotional and psychosocial separation, and living in the urban ghettos of developed countries, most of us are hardly aware that most indigenous peoples have always acknowledged and respected the interrelatedness of humans with all of nature (Metzner, 1999), a sense of relatedness that we can achieve by engaging in processes designed to enhance our natural embodied sense of self.

Institutional separation

Most people in developed countries tend to be proud of a number of aspects of institutionalised separation. In accordance with the currently dominant dualistic worldview, they separate the church from government, the natural sciences from the social sciences and arts, nature from culture, friends from foes, good from bad, right from wrong, and freedom-loving people from terrorists and those that support them. The lack of integration of person and planet is also prevalent in the various scientific disciplines. Medical professionals look after our physical health, psychotherapists help with the identification and the solution of emotional conflicts, priests provide spiritual guidance, and physiotherapists and masseurs help us keep our bodies functioning.

The split between the various scientific approaches is paralleled by our subjective experience of being human. Physical illnesses are still widely considered as discrete from emotional illnesses, just as conflicts and social realities are regarded as widely independent from the cultural and environmental conditions. Muscular tensions are viewed as the products of stress rather than as a complex result of internalised conflicts and physical responses to relational and environmental conditions.

Language

Humans commonly use language to relate to, and connect with, others. Paradoxically, language may also be used to dissect the experience of wholeness into discrete parts. The specialised lexis of conventional medicine, for example, has replaced words that carry strong emotions with specific scientific terms that are devoid of emotional responses. Whereas the use of such language (e.g., replacing the term 'cancer' with 'neoplasm') may prevent us from responding with feelings and emotions to our dis-eases, it may also deprive us of an opportunity to become an active agent in our own healing process. The use of such emotionally disconnected language perpetuates the belief held in conventional medicine that it is possible to cure people by means of external interventions and by asking patients to remain as emotionally disconnected observers in their own healing process.

Fromm et al. (1971) describe the disconnection from nature by using research on a flower as an analogy. In this analogy, Western scientists try to understand the nature of a flower by picking it from its surroundings and by analysing it under the microscope, being unaware that by picking and killing the flower they have already destroyed its essence. Eastern 'scientists', in contrast, might sit and meditate in front of the flower, trying to experience it with their emotional and intuitive senses.

Keeping knowledge separate

Modern people have the tendency to compartmentalise knowledge. A good example of this is our tendency to keep biological knowledge separate from medical knowledge. By withholding from conventional medicine the view that viruses represent an ecologically useful communication system of organisms (Pollmann, 1977), our medical system is able to continue to construct them only as 'enemies' and to operate as an industry whose interest is increasingly in using people's illnesses as a way of earning profits for private investors.

Projection of enemies

Another key feature of egocentric consciousness is the widespread tendency to regard most others as our enemies. As will be described in Chapter 8, this tendency often results from childhood experiences of rejection and hostility and a general lack of loving attention. Many of us project this sense of enmity onto people who hold significantly different values and worldviews. An example of this projection is the so-called 'Axis of Evil', an expression used by the USA Administration for some sovereign countries that continue to refuse to adopt USA values as their modus operandi. Whether or not the USA Administration is using this expression also as a ploy to justify the invasion of other countries is debatable; there can be little doubt, however, that many people in the United States of America and other Western countries project old and current fears onto foreign countries, and more recently, also onto so-called terror networks. Although the threat of terrorist acts is real, it is nonetheless to a large degree the result of exploitative and imperialistic policies that have come home to roost.

Table 7.2 Aspects of the separation metaphor

Physio-emotional	Psychosocial	Environmental	Institutional
Lack of experience of body-mind unity	Lack of contact with others; Pseudo contact (internet chats, mobile phones); Uncaring, ego-centric, self-serving behaviour; Difficulties with seeing sense and purpose in relationships	Stabilising deficient selves through the careless and addictive use of goods and services; Compensating our lack of identity through anthropocentrism	Specialisation; Separation of knowledge; Language; Dualistic worldviews

The pollution/waste metaphor

Keywords:

- Environmental pollution
- Production of waste
- Polluted food
- Unfinished physio-emotional cycles
- Repetitive and unproductive conflicts
- Generating demand for non-essential products and services through advertising
- Invasion of emotional boundaries

The notion of pollution

The notions of pollution and waste suggest that something is superfluous, non-essential, toxic, and wasteful. Pollution and waste usually emerge as side effects, or by-products, of processes such as the driving of vehicles and industrial production (smog), or from practices such as the transport of goods (packaging). Often even the products themselves represent waste, in particular when they are purposely produced with inbuilt obsolescence.

Whereas wastefulness and pollution represent predictable results of our modern capitalistic way of producing goods, a holistic view also acknowledges meaningful analogies between environmental pollution, physio-emotional and psychosocial pollution, and wastefulness. Though disregarded by most environmentalists and ecologists, these manifestations must be addressed if we are to achieve a full understanding of pollution and wastefulness.

Electrosmog

A form of pollution still neglected by most environmentalists is electromagnetic pollution, also called 'electrosmog'. Research has demonstrated that electrosmog can contribute to the destruction of the blood-brain barrier (BBC News, 1999). This barrier is an anatomical structure that prevents germs residing in our bodies from reaching the brain where they may cause inflammations such as meningitis. Furthermore, according to the researchers cited on websites such as *www.wissenschaft-unzensiert.de, www.funksmog.org; www.oekosmog. de*, the technology associated with mobile phones has been identified as capable of leading to:

- increases in the risk of brain cancers;
- biological damage to the brain through heating effects;
- symptoms such as headaches, earaches, bad sleep, fatigue, blurring of vision, short-term memory loss, numbing and tingling;
- single and double strand breaks of DNA in brain cells (it is known that double strand breaks lead to cell death);
- so-called 'hot spots' in the brain that can contribute to the emergence of Alzheimer's disease;
- EEG changes;
- bouts of epilepsy; and
- facial rashes and swelling.

In several European countries, the proliferation of electrosmog has led to the formation of thousands of public initiatives (according to *Wissenschaft Unzensiert*, 11,000 in Germany alone), whose aims are to inform the public about health risks and to prevent the further uncontrolled proliferation of this harmful technology.

Physio-emotional wastefulness and pollution

Nutritionists and other health professionals have provided ample information on the substances currently polluting our bodies. These include food additives, heavy metals, and hormones used in meat production (Ashton and Laura, 1998). Nevertheless, the pollution of our bodies through metabolic waste products resulting from unfinished physio-emotional metabolic cycles continues to be widely ignored. Mona-Lisa Boyesen (1974) and Gerda Boyesen (1980), the originators of the biodynamic approach to bodyoriented psychotherapy, call this pollution of body 'tissue chemostasis'. They regard chemostasis as an integral part of what Mona-Lisa Boyesen (1974) calls the 'somatic compromise'. This is a term for the complex changes in tissue consistency that emerge as result of the systemic repression of feelings, with its associated reduction of flow of physio-emotional energy in the body-mind. Once this somatic compromise is established, and tissue armouring is in place, the lack of energy flow and fluid movement facilitate further accumulation of waste products. With the internal cleansing mechanisms partly disabled by the effects of the somatic compromise, the waste products from unexpressed emotions produced by unfinished physio-emotional cycles as well as toxic substances often ingested in food, or absorbed through the skin, are far more likely to accumulate in our bodies.

Psychosocial wastefulness and pollution

A holistic, perspectivist, and psychosomatic view of being human also recognises that most of us are 'polluted' with the demands of our modern society. These demands, mediated by our parents and other caregivers in our early life, are regarded by our 'self' as foreign and toxic. In this sense, our present conventional system of education can be regarded as wasteful or lacking efficiency because it imparts information that is perceived by many as irrelevant for our daily life, while it neglects to teach students how to be fully embodied, to lead harmonious relationships, and to live sustainably in relation to the natural environment.

A large amount of psychosocial waste arises from the difficulty of many of us in reflecting on our behaviour and unconscious motives and feelings. Since most of us are unconscious of our early personal wounds, and consequently struggle with understanding our projections, we spend considerable time and emotional energies engaged with arguments and conflicts. Such arguments are usually repetitive and often lead to an escalation of conflicts rather than to workable conflict solutions.

In search of real alternatives to more pavement and vehicles, it becomes clear that *non-transportation* solutions are essential: car-free living, ecologically designed towns, and bioregional economic policies that resist unnecessary world trade (Lundberg, Alternative to Oil: Technofix, or Lifestyle Change? (www.culturechange.org/issue10/alternative-to-oil.htm).

Another aspect of this condition is the widespread difficulty in identifying, sensing, and communicating both past and present feelings and emotions, a condition most psychosomaticists call alexithymia (Sifneos, 1964).

Being disconnected from our original traumatic scenarios, and lacking the ability to adequately identify and express feelings and emotions, many of us invest our energies with distorted feelings of hope, regret, anxiety, anger, unrealistic expectations, frustrations, and the like, all of which may be regarded as waste in our body-mind relationships.

Institutional wastefulness and pollution

Advertising

Whereas in the early days of capitalism, the industries struggled with satisfying the demands for the newly emerging mass-produced goods, our present postcapitalist era is beset with the difficulty of finding consumers for the oversupply of goods, many of which being produced to satisfy compensatory self-stabilising wants. To create the demand for excess goods by generating false needs, advertising agencies have been using techniques of depth psychology to associate products with our desire to increase our self-esteem (Lasch, 1980; Hunnicutt, 1988; Kanner and Gomes, 1995). Such advertising is designed to make us believe that consuming a particular product will make us feel satisfied, improve our status, or solve our problems. As pointed out earlier, however, the psychological satisfaction produced by the consumption of inessential goods and services is transient and leaves us susceptible to the next advertising campaign.

The money and time invested in advertising, and the artificial demand that it creates, are major factors of "waste", and are a contributing factor to many aspects of unsustainable living. Like symptom manipulation in conventional medicine (see below), the overconsumption resulting from manipulation and people's self-deficits prevents many of us from seeking wellness, healing, inner peace, and connectedness from connecting to our deep needs, feelings, and emotions, and often also from spending time in nature (Cohen 2003; Logan and Meuse, 2001; Beringer, 1999a, 1999b).

Symptom manipulation

A key feature of institutionalised wastefulness is the practice of substituting healing with the short-term cures typical of modern conventional medicine. This symptom manipulation, the practice of seemingly curing illnesses without assisting people in understanding the deeper meaning of their symptoms and suffering, has become one of the most wasteful and unsustainable features of modern societies. Rather than viewing symptoms of illness as guides to hidden emotional wounds

(Dethlefsen, 1990), and to a deeper understanding of our conflicts and difficulties with embodiment (Alexander, 1950; von Uexkuell, 1963, 1979), the short-term cures provided by conventional medicine maintain a high level of emotional and psychosocial suffering in the public.

In addition to treating physical ailments, symptom manipulation is now increasingly employed in connection with self-esteem. Gergen (1991) and other deconstructionist postmodernists who have been writing on the topic of self point out how changes in society have altered our consciousness. In the framework of deconstructionist thought, we are now asked to believe that whatever we are able to create with new technologies will create a new sense of self, a new identity, and a new consciousness. To achieve this new identity, an increasing number of us now use surgery to reshape our faces, trim our body fat, or modify our breasts in size and shape. These practices fail to consider that our bodies reflect our consciousness and our ability to live sustainably. By creating a pseudo-reality through surgery, we might be able to enjoy our new shape for a short while, but since we have changed our shape without changing our consciousness and lifestyle, we have in effect deepened the split between body and mind, and thereby forced our body-mind to create alternative emotional and/or physical symptoms (Dethlefsen, 1990).

Table 7.3   Aspects of the wastefulness/pollution metaphor

Physio-emotional	*Psychosocial*	*Environmental*	*Institutional*
Chemostasis; Muscular armouring; Symptom manipulation.	Unconscious conflicts; Repetitive and unproductive arguments; Alexithymia.	Pollution; Waste production; Packaging; Goods made not to last; Polluted food.	Conventional, non-psychosomatic, medicine; Advertising; Conventional education.

The growth/excess metaphor

Keywords
- Excessive choice
- Competition
- Invasion
- Proliferation
- Loss of identity

- Growing for the sake of growing
- Population growth
- Expansion of power
- Political superstructures/nation states
- Cancer

Our stalled self and the need to grow

To understand the various manifestations, and the sense of urgency regarding growth in our modern societies, it may help to consider that most of us probably had little opportunity to develop a strong and coherent self during our upbringing (cf. Kohut 1971, 1977, 1984). This would prevent us from reaching, during our ontogenetic socialisation, the maturity and self-reflection that humankind has achieved phylogenetically (Gebser, 1986). The logical consequence of this deficit is a latent need to grow emotionally and spiritually.

Physio-emotional growth/excess

An exploration of the notions of growth and excess at the physio-emotional level has to focus on the non-essential features in our bodies and minds. At the body level, we find widespread excessive body tissue and malignant and benign tumors. Cancer, an illness that produces such tumors, may be regarded as a key aspect of our ecological crises when considering that, in 1999, 35,053 Australians died of cancer (total deaths in 1999: 128,102). In other words, cancer accounted for 27 per cent of all deaths (*Australian Yearbook of Statistics* – Cancer control.pdf). Although people attracting cancer now live longer due to improved medical treatments and prevention, cancer is still one of the leading causes of death in the Western world.

The process of cancer in individuals may be conceptualised as one possible substitute for blocked emotional and spiritual growth. Cancers, as much as the self-destructive effects of unbridled consumerism, may thus be regarded as symbolic manifestations of our failure to develop our self-experience from a fragmented self to a stable emotional self, and from there into the transpersonal domain towards an eco-self (see Chapter 8). As long as societal forces do not encourage and support this development of an eco-self, it is difficult to see how people will cease to act out their needs for growth through behaviour that is unsustainable and finally self-destructive.

Bahne-Bahnson (1982) proposes that people suffering from cancer are experiencing, in a psychosomatic way, old emotional deficits around nurturing. He argues that people suffering from cancer take over the role of the nurturer, whereby the tumor symbolises the inner child that is struggling with the effects of deprivation. Sadly, in this symbolic scenario the growing inner 'baby' is destroying its mother. Bahne-Bahnson notes that cancer patients have often experienced a role-reversal between mother and child during their childhood that deprived the child of the chance of being a carefree child and of developing a coherent sense of self.

A typical feature of cancer cells is their loss of identity and sense of socially responsible behaviour. Rather than identifying with the organ of which it has become a part during the organism's ontogeny, cancer cells grow for the sake of growing. Interestingly, the organism 'programmed' for cancer not only widely refrains from attacking the rampant cells, but also facilitates their growth by supporting them with nutrients. This fact has led Henschel and Vester (1977) to regard cancer as a disorganised way of living, whereas Dethlefsen and Dahlke (1990) describe cancer as a state of anarchy in the organism. The latter authors regard tumors as anarchists who have stopped playing to the rules of the organism, but follow their own 'motives'.

The relationship of modern people to the other-than-human world has been likened to the relationship between tumors and their host organisms (Dethlefsen, 1990). In the same way as cancer cells have lost their identification with the tissue or organ to which they belong and upon which they rely for sustenance, humans have lost their identification with their natural environment, and continue to grow in numbers, extend their ecological footprint, and invade and destroy the last places of wilderness. Both finally destroy the subtle functional order of their host organisms, whether this is the planet or an individual. Our species-wide, crippled emotional development and fixation at the stage of adolescence (Erikson, 1968) is paralleled both by the 'illness' cancer and by our unbridled and addictive push towards economic growth. Weigel (1995, p. xii) writes:

> An invasive and unrestrained malignant cell is to human cancer what an invasive and unrestrained human being is to earth cancer. Both represent an aberrant version of their original constitution; both are permitted to thrive because of a systemic imbalance; both are deadly to the health of the organism. In the same vein, the anthropologist Hern (1990) draws our attention to the growth of London from 1800 to 1955 as an expanding, invasive and malignant tumor, whereas Roszak (2001) describes the spread of urban conglomeration as 'Gaia's City Pox'.

ADD and ADHD

According to the unspecified authors who maintain the website www.add.org at present an increasing number of people in the industrialised world (e.g., about four to six per cent in the USA) suffer from Attention Deficit Disorder (ADD) or Attention Deficit Hyperactivity Disorder (ADHD). These conditions emerge as distractibility, impulsivity, and hyperactivity.

Conventional medical research widely rejects an involvement of psychosocial factors in the etiology of ADD/ADHD. In contrast, a growing number of holistically oriented practitioners believe that this condition is caused by factors such as an excessive watching of TV, food allergies, excessive consumption of sugar, poor home life with little attention given to children, and an underfunded, yet demanding, education system. By insisting on a biological rather than psychosocial etiology, conventional medical scientists continue to ignore that our modern world is in many ways a hyperactive world, one in which most people are subjected to constant background noise, and confronted with emotionally and erotically stimulating images. Most people also have to cope with the exhausting effects of poor quality mass-produced foods, foods that often contain preservatives to postpone their decay and colourings to make them more attractive.

At the same time, many of us are also permanently struggling with debilitating personal conflicts, with increasing demands to perform at work and school, and with a lack of time to relate, relax, and reflect. Here we are not even taking into account issues such as the consumption of hormones in meat and the hazardous effects of electromagnetic pollution. Considering these environmental inputs, it is no wonder that many of us respond with chronic excitation to the constant bombardment with stimuli. The question to pose should not only be what causes ADD/ADHD, but also what are many of us knowingly or unknowingly, doing to buffer the various stressful effects of these environmental inputs.

Psychosocial and institutional growth/excess

Psychosocial growth and excess currently manifests in a wide variety of forms. These include our arrogance and our self-serving behaviour in relation to others around us, exemplified in our Western arrogance in relation to non-Western cultures. This arrogance is currently represented in the belief that Western democracies can serve as ideal models for other countries. Stalled emotional and spiritual growth finds symbolic expressions on the institutional level in activities such as:

- the present Western imperial efforts to secure access to cheap resources and labour;
- the trauma-induced, and habitual, push towards economic growth;
- the merging of corporate companies aimed at securing market share;
- the establishing of powerful monopolies;
- the expansion of power and influence through the association of nation states (for example the European Union); and
- the creation of excessive choices and competition that provides the present huge array of goods and services.

Table 7.4   Aspects of the growth/excess metaphor

Physio-emotional	*Psychosocial*	*Environmental*	*Institutional*
Symbolic growth; Cancer; Inflammations in the body mediated by "invading" antigens; Controlling and taming our emotions.	Aggressive behaviour and attitudes; Expanding at the expense of other people (need for power and control in relationships); Social Darwinism; Boundary conflicts and emotional invasion.	The need to control and tame nature; The idea of progress; Urban sprawl.	Expansion of corporate companies; Globalisation; Colonisation; The unsustainable demand for economic growth.

The exhaustion metaphor

Keywords:

- Deprivation
- Exhaustion
- Lack of energy
- Shallow breathing
- Lack of body contact
- Exploitation
- Starvation in developing countries
- The new class of the working poor
- Emaciating illnesses (AIDS, tuberculosis)
- Exploitation of the natural environment
- Resource degradation, such as soil erosion
- Loss of biodiversity

- The scarcity metaphor
- Depletion of buffer systems

Addictive exhaustion

During recent decades, environmentalists have achieved a profound understanding of the varied aspects of environmental exhaustion. Many now have a detailed understanding of issues such as:

- the processes causing the continuing decrease of biodiversity;
- the continuing loss of precious topsoil;
- the continuing exploitation of natural resources;
- the exploitation of animals for the purpose of maximising profits;
- our nation's ecological footprints; and
- the limits of the carrying capacity of this planet.

Yet most environmentalists still ignore what is referred to here as the physio-emotional, psychosocial, and institutional aspects of exhaustion – a condition associated with the desperate attempts of many people to soothe, or compensate for, their inner emptiness (Kanner and Gomes, 1995). This compensation emerges, for example, as an excessive concern with outward appearances, as the need to fill homes and offices with expensive gadgets, as a liking for big cars, and as a compulsion to accumulate power and influence. Few of us seem able to look behind the smokescreen and realise that working hard to afford these symbols of status and superfluous gadgets only deepens our state of exhaustion (Durning, 1992), which, if not contained and healed, often leads to economic collapse, emotional breakdowns, the break-up of relationships, addictive behaviours, and psychosomatic illnesses.

Physio-emotional exhaustion and the lack of self-regulation

Most of us who live in developed countries significantly lack the self-experience of body-mind unity that would enable us to be self-regulating and streaming beings (see Chapter 8). Since the state of physio-emotional exhaustion is increasingly becoming an all-encompassing phenomenon in these countries, an increasing number of people have lost much of their natural ability to self-regulate. In the following section, we describe some of these occurrences of our struggles with self-regulation.

AIDS

Our general lack of physio-emotional self-regulation, emotional, social, and economic exploitation, and the resulting emotional and spiritual exhaustion have led to the occurrence of a number of psychosomatic forms of exhaustion such as tuberculosis and, more recently, AIDS. Depending on our viewpoint, we may also associate conditions such as depression and heart diseases with physio-emotional and psychosocial exploitation and exhaustion.

It has been calculated that in the next 10 years more people will die of AIDS than have died during the six years of the Second World War. It is expected that by the year 2020, 68 million people will have died from AIDS. In 2001, in the USA alone, more than 32,000 people between 13 and 24 became infected with the HIV virus (Newshour Extra, 12 July 2002).

AIDS has its most devastating effect in developing countries, in some of which now more than 30 per cent of the population are infected with the HIV virus. At the same time, only 36,000 of the 26 million people in these countries have access to the highly effective triple-cocktail drug therapy that people with HIV and AIDS can take for granted in the USA and most other Western countries. According to Strub (2001), this is mainly due to the profit interests of the large pharmaceutical corporations that hold the patents on these drugs.

Psychosomatic research on AIDS is still in its early stages, probably because it involves a viral infection and because of political influence. The few people who have undertaken research and published articles on the psychosomatic and psychosocial causes of AIDS regard it as a manifestation of difficulties with the integration of love and sexuality (Braeutigam and Christian, 1986; Dethlefsen and Dahlke, 1990; Sattmann-Frese, 1992). This can be observed in sub-Saharan African states, where sexuality and promiscuity help many people survive in a climate of poverty inflicted by postcolonial structures and current exploitation by Western nations (cf. McMichael, 2001). In the West, in contrast, AIDS has gained its greatest foothold mainly among drug addicts who share needles, and among those gay men who participate in unsustainable lifestyles.

Lauritsen (1997) contends that only a small subset of gay men appears to be at risk of attracting AIDS. These are, according to him, people who have typically suffered recurring sexually transmitted diseases, have undergone repeated treatments with antibiotics, and are engaged in a highly unsustainable lifestyle that includes the high use of alcohol, tobacco, and other recreational drugs such as amphetamines. Lauritsen's views confirm my own (Werner's) research, during which I, Werner, learned that some gay men engage in excessive sexual activities (e.g., involving up to 30 ejaculations during a weekend), often experienced with unknown partners and under the influence of a multitude of drugs. The emotional and physical exhaustion that people would naturally experience as a result of such emotionally disconnected, and often physically demanding, activities is often masked by the use of recreational drugs.

An increasing number of researchers, such as Ellner and Cort (1997), believe that being a gay man in our present commercialised gay culture is in and of itself likely to be a toxic and dangerous condition that has a high probability of leading to infantile excesses inappropriate for adults. Having become the (sub)cultural norm, this lifestyle, together with the psychological difficulties of being HIV-positive and of living with AIDS, makes life, according to these authors, irrelevant beyond the age of 40. In other words, by then such people will have burnt out, which is what AIDS might be all about.

Depression

A key aspect of the failure to support healthy embodiment and self-regulation is depression. This emotional and energetic condition not only costs our modern societies billions of dollars in lost productivity, it also contributes to the unsustainability of an estimated 340 million sufferers of depression worldwide, and of many more millions of related people. Depression may lead to high levels of emotional and social impairment, and is a major contributing factor to suicide. In 1996, 30,862 people committed suicide in the USA. Australia has one of the highest suicide rates for young males in the Western world. According to Harrison, Moller, and Bordeaux "[t]he rate of suicide among males aged 15 to 24 in 1990 was about three times higher than the rate in 1960. This rate has not risen further since 1990" (http://www.nisu.flinders.edu.au/pubs/bulletin15/bulletin15sup.html).

My clinical experience as a psychotherapist has led me to believe that an important aspect of depression is the often unconscious struggle with self-maintenance and unrealistic internalised and external demands. The most severe cases of depression I (Werner) have ever worked with involved a number of German diplomats who had burnout after years of struggling to build their lives in foreign countries. The symptoms of depression are usually associated with a lack of energy, pleasure, and ease, a continuous sense of struggling with life's demands, a sense of worthlessness and guilt, and thoughts of suicide and impaired concentration. These symptoms make the lives of individuals highly unsustainable and limit their ability to maintain meaningful relationships, to care for themselves, for others, and for the natural environment.

Psychosocial and institutionalised exhaustion

Psychosocial exhaustion is strongly associated with the oral deprivation outlined in the previous chapter. Within a cultural context, psychosocial and institutionalised exhaustion emerge as results of a neglect of the basic aspects of being human. Psychosocial exhaustion may be regarded as one result of exploitation. Emerging as a predictable result of the oral and narcissistic conditions described in the previous chapter, the exploitation/exhaustion scenario lies at the core of our ecological crises. It emerges, for example, as exploitation of:

- socially and economically dependent workers in all countries;
- children and women, both for cheap labour and sex;
- people in Third World countries by Western elites (Sachs, 1993); and
- women by societal structures based on male values and power structures.

As indicated in the previous chapter, exploitation has become so all-encompassing that it is literally impossible to avoid participating in it. Whereas most people find themselves most of the time on the side of the exploited, a minority of people manages to join the side of the exploiters. At the same time, there are no sharp demarcation lines, since modern societies are structured as hierarchies in which most of us find ourselves not only in exploitative positions of relative power, but also on the receiving end of power. In other words, most of us are exploited and act as exploiters at the same time ('the oppressed will oppress').

Table 7.5 Aspects of the exhaustion metaphor

Physio-emotional	Psychosocial	Environmental	Institutional
Shallow breathing; Reduced physiological and emotional charge; Reduced aliveness; Tissues deprived of energy and vibrations; AIDS;	Lack of empathy; Exploitative relationships; The world owes me a living attitude; Self-exploitation; Viewing relationships	Assumption of never-ending resources; Unbridled consumerism; Loss of biodiversity; Exploitation of the biosphere (tree-logging, etc.); Loss of	Exploitative ways of producing goods and services; Appropriation of labour; Stock exchange; Competition for markets

| Tuberculosis; Lack of self-care | as places of competition | topsoil; Experience of competition projected onto the environment; Competition for allegedly scarce resources | |

'Enworlding' our embodiment

When considering the topics described in this chapter, it becomes increasingly obvious that we not only take the world around us into our body (e.g., by digesting poisonous substances, adopting cultural attitudes and behaviour, or by being stressed by ambient noise), we also unconsciously shape the world as a mirror image of our egocentric body-mind reality. The psychological processes at work externalise inner conflicts as conflicts between nations and ethnic groups. Muscular tensions are paralleled by political tensions and tensions between different worldviews and paradigms. Collapsed (hypotonic) tissue finds a synergy in barren and deserted landscapes, whereas overcharged (hypertonic) tissue has a striking parallel in our dense and overcrowded cities. Our internal pollution with the metabolic remnants of unprocessed physio-emotional cycles and with internalised super-ego demands finds its analogy in the various aspects of environmental pollution, whereas the current increase in simplism and polarisation in thinking has its equivalent in the declining biodiversity. Whereas such vertical thinking and intuiting might sound far-fetched for many of us, many people engaging in psychotherapy to heal from their traumatic experiences and their body-mind and person-planet splits frequently make such associations between their inner experiences and their outer realities.

The metaphors employed in this chapter not only allow us to draw synergies between body and mind, and person and planet, but also deepen our understanding of possible compensatory structures. Space permitting, we include here only two examples of this system.

Table 7.6 Body-mind and person-planet synergies and compensatory structures

Topic	*Body-mind*	*Person-planet*	*Compensatory structures*
Lack of communication	Body-mind split; Left-right split, head-body split,	Lack of awareness of interdependency; Difficulty in	Notion of globalisation; The Internet;

	etc.; Disowned parts of the body.	experiencing person-planet unity; Lack of empathic dialogue between nations.	Anonymous meetings on chat sites.
Shallow breathing	Neurotic breathing patterns leading to a lack of internal ventilation and a low level of emotional charge.	Declining wealth and influence of common people; declining oxygen levels.	Glorification of notions of power; Powerful workshops, cars, countries, people, etc.

In this chapter we have conceptualised key synergies and analogies between seemingly unrelated aspects of human struggle and suffering. Using holistic and systems thinking, we applied four typical metaphors of human suffering to cross the levels of physio-emotional, psychosocial, ecological, and institutional sustainability. This served to highlight the interrelatedness of these four levels and to remind us that we live in a cosmos, in an ordered system and a whole. Whether or not this whole is chaotic and unsustainable, or harmonious and sustainable, is a question of our willingness to expand our consciousness towards higher levels of eco-self.

In the following chapter we describe the sixth and last level of eco-self consciousness in the system proposed here we will show that, at this level of consciousness, we have to expand our perception of the world from a holistic and intellectual one to one of a direct experience of person-planet unity.

8 Person-planet Unity Consciousness (Stage 6)

In this chapter we describe the provisional final stage in our proposed system of eco-self development. At this stage of consciousness development, we move beyond intellectual meaning-making and constructed worldviews to a felt sense, and a direct experience of, person-planet unity. Key aspects of this form of self-experience have been described, for example, by Watts (1961) and Moore (1996). This self-experience, often also called ecstasy, enlightenment, satori, or grace, is based on our ability to experience ourselves as energetically 'streaming beings' Boadella (1987). It involves the ability to allow physio-emotional charge (chi) to flow freely through the body-mind, an ability that is often hampered by chronic muscular tension, shallow breathing, and pathological variations in tissue tonus. Here we will provide descriptions of experiences of streaming, and of person-planet unity, and examines historical accounts of these phenomena.

Whereas at the fourth level of eco-self development ecological crises were conceptualised as predictable results of emotional defences and a search for a coherent sense of self, and at the fifth level this was enhanced by a broader understanding of the synergies between inner and outer pollution, exploitation, and other issues, at this sixth level, our aim is to experience a deep felt sense of oneness with the biosphere.

The epistemology for this chapter includes a critical examination of the notion held by object relation theorists such as Kaplan (1978) that ego-development is naturally associated with an alienation from the body, a phenomenon often called desomatisation (Schur, 1974). This view suggests that the ontogenetic development of humans is a process during which we have to leave much of our animal nature behind, including our ability to experience the world as streaming beings.

In contrast to this view, we will argue that the loss of person-planet unity is not a necessary prerequisite to self-development, and that many key aspects of our ecological crises are based on people's difficulty with experiencing an embodied sense of person-planet unity. The argument will also include aspects of ecological crises that result from our lack of understanding, and the consequent rejection, of a simultaneousness of personal and transpersonal self-experiences. The chapter will conclude with a description of the ways in which we unconsciously compensate for the lack of person-planet unity experiences through symbolic forms of connectedness.

Six person-planet unity experiences

In the following, we briefly describe six personal experiences that go beyond the currently accepted and normalised personal experiences.

(1) Self-dissolution and touching

Those body-oriented psychotherapists and bodyworkers who work with touch, and who also have a high level of body-mind integration (bioenergetic flow), frequently experience a blurring of self-boundaries when they gently hold their hands on people's bodies for an extended time. During such experiences, it becomes difficult to tell where the practitioner's body ends and the body of the client begins. When these practitioners close their eyes and deepen their breathing, they might even experience a softening of the perception of their personal self. Some even sense that they share an energetic life force with their clients, and often experience synchronised physical expressions such as rumblings in their guts (borborygmi). These practitioners may interrupt or limit these experiences of self-dissolution by moving their hands to create friction between their hands and the clients' bodies, by focusing on objects in the room, and by decreasing the depth of their breathing.

(2) Self-dissolution and meditation

Many of us who meditate extensively often experience a dissolving of self-boundaries as part of their contemplation practice. The deep and slow breathing associated with deep meditation and the gradual disappearance of the chatter in one's mind produces a state of being in which the sense of self transcends both self-boundaries and space-time. People practising body-mind exercises, such as Kum Nye (Tulku, 1977, 1981), often also report a deepening of their energetic connectedness with the environment. Such exercises enable them to sense an energetic connection to the ground, a feeling of becoming one with the earth they stand on.

(3) Sneezing and bliss

Probably few modern people are aware that sneezing is one of the most powerful mechanisms of physio-emotional self-regulation. Besides being a physio-emotional overflow valve that humans often unconsciously use to maintain a natural level of physiological and emotional charge, repeated sneezing also has the capacity to harmonise energies to the extent that people experience strong energetic streamings and a strong sense of peace and harmony.

(4) Haydn Washington's experience

Haydn Washington (2002, p. 7), a colleague in our School, describes an early morning experience with a lyrebird as follows:

> I opened my eyes to stare into deep black eyes a few metres away. Fascinated eyes. Eyes of otherness. There was no fear...none at all. We watched in mutual astonishment at the incredibility of our 'being'. We existed at this moment in time, and the gulf between our histories and separate evolution was gone. [...] There was no thought, nothing but the startling desire to hang on to a connection that we knew could not last...holding on to our harmony for yet another unlikely moment...

(5) Psychosomatic identification

In 1988, I (Werner) provided bodywork sessions over several months to five people infected with the HIV virus as part of a project for a German AIDS and drug management agency. On one occasion, after treating a young man suffering from full-blown AIDS with holistic bodywork, I experienced a severe depletion of my energies and had to stay in bed for two days. On a different occasion, I developed some hours after the bodywork session about 40 Kaposi sarcomas on my torso that faded after approximately two days. Any experienced medical doctor would have diagnosed me with these sarcomas as being in the last stage of full-blown AIDS. Yet I was then, and I still am now, HIV-negative.

(6) Person-planet unity and shared pain

In 1983, I (Werner) attended a residential training at the Gerda Boyesen Centre for Biodynamic Psychology in Acton (West London) as part of my ongoing psychotherapy training. Waiting for the trainer to appear, I was sitting on the carpeted floor, gaily throwing both feet up in the air. When my heels touched the floor, I felt a sharp pain in my right heel, and I immediately thought, and felt, that I would be in pain for the whole weekend.
Puzzled about the event and the fact that the other heel was perfectly healthy and free of pain, I massaged my heel for the whole weekend, hoping that the swelling that had emerged would not disable me for an extended time.

Limping home to Ealing Broadway on late Sunday afternoon, I opened the door of the house that I shared with some flatmates, when one of them approached me, obviously upset about something. She told me that she had just released our cat from a trap in which she must have been stuck for some time. Puzzled and upset, I asked my flatmate whether the cat had been trapped with her right back leg. She agreed, wondering how I knew. I replied that I had treated her for the last two days to help her ease the pain.

Issues of transpersonal psychology

The above stories, which probably sound weird and unbelievable to people committed to a purely rational and scientific worldview, are nevertheless quite ordinary experiences for people who cultivate their felt sense of body-mind unity and are able to accept thoughts, feelings, and experiences without preconceived judgments. The six stories may be regarded as what transpersonal psychologists might call supernatural experiences, an expression that we regard as problematic. This is because such experiences are quite ordinary for people who have retained or gained a capability for experiencing high levels of energetic streaming and pulsation (Reich (1933, 1942), Boadella (1976, 1987), G. Boyesen (1976, 1985), and who are consequently more in touch with their needs and feelings than the average person.

This state of consciousness that all of us would have experienced in the womb and as small children, but that most of us have lost during our upbringing, may be regarded as the *natural* state of consciousness, and not a supernatural one. If infants had a chance to experience full attachment to a love object (Bowlby, 1997), and if they were spared the traumatic experiences that led to their energetic fragmentation, they would likely be able to retain their energetic connection to the biosphere. Yet, having grown up in modern cultures, most of them have to a large degree lost this connectedness as a continuous experience. Lacking energetic streamings and trust, they experience a partial numbness of the body-mind, are chronically torn by conflicts and doubts, and have an insatiable yearning for fulfilment as well as a general feeling of disconnectedness from nature. In other words, ego-centred experience, psychosomatic numbness, and a sense of separation from the cosmos have become the norm – a norm that is constantly reproduced and perpetuated by both modern and deconstructionist postmodern ideological beliefs.

Consequently, rather than speaking about the natural and the supernatural, it would make sense to refer to these states of being as natural and less-than-natural, that is, as 'infranatural'. In other words, the self-experience associated with the egocentric condition represents the unsustainable, psychosocially and physio-emotionally impaired, and less-than-natural norm, whereas one based on body-mind and person-planet unity represents the natural, but still marginalised, condition in modern society.

This is not to say that egocentric and ecocentric self-experiences are polarised without grey-areas between them. People such as Watts (1951, 1958, 1961, 1962, 1968), Moore (1996), Abram (1997), Evernden (1992), Csikcentmichaily (1992), and others describe varied aspects of this grey-area. These descriptions suggest asking why some of us more than others have gained or retained a felt sense of connectedness with the other-than-human environment. Although the answer to this question is probably as complex as the experiences are varied, it is possible to associate the impairment of our ability to experience person-planet unity with key aspects of the oral-exploiting and narcissistic-shaming conditions examined in Chapter 6, and with the schizoid-terrorising condition explored in this chapter.

Transpersonal psychology is concerned with 'direct experiences', the ability to experience the world directly, undiminished and uncompromised by cultural interpretation. Both the modernist and deconstructionist postmodernist worldviews undermine and often vilify such experiences. For modernists, direct experiences are far too subjective to be taken seriously, whereas for deconstructionists these experiences lack cultural interpretation and are too infused with essentialism.

Acknowledging that a comprehensive description of all key issues of transpersonal psychology would be beyond the scope of this study, we will restrict ourselves to a brief outline of some key aspects of transpersonal psychology that we believe have immediate relevance to this study.

Archetypes

Scholar and psychotherapist Carl Gustav Jung bridged depth psychology and transpersonal psychology, and he emphasised that the stories of our psychological development follow certain patterns, which he called archetypes. Not denying that children suffer traumatic experiences during their upbringing, Jung suggested that human experiences also follow archetypal patterns that are alive in myths, legends, and fairy tales. These archetypal stories describe traumatic stories not from the point of view of a pitiable accident, but from the viewpoint of healing journeys. Jung, probably more than his contemporaries, also believed that people's selves are not restricted to their bodies and skin surface, but extend into the universe. He may thus be justifiably called the (modern) father of the eco-self.

Religion

Transpersonal psychology is not concerned with particular brands of religion but acknowledges that "religio" stands for rootedness. Potentially, it is thus associated with our efforts to connect our consciousness with our spiritual, physical, and ethnic roots. In contrast to most religious systems that are predominantly based on worshipping practices, transpersonal practices are more akin to the branches of religion that work with direct experience and meditation, such as Zen in Buddhism, the Sufi tradition in Islam, and the Gnostic tradition in Christianity.

Anthropocentrism

There has been an ongoing debate among transpersonal psychologists as to whether transpersonal psychology should take a human-centred or naturalistic direction. Although Maslow (1964) clearly states that transpersonal psychology should be non-anthropocentric and naturalistic rather than anthropocentric and transcendental, Fox (1990) believes that most scholars, including Maslow, predominantly employ anthropocentric formulations in their writings, in which case, as Fox (1990) puts it, transpersonal psychology would still have to be 'ecologised'.

Streamings and transpersonal experiences

My (Werner's) experience with both meditation and bodywork has taught me that there exists an intimate link between body-mind and person-planet unity. Deep meditation, the Neo-Reichian body-oriented psychotherapies, shamanic practices, and systems such as Yoga and Kum Nye (Tulku, 1977, 1981), offer ways of deepening people's ability to generate physio-emotional streamings and to harmonise their energies. It is this ability to charge and move subtle biophysical energy that enhances people's ability to experience a felt sense of person-planet-unity. Boadella (1987, p. 32) writes:

> When the condition of serenity and tranquility in the womb is recovered, it is experienced as a state of tension-free, melting, oceanic ecstasy. Grof relates this to the experiences of mystic unity and merging, to the peak experiences of later life. Freud similarly spoke of 'oceanic feelings' and Reich of 'cosmic streamings'.

Both the experience of energetic streamings and the mentioned experience of dissolving ego-boundaries are viewed by modern societies as pathological because relatively few people have experienced these phenomena while retaining an intact sense of self. For this reason, energetic streamings and self-diffusion experiences are viewed by most psychiatrists as symptoms of schizophrenia, an emotional state in which people experience a breakdown of their emotional defences and in which the 'phren' (diaphragm and soul) allows traumatic experiences to press into their consciousness. In other words, and as Barrows (1995) pointed out, the Western natural and social sciences still lack a concept of the possibility of a simultaneousness of a coherent personal self and an ecological and transpersonal self.

Traumas and loss of person-planet unity

The issues raised in the six stories presented above serve to illustrate that having or being an eco-self denotes a form of consciousness that is based on a felt sense of body-mind and person-planet unity. They highlight that the understanding of eco-self currently favoured by environmentalists and environmental educators is significantly limited because it is based on a mechanistic rather than an energetic perception of the world. An understanding of an eco-self that is not limited to behaviourist and cognitive perspectives has to include the insight that solving our ecological problems will also require us to:

- reclaim our bodies and to understand and respond to its signals;
- allow free expression of its sounds;
- deepen our ability to experience energetic streamings;
- understand our ecological crises as manifestations of the unhealed wounds of individuals living in modern societies;
- experience a stable sense of self based on embodiedness, mutual support, and nurturing; and
- deepen our breathing and become comfortable with non-erotic human touch.

Experienced in such a way, eco-self consciousness represents the awareness that our selves do not stop at the limits of our physical bodies. In the same way in which our subtle energies extend into the interpersonal space, so an eco-self consciousness enables us to experience the rest of nature as integrated parts of our being. With this awareness, we feel and understand, without having to resort to ethical constructs, that we cannot hurt other beings and nature as a whole without hurting ourselves.

The current possibilities to enhance one's ability to experience body-mind and person-planet unity through body-mind practices demonstrate that adults can be enabled to experience a lasting sense of connectedness to the universe. This is in contrast to the fleeting experiences of ecstasy after the achievement of a difficult task or the one of falling in love. Whereas these and similar experiences can trigger a strong momentary feeling of elation and excitement, they usually do not last over an extended time.

Loss of person-planet unity

There has been a lot of speculation on the historical processes that have led to the gradual loss of people's ability to experience physio-emotional streamings. Acknowledging that a comprehensive discussion of this topic is beyond the scope of this study, we wish to assert here that it makes sense to associate this loss with the emerging loss of the 'hearing of the voices of gods', an era that Jaynes (1976, p. 436) associates with the second millennium BC. The notion of hearing the voices of the gods is here equated with the ability of undistressed humans to experience body and mind, and person and planet as a unity. In the same vein, the notion of obeying our lost divinities is probably paralleled by our acceptance of limitations imposed by our bodies and nature (Fisher, 2002, p. 119). Other milestones of this loss of unity experiences would have been the Enlightenment and the emergence of the scientific revolution. An interesting detail of this development is that in 1847 von Helmholtz, a German physiologist, formulated an exclusively mathematical view of energy transformation. As Jaynes (1976, pp. 437, 438) remarks:

> His [Helmholtz's] mathematical treatment of the principle coldly placed the emphasis where it has been ever since: there are no outside forces in our closed world of energy transformations. There is no corner in the stars for any god, no crack in this closed universe of matter for any divine influence to seep through, none whatsoever.

The complete erosion of a spiritual view of the cosmos expressed in Helmholtz's work, a phenomenon that Jaynes calls the breakdown of the bicameral mind, was (interestingly or predictably) soon followed by Darwin's work on genetic change through random mutation and the survival of the fittest. Tragically, the transition from the holistic-medieval worldview to the modern worldview, a transition often described as 'the passage from the Dark Ages to the Enlightenment' (Spretnak, 1997, p. 44), did not deliver what people probably, consciously or unconsciously, had hoped for. Rather than leading to a reclaiming of the body and an increased experience of body-mind and person-planet unity, the rejection of spirituality led to the mechanistic and scientific modern worldview with all its negative ecological consequences. The 'spirituality-embodiment-coin' had been flipped over without any integration between the two taking place.

Cosmic consciousness

Ancient people have known about the experience of cosmic consciousness (Bucke, 1991) for a long time, and have described them with terms such as *satori* (Zen), *nirvana* (Buddhism), *samadhi* (Yoga), *shema* (cabbalism), and *unio mystica* (Catholicism). Watts (1973, p. 17) writes about cosmic consciousness:

> There is no really satisfactory name for this type of experience. To call it mystical is to confuse it with visions of another world, or of gods and angels. To call it spiritual or metaphysical is to suggest that it is not also extremely concrete and physical, while the term "cosmic consciousness" itself has the unpoetic flavor of occultist jargon.

Many mystics and poets have described the possibility of a real and felt connection with the creation. Yet, it is often said that this state of consciousness only occurs coincidentally, unless we reproduce it by means of psychedelic drugs.

What then does, for example, the experience of ecstasy feel like? How do we know that we experience this state of being? Watts (1973, pp. 17,18) puts it this way:

> To the individual thus enlightened it appears as a vivid and overwhelming certainty that the universe, precisely as it is at this moment, as a whole and in every one of its parts, is so completely right as to need no explanation or justification beyond what it simply is.

And further on, he remarks:

> At the same time it is usual for the individual to feel that the whole world has become his own body, and that whatever he is has not only become, but always has been what everything else is (1973, p. 18).

The cosmic consciousness described here is very similar to what is often called mystical consciousness (Noyes, 1974) or ontological identification (Fox, 1990). This kind of self-experience consists, according to Noyes (1974, p. 397), of "ineffability, transcendence of time and space, sense of truth, loss of control, intensified emotion, transience, and disordered perception". For Fox (1990, p. 250), "[o]ntologically based identification refers to experiences of commonality with all that is that are brought about through deep-seated realization of the fact *that* things are". It has to be noted again that notions such as loss of control, diffusion of boundaries, and disordered perception are associated here with people who are able to experience a stable sense of self. In relating to these people, they differ from similar symptoms suffered by people who lack a coherent sense of self. The lack of understanding of this distinction, which is often referred to as pre-trans fallacy (Wilber, 1983), has led many psychiatrists to pathologise transpersonal experiences.

In a similar vein, Livingston (1981) writes about the importance of our ability to identify with animals, but also acknowledges modern people's difficulty in experiencing a deep connectedness with non-human creatures. He suggests that the ability to identify with wild animals would mark an engagement in a process of recovery.

Berry (1988), a theologian and geologist, on the other hand, believes that humans have become autistic in relation to the rest of the biosphere because of the adoption of, and belief in, the Cartesian mechanistic worldview. He suggests that belief in this mechanistic view destroyed the loving bond that humans once experienced with nature.

In a similar vein, Roszak (1981), one of the originators of ecological psychology, makes us aware of the many connections between humans and the rest of the biosphere. He suggests that humans are mothered out of the substance of this planet, and that this heritage inextricably shapes who we are.

Shepard was one of the first scholars who conceptualised the psychopathological underpinning of our exploitative relationship with the Earth. In his (1982) book *Nature and madness* he describes the beliefs and practices of our Judaeo-Christian civilisation as the predictable result of what he calls 'ontogenetic crippling', a deficit of self-development that has affected us as a culture since we left the cultural stage of hunter-gatherers behind. Pointing at the relatively long neoteny of human beings and the prolonged period of dependency of children on their caregivers, Shepard suggests that with the domestication of animals and the emergence of agriculture humans started to neglect the developmental needs of their offspring, thereby creating the emotional distortions now widely responsible for our ecological crises.

Walker (1979, p. 102), on the other hand, writes of cosmic consciousness that "all objects and elements forming the universe share in a kind of common mind", whereas Averroes (d. 1198) held that we have separate bodies, but not separate minds. He contended that all of humanity shares in a universal soul, and believed that being aware of, and having access to, this universal mind is a profoundly mystical experience that leads to an indescribable depth of knowing.

As briefly mentioned, cosmic consciousness has often been associated with the notion of ecstasy. Johnson (1989, p. vii) notes:

> Ecstasy. It was once considered a favor of the Gods, a divine gift that could lift mortals out of ordinary reality and into a higher world. The transformative fire of ecstasy would burn away the barriers between ourselves and our souls, bestowing on us a greater understanding of our relation to ourselves and to the universe.

Those who have used the psychedelic drug MDMA would certainly agree to the above comment on ecstasy. In the state of ecstasy and under the influence of this drug, most claim to experience themselves as part of the cosmos, which suggests that one of the main features of being neurotic is a self-experience of ego-encapsulation.

Another term sometimes used for the experience of person-planet unity is the term *enchantment*. Moore (1996, p. ix) writes:

> An enchanted life has many moments when the heart is overwhelmed by beauty and the imagination is electrified by some haunting quality in the world or by a spirit or voice speaking from deep within a thing, a place or a person. Enchantment may be a state of rapture and ecstasy in which the soul comes to the foreground, and the literal concerns of survival and daily preoccupation at least momentarily fade into the background.

Person-planet unity and energy

The experience of person-planet unity is associated with a worldview that includes an awareness of subtle energy flowing through the whole cosmos. Whereas in modern cultures we have almost entirely lost this awareness of subtle energies, most Eastern cultures have retained, at least to a certain extent, an awareness of this energy. Unlike energy as it is conceptualised in physics, physiology or biochemistry where it denotes physical or metabolic energy, this understanding of energy is probably best described as cosmic energy. Mann (1973, p. 163) writes:

Simply put, the theory is that the human organism is responsive to the total external environment – that is, that a man is linked to a cosmic vital energy. If there is a change in the energy envelope around man, he will be affected by it; the vital energies in the body resonate to these changes and they in turn affect the physical body.

The idea of a vital or cosmic energy is probably more than 5000 old. It was known as *prana* by the Hindus and as *mana* by the native Hawaiians. Mesmer (1734–1815), who earned his medical degree in Vienna in 1766, formulated a theory of an invisible magnetic current (animal magnetism) that flows through all objects in the universe, including the human body.

Paracelsus (1493–1541), a doctor and natural philosopher, is best known for the introduction of chemicals in medicine. Less known is that he also believed in what he called "*munia*", a magnetic force or energy that all people potentially own, and that can be used to heal diseases in others. He viewed *munia* as radiating within and around people, and as a force that can be directed by them.

Conventional scientific disciplines, such as psychology, physiology, medicine, and education, have yet to acknowledge the existence of this universal cosmic energy and the experience of streamings as the most basic and profound ways of being in the world. Such streamings, and their relation to the experience of body-mind unity and person-planet unity, have been documented for a long time. Devall (1990) describes Naess' concept of the oceanic self, which seems to describe a subjectively 'feelable' way of being connected with nature. Already Freud was confronted with this phenomenon when the Ramakrishna biographer Rolland approached him to analyse this mystical experience. Freud, critical of religious experiences, doubted that these experiences were real or that the exploration of such states could benefit people in developing a strong ego. The observed disappearance of oceanic streamings in adults living in modern cultures was consequently viewed as 'natural desomatisation' (Schur 1955) and associated with normal ego-maturation. However, as mentioned earlier, Boadella (1987), Conger (1994), and G. Boyesen (1976, 1985) have demonstrated that adults are able to experience these streamings after having worked for some time with a body-oriented psychotherapist – an experience that I, (Werner) can confirm both from my experience of being human and from more than 20 years of working with this therapeutic modality. They conclude that the experience of streamings rather than numbness is actually the natural way of being in the world.

We can experience these streamings in a number of different ways. At one end of the spectrum, we find spontaneous jerky movements when, for example, in somatic psychotherapy, muscular and tissue armouring begin to dissolve. At the other end of the spectrum, we find streamings in the form of very fine (flour-like), continuous and pleasant vibrations in people who have experienced bodywork and psychotherapy over an extended time. In between these two extreme positions, we can locate vibrations of various amplitudes that have the basic tendency to become finer as people learn to live with higher levels of emotional and physiological charge and become more energetically and emotionally integrated.

Such a refinement of vibration is highly dependent on our ability to maintain a deep level of connected breathing. However, very few people breathe fully and in an uninterrupted fashion. Reich (1933, 1942), Lowen (1958, 1972, 1980), and Dychtwald (1986) have described how human beings unconsciously restrict their breathing in order to protect themselves against the experience of unmanageable feelings. Most of us show a combination of the four common breathing patterns:

- shallow breathing
- disconnected breathing
- isolated chest breathing
- isolated belly breathing

It is not exaggerated to say that our difficulties in experiencing streamings, and the consequent lack of energetic connectedness to the biosphere, are at the very core of the emotional and spiritual misery experienced by most modern people today. Having widely lost their deepest and most reliable sense of beingness, they seek meaning and fulfilment in the compensatory scenarios described in earlier chapters.

Redefining object-relations theory

The experiences and issues described so far in this chapter question some of the key notions of object-relations theory. Although object-relations theory represents a useful concept in the broad framework of depth psychology, when viewed from a psychosomatic and transpersonal perspective, it shows a number of serious limitations.

- It neglects the natural processes working in the infant's body and adopts the view that ego maturation is automatically associated with a process of desomatisation (Schur, 1974).

- It confirms Freud's view that the ego is principally situated on the surface of the body.
- It uncritically adopts many aspects of the modern worldview, which is based on subject-object dichotomy, atomism, and notions of disconnectedness.
- It limits its focus to interactions between mother and child, when there are strong indicators suggesting that there are at least three 'factors' influencing the ontogeny of humans: mother, the family, and the wider natural and cultural environments into which a child is born.
- It neglects the possibility of a karmic purpose in life, that is, that we might 'choose' our parents and the environment we are born into as a challenge to heal past experiences.
- It neglects the consideration that children are actually not becoming less dependent as they develop, but rather shift the focus of their dependency towards other family members, the community, and the natural world.
- It creates an ideal of an independent wellbeing at the same time as we are becoming painfully aware of how dependent we are both on one another and on the integrity of the biosystems of this planet.

In the following section, we describe in greater detail some of the points listed above.

The role of nature in child development

Object relations theory has yet to consider that infants are not only interacting with their mothers but are also in meaningful relationships with animals and other features of the natural environment. It has so far failed to embrace the notion that the environment is magic to children in a similar way to indigenous people's experience of the land around them, such as that of Australian Aborigines. Recently, Verny (1981), Josselson (1996), Hill (2003a), and others have elaborated on the importance of the various influences of the nonhuman environment on human self-development.

Lack of awareness of subtle energy

As a theory mainly situated in ego psychology, object-relations theory has still to acknowledge the bio-energetic processes taking place in human beings. Defining a widely desomatised way of being (numbness) as the normal energetic state of being, it has developed a short-sighted and biased focus both on the external world and on the ways in which newborns find attachment (Bowlby, 1997) and bonding with mother.

The view held by object-relations theorists that we meet others through skin-to-skin contact, through sound, smell and visual perception, fails to consider that babies are not just empty minds, but beings who live in a state of enchantment by having an energetic connection with 'objects' beyond their skin boundary. In contrast, a more holistic view on eco-self development would acknowledge that babies not only need fulfilment of their needs from human beings, but are also embedded in a complex ecological landscape. As Barrows (1995, p. 103) notes:

> It [a theory of child development] must acknowledge that, from the earliest moments of life, the infant has an awareness not only of human touch, but also of the touch of a breeze on her skin, variations in light and colour, temperature, texture, sound. No one who has spent time watching an infant could fail to know this; yet the theorists on whose work our current understanding (and therapies) have been based fail to account for its importance - indeed, even for its presence.

And in relation to the cultural values reflected in mainstream psychology, she writes:

> Our culture's insistence on independence, mastery, and competition has led to the popularity of a psychology that emphasizes only the first aspects of a child's task: the theory of Margaret Mahler, for instance, which traces the development of the child as a process of separation and individuation (1995, p. 105).

This critique of object relations may be extended to a questioning of the very notion of the object as the 'outside' that is the 'not me' (Barrows, 1995, p. 106). As indicated in the six stories with which we introduced this chapter, there is ample evidence that adults, if enabled to do so, can have a self-experience not based on individuation and separation, but on a merging experience that retains personal boundaries at the same time, that is, on a simultaneousness of a personal and a transpersonal self-experience.

The schizoid-rejecting condition and the natural environment

At this point, it will be useful to provide, from a character structure perspective, a brief outline of issues relating to the first months of a newborn. we suggest that the traumatic experiences of this formative period, a period that can contribute towards the formation of what has been called the schizoid condition, has a strong influence on the child's emerging relationship with the natural environment. Considering that terror is often a key emotion experienced in this phase of child development, we shall also relate this condition to terrorism, a phenomenon that has become an increasing threat to the integrity of social life and the natural environment. For clarity, we shall call this condition here the schizoid-terrorising condition to indicate the significant link between the experience of terror and the subsequent development of certain feelings, values, and attitudes towards people and the natural environment.

The environmental causes of the schizoid-terrorising condition

Guntrip (1980, pp. 17, 18) describes schizoid phenomena as follows:

> Complaints of feeling cut-off, shut off, out of touch, feeling apart or strange, of things being out of focus or unreal, of not feeling one with people, or of the point having gone out of life, interest flagging, things feeling futile and meaningless, all describe in various ways this state of mind.

These self-experiences describe an emotional condition that is caused by the effects of an external world experienced as hostile, harsh, threatening, and terrorising. A character-analytical perspective comes to the same diagnosis by associating this condition with:

- fear
- terror
- harshness
- rough handling
- threats
- painful stimulation
- lack of safety
- cold, distant, unattuned or hostile caregivers
- rejection

The above keywords, taken from Johnson's (1994) book *Character Styles* provide a sketch of the environment experienced by newborns that are likely to develop the schizoid-terrorising condition. In such an environment, newborns are severely deprived of the two most basic ingredients for the formation of a strong self, and even for survival – love and safety. Feeling deeply unloved and rejected, newborns instinctively withdraw and split off from the surrounding harsh and uncaring environment.

Ambivalence and rejection in the womb

One of the scenarios likely to contribute to the creation of the schizoid-terrorising environment is the experience of trauma and ambiguity in the womb. Referring to the fetus' life in the womb, Campbell (1981, p. 3) writes:

> The intrauterine experience of the fetus is the initial basis for the acceptance or rejection the child carries into its world. Maternal ambivalence is transmitted to the fetus in the state of inner turmoil. A longing to return to the womb, either as the only known refuge or in an attempt to gain what was never initially given (i.e. warmth) is displayed in the regressions of this character structure. Disturbances in sucking and breathing may arise from an insecure environment of the womb.

In such an environment, the child is deprived of the opportunity to develop a symbiotic bond with the mother, which in turn leads the child to experience difficulties with relating to others as an adult and with feeling at home in the outside world. Losing its bond due to these physio-emotional mechanisms, and feeling rejected by the external world, the child fails to develop a coherent and trusting self. If not healed, a child rejected in this way is likely to face lifelong difficulties in trusting that relationships, or the world as a whole, are able to provide the basic safety and nurturing for a pleasurable existence, free of fear and terror.

The experience of fear in the social world

One of the key experiences that lead to the schizoid-terrorising condition is fear. Newborns experience fear when parents or other important caregivers fail to provide a welcoming and save environment for them. When they experience fear associated with malicious and life-threatening activities by important caregivers, they may experience terror. The experience of fear not only results from emotional rejection and rough handling, but also from an unsafe and violent environment, such as one affected by war and natural and ecological catastrophes. In many countries, we still find people suffering from various traumas relating to wars. These people still embody the terror of the experience of sheltering from bombs, of being raped by foreign soldiers, of being on active duty as soldiers, or of starving and watching family members and fellow citizens die and suffer.

The integrated person

The presentation of the six transpersonal stories, my arguments about the necessity to rethink many aspects of object relations theory, and the description of key aspects of the schizoid-terrorising condition, provide a conception of two essential ways of being in the world – ways of being that are, of course, not sharply defined. These ways of being in the world are listed in Table 8.1 on the following page.

Effects of schizoid-terrorising experiences on the environment

Literature on our ecological crises and depth psychology often describe notions of a hostile, dark, and threatening natural environment. These notions share Freud's belief that the natural environment needs to be tamed and confirm the view of some feminists on the so-called dark side of nature. Holdgate (1996), for example, writes that nature must have impinged on people's consciousness as an enemy, as the bringer of storms and droughts and of cold and famine. He suggests that people were often killed and hurt while hunting large animals, and in the absence of sophisticated surgery even small wounds must have had lasting and debilitating, if not fatal, effects.

People, and whole nations, who experience the world as dark, hostile, and threatening, often tend to embark on attempts to make the world a safer and more secure place. Psychologically, such an undertaking is likely initiated by a projection of their schizoid-terrorising experiences onto other people or onto nature. Johnson (1994, p. 23) writes that:

> to the extent that the early environment is indeed harsh, the theory simply asserts that the individual will be inclined to generalize his early experience and anticipate harshness in subsequent social situations.

He also refers to this point when he writes that people "often tend to gravitate towards relationships and environments that are themselves harsh" (1994, p. 23).

Whether we apply the psychoanalytic concept of 'repetition compulsion' or other aspects of holistic thinking, they all suggest that those struggling with this kind of emotional condition are also the ones most likely to be unconsciously drawn to seeking social and natural environments that match their early harsh experiences and that confirm their expectations of a harsh and fear-instilling world. Caught in this emotional condition, they may often see harshness, danger, and rejection where it does not exist, and may respond by attacking the perceived danger to survive in this seemingly harsh and dangerous environment. A case in point here is the present war in Iraq, which was to a great extent justified by referring to Saddam Hussein's armaments as weapons of mass destruction. Whereas weapons of mass destruction have not been found, the USA, however, has demonstrated a level of cruelty and contempt towards Iraqis and to prisoners (e.g., at the Abu Ghraib prison) that replicates Hussein's systems of torture. It is ironic that by projecting our schizoid-terrorising expectations onto the external environment, we often create self-fulfilling prophecies. Iraq, to use this example again, is only *now* attracting non-Iraqis as opposing combatants - the very people the Bush Administration used as one of the justifications for going to war.

Table 8.1 Comparison between the disconnected and the integrated child

	The disconnected child	*The integrated child*
Relationship to the external world	Experiences the external world as incompatible with its spiritual and emotional needs, and loses trust in the external world; also loses the experience of energetic streamings; develops a surface existence.	Is able to retain his or her body-self; retains the energetic connection to biosphere and develops a functioning personal and transpersonal self in the external world (an eco-self).
Trauma	Parents fail to provide the warmth and bonding for the child to feel welcomed in the external world.	Parents are able to provide a loving and welcoming environment for the child.
Worldviews held	The world is a harsh and cold place; I will have to struggle hard to justify my being in the world.	The whole world is a friendly and nurturing place and a meaningful and interconnected cosmos.

The schizoid-terrorising condition and the new capitalism

There is a growing recognition that the phenomenon called the new economy, or the new capitalism, is causing a tremendous amount of fear and uncertainty in increasing numbers of people in the Western world. Sennett (1998) has pointed out that the new economic order, sold to the public as a chance to be part of a flexible workforce, also has a very grave downside. Like Beck (1992, 2000), he is concerned about the decline of opportunities to build life stories around meaningful careers. According to these authors, the downsizing of jobs and other a key aspects of the new economy often leads to:

- a corrosion of trust, loyalty, and mutual commitment between employers and employees;
- a corrosion of character, and in "particular those qualities of character which bind human beings to one another and furnishes each with a sense of sustainable self" (ibid., no page number);
- an undermining of long-term virtues, such as trustworthiness, formal obligation, commitment, and purpose;
- a neglect of skilling and supports drifting in "time, from place to place, and from job to job" (ibid.);
- a growing inequality with its consequently arising problems;
- increased exploitation; and
- a drop of morale and motivation of workers.

It leads, in other words, to a significant reduction in social and emotional capital. Paradoxically, companies continue with their restructuring efforts despite data from many studies that suggest that repeated downsizings not only create long-term sustainability problems, but often also produce lower profits and declining worker productivity in both the short and medium term. Lopez, Regier, and Holder-Webb, for example, have researched the operating performance after restructurings and report no significant operating advantage. They write:

> Our empirical analysis suggests that restructurings *at best* have no effect on firm operating performance in the years subsequent to the restructuring. The following empirical evidence provides support for this conclusion. [...] Most importantly, empirical tests using the restructuring metric suggested by Smart and Waldfogel (1994) to control for firm and industry performance in the absence of a restructuring indicate that operating margin for restructuring firms is significantly negative in years 3 through 5, and return on equity is not significantly different from zero in the same periods (http://www2.owen.vanderbilt.edu/fmrc/Activity/paper/HolderWebPaper.pdf)

This lack of performance improvement suggests that downsizing may in many cases represent an irrational practice that may serve managers to demonstrate good managing skills in their CVs, but that may have no or very little positive effect on the wellbeing of society.

The schizoid-terrorising condition and alienation

A key notion used by environmentalists to describe our relationship with the natural environment is 'alienation', the state of being dissociated from nature. In comparing human beings with animals, Fromm (1974, p. 303) writes:

> Self-awareness, reason and imagination have disrupted the 'harmony' that characterizes animal existence. Their emergence has made man into an anomaly, the freak of the universe. He is part of nature, subject to her physical laws and unable to change them, yet he transcends nature.

Fromm seems to suggest in this citation that the typical qualities that we associate with being human also cause the dissociation from nature. He clarifies this point when he continues:

> Man is the only animal who does not feel at home in nature, who can feel evicted from paradise, the only animal for whom his own existence is a problem that he has to solve and from which he cannot escape. He cannot go back to the pre-human state of harmony with nature, and he does not know where he will arrive if he goes forward. (1974, p. 303).

This citation implies that Fromm, like many other scholars, seems to have become resigned to the impossibility of human beings attaining a state of harmony with nature. Probably lacking the experience of a felt sense of connectedness with the rest of the creation himself, he declares that a felt sense of person-planet unity is a pre-human experience and thus no longer possible to achieve. His view stands in strong contrast to the views of the scholars mentioned in a previous chapter, who clearly state that connectedness, and not dissociation, is the natural way of perceiving the world.

The schizoid condition and terrorism

The strong association of the schizoid condition with the emotions of terror and fear suggests a significant association of the phenomenon of terrorism with this condition. My aim is to examine this association from the depth psychology and holistic perspectives employed here. We argue here that the phenomenon terrorism may be associated with some of the typical emotional scenarios that lead to the formation of the schizoid-terrorising condition, as well as with key aspects of the narcissistic-shaming and oral-exploiting conditions. Before proceeding, we wish to state clearly that our aim is to contribute to a deeper understanding of the phenomenon terrorism, not to support and condone it.

Western bias on terrorism

Terrorism is, according to the *Encyclopedia Britannica* (2002 edition), the "systematic use of terror or unpredictable violence against governments, publics, or individuals to attain a political objective". The same source also states that terrorism "has been used by political organizations with both rightist and leftist objectives, by nationalistic and ethnic groups, by revolutionaries, and by the armies and secret police of governments themselves" (2002 edition).

Socio-psychological aspects of terrorism have been explored by authors such as Hudson (1999), Gurr (1970), Berkowitz (1973), Davies (1973), Post (1984, 1985, 1987, 1990), Knutson (1981), and DeMause (1982, 2002). Many of these authors, however, are biased towards a Western perspective of terrorism in that they fail to relate the cause of terrorism to Western economic exploitation and imperialism. They consequently subscribe to the simplistic trope that says, 'when it is done by the enemy, it is an act of terrorism; when it is done by us, it is not'. This uncritical treatment of terrorism is also evident in the ways in which these authors adopt the language used by Western administrations, which is, by denouncing people fighting against exploitation and for independence as insurgents, extremists, and terrorists.

Psychiatric views on terrorism

The debate around the root causes of terrorism is polarised into two broad views. One view assumes the existence of a psychopathology that destines people to become terrorists, whereas the other assumes environmental causative factors. Many authors generally rely on a standard psychiatric psychopathology or on social psychological analyses. Berkowitz (1972), for example, describes six psychological types of people who are most likely to threaten or to try to use weapons of mass destruction: paranoids, paranoid schizophrenics, people with borderline personality disorder, schizophrenic, passive-aggressive and sociopathic conditions. In the following section, we present a brief overview of present thinking about terrorism.

(1) Physiology Hypothesis

Hubbard (1983) takes a physiological approach to analysing the causes of terrorism by suggesting that people engage in terrorist activity because of the occurrence of stress-related substances such as norephinedrine, acetylcholine, and endorphins in their bodies. Such an explanation serves to distract people from asking what actually causes people's high levels of stress. They also neglect a consideration of the psychosocial and socioeconomic aspects of stress, such as poverty as result of exploitation, the emotional effects of the continued humiliation of people in occupied countries, and the loss of pride of people who have lost control of their homeland.

(2) Frustration-aggression hypothesis

Several psychological explorations of terrorism have focused on frustration and aggression. The so-called 'relative deprivation hypothesis', developed by Gurr (1970) and reformulated by Davies (1973), suggests that people respond to experiences of frustration with terrorism because of a gap between their expectations and the chances to satisfy their needs. Yet, the authors fail to notice that many so-called terrorists belong to the affluent social class in their countries, and have in comparison little reason to be frustrated. As the discussion around the Baader-Meinhof group in Germany in the 1970s showed, many so-called terrorists in fact want to make a point by rejecting consumerism as a way of soothing their concerns about social inequality and exploitation.

(3) Negative identity hypothesis

Knutson (1981) hypothesises that political terrorists consciously assume a negative identity. Referring to Erikson's (1968) theory of identity formation, she suggests that some people become terrorists after experiencing disappointment about not being able to achieve their goals, such as a particular education. Whereas Knutson's hypothesis makes good sense if we consider that a society is indeed responsible for providing easy access to education, reports in the media show that many so-called terrorists are well-trained professionals, who are prepared to become suicide bombers for the honour of their religious beliefs, their country, or their family.

(4) Defective childrearing

DeMause (2002) believes that the global battle of terrorism against liberal Western values is occurring because the world outside the West has fallen behind in the evolution of their childrearing practices. Dismissing any links of terrorism to global exploitation, the American striving for global hegemony and American foreign policy, he suggests that the USA should back a kind of UN-sponsored Marshall plan aimed at teaching Muslims more humane childrearing practices. His view is based on the assumption that most Western nations do generally have superior childrearing and educational systems. Events such as the Columbine massacre, the high ratio of suicides among young people, and the perceived necessity to treat millions of children with psychotropic drugs, cast serious doubts on the ideal American, and more generally on Western, ways of raising children.

(5) A depth psychology perspective of terrorism

Post (1984, 1985, 1987, 1990), Crayton (1983) and Pearlstein (1991) regard terrorism as a consequence of the failure to adequately deal with primary narcissism and the grandiose self. They suggest that terrorist tendencies can emerge in people who have become sociopathic, arrogant, and who lack regard for others due to a lack of reality testing. According to these authors, aggressive behaviour may then emerge as result of feelings of helpless defeatism and a wish to destroy the source of the narcissistic injury.

Although raising many important issues, the abovementioned authors decontextualise terrorism by omitting its psychosocial and socioeconomic contexts. Hudson (1999), for example, focuses primarily on the psychological conditions experienced in Muslim countries, without making efforts to explore the prevalent psychological conditions experienced in Western countries that facilitate imperialist enterprises and the deterioration of the natural environment.

Contextual views on terrorism

In contrast, a view that aims to understand wider contexts might regard terrorism as a predictable result of multiple causal factors, such as economic, religious, and sociological factors. Wilkinson (1974, 1986), for example, views factors such as ethnic conflicts, poverty, modernisation stresses, social inequities, governmental weakness and ineptness, and lack of peaceful communication channels, as contributing factors to terrorism.

An increasing number of psychologically literate political analysts and ecologists acknowledge the strong connections between imperialism, globalisation, and terrorism. Authors such as Blum (2003), Chomsky (2003), Herman (1982, 1992), Fanon (1969, 1986), Ahmad (2000), and Parenti (1995) highlight the effects of imperialism and colonisation on the emotional and social experiences of both the colonised and the colonisers.

Fanon (1967, cited in Watkins, 2002), for example, views terror as the weapon of choice of the disempowered. He describes vividly how colonisation has instilled in the colonised a sense of worthlessness, despair, and abasement. Fanon's view is echoed by Memmi (1991) who describes how colonisation has led to a historical and social mutilation that has severed people from their history, culture, and language.

In a similar vein, Mathiesen (2002) notes that what is being defined as terrorism at this moment may be subject to change over time. As an example, he mentions demonstrations and actions carried out by the Norwegian labour movement in the early 1900s, which at the time were regarded as acts of terrorism, whereas "in retrospect they are now seen as having been legitimate and necessary attempts to change Norwegian politics and social structure" (2002, p. 85). When viewed from such a contextual perspective, terrorism is a predictable expression of the need of the colonised to expel the colonisers from their territory, to stop the invaders from getting access to their resources, and to free themselves from emotionally and socially humiliating rule.

A major hurdle to overcoming the causes of terrorism lies in the total lack of empathy of the colonisers with the colonised. Being caught in the schizoid-terrorising, oral-exploiting, and narcissistic-shaming conditions, they lack the emotional sensitivity that would enable them to sense and understand the exploiting and humiliating effects of their enterprises.

These psychological considerations support the political analyses and well-researched propositions of Chomsky (2002, 2003), and Ali (2003), people who hold that terrorism is:

- the predictable result of decades of Western cultural and economic domination based on our modern worldview;
- fuelled by the Western arrogance that ignores the values and spiritual assets of other countries;
- the consequence of state terrorism committed by the West to get access to resources such as oil, and to establish unchallenged hegemony;
- a way of fighting for freedom and dignity of the dispossessed; and
- the consequence of the USA's lack of willingness to reflect on the effects of their foreign policies.

A view held in common by these authors is that a key cause of terrorism is the arrogance that the USA has demonstrated towards the rest of the world, and in particular towards non-Westerners. The following quotation by Brookhiser (2001, quoted in Sardar and Davies, 2002, p. 19) is a good example of this arrogant way of relating to the rest of the world. According to Brookhiser, the USA is perceived:

> correctly as the incarnation of a dominant world system – an empire of capitalism and democracy. New York City is also perceived as the hub of one of those subsystems, the roaring dynamo of wealth. Anyone who looks at his lot and is unhappy, looks at us – country and city – and sees an alternative. If he has an aspiring frame of mind, he may come here or imitate us. If he has an aggrieved frame of mind, he will hold us responsible. If he has the resources of a hostile nation, or his functional equivalent, he will try to kill us... The world's losers hate us because we are powerful, rich and good (or at least better than they are).

Brimming with arrogance, self-righteousness, and rhetoric, this quotation expresses what many Americans believe that foreigners think about their country. Immersed in the oral and narcissistic condition, many Americans seem unaware that many people in the rest of the world have a highly sophisticated view of the complexities of American society. They are not only aware that the 'roaring dynamo America' also has a huge hub of disfranchised people who struggle to make ends meet, they are also aware that much of America's wealth is the result of exploitation and the protectionist policies that refuse to meet other nations economically on a level playing field.

The conclusion from what has been said above, and previously in Chapter 7, is that colonising forces are often acting out unrealistic feelings of entitlement resulting from unconscious oral frustration. Being unconscious of their early oral deprivation, colonisers are unable to understand how they project their emotional struggles onto people in their own country and/or other nations by aggressively forcing them to provide the metaphorical nipples needed to soothe their emotional pain. The irony of this situation is that the colonising forces, which generally have a self-image of being superior and more sophisticated than the members of the colonised country, expose in the act of colonisation their infantile oral and narcissistic deficits and their lack of ability to lead emotionally, psychosocially, and economically sustainable lives. The predictable resistance that emerges as reactive terrorism is then experienced by colonisers as a refusal to provide soothing and nurturing self-support, which, in turn, unleashes the oral and narcissistic rage that justifies further punishment of the people resisting their exploitation and humiliation.

In this context it is interesting that the oral-exploiting motivation for terrorist imperial enterprises is rarely openly discussed and justified, whereas the narcissistic-shaming motivation is openly used as justification for a subjugation of other countries. In other words, it is not possible to publicly argue that Western nations deserve political and economic control over the Iraqi oil, but it is acceptable to argue that we have the better political and social system, and that it is acceptable to colonise Iraq (and other countries) to establish our allegedly superior democratic system there.

Terrorism and the schizoid condition

Having described state terrorism and reactive terrorism as unsustainable expressions of our modern egocentric condition, and having outlined the connection to the oral-exploiting and narcissistic-shaming conditions, we will argue in the remainder of this chapter that the phenomenon of terrorism is also to a significant extent underpinned by the schizoid condition. Recalling that the schizoid condition emerges as a child's response to hatred, painful stimulation, rough handling, rejection and a lack of a sense of safety (Johnson 1994), it makes sense to trace the roots of the phenomena of terrorism back to such experiences in childhood. These experiences would predictably lead to:

- the earlier described expectation that the Earth is a dangerous and hostile place (being subjected to violence);
- the expectation of being attacked from the outside and a perceived necessity to pre-empt these attacks (e.g., Saddam Hussein's alleged weapons of mass destruction and the necessity of a pre-emptive strike);
- the expectation of having our sense of place violated;
- the expectation of being annihilated; and
- the expectation of having to struggle for sheer survival.

A psychoanalytic and holistic view on terrorism suggests that people engaging in terrorist activities must have been terrorised themselves, or must at least have repeatedly witnessed terrorising activities against people they care for. Acts of terrorism are currently occurring in the context of conflicts between Iraqis and the USA, between Israel and Palestine, Russia and Chechnya, Basque and Spain, and the UK and Northern Ireland. Common to these conflicts is a struggle for independence and ethnic identity, for ownership of land, and for emotionally, psychosocially, and economically sustainable living conditions, conditions that include the ability to be proud of being alive, of belonging to a certain place, and to a community of people. In other words, these struggles revolve around the right to exist, which is, as pointed out, a central issue of the schizoid-terrorising condition.

We propose that the scenarios described here, when combined with the greed resulting from oral deprivation and the ignorance stemming from a narcissistic mindset, form the psychological foundation for the emergence of Western state terrorism. This mindset may be contrasted with the following list of the experiences of growing up in colonised countries.

- People living in occupied countries experience the occupation as a violation of their sense of identity and as an intrusion on their right for self-determination.
- People grow up with a permanent sense of shame and humiliation.
- People live with a permanent sense of being emotionally and economically exploited for the psychological and economic benefit of a foreign county.
- People grow up knowing that they can survive only if they quell their pride and abandon their sense of human dignity. Speaking up would mean to risk being punished and further terrorised by the foreign authority.

An understanding of terrorism based on depth psychology described here supports the still marginalised, but growing, view that our present ways of fighting terrorism will not achieve the goal of 'ridding' the world of terrorism. As much as we cannot 'fight' illness, we will have to embrace the idea that terrorism needs to be made redundant by addressing its underlying root causes. To achieve this goal, a large number of people in Western societies may have to dramatically improve their ability to lead physio-emotionally and psychosocially sustainable lives, since as long many people maintain their character defences, they may have to exploit, humiliate and rule people at home and in other countries. Without deep emotional healing, the gulf between the developed and the developing countries is likely to threaten a major social catastrophe will destroy the very foundations of our modern societies

In concluding these considerations on terrorism, it needs to be emphasised that terrorism not only relates to the schizoid-terrorising condition, but also to the oral-exploiting and narcissistic-shaming conditions explored in Chapter 7. Its association with exploitation and power issues can be traced back to the earliest occurrences of terrorism (Sinclair, 2003).

Technology and addiction

A similar phenomenon that has relevance to all three psychological conditions is technology. Along with colonialism, it may serve to satisfy our needs and wants for goods, enable us to hold power over other humans, and allow us to tame nature, which many of us perceive as hostile and threatening. Paradoxically, and unbeknown to many of us, technology is instrumental in creating many of the problems against which we need to protect ourselves in the first place. Glendinning (1995), an American ecopsychologist, charges that many of us have become addicted to technology. She suggests that we need to re-examine the role that technology plays in the lives of modern people, because it has become part of our lives to an extent that threatens our wellbeing at many levels. At the same time as proponents of technology and technological progress highlight the ways in which it apparently makes our lives more enjoyable, they hide from us the fact that the side-effects of technology and industrialisation continue to turn this planet into a barren and poisonous wasteland, into the harsh and hostile environment that lies at the heart of the schizoid-terrorising condition. Glendinning associates our relationship with technology with the emotional issues of control, denial, grandiosity, dishonesty, disconnection from feelings, and irrational techno-addictive thinking; that is, with many, if not all emotional conditions explored in the previous chapters.

Why should we aim to achieve person-planet unity?

In concluding this examination of person-planet unity and sustainable living, we wish to emphasise that our ability to live sustainably on this planet is likely to be highly dependent on our ability to deepen our felt sense of person-planet unity. This will require from us to acknowledge that, in Conn's words:

> we have [...] cut ourselves off from the connection to the Earth so thoroughly in our epistemology and our psychology that even though we are "bleeding at the roots," we neither understand the problem nor know what we can do about it.

When conventional object relations theory implicitly suggests that we need to leave our oceanic streamings behind in order to develop a mature ego, it fails to consider that all human beings retain their ingrained need to be connected to both their bodies and the biosphere. Yet, having widely lost our biophysical ability to experience a felt sense of person-planet unity, we currently compensate this loss by overemphasising experiences, such as:

- person-to-person love;
- mateship;
- affiliation with clubs and organisations;
- alcohol and psychotropic drugs;
- memberships in religious faiths or sects; and
- other compensatory ways of achieving a sense of connectedness.

As most people in modern societies have widely lost their sense of enchantment about simply being alive, and as they consequently project their need for person-planet unity onto scenarios such as the ones listed above, they overemphasise the importance of these features and at the same time make themselves vulnerable to the continuous experience of conflict. This suggests that an 'education for sustainable living', a notion explored in more detail in Chapter 11, will require us to deepen our experience of person-planet unity beyond the transient way in which we currently experience this state in certain situations (Moyes, 1974).

In Chapter 8, we have examined the last stage of eco-self transformation proposed in this study, a state of consciousness based on the experience of a high level of body-mind integration and a felt sense of person-planet unity. Suggesting that the difficulties in experiencing this felt sense of unity are related to what is called the schizoid-terrorising condition, we have also examined related issues such as our ill-conceived fight against terrorism.

Having described a possible framework for a deep understanding of the complex and synergistic issues relating to our ecological crises, in the following chapter we shall place this system of consciousness transformation in a larger context and use it to critically examine some of the currently dominant views on, and practices of, environmental and social change.

9 Placing the Six-stage Model in Larger Frameworks

In this chapter we place the six-stage model of consciousness transformation described in the previous six chapters in a wider context by:

- comparing the model with a circular model of consciousness development;
- exploring key issues relating to a shift from education towards change to enabling sustainable living;
- exploring the psychological resistances to deep change;
- examining the limitations of each of the six stages of consciousness transformation in the light of the knowledge of the whole spectrum; and by
- examining key similarities and differences to the three existing disciplines of radical ecology: social ecology, deep ecology, and ecofeminism.

Linear and Circular Models of Consciousness Transformation

Gebser's (1986) *System of Unfolding Consciousness*, Wilber's (1995, 1997) *Four Quadrant System*, and Beck and Cowan's (1996) *Spiral dynamics Model*, briefly outlined in an earlier chapter, describe a linear model of consciousness development. There seems to be, however, a second process of development that does not follow this clear evolutionary path. Hammond (2004), for example, proposes that society cycles through stages of decadence and renaissance. Using what he calls an 'organic theory of society' – based on the Freudian notions of life-instinct (eros) and death instinct (thanatos) – he differentiates between Dionysian-amoral and Apollonian-moralistic eras. Although not agreeing with many of the notions on which Hammond bases his arguments, and strongly disagreeing with his view that war can improve humanity and is an expression of the renaissance spirit, he has a point when he argues that nations and ethnic groups go through cycles of what may be called egocentric and ecocentric phases.

By referring to the work of Kirk (1988), Whitney (1997) writes that the final decades of the Roman Empire were in a phase of decadence, characterised by:

- a breakdown of faith and morality;
- unchecked power;

- overcentralised governments;
- lethargic bureaucracies;
- a decline in self-reliance;
- a shrinking of the middle class;
- an increased use of cheap labour to increase profits for the wealthy;
- an increased appetite for violence, drugs, distraction, perversity, cruelty and sensation;
- an erosion of civil society;
- a loss of higher purpose in human life;
- the trivialisation of art; and
- the breakdown of the family as an institution.

Whereas the above-listed features of social life have been present during the final decades of the Roman Empire, many, if not all, of these features described by Kirk and Whitney also apply to our hypermodern era – an era that Swimme and Berry (1992) call the 'terminal cenozoic'. The latter use this term to denote the last phase of the cenozoic era that commenced approximately 65 million years ago with the emergence of mammals. In a similar vein, O'Sullivan (1999) associates this notion with the effects of globalisation, the new global economy of transnational business that according to Saul (2005) is currently in the process of collapsing. Echoing these views, Berry (1988), in the same vein, associates the notion of the terminal cenozoic with the practice of advertising, which turns our present 'wasteworld' into 'wonderworld' by extolling consumerism as a creative process by which we can achieve freedom and happiness. Ellul (1964), finally, associates this time with technological industrialism and the problems that it creates.

The transition from the terminal cenozoic to the emergent ecozoic era, then, is, according to Swimme and Berry (1992), associated with the features of ecological unsustainability typical for our present time. At the ecological level, these features include features such as global warming, ozone depletion, and the increasing accumulation of toxic waste. At the level of societal development, this transitional phase can be associated with terrorism, the continuing decline of civic engagement, the search for solace and meaning through consumerism, and many other unsustainable practices mentioned in this study. We can also associate the hypermodern era with notions such as 'late capitalism', a time of a turning away from cosmological questions (O'Sullivan, 1999; Spretnak, 1991, 1997).

At first glance, it sounds contradictory to propose a linear model of eco-self transformation, and to suggest that societies also move through circular phases of ego-self and eco-self consciousness. Whereas the linear model can be associated with notions of growth, progress, and development, the circular model is associated with notions of pulsation, repetition and spiral development. Linear development can be traced to a Judeo-Christian heritage (Eliade, 1959), whereas cyclical/spiral repetition probably has its roots in Taoism, with its notion of Yin and Yang. A closer look, however, suggests that pulsation and development are not necessarily antithetical, rather that pulsation is, in fact, embedded in larger linear developmental processes. The hearts of animals and human beings can be regarded as a typical symbol of pulsation; yet, they also grow, age, cease to function, and finally disintegrate.

The point of concern in this chapter is that in modern societies most people have emotionally and spiritually fallen behind relative to the technological progress achieved over the last centuries. At the same time that we in the Western world have become engaged in tremendous technological evolution and increased the complexity of matter (Swimme and Berry, 1992), we have failed to evolve in a harmonious manner in ways that would enable us to use our scientific and technological achievements wisely and cautiously.

A number of reasons for this process of 'neurotisation' of humans have been proposed. Shepard (1982), for example, asserts that the process he calls 'ontogenetic crippling' predictably started with the transition from the era of the hunter-gatherers to the era of domestication, which took place approximately 12,000 years ago. In contrast, other scholars hold that our present state of consciousness is the result of prolonged suffering. This may have been caused by cataclysmic disasters such as earthquakes (Muck, 1983) or by emerging imbalances between population growth and changes in the natural environment (Diamond, 2005). Whatever it was that has put the process of 'neurotisation' in train, it has led to an excessive evolution of the cortex of the brain. It is, as Pelletier (1979) explains, purely culturally constructed, without a biological basis, and it asserts excessive control over subcortical, diencephalic processes.

A possible way of gaining a deeper understanding of the processes that has led to our present predicament is to conceptualise the history of human culture and the psychological development of human beings as a parallel process. Gerald Heard (http://home.wxs.nl/~brouw724/ GeraldHeard/html), for example, suggests that "ontogeny (the inner state of our individual being) has followed the same evolutionary blueprint as phylogeny (the development of cultural consciousness in our human race)". Heard categorises the consciousness development of humans into what he called the 'five ages of man'. These are the pre-individual (coconscious), proto-individual (heroic), mid-individual (ascetic), total-individual (humanic), and the post-individual (leptoid) man.

From education towards change towards an enabling of sustainable living

Kolb's problem-oriented learning

The question, then, is how to enable people living in our modern societies to live satisfying and sustainable lives without destroying the surrounding human and other-than-human environments. As outlined in previous chapters, education is currently regarded as one of the key elements of change, and our present approaches to environmental education often build on Kolb's (1984) views on problem-oriented learning. Distinguishing between two different forms of learning, an experience-distant learning of facts, and an experience-related learning, Kolb suggests that we should conceive of learning and problem-solving as a single process. He posits that this integrated way of learning may be demonstrated by means of a cycle that consists of four stages. According to Kolb's model, concrete experience (step 1) naturally leads us to observe and reflect on our experience (step 2). This reflection, in turn, will lead us to the formulation of general concepts and ideas on why we perceived our concrete experience as problematic (step 3). These concepts, Kolb asserts, lead, after further consideration, to a new hypothesis (step 4), which we can test in a new concrete experience (step 1 of the next cycle). Kolb's concept is appealing because it supports the belief that life is a process of continual change, and a process that can be broken down into understandable and workable stages that we can learn and use.

Yet, when viewed from the vantage point of the psychological perspectives employed in this study, Kolb's concept of learning may be severely limited by a lack of understanding of the effects of our unconscious feelings and motivations. A consideration of those factors suggests that Kolb's model of learning only works within the confines of a given psychological structure, such as a particular character structure. 'Vertical learning', in contrast, would consequently be a useful term for a form of learning in which, to put it in Jungian terms, people integrate their shadow and transgress their egocentric patterns in order to make their emotional defences redundant (Jung, 1971). Such learning frequently takes place in psychotherapy, in emotionally supported meditation, and in the emotional and biospiritual work done with shamans (Harner, 1973; Eliade, 1989; Goodman, 1990; Heinze, 1991; Kalweit, 1992).

Kolb's system fails to consider that the unconscious is 'really unconscious', that most of us, in the absence of a significant emotional integration, are only able to make 'conscious' choices within the limitations imposed by our traumatic life experiences and by the anxiety that is created when compensatory mechanisms have to be abandoned. 'Vertical learning', in contrast, would enable us with the assistance of qualified support to transgress the emotional limitations imposed by developmental traumas.

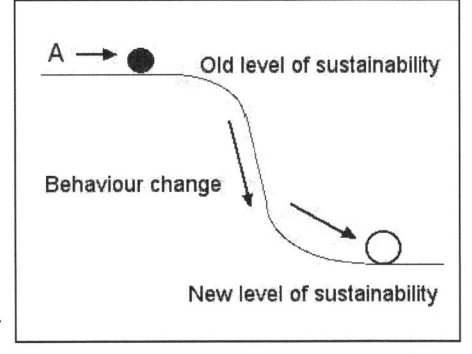

Figure 9.1 System on different levels of sustainability

Vertical learning is often experienced as an uphill struggle against emotional resistance resulting from anxiety experienced as part of emotional integration and expansion of consciousness. The recognition of this uphill struggle or resistance against change is a key distinction between a learning-oriented paradigm and a paradigm oriented towards enablement and maintenance. The key assumption behind horizontal learning is that an input of appropriate knowledge will be able to create change. This assumption is depicted in Figure 9.1, in which a system, here displayed as a ball, will move towards a slope when it is pushed by a force (A).

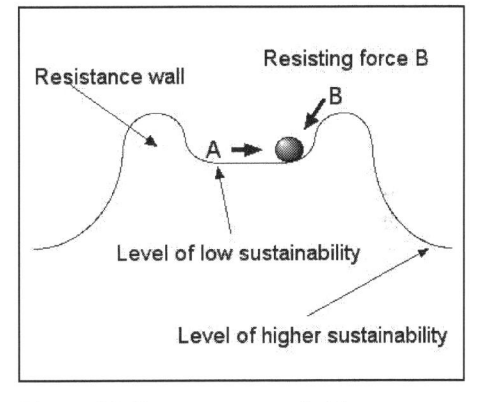

Figure 9.2 System surrounded by resistance walls

Vertical learning, on the other hand, acknowledges that deep change requires people to overcome some emotional resistance towards deep change. This resistance emerges as anxiety when our ways of thinking and perceiving the world are being challenged, and when we are asked to abandon self-stabilising compensatory mechanisms.

In a graphic representation this resistance forms a wall around a level of sustainability, and by doing so creates what Resilience Alliance theorists call a stability landscape (Holling, 1973; Ludwig, Walker and Holling, 1997; Walker, Holling, Carpenter and Kinzig, 2004). This stability or sustainability platform is illustrated in Figure 9.2, which also illustrates the resisting force (B) that prevents the system from reaching the downward-sloping area of consciousness and behaviour change.

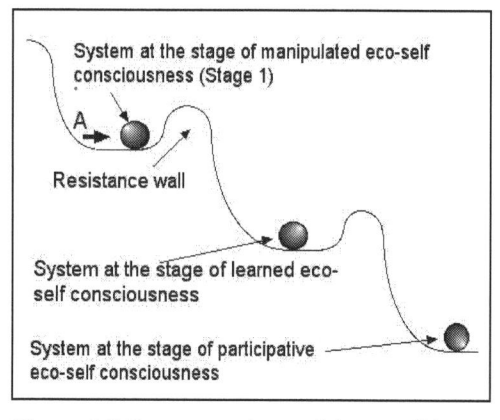

Figure 9.3 System on three of the possible six stages

In Figure 9.3 the above-described scenario is applied to the shifts from manipulated eco-self consciousness to learned eco-self consciousness, and from there to the stage of participative eco-self consciousness. The graphic illustrates how each level of consciousness is surrounded by a resistance wall, a wall that needs to be negotiated for the system to move further down to a higher level of eco-self consciousness.

The notion of moving *down* to a *higher* level of sustainability may at first glance appear contradictory. This apparent contradiction makes sense, however, if we consider that healing and bodymind and person-planet unity are usually experienced as a sense of grounding or coming *down* to earth. In this sense, a higher level of eco-self consciousness is associated with lower levels of stress, with reduced levels of addictions, and a reduced need to engage in compensatory self-stabilising activities.

What, then, do the resistance walls represent? The following considerations list some of the features of these resistance walls. A more detailed description of many of these points is provided in subsequent sections of this chapter.

Resistances towards a shift from ego-self consciousness to manipulated eco-self consciousness

People asked to shift from the currently dominant ego-self consciousness to the first level of eco-self consciousness:

- are challenged to break with the modern belief that science and technology will support our well-being and allow us to have more leisure time;
- have to abandon the belief that technological progress will be all that is needed to solve our ecological problems; and
- have to accept that a curtailing of personal freedoms and a regulation of behaviour are necessary to achieve a more ecologically sustainable society.
-

Resistances towards a shift from manipulated eco-self consciousness to learned eco-self consciousness

People operating at this level of consciousness believe that a sustainable world may be achieved through manipulation strategies and a management approach to change. If challenged to adopt a learning paradigm, they have to:

- question the belief that societal regulation is all that is needed to create a more sustainable society;
- acknowledge that power structures are continuously undermined by people's egocentric consciousness;
- question the belief that change must be readily measurable, quantifiable, and explainable; and
- confront the feelings and experiences relating to an upbringing in which love and support may have often been replaced by manipulation and control.

Resistances towards a shift from learned eco-self consciousness to participative eco-self consciousness

People experiencing the world at this level of consciousness are committed to the belief that a sustainable society may be achieved through providing children and adults with knowledge about unsustainable and sustainable forms of behaviour. People challenged to expand their consciousness towards a participatory perspective to sustainable living will have to:

- question the belief that knowledge should be generated and disseminated by specialists;
- address the imbalances of power between teachers and learners;

- question the idea of the existence of an objective truth, and adopt the view that 'truths' may have to be negotiated between stakeholders;
- address the psychological structures in their own psyche that make them believe that holding knowledge also justifies the exercising of power; and
- acknowledge that to create a sustainable society may require us to replace the currently dominant modern capitalistic system with a system based on a more advanced ecocentric consciousness, on a sense of place, and on local economies.
-
-

Resistances towards a shift from participative eco-self consciousness to deep eco-self consciousness

The shift towards deep eco-self consciousness requires people experiencing the world at the level of participative eco-self consciousness to:

- develop a strong interest in the effects of developmental trauma on people's perceptions and behaviour;
- acknowledge that even a profound knowledge of ecological issues acquired through participatory processes may not necessarily lead to deep changes in the perception of the world and to behaviour change;
- accept that the creation of a sustainable society will also be dependent on their willingness to address issues of personal (physio-emotional and psychosocial) sustainability; and
- acknowledge that planetary recovery may be dependent on our willingness to engage in personal recovery.

Resistances towards a shift from deep eco-self consciousness to holistic eco-self consciousness

The expansion of consciousness from deep eco-self consciousness to holistic eco-self consciousness requires people to:

- expand their perception from a psychological worldview towards a more inclusive worldview grounded in synergies, parallels, purpose, and essence;
- acknowledge synergies and parallelisms of various manifestations of both unsustainable and sustainable structures;

- commit to a postmodern spirituality that grounds spiritual thinking and experience in spiritual energy, human embodiment, natural environment, and society (cf. Holland, 1988); and
- address the personal psychological scenarios resulting from an upbringing that compelled them to resort to compartmentalisation as an emotional defence mechanism.

Resistances towards a shift from holistic eco-self consciousness to experiential eco-self consciousness

At the level of holistic eco-self consciousness we are able to identify the meaningful interrelationships and synergies between the various manifestations of ecological unsustainability. An expansion of consciousness from there towards the last stage of eco-self consciousness described in this study will require people to:
- overcome their fears of the body and its biological energies and signals;
- maintain a constant practice designed to harmonise body, mind, heart, and spirit;
- enhance their ability to live with a high level of emotional charge; and
- maintain a spiritual practice in a discipline that supports a holistic and integrated worldview.

The realisation that, as a society, we have not progressed further in recent decades, and that ecological degradation is continuing in many areas, highlights the difficult task we face in working with these resistances towards a transformation of consciousness. Each shift to a higher level of consciousness may be experienced as a 'little death', or as Metzner (1986, p. 152) says, as "a practice in letting go and releasing attachments".

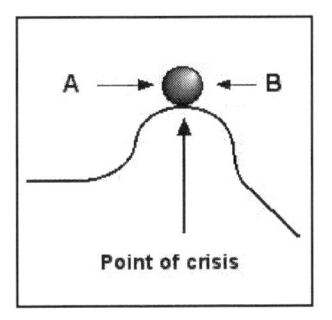

Figure 9.4 Forces acting at a point of crisis

Deep and shallow change

The above explorations also enable us to attain a graphic understanding of the notions of deep and shallow change. A system in crisis showing the two key forces that may be applied to effect change is illustrated in Fig. 9.4. Force A has the capacity to push the system towards a higher level of sustainability (down the slope to the right), whereas Force B aims to maintain the position from which the system moved into crisis mode, or even regress. We suggest that a system in crisis is one in which certain circumstances have forced the system to leave the platform of relative stability and pushed it on top of the resistance wall. At this critical and unstable point it depends on the balance between the two forces whether the system will be moved back to the original platform or progress to a level of higher sustainability.

This systemic view of a crisis may be applied to many different systems, to individuals and to institutions. For example, a person suffering from an illness may be treated by the medical system to reinstate the original state of relative wellness through conventional medical interventions (Force B), or he or she may choose to use the illness in a psychosomatic learning process to achieve a higher level of wholeness, physio-emotional and psychosocial integration, and sustainability (Force A).

A health system in crisis, to use another example, might be restored by providing the health sector with additional funding and improved organisational structures, or the crisis might be used to enable all people involved to achieve a higher level of psychosomatic literacy and psychosocial self-regulation. The latter approach would achieve an increased level of public health, possibly even without having to provide additional funding.

A macro perspective of consciousness development

In the previous discussion we have suggested that the ultimate goal of Learning for Sustainable Living (LfSL) is to enable people to attain experiential eco-self consciousness, a form of consciousness that includes the positive aspects of the preceding stages. This relatively linear transformation of consciousness, however, suggests that people will most likely progress along the continuum proposed in this study. A schematic graphical representation of the proportion of the population in a typical industrialised country at the various stages of eco-self consciousness is provided in Fig. 9.5 on the following page.

The views on the emotional and psychosocial background of our ecological crises explored in this study suggest that ESD will lead to an increase of people perceiving the world at the levels of manipulated, learned, and participative eco-self consciousness, but will not necessarily have a significant impact on a transformation of consciousness beyond these stages. A schematic graphic representation of this scenario is presented in Figure 9.6 on the next page.

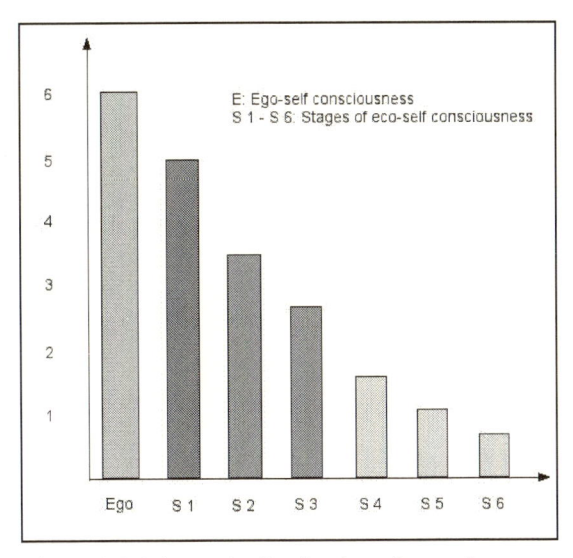

Figure 9.5 Schematic distribution of consciousness among modern people

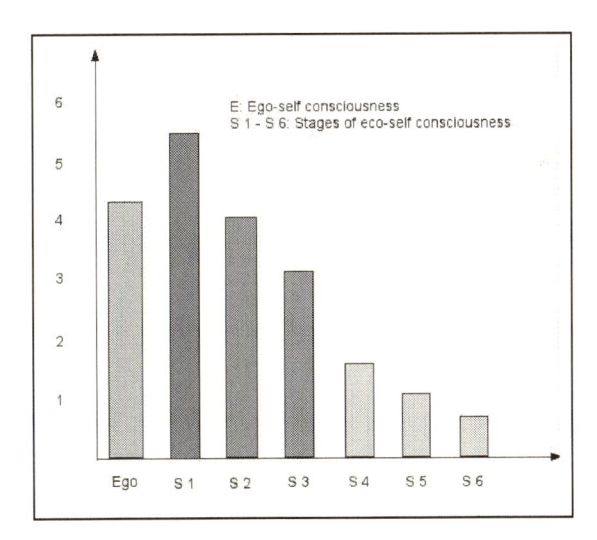

Figure 9.6 Schematic distribution of consciousness achieved through Education for Sustainable Development

Figure 9.6 shows a shift in the number of people operating at the currently dominant ego-self consciousness towards the adjacent levels, with the peak probably remaining for quite some time at the levels of manipulated and learned ego-self consciousness.

In contrast, the application of the more inclusive *Learning for Sustainable Living* approach has the potential, if implemented on a large scale, to lead to a further shift towards higher levels of eco-self consciousness.

A schematic representation of this scenario is presented in Fig. 9.7 on the next page. This graphic shows a significant increase in the numbers of people operating at the levels of participative, deep, holistic, and experiential eco-self consciousness.

This shift would result in a sizeable reduction in the number of people operating at the levels of ego and manipulated eco-self consciousness. Such an expansion of consciousness would be important for the global sustainability of a society, because it would indicate that a large number of people would have moved beyond the stage of symptom manipulation, the stage at which they simply shift their unsustainable behaviour from the natural environment to other areas. We believe that Figure 9.7 probably illustrates the distribution of public consciousness at which deep sustainability is likely to really commence.

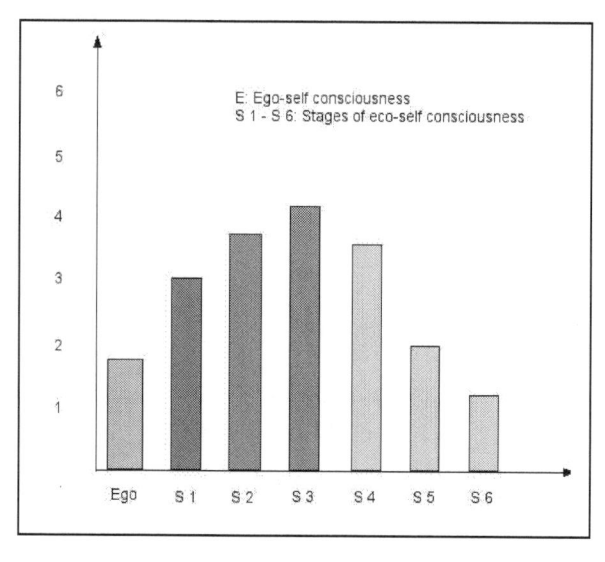

Figure 9.7 Schematic distribution of consciousness achieved through Education for Sustainable Living

Enabling sustainable living

The arguments presented above suggest that learning about ecological functions and environmental deterioration will not be sufficient to negotiate deep-seated resistances to change. They suggest that to achieve deep change, ecological 'education' will have to embrace the notions of inner work (Jones, 1993), enablement (Hill, 2004), community learning, and self- and group-maintenance and nurturing (Hill, 2005).

As outlined in previous chapters, the current role of education is predominantly to convey knowledge and to generate understanding of events and processes. Although it is important to acknowledge the significant differences between the conventional and progressive approaches to environmental education, (e.g., EE and EFS), education as a whole predominantly addresses the mind, and thus fails to enable people to generate the sense of self that is required to make the deep changes necessary to create a more psychosocially and environmentally sustainable society.

Whereas the key requirement for the development of manipulated eco-self consciousness is a willingness to be manipulated, the requirement for developing learned and participative eco-self consciousness a willingness to learn from, in, and about, the environment, the requirement for shifting towards deep eco-self consciousness and beyond, is to engage in what Minelli and Schroll (2003) call self-confrontation and self-examination. This shift from stage 3 to stage 4 of eco-self consciousness is marked by the transition from an extroverted and ethics-oriented approach to solving our ecological crises to an introverted and experience-oriented one, and by the necessity to engage with our personal histories and the phylogenetic processes that have contributed towards the development of the dominant egocentric (neurotic) consciousness.

The question, then, arises whether or not this shift will require us to engage in psychotherapy and other practices designed to enable the experience of body-mind and person-planet unity. The examination of the psychological foundations of unsustainable living presented in Chapters 7, 8, and 9 indeed suggest that a large number of people may have to engage in psychospiritual work to be enabled to create a significant planetary recovery. At the same time, it is also important to consider that consciousness transformation is an organic process, which means that people at the level of ego-self consciousness may not be able to leap to deep eco-self consciousness without first engaging in the intermediary steps. In other words, it will be important to create the structures and processes that will enable us to identify where people are and which steps they can reasonably be expected to take.

Limitations of approaches to change based on behaviourist psychology

Having outlined the key possibilities of a behaviourist approach to ecological change in Chapter 3, we will examine in this segment important limitations of practices based on behaviourist psychology. In his book *Beyond Freedom and Dignity* Skinner writes:

> We can point to remarkable achievements in these fields [science and technology], and it is not surprising that we should try to extend them. But things grow steadily worse, and it is disheartening to find that technology itself is increasingly at fault. Sanitation and medicine have made the problems of population more acute, war has acquired a new horror with the invention of nuclear weapons, and the affluent pursuit of happiness is largely responsible for pollution (1971, p. 3).

Skinner's citation demonstrates that he had a remarkably deep understanding of many of our ecological problems and was highly critical of many scientific achievements. In his novel on a fictitious utopia built on behaviourist principles, *Walden Two*, he demonstrates a deep understanding of unsustainable practices that keep our economy operating at high speed without, however, delivering real happiness and satisfaction. These include:

- style of clothing;
- unused capacities of equipment and buildings;
- our attraction to unnecessary goods and services; and
- advertising used to stimulate artificial demands for unessential goods and services.

Skinner's belief in the equitable sharing of menial work and of providing work for every member of a community have made him an important proponent of a more humane and sustainable society.

Whereas many of Skinner's goals are worth pursuing, his means of achieving them pose a number of significant problems. Although behaviourist psychology has enjoyed a great deal of attention and has led to a number of useful change strategies, it also has attracted profound criticism. From the depth psychology perspective employed in this study, it appears that behaviourist strategies fail to address the levels of psychological functioning below the level of the mask, to frame this point in here terms of Reich's three-layer model.

A point of critique particularly relevant to this research project is the charge that the process of operant conditioning described by Skinner (1948, 1953, 1971) is a key contributing factor in the creation of egocentric consciousness and thus part of the problem. It appears that change agents advocating the use of operant conditioning as a tool for change are apparently not aware of the fact that this very psychological mechanism is at the heart of the creation of egocentric consciousness. In referring to Winnicott (1979) Orbach (2004, p. 27) writes:

> A Winnicottian statement of this position might be that when a baby's own gestures are repeatedly ignored or remain unreflected on, it finds the part of itself or develops those aspects of self through bringing forth attributes, activities, and emotions acceptable and pleasing to its primary care-giver.

If repeatedly forced to make these compromises, the baby develops what Winnicott (1960) has called a false self. This self, often also called adapted self (Orbach, 2004; Hill, 2003a), constitutes the mask or third layer in Reich's three-layer model of psychological functioning. At the same time, this process of adaptation also generates other phenomena relating to the secondary layer in Reich's model: self-blame (Fairbairn, 1994), pain, and anger.

Although a methodical examination of the emotional experiences leading to the behaviourist mindset is beyond the scope of this study, the study of the practices employed by behaviourists using holistic and depth psychology principles suggests that people who subscribe to behaviourism are likely to have been subjected in their childhood to significant levels of emotional pain and frustration. In the absence of adequate soothing and empathic meaning-making of this pain and frustration they had to intuitively develop the emotional defence strategies that they then as adults rediscover as part of their scientific pursuits. These are desensitization and stimulus control, the very scenarios that would have allowed them to escape their painful experiences. Having developed these strategies as their key defences, most behaviourists seem to be unaware that in their well-intentioned pursuit for the creation of happier and more content people they have embarked on a witch-hunt aimed at controlling emotions and feelings at various levels of occurrence through social and behavioural engineering. The ethical training described by Skinner (1948) in *Walden Two*, where young hungry and exhausted children have to stand for five minutes in front of their steaming soup before they can satisfy their natural needs, re-enacts the traumatic experience of the behavioural engineers and perpetuates the deep roots of egocentric consciousness.

The point we wish to stress here is that the above-described psychological mechanism of adaptation is the same as the one described by Skinner as operant conditioning, a form of self-development in which a child learns to adopt the psychological realities of other people because their own needs, desires, and emotional expressions fail to attract sufficient positive affirmation. In behaviourist terminology we would say that parents and other caregivers usually reinforce self-compromising behaviours rather than encourage their children to fully be themselves.

The reasoning applied here also demonstrates that operant conditioning has grave side-effects. In young children it is an integral factor in the creation of neurosis, whereas in later years it deprives individuals of the deep healing that would enable them to enhance their ability to lead ecologically sustainable lives as a natural expression of their physio-emotional and psychosocial sustainability. The effects of this deprivation of healing can, for example, be seen in the widespread incongruity between attitudes and psychological maturity as described, for example, by Jones (1993) in his comments on the meetings of green parties.

Claiming superior knowledge

In recent decades, behaviourism has attracted considerable criticism because of its mechanistic explanations of human behaviour, its affront to human dignity, and its failure to consider issues of ethics and power (Huxley, 1992; Bertalanffy 1960). Behavioural technologies of persuasion and influence have also been criticised because of the assumption that behaviourists have the right to manipulate people into doing something that they would not do without external influence. Werner (1999, p. 228) writes that:

> [I]n theory, if we can understand why they [people] are not conserving, we can change the situation or change their attitudes in ways that increase conservation.

The wording of this and many similar quotations highlights the behaviourists' claim to possess the right knowledge and the right attitude. It also carries the implicit assumption that behaviourists believe that they are entitled to use psychological manipulation as a means of effecting change. A holistic approach to change, in contrast, questions this right and the value of manipulative and power-exercising methods of achieving sustainable behaviour.

Behaviourists have recently developed strategies which, when viewed from a depth psychology perspective, can be likened to psychological warfare and brainwashing. Referring to changes of attitudes that have an extensive intra-attitudinal structure, Eagly and Kulesa (1997, p. 131) write that:

> successes in changing strong attitudes have involved bombarding the target audience with a large amount of information consistent with the desired attitude(s) and, at least sometimes, isolating these individuals from competing influences.

Suggesting that not all means can justify the ends, my critique here relates in particular to two problems arising from such manipulative interventions: a concern with empowerment, and the belief that changes achieved by means of manipulation actually increase egocentric functioning, with all its resulting effects.

In her article, 'Psychological Perspectives on Sustainability', Werner (1999) suggests that citizens may become psychologically helpless when authorities make decisions for them. Yet, if this is true, then being manipulated and influenced towards changing attitudes and behaviour must also be perceived as equally disempowering. Using interventions for a good cause, such as persuading people to recycle, does not necessarily lessen the manipulative and disempowering character of the interventions in question. Werner thus would employ an 'holistic' approach that would try to persuade people:

- to understand that their happiness is largely independent upon the amount of goods they consume (cognitive intervention);
- to change their values from a perceived right to consume towards a perceived responsibility to conserve and share resources;
- to take pride in being a responsible member of the community of living beings rather than taking pride in possessing power and wealth; and
- to establish their sense of self on being rather than doing and owning.

Yet, as progressive as this list may look at first glance, closer scrutiny based upon depth psychology suggests that all of these interventions represent a manipulation on the symptom level because people are asked to display a behaviour that lacks consistency with their embodied self-experience. The following list highlights some of the possible consequences of such manipulative and persuasive approaches to change.

Being persuaded to, or seduced into, behaving sustainably constitutes a manipulation at symptom level. The emotional experience (inner reality) expressed in unsustainable behaviour is likely to emerge in other forms of unsustainable behaviour.

Until the emotional energy discharged through a particular behaviour finds expression in a new expression (symptom), people usually experience a deepened sense of conflict between outer demands and their conscious, and unconscious, need to express their inner reality.

Unless advertising campaigns that continually seduce people into purchasing non-essential goods and services are abandoned as well, many people will experience increased conflict through being seduced into stabilising their sense of self through consumption, while at the same time being persuaded to refrain from acting upon it.

People persuaded to display behaviour imposed by the expectation of external forces are likely to experience their personal lives as even less sustainable because they are meant to conform to outer demands without getting a chance to engage in a personal healing process.

One-approach-fits-all-people campaigns fail to understand that people need to arrive at ecologically sustainable behaviour simultaneously with an increased capacity to lead psychosocially and physio-emotionally sustainable lives, and with the feeling that they were able to arrive there as a result of their individual healing journeys.

Failing to ask the question 'Why?'

Approaches to change based on behaviourist (and cognitive) psychology usually neglect to ask *why* people do what they do. A study undertaken by Jason, Zolik and Matese (1979) that explored littering behaviour with dog faeces, established that the number of people picking up their dog's faeces increased when they were shown effective and hygienic ways of cleaning up after their dogs. Although the study appears statistically impressive in that the number of dog owners who cleaned up initially increased from five per cent to 84 per cent, the authors of the study admit that many dog owners avoided the target area of the investigation after the initial modelling procedure. Geller et al. (1982) suggest that the frequency data indicated that avoidance behaviour occurred, and that part of the apparent efficacy of 'pooper-scooper modelling' was a result of a redistribution of dog defecation outside of the target area. In other words, many dog owners investigated in this educational study left the target area to continue their habit of polluting the environment without fear of being observed and having to justify it.

This active evasion questions the widely held view that destructive behaviour towards the environment is a result of a lack of information, knowledge, and effective modelling. The resistance suggests, however, that providing information and behaviour modelling are not necessarily sufficient to change people's behaviour, and that we have to consider that people's behaviour is informed by deeper psychological mechanisms. A depth psychology perspective on ecologically unsustainable behaviour, in contrast, suggests that many dog owners experienced the demands of the environmental educators as an invasion into their sense of freedom and self-determination, a demand they resisted by evading the target area.

Limitations of a cognitive approach to environmental change

In this section, we discuss key limitations of the cognitive approach to environmental change.

Overemphasis on knowledge and education

Current environmental education is mainly concerned with knowledge and mental understanding. Although agreeing that a profound knowledge of ecological processes is useful, this study has demonstrated that educational approaches based on the belief that we can fight 'wrong' behaviour by providing the 'right' kind of information is limited in its potential to achieve deep sustainability. For instance, our knowledge of the harmful effects of substances such as alcohol and nicotine has so far not prevented us from continuing in our self-destructive and unsustainable habits. Knowing that it is more sustainable to produce goods that can be easily serviced and repaired has not led companies to produce long-lasting and repairable goods. These, and many other examples, demonstrate that it is difficult to establish a linear relationship between knowledge and behaviour.

Research on links between ecological consciousness and sustainable behaviour presents a confusing picture. On the one hand, behaviourist research based on behaviourist and cognitive psychology claims to have established a positive correlation between ecological consciousness and sustainable behaviour towards the environment (Diekmann and Preisendoerfer, 1991), whereas on the other hand there appears to be an inconsistency between people's attitude and their actual behaviour towards the environment (Spada, 1990). According to Meohring (1996), recent empirical research suggests that the traditional behaviourism-based educational approaches to environmental education in schools so far have had very little impact on behaviour towards the environment. Concluding that present environmental education is in a dead-end street, he questions the predominant belief that humans need to be morally educated (Sueddeutsche Zeitung No 106, 10 May 1993). Moehring also critiques Giesecke's (1982) view, which suggests that human beings are naturally in need of education, and that education naturally implies a power relationship of some people over others, a relationship justified by the necessity to care and to be cared for. He also questions the assumption held by most conventional environmental educators that sustainability can be learnt by being educated to 'do the right thing' by the environment. Agreeing with his view, we suggest that 'learning sustainability' requires adopting an approach to change that considers, at least to a certain extent, all steps of eco-self development outlined in this study.

Learning self-knowledge

Educational theories and practices that go beyond the idea of providing students with abstract and decontextualised knowledge have existed for some time, and have gained some influence in the educational systems of Western societies. People such as Steiner, Neill (1984), Freire (1970), Illich (1972), Pestalozzi (1894), Rousseau (1979), and Tolstoy (1861, 1872, 1874), devised ways of educating children without the currently accepted cultural influences, the aim of which is to form children into outward-oriented beings (Hill, 2003a). More interested in dialogue than instruction, Tolstoy argued that as soon as we assume the right to educate, we educate children for our own interests (cf. Klemm, 1984). These libertarians insist that nobody has the right to educate, and yet there can be little doubt that children are in need of guidance and support. Goodman (1979) conceptualised the notion of incidental education, a form of education that is informal and based on culturally perpetuated and widely used patterns of instruction. Such instructions are usually employed by traditional communities to teach living and language skills (Roszak, 1979).

Although such 'de-schooling' (Illich, 1972) may not be a realistic endeavour at a time when six billion people on this planet need to be fed, there is certainly a necessity to address the grave imbalance between an 'education for living and sustainability', and the currently practised education for knowledge. Roszak (1979) addresses this imbalance by suggesting that we are in need of what he calls affective education, a form of 'education' often called personal growth, or the realisation of human potential.

Failure to provide healing

It appears that people continue their destructive behaviour because educational interventions have not helped them to understand the deeper motivations and conflicts behind their unsustainable behaviour. Many of our current educational and behaviourist interventions make people feel guilty by pointing at the destructive effects of their actions and by suggesting that people have to change in order to save the planet. In conversations with many people about this subject, we have learnt that many of us feel unfairly singled out to do the 'heavy lifting', the changing, whereas wealthy people and people in power seem to get away with far more severe unsustainable behaviour. These people have, understandably, a deep need to be treated fairly and resist changing their actions towards the environment when people in power are at the same time allowed to continue committing grave offences against the natural environment.

A predominantly educational approach to solving our ecological crises also neglects people's need for healing, a view echoed, for example, by Naess (1973), and Naess and Rothenberg (1990). Naess regards his approach to change – Deep Ecology – not only as a campaign to save our diminishing wilderness areas and to protect biodiversity, but also as a movement to liberate humanity from enslaving attitudes and practices. Oriented as we are towards external changes, such as natural resource management, air quality management, environmental economics, waste management, and site remediation and rehabilitation, our present approaches to environmental education are not concerned with personal healing. Having widely adopted a corporate management approach to sustainability, the currently dominant ESD programs invariably lack psychological considerations, reflections on learning, ecofeminist concerns, and considerations of notions such as psychosocial sustainability and healing. The underlying assumption contained in many curricula used in tertiary education is that environmental deterioration is a problem that can be managed by means of technical and social engineering and by providing knowledge-based (EE) or process-based (ESD and EFS) education. An alternative approach, based on depth psychology, holism, and transpersonal psychology, is described in the next chapter.

Failure to provide nurturing and a sense of connectedness

Our present educational approaches to sustainability still widely fail people's needs to deepen the experience of love towards the world around them. Even profound knowledge of the interrelationships between humans and the rest of the biosphere does not automatically facilitate the body-mind integration necessary to experience the physio-emotional streamings that are needed to enable people to experience an embodied sense of self and an energetic connection to the rest of the biosphere.

The depth psychology perspectives of our ecological crises advocated in this study question whether we will be able to lead truly ecologically sustainable lifestyles as long as we are still energetically disconnected from nature. To achieve such a sense of connectedness and to overcome the energetic autism (Metzner, 1999) from which most of us are suffering, many of us will have to engage with some of our deep conflicts and unconscious traumas to deepen our ability to unify body and mind and to enhance our ability to experience a felt sense of person-planet unity.

Educating the wrong people

Most approaches to environmental education are based on the assumption that environmental sustainability can be improved by teaching children and adolescents sustainable behaviour. Yet, as Moehring (1996) and others have noted, such environmental education has been shown to be of limited effectiveness. This is not surprising, considering that conventional environmental education places the responsibility to change mainly in the hands of the ones with the least power and least able to harm the environment. A lopsided focus on educating children and adolescents based on the hope that future generations of decision makers will be able to create a more sustainable world may be an admission of powerlessness in relation to changing the behaviour of adults. Yet, considering that most young people already struggle with many social pressures and self-formation issues it is questionable whether or not they will have the emotional strength to become the sustainable human beings that will create a more sustainable society.

Another questionable view held by many environmental educators is that students may be able to teach their parents sustainable behaviour. While agreeing that most environmentally aware parents will be open to learning from their children, the parents who unconsciously stabilise their sense of self through physio-emotionally, psychosocially, and environmentally unsustainable habits are likely to feel emotionally challenged if their children question their consumption habits and other forms of environmentally damaging behaviour. For these children, the demand to teach their parents sustainable behaviour can easily become an emotional minefield leading to increased conflict in their families.

A possible way out of this dilemma has been suggested by Gugerli-Dolder, a Swiss environmental educator and deep ecologist. In her (2002) paper entitled *Denken wie eine Spinne* (Thinking Like a Spider), she suggests that environmental education at schools and the development of schools into a nature- and experience-oriented environment will be dependent on a cooperation between teachers, associated school staff, parents, and educational institutions. Such a co-operation would include parents in the educational processes and thus prevent the possible emergence of conflict in the family. Gugerli-Dolder, however, notes that schools only rarely utilise the potentials emerging from such cooperation.

Depth psychology and postmodern environmental education

In this section, we discuss key limitations of the deconstructionist postmodern worldview and its associated approach to environmental education.

Deconstructionist and constructivist views on ecological issues

Education for Sustainability (EFS), the postmodern approach to environmental education, may be regarded as the most progressive, innovative, and self-reflective approach to environmental education employed so far. There is no doubt that its insistence on teaching sustainability by exploring local agendas, and its empowering teaching strategies lead to deeper and more integrated learning. Yet, an examination from a depth psychology perspective shows some significant limitations of this approach. These arise mainly from deconstructionist postmodernism's rejection of the importance of a stable sense of self.

Proponents of deconstructionist thinking regard the present ecological problems as the result of the social, political, and economical organisation of modernity. They regard this brand of postmodernisms the philosophical platform that will recognise and help overcome the excesses of materialism, individualism, patriarchy, scientism, technocentrism, secularism, anthropocentrism and ethnocentrism (Huckle, 1996). This thinking includes a commitment to a "rejection of the doctrine of the supremacy of reason, the notion of truth, the belief in the perfectibility of man, and the idea that we could create a better, if not perfect, society. It holds that reality is merely socially constructed, and that ideas such as God, democracy, and soul are "framed as contingencies, textual artifacts" (Oelschlaeger 1995, p. 6). Yet, Oelschlaeger also points out that because deconstructionism decries all foundational claims, it tends to be self-defeating, since "we are, after all, biologically underdetermined" (ibid).

In contrast to deconstructionism, constructive or affirmative postmodernism does not reject modernism, but seeks to revise its premises and traditional concepts. According to Madsen (2005), it tries to offer a unity of scientific, aesthetic, ethical, and religious intuitions, and rejects approaches to science that exclusively rely on data made available by the modern natural sciences. A summary of Madsen's views on constructive postmodernism suggests that it seeks to:

- revive our interest in premodern notions of reality;
- provoke our interest in cosmic meaning and the re-enchantment of nature;
- include an acceptance of alternative (non-sensory) ways of perceiving the world; and
- make an important contribution to the revision of modernity to ensure the survival of life on this planet.

Oelschlaeger (1995, p. 6) locates a key difference between the two brands of postmodernism in the depth of scepticism on the 'possibility of a coherent meaning in language' and in the denial of the possibility of critical judgment, history, and scientific truth. In other words, affirmative postmodernism does not deny the value of such notions outright, but regards science as "a textual enterprise that continually reshapes itself through discourse that occurs in communities" (Oelschlaeger, 1995, p. 7). Another distinction can be made in relation to claims on truth. Whereas deconstructionist postmodernists criticise all claims on truth as expression of essentialism, affirmative postmodernists hold that statements of truth can be made by groups of people adhering to particular worldviews or belonging to particular professions.

Deconstructed selves

The approach to making sense of our ecological crises employed in this study is critical with some of the beliefs held by deconstructionist postmodernists. Gergen (1991, p. 139), for example, writes:

> In the postmodern world there is no individual essence to which one remains true or committed. One's identity is continuously emergent, re-formed, and redirected as one moves through a sea of ever-changing relationships. In the case of "Who am I?" it is a teeming world of provisional possibilities.

A depth psychology critique of deconstructionist postmodernism suggests that, by denying the existence and necessity of a coherent self-experience, deconstructionism implicitly justifies egocentric living with its associated fragmented self-experience as the normal way of being in the world. Whereas Gergen rejects the view that there is a stable self and suggests that people embody different selves in relationships with different individuals, the perspective proposed here recognises that people experience the world and act in it with a high level of characterological constancy. It recognises that beyond the different surface appearances, people present consistent patterns in most social and emotional contexts. Whether we call these patterns character structures or defence mechanisms, they represent a self-formation that is highly reliable, in particular when we include the emotional and psychosocial meanings expressed through posture (Lowen, 1958, 1972, 1980), skin and connective tissue consistency (G. Boyesen 1976), and the various patterns of physio-emotional armouring (Reich, 1942).

Whereas the views on ecological crises expressed in this study leave ample room for many different lifestyles, they are nevertheless critical of the deconstructionist habit of defining self by means of designer clothes, cars, houses, and other consumables. Gergen indeed suggests that

> [I]n this context, the replacement of department-store-reliable clothing by the remarkable array of apparel served up by 'unique' boutiques becomes intelligible (1991, p. 154).

His suggestion to define ourselves through our clothing and other lifestyle choices supports the unconscious compensatory self-definition strategies that are a major contributing factor of ecological degradation. The short-term self-support championed by Gergen and other deconstructionists also uncritically supports addictive behaviour, the exploitation of workers, and the maintenance of inequitable class differences. Gergen's view even questions the necessity to work towards a more sustainable world. Winter (1996, p. 289) addresses this point by noting that:

> [f]rom the vantage point of the deconstructionist, nothing is real. Everything we know is the result of our limited and distorted constructions. [...] For if nothing is real, there is little sense in committing oneself to any particular set of values, including the value of sustaining human existence on the planet.

By categorising deep feelings and the need for committed relationships as outdated, many deconstructionists remain committed to the dualistic thinking that, through its negative labeling of feelings, needs, and behaviour, supports the disowning of important aspects of people's identity. It appears that deconstructionists have simply reconstituted, or recycled, duality by redefining the qualities in the service of their particular worldview. In Table 9.1 we present some of the qualities excluded from conscious experience by deconstructionist postmodernists. Qualities preferred in the postmodern worldview are listed in column 1; the disowned qualities in column 2; and the typical ways in which disowned aspects of our life might manifest as symptoms in the third column.

Table 9.1   Comparison of deconstructionist and depth psychology values

Preferred discourse	*Marginalised discourse*	*Compensatory manifestation*
Superficiality	Depth	Manifestations of passion, psychosomatic illness, nervous breakdowns
Relative truth	Absolute truth; meta-narratives	Emergence of fundamentalism
Chaos	Order	Pathological need to control and tame life and nature
Context	Essence	Addictions
Fleeting encounters	Commitment to friendship and relationships	Loneliness, compensatory consumerism
Superficial encounters	Deep love	Tuberculosis, AIDS

Environmental education – deconstructionist or reconstructionist?

Although environmental educators such as Sterling (1996, 2001), Huckle (1983, 1990, 1996), A. Gough (1996), N. Gough (1987), Tilbury (1993, 1995), Tilbury and Stevenson (2002), Robottom (1988), and Robottom and Hart (1993) base their theories and practical applications on postmodern epistemology, they do not necessarily commit themselves to being deconstructionists. An examination of the worldviews underpinning Education for Sustainability shows a rather confusing picture. What we can ascertain is that Education for Sustainability is situated somewhere in between a mechanistic and a depth psychology model of education. Table 9.2 on the following page, which is based on Sterling's (2001) book *Sustainable Education: Revisioning Learning and Change*, highlights some of the differences between the three approaches, whereas specific differences between postmodern and depth psychology approaches to working towards sustainability are highlighted in Tables 9.3, 9.4, 9.5 and 9.6. The issues briefly summarised in these tables highlight that EFS is leaning strongly towards the deconstructionist approach, whereas the psychological and holistic approaches to deep change and healing described in this study are associated with the more spiritual aspects of the reconstructionist postmodern worldview.

Table 9.2   Comparing environmental education based on a mechanistic, postmodern, ecological, and depth psychology worldview

Mechanistic worldview	Ecological worldview	*Depth psychology worldview*
Goal oriented	Direction oriented	*Healing oriented*
Controlling change	Facilitating change	*Facilitating healing*
Awareness of causal relationships	Awareness of emergence	*Awareness of underlying psychological traumas, motivations, and analogies – ecological crises as manifestations of a lack of sense of self*
Adaptive learning	Adaptive, critical and creative learning	*Learning to embrace past traumatic events; Learning from reparenting; Learning to deal with strong emotional charge; Learning about the interrelationships between the personal, the social, and the environmental aspects of living.*
Planning	Design	*Experience and emotional integration*
External evaluation	Self-evaluation with support	*Supported healing journey*
Poor ability to respond to change	Flexibility and responsiveness	*Change beyond the limitations of character fixations (healing)*
Unsustainability	Greater Sustainability	*Sustainable living on many different levels*

Table 9.2 is based on Sterling's table (2001, p. 47) on this subject. The first two columns are reproduced from Sterling's book, whereas the third column represents our addition (in italics).

Table 9.3 Theoretical framework, schools of thought, and aims of postmodern, cognitive psychology and depth psychology

	Deconstructionist Postmodern	Depth Psychology/Transpersonal Psychology
Focus	Education as an agent of change supporting improved 'constructions'	Our past and present feelings, and the ways these alter our behaviour, both to others and the natural environment
Theoretical framework	Deconstructionism (Derrida, 1978); New environmental paradigm (Milbrath, 1989); Critique of the dominant scientific paradigm (Gough, N. 1987; Elliott 1991; Fien, 1992, 1993; Robottom and Hart, 1993); Postmodern education (Huckle and Sterling, 1996); Education in the senses (Emery, 1981)	Theories of conflict (Freud, S. 1923); Theories on the repression of feelings, and their emergence as symptoms, body structure and behaviour (Reich, 1933, 1942); The understanding of psychological defence mechanisms (Freud, A. 1937), and character structures (Reich, 1933; Johnson, 1985, 1994)
View of nature	Nature is socially constructed – its causal powers and objective properties are mediated by social processes (Huckle, 1996)	Humans and non-humans are bound by basic natural laws. Failure to observe these laws, as prevalent in the ego-centred (neurotic) human condition, leads to continuous suffering and ecological degradation
Aims	Social and cultural change; Overcoming unsustainable practices through an integrative, contextually sensitive, process-oriented and reflective critical process of learning sustainability	Integrating disowned feelings (Jung, 1971), resolving conflicts, and developing an ecological self that is capable of living sustainably

Table 9.4 Assumptions concerning causes of environmental degradation

	Deconstructionist Postmodern thinking	**Depth Psychology and Transpersonal Psychology**
Assumed causes of environmental degradation	Logical result of capitalism's inherent tendency to discount present and future environmental costs (Huckle 1996); Focus on capital accumulation, destruction of common property; Private ownership of land the means of production and reproduction; Focus on atomistic and materialistic Western science	Ecological degradation emerges as predictable side-effects of our struggle for a coherent, integrated, and embodied sense of self
View of self	Identity is continuously emergent, re-formed, and dependent on social contexts (Gergen, 1991)	Development of a coherent personal and transpersonal self
Distorted behavioural strategy	Lack of holistic thinking, replacement of intrinsic values with instrumental values, and exclusive reliance on positivistic and empiricist science	Compensatory, often addictive, and unsustainable behaviour (e.g., consumerism) serve to provide temporary relief from anxiety and a short-term sense of self

Table 9.5 Strategies for supporting behavioural change

	Postmodern thinking	*Depth psychology*
Assumptions underlying strategies for change	Ecological crises result from modern ways of perceiving the world and producing goods and services	Sustainable behaviour, and supportive institutional structures and processes, are emergent and develop naturally in psychologically healthy individuals and populations
Central approach to change	We will change our behaviour if we adopt and embrace ecological issues by means of problem-	The natural environment will improve as we learn to develop a coherent sense of self and thus do not need to

	solving, action-based activities that deal with real-life and local issues	resort to coping strategies and compensatory behaviour to achieve pseudo self-stability
Dominant change strategies	Achieving change through participating in direct action aimed at improving ecological conditions	Enabling people to experience themselves as part of the natural environment and to developing their eco-self identity, thereby extending a focus of concern from the personal self to others and the planet as a whole
Basis for change	Empowerment, development of a contextual worldview, critical and reflective thinking; changing values	General healing and development of the self

The issues listed in the third column of the previous tables show similarities with Spretnak's (1997) version of postmodern thinking, an approach she calls ecological postmodernism. Excerpts of a table in Spretnak's (1997) book *The Resurgence of the Real: Body, Nature and Place in a Hypermodern World* are presented in Table 9.6 on the following page so that deconstructionist, ecological postmodernism and a depth psychological approach to ecological crises (in italics) may be compared. A curriculum for such a *Learning for Sustainable Living* is currently being developed. It:

- is concerned with the personal, social, and ecological aspects of sustainable living (Hill, 1991, in press a) rather than with the current goals of sustainable development;
- focuses mainly on people who actually harm the natural environment, and in particular on those who make far-reaching decisions on the fate of our Earth;
- works on modelling sustainable behaviour rather than on teaching behaviour, thus requiring educators to also examine their own personal, psychosocial, and ecological sustainability;
- acknowledges the positive value of many other interventions, such as energy-saving technologies, but suggests that we have to both deepen our personal sense of self and our ability to identify with the biosphere;
- asks educators to base their theorising and practices on a very broad, and holistic, perspective of sustainability, one that expands the notion of ecological crises by including an awareness of the

roles of psychosomatic illnesses, addictions, and our legal system; and it
- enables people to develop a friendly, non-exploiting relationship with their bodies, as a foundation for a sense of self based on simple beingness, rather than on power and wealth.

Table 9.6 Comparison of deconstructionist, Spretnak's ecological postmodernism and an ecology based on depth psychology and transpersonal psychology

Deconstructionist Postmodern	Ecological Postmodern	*Depth Psychology approach*
Extreme relativism	Experientialism	Experience, deep meaning, stable and transpersonal sense of self
An aggregate of fragments	A community of subjects	*A community of subjects enabled to experience body-mind and person-planet unity*
Social construction	Dynamic relationship	*Learning from relationships, from our projections onto the natural environment, and from our struggles with our sense of self*
Nature as wronged object	Nature as subject	*Nature as our extended self*
"Erasure of the body" (It's all social construction)	Trust in the body	*Trust in the body's self-regulation mechanisms, in the harmonising of our body energies as basis for sustainable living*
"Gesturing towards the sublime"	Creativity in the cosmos, ultimate mystery	*Creativity in non-judgment; Focus on emotional growth and self-development*

Source: (Spretnak 1997, p. 73), Citations in columns one and two taken from Spretnak book; column three added by the authors (in italics).

Critique of aspects of constructive postmodernism

In the previous segment, we briefly described the distinction between deconstructionist and constructionist postmodernism by citing some of Madsen's (2005) and Oelschlaeger's (1995) views on this distinction. Many radical ecologists define affirmative postmodernism in far more radical terms. If postmodernism is about being critical with the mechanistic and reductionist modern paradigm, then it is possible to subsume esoteric psychologists, such as Dethlefsen, and many New-Age theorists, such as Wilber, under this category. Smith (1995, p. 261) would probably support such a view by suggesting that postmodernism "represents a long awaited return to a primitive understanding of our place in the world". He holds that the premodern and postmodern worldviews share many similarities, for example, in the strong female influence on, and the contextual thinking in, premodern societies (1995, p. 262).

From this viewpoint, constructive postmodernism becomes the epistemological container for all views that are critical towards the modern project without rejecting deep feelings and meaningful analogies and without limiting themselves to a sociopolitical analysis of modernity. Such a definition would subsume deep ecologists, social ecologists, spiritual ecofeminists, many New-Age theorists, and many other people in this field, whether or not they might call themselves postmodernists (Zimmerman, 1994).

As pointed out, constructive postmodernism is highly compatible with the psychological views put forward in this study, particularly if the views held by these postmodernists include an awareness of the psychological forces underlying our ecological crises. A depth psychology critique of constructive postmodernism is thus mainly concerned with issues arising from a failure of deep ecology, social ecology, ecofeminism, and New-Ageism to address depth psychological and holistic perspectives in educational theory and practice.

A scanning of these worldviews through the lens of the perspectives put forward in this study acknowledges that a comprehensive critique of constructive postmodernism is beyond the scope of this project, and will therefore have to form part of a later, extended version of this study. This being so, only a small, but critical, number of key issues will be addressed here.

Deep Ecology's cultivation of ecological consciousness

As outlined in the introduction, one of the key aims of Deep Ecology is the cultivation of an ecological consciousness. After exploring in the present study six distinct levels of ecological consciousness, it is the aim of this small segment to examine the level of consciousness Deep Ecology is referring to.

An examination of Deep Ecology thinking suggests that deep ecologists knowingly, or unknowingly, mainly apply a behaviourist model of change. This assessment emerges from Deep Ecology's belief that the necessary deep changes will have to be achieved through practicing self-discipline. This request to practice self-discipline indicates that deep ecologists struggle with conceptualising the psychological underpinnings of our ecological crises and the consequent necessity to heal our psychological conditions. Suggesting self-discipline as a key modality for change makes one wonder whether deep ecologists are aware of the possibility of a deep experience of body-mind and person-planet unity, an experience from which a caring behaviour towards other people and nature would flow naturally without the need for discipline and restraint. A depth psychology understanding of our ecological crises, in contrast, would suggest replacing Deep Ecology's notions of discipline and restraint with the notion of emotional integration.

The critique of Deep Ecology's suggestion to base change on self-discipline rather than on a deep understanding of the need to heal people's egocentric condition is also implied in Plumwood's (2000, p. 266) suggestion that:

> [t]he real basis of the discontinuity [of humans from nature] lies in the concept of an authentic human being, in what is taken to be valuable in human character, society, and culture, as what is distinct from what is taken to be natural.

Charging that deep ecologists attempt to address this discontinuity by obliterating distinctions and boundaries between humans and nature, Plumwood shares the view held here that an expanded self has to be based simultaneously on personal and transpersonal self-experiences.

Depth psychology perspectives and self-realisation

Both New Paradigmers and Deep Ecologists regard self-realisation as an important aspect of reflexivity that supports attempts to create an ecologically sustainable world. More than new paradigmers, who tend to employ chaos theory as a conceptual foundation for change, the depth psychology perspective put forward here joins deep ecologists and transpersonal psychologists in the belief that emotional maturation and self-realisation will be crucial factors for the enabling of societal changes. If the view that we have created our environment as a mirror of our inner world is true, then we must alter our consciousness in order to create a more sustainable world.

The approach to healing our ecological crises proposed in this study also shares Roszak's belief that Eastern religions, alternative psychotherapies, paganism, esoteric science, bodywork, and other practices, have played important and beneficial roles in assisting and ameliorating "Western society's troubled passage through a crucial stage in the evolution of the human race" (Zimmerman, 1994, p. 81). It is suggested here that these worldviews and practices will become increasingly important as environmental education moves towards a more inclusive, psychologically aware ecological education, one concerned with enhancing eco-self consciousness and self-realisation.

Important here is that self-realisation involves the self-realisation of all beings (Devall and Sessions, 1985; Sessions, 1995). A high level of self-realisation cannot be achieved, however, as new paradigmers suggest, by simply identifying with the larger cosmic unity. Although agreeing with the view held by new paradigmers and deep ecologists that it is necessary to work on many different levels towards a healthier and more harmonious environment, so far only very few radical ecologists regard the harmonisation of body and mind as an important precondition for a felt experience of person-planet unity. Deep ecologists, for example, appear to lopsidedly advocate direct action, a term that includes personal and political action, but fails to clearly articulate whether or not such personal action also includes working towards a felt sense of body-mind and person-planet unity, as described in this study.

Depth Psychology and the romantics' need to be emotional about nature

Ecofeminism, Deep Ecology, and Social Ecology have had, and continue to have, a strong influence in the advancement of our thinking about the natural environment and associated psychosocial issues. Interestingly though, many ecofeminist authors seem to struggle with the notion of romanticism, a social movement that has played an important role in the formation of ecological thought.

Spretnak has taken on the task of defending romanticism and the ecological ideas it stands for. She observes that 'romantic' in these days is a pejorative label used by those in power to discredit the critics of core concepts of modernity, such as economism, materialism, and scientism. Spretnak (1997, pp. 132-133) remarks that "an entire lineage of resistance to modernity is blurred, diminished, and distorted by regarding it as mere recurrences of romanticism."

Romantics have met much contempt for being emotional about nature both by modernists and deconstructionists. Yet, at a time when many of our modern and deconstructionist postmodern practices threaten to destroy the environment, we have to ask what is wrong with being romantic and getting emotional about nature? As a result of the research presented here, we have come to think about romanticism as a general term for a resistance against the psychosocial and emotional deterioration of humankind. Because of its concern with healthy and socially and spiritually connected living, romantic ideas will continue to play an eminent role in our attempts to create a psychosocially and environmentally sustainable society. Below are seven issues relating to this that we currently regard as pre-eminent:

(1) Romantics argued in defence of the belief that all people are unique and incomparable, and that they should not be subjected to what Spretnak calls 'uniformitarianism' (Spretnak, 1997). Reframed in psychological terms, this means that romantics argued against the institutionalisation of the psychological experiences that have led to what is now being called narcissism.

(2) The Romantic movement emphasised the belief that all people possess a good core, a belief that re-emerged in Reich's (1933, 1942) critique on Freud's negative views of the id.

(3) Romantics were concerned about the loss of qualitative experience that emerged with the move towards reductionist empiricism. Goethe, for example, argued against Newton's emphasis on measuring phenomena by insisting that people should retain their ability to subjectively experience form, light, and colour.

(4) Romantics resisted the belief that modernity, with its emphasis on science and technology, would lead to an improvement of the living conditions of society. Unless we equate these living conditions with the consumption of non-essential goods and services, this improvement certainly has not happened.

(5) Romantics resisted the attempts made by modernists to master and control nature.

(6) Romantics resisted modernity's attempt to apply the principles of natural science to the complexity of being human. This application has led to a loss of an integrated psychosocial and psychosomatic understanding of what it means to be human and to be embedded in meaningful relationships. The emerging modern discipline of psychology, for example, replaced complex analogous and paradoxical functioning with concepts based on linearity, and causes and effects.

(7) Romantics questioned the value of scientific inquiry that takes the object of research out of its context.

We suggest that an emotional involvement with nature, both internally, spiritually and psychosomatically, and externally, environmentally, will be an important and necessary aspect of our successful attempts to create a sustainable world. In other words, we might be well advised to turn to the wisdom of romantics such as Goethe, Rousseau, Montessori, Pestalozzi, Coleridge and Wordsworth to tap into their rich and intuitive knowledge of people's passion for nature.

Ecological psychotherapies

Psychological interventions aimed at facilitating ecological awareness and emotional maturity are not new. People such as Roszak (1995), Winter (1996), Fisher (2002), Clinebell (1996), Macy (1991, 1995), Conn (1995), Shapiro (1995), Cahalan (1995), Greenway (1995), O'Connor (1995), Gray (1995), and others have argued for an integration of ecology and psychology. Defying a present trend in the USA and other Western countries that aims to dilute the healing aspect of psychotherapy by shifting it towards the managed care paradigm, these scholars and practitioners have taken on the challenge of creating a new therapeutic paradigm. Conn's main concern, for example, is to "work toward an ecopsychological transformation of theory and practice in psychotherapy" (1995, p. 160). Suggesting that we are still operating from a view of psychotherapy that focuses on the development of the individual and that pathologises feelings and concerns about the environment, she writes:

> We have not been taught how to move out of the office, in our theories or in our practice. Most of us are still operating out of old paradigms that constrict our professional movement (1995, p. 160).

When she asks *When The Earth Hurts – Who Responds?* she believes that all of us are now, in one or the other way, experiencing the pain of the Earth (1995, p. 162). A defining feature of this new therapeutic paradigm is the understanding that emotional pathology is one of many symptoms of a wider and more complex ecological scenario. She notes that:

> As an ecopsychologist, I would like to see a revision of the DSM that looks at individual symptoms as "signals" of distress in our connection with the larger context or as a defect in the larger context itself. For example, I would interpret what I have called "materialistic disorder," the need to consume, as a serious signal of our culture's disconnection from the Earth.

Conn also addresses another unsustainable key metaphor, which is the cultural emphasis on what is often referred to as the self-contained individual. She writes:

> The focus on the self-contained individual is accompanied by a cultural overemphasis on rational thought to the exclusion of emotional responsiveness, so that pain, or indeed emotional experience of any kind, also tends to be pathologized or truncated rather than validated, encouraged, and fully felt (1995, p. 163).

This construct still informs the work of most psychotherapists, who are generally more interested in insights than in 'outsights' or in the integration of both. In the same vein, Theodore Roszak (1995) suggests that modern psychotherapy has so far failed to reach beyond family and society to address the nonhuman habitat with which we continuously interact. Psychotherapy is indeed still predominantly based on individualistic pathology, which regards the individual as aloof from political decisions and the influences of the natural environment (Hillman and Ventura, 1993). In summary, most current approaches to psychotherapy lack an understanding of sustainable living and ecological effectiveness because:

- they are driven by theory rather than by experience (Polkinghorne, 1992);
- they often operate from a mono-causal etiology (for example, all problems are caused by the oedipal conflict);
- they fail to conceptualise the influence of the natural environment upon people's wellbeing;
- except for the Neo-Reichian ones, they fail to assist people in enhancing their ability to experience body-mind and person-planet unity;
- they have a limited understanding of the ways in which our egocentric consciousness manifests as symptoms of our ecological crises;
- they usually regard people who express caring for the environment and who experience pain about natural disasters and the killing of animals and people, as creating distractions from the *real* issue, which they believe has to be about personal pain *exclusively* stemming from historic, personal traumatic experiences (Conn, 1995); and

- many psychotherapists still discourage people from taking political action on the grounds that people's feelings are highly symbolic and therefore not also grounded in real and present experiences.

An ecological view of dis-ease and wellness acknowledges that much of our behaviour is a manifestation of past traumas, but that our social and natural environments also play important roles in our lives through the generation of feelings, values, and attitudes. At a time of continuing ecological degradation, we also have to consider that many people might empower themselves by unconsciously generating interpersonal conflicts as a compensatory maneouvre of avoiding the experiences of conflict and fear in relation to environmental degradation. After all, it is much easier to leave a relationship than the planet. In other words, we cannot be sure that experiences of conflict in relationships are not also transferred from the outside world to the interpersonal social space. Here the notion of transference, often used in depth psychology, attains a new meaning as an expression of a translocation of ecological conflicts.

Doing psychotherapy in nature

Shapiro (1995) is one of the therapists who aims to facilitate emotional growth through habitat restoration work. By operating from the assumption that people's psyche cannot be separated from the natural environment, he envisages the relationships between humans and the natural environment as a continuation of circular processes. In this view, people's efforts to heal the environment will bear fruit by enabling them to develop a sense of pride and by improving the conditions for healthier living.

Ecoalienation and Ecobonding (Ecotherapy)

Clinebell (1996) developed a theoretical foundation for a therapeutic approach that draws upon object-relations theory, Jungian depth psychology, and in some sense, also on somatic psychotherapy. Regarding what he calls ecoalienation as one of the fundamental causes for the Earth's suffering, he writes:

> The central premise of ecotherapy is that our early relationships with the natural world have a profound shaping impact on a grounded sense of identity for our whole body-mind-spirit organism. Our identity formation is influenced at a deep, pre-verbal level, by our

early experiences in nature, but also by our culture's views of the natural world as these are experienced by us directly and also through our parents' feelings, attitudes and ways of relating with nature (1996, p. 27).

Clinebell's ecological personality model is based on a concept of body-mind-spirit unity, to which he adds a biosphere dimension. Taking Winnicott's (1969) concept of the transitional object and extending it into the natural realm, he (1996, p. 29) notes:

> In parallel ways, it is my view that transitional objects from nature are very important throughout life. This throws light on the intense bonding that many children and adults sustain with their pets and plants, their flowering window boxes and their gardens.

Clinebell conceptualises what he calls "a dual distancing, a splitting of humans from their connectedness with the natural world, a world that they are in, and that is in them" (1996, p. 35). Believing that inner and outer ecoalienation are resonating with one another, he considers that much of the anxiety in humans can be neutralised through making conscious efforts to bond with nature (ecobonding). He also shows a deep understanding of the body-mind-spirit unity when he parallels ecoalienation and alienation from our inner wildness (1996, p. 29).

Through interactive exercises, we practice letting go of the socially constructed, isolated self and come home to our interexistence with all forms of life. We retrace our steps through our evolutionary journey and allow other life forms to speak through us. We shed our solely human identification and feel deep empathy for the myriad species and landscapes of the Earth (http://www.rainforestinfo.org.au/ deep-eco/coab-flier.htm).

Joanna Macy's work

Joanna Macy is one of the leading protagonists in movements for peace, justice, and a safe and healthy environment. An eco-philosopher and scholar of Buddhism, she has been involved in the creation of both a new paradigm of personal and social change and of powerful workshops, which she teaches in America, Asia, Europe, and Australia. She has authored and co-authored many books, including *Despair and Personal Power in the Nuclear Age* (1983), *Dharma and Development* (1985), *Mutual Causality in Buddhism and General Systems Theory* (1991), and *World as Lover, World as Self* (1991). Together with John Seed, an

Australian environmentalist, she created the Council of All Beings, a series of re-Earthing rituals designed to address the sense of alienation from the biosphere that many people currently feel.

A central feature of Macy's work is her notion of the 'Great Turning', a term that denotes the currently occurring shift towards sustainability and planetary healing. Macy suggests that this shift is simultaneously taking place at the level of policies and legislation aimed at slowing ecological deterioration, at the level of social and economic arrangements (for example, consumer cooperatives), and at the level of spiritual change and expansion.

Although not suggesting that our efforts will necessarily save humankind from extinction, Macy has been instilling hope in thousands of people during her 20 years as author and facilitator of workshops and groups. In these groups, she assists people in facing the despair that she believes we all feel in the face of continuing ecological deterioration.

In this chapter, we have placed the psychological scenarios explored in the Chapters 3 to 8 in a larger context by examining the possibilities and limitations of the various stages of eco-self consciousness, and by highlighting the difficulties associated with shifting from lower to higher levels of consciousness. We have also briefly sketched out some of the defining features of the newly emerging ecopsychotherapy paradigm.

Before proceeding to connecting the transformation of consciousness described in the previous chapters to the notions of sustainability and sustainable development, we wish to point out that the model proposed in this study is in many ways similar to notions that Metzner associates with the industrial and the ecological age. In the chapter entitled *Transition to an Ecological Worldview* in his (1999) book *Green Psychology*, he succinctly summarises aspects of this transition by comparing key notions relating to these two opposing ages. Under the heading *The Role of the Human* he juxtaposes opposing pairs such as conquest of nature with living as part of nature, dominion and control with co-evolution and symbiosis, and exploitation and management with stewardship and restoration.

What we hope to have achieved in the preceding chapters is to break these opposing positions down into manageable steps, steps that can lay the foundation for the design of 'stage-appropriate' courses and processes aimed at enhancing people's personal and environmental sustainability by transforming their consciousness. A number of courses that have been designed for this purpose are outlined in Chapter 11. Many others may be designed by ecological educators.

10 From Sustainable Development to Sustainable Living

Having critically reviewed in the previous chapter some of the key approaches to environmentalism and ecological thinking, we proceed in this chapter with a critical review of the notion of sustainable development. This notion has received much criticism for being a rather shallow approach to ecological change, one that is unlikely to lead to a significant planetary recovery. Acknowledging the limitations of this approach, we will formulate key aspects of sustainable living, an approach to deep change and healing based on the psychological perspectives employed in this study to make sense of our ecological crises. We will conclude the chapter with a tentative attempt at formulating an outline of a 'Sustainology', a field of inquiry that integrates the existing approaches to radical psychology with the psychological views explored in this study.

Sustainability and sustainable development

The notion of sustainability

Sustainability has become one of the buzzwords among environmentalists and environmental educators. During recent decades, we have mainly used it as a generic term for practices that can be sustained without exploiting people, animals, or natural resources. Although it has become one of the key concepts in ecology and environmental education, it still eludes a clear definition. Sterling (1996, p. 18) writes:

> To begin with, education for sustainability (EFS) begs the question of what is meant with sustainability. A seemingly useful definition like 'sustainable wellbeing', which suggests that both the human condition and the condition of the ecosystems are satisfactory and improving, still leaves room for interpretation.

Huckle (1996, p. 3), on the other hand, remarks:

> Like liberty, justice, and democracy, sustainability has no single and agreed meaning. It takes on meaning within different political ideologies and programmes underpinned by different kind of knowledge, values, and philosophy.

The notion of sustainability, often used synonymously with sustainable development, has recently been expanded to include a range of social concerns, such as social equity.

The notion of development

The notion of development has gained political relevance with the inauguration speech with which USA President Harry Truman commenced his post-war administration. Sachs (1992) has pointed out how Truman reduced the emotional and psychosocial complexity of the South into one metaphor or category: underdeveloped (O'Sullivan, 1999). The implications of this notion have been complex and have significantly shaped post-war USA policies.

From the perspective of US economic interests, the view of calling the South underdeveloped has been an ingenious move. It has established the American money-oriented way of life and doing business as the dominant economic paradigm, and paved the way for the USA to become the predominant imperial force that it has been for some time now. By defining frugality as poverty and a problem (Sachs, 1992), and by defining economic growth and development as the solution to the problem, Truman's administration had found a way to disguise colonial enterprises and economic exploitation as development aid. With this ingenious move, the USA had found a way of exploiting the human and natural resources of the so-called underdeveloped countries without having to occupy them with military force.

Ekins (1992) outlined how the use of debt, trade, and aid became the *modus operandi* of modern imperialism. Countries are provided with loans that are usually used to establish the infrastructure needed for the exploitation of human and natural resources. Markets are also established for the importation of cheap consumer goods that provide people in the developing countries with some benefit from the promised development. But, as Ekins (1992) points out, common people usually remain impoverished because they have to pay the bill for the development through repayments imposed under the structural repayment policy imposed by the World Bank and the International Monetary Fund.

In the same vein, the trade liberalisation resulting from the GATT[5] agreement, first signed in 1947 to provide an international forum that encouraged free trade between member states, hailed by the 1992 Rio Declaration as a means of promoting sustainable development, has turned out to support a race to the bottom in social and environmental standards

---

[5] GATT - General Agreement on Tariffs and Trade

(Leveson-Gower, 1997). It has led in many Western countries to a pressure to accept lower wages, reduced rights to strike for workers' interests, and other work-related disadvantages. The physio-emotional, psychosocial, and environmental consequences of trade liberalisation, such as reduced job security and increased competitiveness are yet to be investigated.

When viewed from a psychological perspective, development has served many people in Western countries well by providing them with the cheap goods and services needed to soothe their oral dilemma and by providing narcissistic self-support. By accepting that they need (economic) development without insisting on sharing their cultural assets with the West as part of the deal, the so-called underdeveloped countries devalued their own cultural assets and behaved in effect like colonised subjects. Yet, it is probably fair to say that a real exchange of assets has never been the issue since many of us in the Western countries rely on these aspects of colonisation as a way of bolstering our defective selves. Whereas Western development aid has provided the so-called underdeveloped countries with some meagre crumbs of our big cake, it has pulled them down to our Western emotionally and psychosocially unsustainable individualistic way of life, leaving them with the worst of both worlds. Western interference has also significantly disturbed community life in these countries through providing easy access to television sets and other gadgets, gadgets that are increasingly regarded as having been instrumental in the decay of community spirit in the West.

Limitations of the notion sustainable development

A number of events have shaped the sociopolitical landscape in relation to environmental degradation: the Stockholm Conference on the Human Environment in 1972, the World Conservation strategy (IUCN[6]/UNEP[7]/WWF[8]) formulated in 1980, the Brundtland report (WCED[9]) in 1987, and the UNCED[10] summit in Rio de Janeiro in 1992. Now, thirteen years after this summit, and three years after the more recent similar event in Johannesburg in 2002, we can say with some certainty that the outcomes of these conferences have failed to make the world a more sustainable place. Regarding the above-mentioned events as failures, many environmentalists suggest that the so-called UNCED process that

---

[6] IUCN - International Union for Conservation of Nature and Natural Resources
[7] UNEP - United Nations Environment Programme
[8] WWF - World Wildlife Fund
[9] WCED - World Commission on Environment and Development
[10] UNCED - United Nations Conference on Environment and Development

led to the summit in Rio de Janeiro, with its outcome entitled Agenda 21, has handed much of the control over the global environment to the nation states and has installed them as legitimate actors to deal with our environmental crises (Finger, 1993). Since these nation states, in turn, have widely handed over the task of looking after the environment to the transnational corporations (TNCs), the responsibility is now resting in the hands of those people and institutions that are responsible for much of our ecological crises in the first place (Sachs, 1993). This co-opting of attempts to improve our environment through TNCs has given the control of the chickens to the foxes that now control many of the activities that were once controlled by grassroot movements.

One of the key outcomes of this political maneuvering is the notion of sustainable development, which through the widespread adoption of a broadly accepted definition is now generally accepted as standing for our ability to meet the needs and demands of human populations without undermining the resilience of life-supporting properties. Although such a definition makes sense at first glance, considered at a deep level, it fails to clarify what kinds of needs are being referred to, and which needs can, and should, be sustainably satisfied. In failing to ask these questions, this definition of sustainable development neither questions the excessive consumerism of Western societies, nor does it address the huge discrepancy in wealth and power between the developed and the developing countries. Although this notion of sustainable development has informed political practice now for almost a decade, there seem to be few significant signs of improvement of our natural environment. Sachs (1993, p. 34) writes:

> Reaffirming the centrality of 'development' in the international discussion on the environment surely helps to secure the collaboration of the dominating actors in government, economy, and science, but it prevents the rupture required to head off the multifaceted dangers for the future of mankind. It locks the perception of the ecological predicament into the very world-view, which stimulates the pernicious dynamics, and hands the action over to those social forces – governments, agencies and corporations – which have largely been responsible for the present state of affairs.

Research concerned with the notion of sustainable development (SD) usually stays well within an inquiry that is more interested in the questions of 'how' and 'how much' rather than in the question 'why' and 'whether to'. Outcomes of conventional SD research have so far mainly favoured the interests of the large corporate companies, which during this time have considerably expanded their power base under the guise of globalisation. Realpolitik in 2005 shows that in most Western countries the overriding issue in economics and society is still the satisfaction of the 'needs' of investors, who expect and demand ever-increasing returns on their investments. Framed in terms of depth psychology, this means that the focus is still on Western people's egocentric needs to stabilise their sense of self through retail therapy and empowerment at the expense of people in the developing world, and at the risk of compromising the living conditions of future generations.

Besides producing the Earth Charter, a series of principles intended to govern the relationship of people and nations with each other, and with the Earth, the UNCED process produced the so-called Agenda 21, a program of action for the implementation of the principles contained in the Earth Charter. Although environmentalism has in recent years undoubtedly shifted some of its perceptions of our environmental crises, it still retains an understanding of environmental concerns based on economic expansion in a global free-market economy (Winter, 1996; Simon, 1981). As Sachs (1993) points out, Agenda 21 uses many holistic-sounding terms such as 'integrated approach' and 'increased co-ordination', but dismisses alternatives as irrelevant if they do not conform to the limited ideas of sustainable development. Self-development, as it is described in this present study, has not been a consideration of Agenda 21 and has so far only been addressed by a small group of radical ecologists and ecological psychologists.

In considering the agendas raised in Agenda 21, as outlined, for example, by Keating (1993), we suggest that conventional environmentalism has so far failed to:

- distinguish between egocentric (neurotic) wants and naturally sustainable needs;
- acknowledge that increases in income and personal power above a critical threshold do not automatically translate into an increase in happiness and wellbeing;
- acknowledge that much of our ecological deterioration is the result of our addictive drive to stabilise our fragmented selves;
- more widely embrace the idea that to create a sustainable society we may have to shrink our economies, while at the same time ensuring that work, which needs to be meaningful, is distributed fairly and evenly among the members of a society;

- deepen our understanding of sustainability and acknowledge that sustainable living is a phenomenon that operates at personal physio-emotional, psychosocial, environmental, and institutional levels;
- acknowledge the wasteful and destructive role of advertising, which continues to turn essential human needs into unsustainable and addictive desires; and
- force our industries to produce high-quality products that survive beyond the warranty date[11] and that can be properly repaired if they break.

Although proponents of sustainable development are aware of many aspects of the wasteful consumerism in the Western industrialised nations, and of the difficulties experienced in the developing countries to provide for even basic human needs, they have widely failed to conceptualise the psychological strategies that would enable us to stop the present uneven development and to commence an equitable downsizing and fundamental redesign.

Aspects of sustainable living

Defending the notion of growth

Issues such as the ones mentioned above have led to a deep criticism of the notions of progress, growth, and development. Such criticism, however, often generalises the use of these notions, and thus fails to consider that progress, growth, and development *per se* are not unsustainable constructs. What is unsustainable is the exclusive application of these notions to the field of economy rather than to personal, emotional and spiritual growth and development. These aspects of growth have been replaced in modern societies with a cultural commitment to economic growth and development, which has led to the addictive consumerism that is now threatening the integrity of this planet. Where economic growth and development in egocentric societies are the problem, we suggest that emotional and spiritual growth and development are important aspects of the solution.

---

[11] At the time I (Werner) wrote this, I had to take our malfunctioning television set to a repair shop. It has only lasted 16 months, whereas our previous TV lasted more than 16 years before it developed a similar problem!

The notion of sustainable living

The year 1991 saw the launch of a follow-up to the World Conservation Strategy – Caring for the Earth: a strategy for sustainable living. In a thoughtful adoption of the theme of this event, the term 'sustainable living' appeared for the first time in an international written document. The text reads:

> The aim of Caring for the Earth is to help improve the condition of the world's people, by defining two requirements. One is to secure a widespread and deeply-held commitment to a new ethic, the ethic for sustainable living, and to translate its principles into practice (IUCN/UNEP/WWF, Palmer, 1991, p. 67).

This new notion, which earned some more attention at the following summit in Rio de Janeiro, was intended to mark a shift from a focus on development towards a focus on changes towards sustainable living or sustainable lifestyles (Tilbury, 1995). However, this shift has not occurred, and the notion of sustainable development continues to be the predominant paradigm. At the same time, the notion of ESD was broadened to include issues such as social equity, the right to be properly educated, and equal rights for people of different skin colour. ESD consequently achieved greater recognition because it was adopted by the United Nations as the overarching term for all attempts at creating a more sustainable society and natural environment. In contrast, the notion of sustainable living has so far failed to achieve wider consideration of its emotional, social, and political dimensions. An Internet search on this topic, which is a good indicator of what is being currently discussed in public, primarily brings up web pages on solar panels, mud bricks, energy-efficient technologies, organic gardening, and a whole host of other 'alternative' practices. In other words, ESD has incorporated many issues of social change and community health, but has remained oblivious to the depth psychological underpinnings of our ecological crises, whereas the notion of sustainable living remains limited to a focus on the marketable aspects of sustainable living.

Physio-emotional, psychosocial, environmental, and institutional sustainability

Having referred in a previous chapter to the physio-emotional, psychosocial, environmental, and institutional aspects of unsustainable living, we propose to reframe the notion of sustainability in relation to these four terms. This can provide us with an interdisciplinary framework that enables a deep understanding of the interrelationships and analogies between the ecological processes at work on this planet. This also provides an opportunity to include a discussion of the complex relationships between child-development theory, psychosocial behaviour, psychosomatic expression of conflict, our relationships with the natural environment, and the formation of beliefs, attitudes, and social structures. These four areas also emerge naturally as the ones most demanding attention with a shift in thinking from sustainable development towards sustainable living. In the following section, we will highlight key aspects of these four aspects of sustainability and unsustainability.

Physio-emotional sustainability

The concept of physio-emotional sustainability can be employed to denote our ability to have a friendly and nurturing relationship with our bodies, to understand their signals, to experience pleasure through them, and to cope with life's demands without resorting to compensatory, and often destructive, behaviour such as consumerism. It also represents our ability to understand the psychosomatic meaning of our illnesses, to work creatively with our physical and emotional boundaries and limitations, and to experience a high level of body-mind and person-planet unity.

This notion addresses our difficulties in relating to our bodies in respectful and nurturing ways, and it draws attention to the many common misconceptions and unsustainable beliefs about the meaning and functioning of our bodies. It also describes the ways in which we neglect the activities necessary to experience a sense of body-mind and person-planet unity, and to maintain physical and emotional health.

Psychosocial sustainability

We can employ the term 'psychosocial sustainability' to describe the emotional and structural features and mechanisms governing the relationships between human beings. Relationships are psychosocially sustainable when they provide support, nurturing, emotional holding, and emotional and spiritual growth for everyone involved (Shem and Surrey, 1998; Hill, Wilson and Watson, 2004). Relationships between partners may also be regarded as sustainable when they provide a safe container for the respectful and adequate raising of children (Solter, 1989).

Relationships are psychosocially unsustainable when traumas, internalised emotional conflicts, and environmental issues, lead to suffering in relationships, in families, and in the wider community. This suggests that we live psychosocially unsustainable lives when we lack the self-esteem and ecological and emotional skills to recognise how past traumas and current relational and environmental influences lead us to form and maintain relationships based on self-preservation and character defenses, rather than on curiosity, respect, and mutual support.

Environmental sustainability

Environmental sustainability is the aspect of sustainable living that has so far attracted the lion's share of the attention of environmentalists and environmental educators. Many key issues have been mentioned in the introduction to this study. In summarising, one could say that there is beginning to be agreement that our society will be environmentally sustainable when we will:

- implement our present technological possibilities to produce high-quality goods that have a long lifespan and can be easily repaired and serviced;
- acknowledge the planet's finite resources and the necessity to move from non-renewable to renewable resources;
- observe limitations imposed by the carrying capacity of this planet
- nurture and protect the soil in ways that allow it to maintain its power to grow food for future generations;
- ensure that water and air remain unpolluted; and
- keep access to the seed pool in public hands rather than have it controlled by profit-oriented companies, so that genetic diversity may be maintained.

A society is environmentally unsustainable when it compromises any of the above key areas, and will predictably contribute to further environmental degradation.

The problem with renewable energy is that it's not so renewable. The energy production ration of non-oil energy extraction is comparatively poor. Additionally, the present infrastructure is entirely geared toward petroleum, which allows for our vast, consuming population size. Renewable energy will have its niche in local applications, but it will never power a global economy (Lundberg, 27 June, 2005).

Institutional sustainability

Institutions and worldviews are sustainable when they:

- promote healing and emotional integration rather than superficial change (Hill, 2003a, 2003b; Stettbacher, 1991);

- are concerned with creating level playing fields for the fair exchange of goods and services;
- foster a movement towards power-sharing and social equity
- adhere to democratic principles and open dialogue;
- facilitate the sharing of knowledge and the development of meaningful skills; and
- focus on fostering social responsibility rather than on personal enrichment.

For institutions to be truly sustainable, they also have to practice sustainability within their own hierarchical structures. This may mean that people in leading roles use their power not to maintain and increase their power base, but to allow everyone to benefit from the leadership. Institutions are unsustainable when they fail to achieve the abovementioned objectives.

Sustainability indicators

The reframing of sustainability from the currently dominant triple-bottom-line system of economic, social, and environmental sustainability to the four-tier system described here requires an examination of the possible limitations of the currently used sustainability indicators and frameworks. Following the creation of Agenda 21, the Commission on Sustainable Development (CSD) was formed to oversee and coordinate the development of sustainability indicators that can be used to monitor the state of the environment and the progress towards sustainability achieved in a particular time frame. The CSD then contracted a host of organisations and scientists working at universities and other research organisations to develop suitable sets of sustainability indicators. These groups met at various locations to discuss and develop measuring devices (e.g., Wuppertal Institute, Balaton Group, UNEP, Eurostat, and others). The following text briefly outlines a small number of indicator sets, and frameworks and discusses some of their possibilities and limitations in the light of the approach to sustainability taken in this study.

Sets of sustainability indicators

An example of such a set of indicators is described by Moffat et al. (2000). They describe an evaluation system consisting of the following seven indicators:

- Approximate Environmentally-adjusted National Product (AENP)
- Genuine Savings (GS)

- Ecological Footprint (EF)
- Net Primary Product relative to Consumption (NPP/C)
- Environmental Space (ES)
- Index of Sustainable Economic Welfare (ISEW)
- General Progress Indicator (GPI).

Similarly, in 1999, the British Government (UK Defra Quality of Life Count) published a revised edition of 150 sustainability indicators and 14 key headline indicators. The key headline indicators presented in this revised edition include:

- Total output of the economy (GDP)
- Investment in public, business, and private assets
- Proportion of people of working age who are in work
- Qualifications at age 19
- Expected years of healthy life
- Homes judged unfit to live in
- Level of crime
- Emission of greenhouse gases
- Days when air pollution is moderate or high
- Road traffic
- Rivers of good or fair quality
- Populations of wild birds
- New homes built on previously developed land
- Waste arising and management.

An updated version of this system, the *Quality of Life Counts*, was released in 2004.

In November 1996, researchers from five continents came together at the Rockefeller Foundation's Conference Centre in Bellagio, Italy, to identify practical guidelines for the development of suitable indicators. The guidelines were developed to:

> ... serve as guidelines for the whole of the assessment process including the choice and design of indicators, their interpretation and communication of the result (www.iisd.org/measure/principles/bp_full.asp).

The principles were structured under the following 10 main topics:

- Guiding Vision and Goals
- Holistic Perspective

- Essential Elements
- Adequate Scope
- Practical Focus
- Openness
- Effective Communication
- Broad Participation
- Ongoing Assessment
- Institutional Capacity.

Although the principles are progressive within their scientific framework of reference (e.g., by demanding that the methods used and data attained should be accessible to all), they lack an awareness of the psychological underpinnings of our ecological crises.

Indicator frameworks

Several analytical frameworks have been used to identify, develop, and communicate sustainability indicators. According to Gallopin (1997, p. 21), these include the:

- Media approach (measures air, water, land, and living resources)
- Goals approach (used to select indicators according to legal and administrative mandates)
- Sector approach (examines indicators of environmental impact from the perspective of various economic sectors).
- An indicator framework that is gaining increasing attention is the so-called Pressure–State–Response framework that is based on Friend's and Rappaport's (1979) Stress–Response-Framework.

Sustainability indices

Sustainability indices such as the Environmental Sustainability Index (ESI), the Environmental Footprint Index (EFI), and the Environmental Vulnerability Index (EVI) were developed to compare the progress towards sustainable development achieved in different countries (www.ciesin.org/indicators/ESI.html). Sustainability indices represent mathematical calculations using available data of indicators to compute comparable numerical values. To attain the Ecological Footprint Index, for example, a country's total resource consumption is converted into the equivalent of hectares of biologically productive land and then divided by its population. The result is the value of hectares per capita, which then may be compared with the ESIs of other countries. The complex ESI framework developed by the Yale Center for Environmental Law and

Policy (www.ciesin.org/indicators/ESI.html) also covers socio-institutional capacity indicators and international collaboration and stewardship indicators, and thus is more able to represent a country's complex and interrelated sustainability issues.

The veracity and usefulness of sustainability indices is limited by the usefulness of the indicators chosen to create them. The following considerations outline some of the difficulties associated with these choices.

Critique of selected sustainability objectives

The variance between the many available sets of indicators and frameworks highlights that they are societally constructed, or as Meadows (1998, p. 6) puts it, "they are abstractions from abstractions, from models, or sets of assumptions about how the world works, what is important, what should be measured." As the following considerations suggest, the choice of indicators and frameworks, and the value judgments we attach to them, may decide upon whether or not we will manage to move towards deep ecological recovery.

Whereas most of the above described indicator sets and frameworks appear profound and cohesive when viewed from within the currently dominant scientific paradigm, they appear a lot less impressive when viewed from the psychological perspective employed in this study. This view suggests that many of our current sustainability indicator sets are based on a limited understanding of the underlying factors contributing to our ecological crises.

The most comprehensive and progressive example that we could identify is Bossel's (1997) set of sustainability indicators. In his contribution to Moldan and Billharz's book, *Sustainability Indicators*, he lists indicators such as:

- Anxiety related to problems of the economic system (poverty, unemployment) (pct of population seeing 'serious problem')...
- Percent of individual life determined by external forces: bureaucracy, customs, social norms)...
- Work satisfaction (sick days per employee per year)/(sick days per avg. adult per year)...
- Political alienation: pct of population not identifying with any of the political philosophies represented in elected bodies of government (1997, pp. 101-109).

These four sustainability indicators demonstrate that it is possible to define indicators that relatively accurately reflect the psychological and social struggles of most people in Western societies. All that is needed is a relatively unbiased awareness of people's psychosocial and economic situation and a willingness to offer these indicators to the scientific community. Yet, eight years after the publication of Bossel's set of sustainability indicators, the UN agencies are still operating with sets of indicators that are progressive in name only. This is most likely because the notion of sustainable development, with its assumption that our Western economies must continue to grow, is still regarded as a cornerstone of development. Public debate revolves around the amount of growth, whereas the fact of growth is still treated as a 'holy cow'.

The views outlined in this study suggest that to achieve deep sustainability our economy must shrink, and that it could safely shrink in accordance with an emerging transition from an economy geared towards the satisfaction of egocentric wants to an economy oriented towards ecocentric needs. There is no reason why it should not be possible to downsize and redesign whole economies in the same way that many ecologically aware individuals have already done this personally (cf. May 2004). In other words, we will only be on the path to a significant planetary recovery when we manage to be proud of economic figures indicating an equitable shrinking of our economies. That a prolonged recession is not necessarily the end of the world is currently demonstrated by Japan, which has been in economic recession for four years.

Viability

Bossel (1999, p. 26) writes about the viability of systems: "Sustainable development is a property of viable systems: if a system is viable in its environment, it will be sustainable". Although this statement is true in many ecological contexts, it is of limited validity when viewed through the lens of the psychological perspective promoted in this study. This suggests that to fully understand the complex relationships between systems and their environments, we may have to consider four different scenarios. These are:

- an individual with a high level of sustainability lives in an ecologically sustainable environment;
- an individual with a high level of sustainability lives in an ecologically unsustainable environment;
- an individual with a low level of sustainability lives in an ecologically sustainable environment; and

- an individual with a low level of sustainability lives in an ecologically unsustainable environment.

We are able to apply Bossel's statement to the narcissistic-shaming and the oral-exploiting conditions described in Chapter 8. There it was outlined that people (systems) with these conditions may all be recognised within our modern societies. They are therefore, at least in the short term, to use Bossel's word, viable. Yet, although they may be economically viable, they are hardly sustainable, because ultimately the exploitation of other systems will lead to a breakdown of the unsustainable structure. We have here the scenario outlined under d) in the above list, a scenario in which an unsustainable system maintains or even accelerates the unsustainability of an environment.

In contrast, as outlined under b), a person with a high level of sustainability who lives in an unsustainable environment may contribute to an increase in sustainable development, but may do so at the expense of his or her economic and psychosocial viability. This is the scenario of the idealistic change agent, who is engaged in an uphill struggle to achieve social change and healing. Predictably, many of these people become worn out by the destructive forces immanent in unsustainable environments (hence the widespread phenomena of 'burnout' among change agents: Shields, 1993).

The third scenario outlined above is one in which a person with a low level of sustainability (i.e., a highly traumatised person with a significant self deficit presenting many compensatory defence strategies) lives in a relatively ecologically sustainable environment. Such a person may increase his or her viability and make a positive contribution towards the flourishing of his or her environment. As has been pointed out in Chapter 7, however, many people are not able to make use of such an environment. Often their emotional condition rather leads them to undermine the sustainability of the environment. The greed, hatred, and ignorance contained in their body-minds may urge them to sabotage existing ecological sustainability, often for their short-term personal benefit, as can be seen, for example, in the undoing of much of the ecological progress achieved in the '60s and '70s in the USA especially over the past 20 years (Pope and Rauber, 2004).

The last of the four scenarios listed above under a) is the one Bossel presumably favoured in his exploration of the viability of systems. This scenario rarely exists in modern societies, but remains the goal of our efforts to create a sustainable world. Useful additional indicators arising from this issue include statistics on:

- burnout of change agents and environmental educators;
- existing change agents in a given country;
- rollbacks of achieved ecological progress;
- people engaging in psychotherapy and similar work;
- people in psychiatric institutions; and
- the number of political prisoners in a country.

The above examples highlight the importance of choosing appropriate objectives and sustainability indicators. They also make us aware that the choices we make are based on our values. Meadows (1998, p. 2) puts it succinctly when she writes:

> Indicators can be tools of change, learning, and propaganda. Their presence, absence, or prominence affects behaviour. The world would be a very different place if nations prided themselves not on their high GDPs but on their low infant mortality rates. Or if the World Bank ranked countries not by average GDP per capita but by the ratio of the incomes of the richest 10 percent to the poorest 10 percent.

Alternative indicators

The approach to understanding our ecological crises examined in this study not only questions the validity of some of the objectives championed by sustainable development initiatives, but also suggests that the currently available sustainability indicators do not cover enough ground to deliver a coherent picture of the ecological predicaments both in the developing and the developed countries. Sustainability indicators have to be regarded as societally constructed in that they not only reflect diverse scenarios in different regions but also diverse levels of consciousness and worldviews. In comparing, for example, the set of indicators currently used in Finland, which is ranked first on the UN Environmental Sustainability Index (ESI) scale, with those used in the USA being ranked 45, it appears that Finland's set is more comprehensive and socially responsible. Consisting of 85 indicators, grouped under 19 headings, this set has a strong focus on socio-cultural development. Although Finland has a relatively high rate of suicides, long-term unemployment and an increasing rate in violent and drug-related crimes, it can be proud of a decreasing rate of immigrant unemployment and an improvement in air quality. Considering that Finland is, despite of all its unresolved ecological problems, the world leader in sustainable development (cf.www.ymparisto.fi/eng/environ/

sustdev/indicat/inds2000.htm), one can imagine how bad the situation must be in so many other countries.

A possible set of indicators for sustainable living, the approach to healing and change advocated in this study, is presented in Tables 10.1 to 10.4 on the following pages. These tables build on UK Defra's set of indicators (UK Defra, *Quality of Life Counts, 2004*).

Social sustainability indicators, such as the ones presented in these four tables, produce a more sophisticated picture of our emotional and psychosocial sustainability than is currently available. It is acknowledged here that some of the statistics mentioned in the above list are not readily available and that psychosocial research may have to be undertaken to collect additional data on issues such as breastfeeding, addictions, alternative schooling, and psychosomatic illnesses. Such data may, for example, be obtained by employing sustainability-testing questions, such as the one presented in Tables 10.5, 10.6, and 10.7.

Table 10.1 Issues relating to health (added features appear in italics)

Sub-theme	*Indicator – statistics on:*
Mortality	Mortality Rate Under 5 Years old Life Expectation at Birth
Healthcare Delivery	Percentage of Population with Access to Primary Health Care Facilities; Immunisation Against Infectious Childhood Diseases
Medical Drugs	Use and Abuse of Prescribed Drugs
Illicit Drugs	Drug-related Crime Drugs Confiscated by Police
Alcohol consumption	Alcohol Consumption Alcohol-related Illnesses Alcohol-related Accidents
Psychosomatic Illness	*Psychosomatic Illnesses*
Environmental Illness	*Illnesses caused by environmental health hazards*

Table 10.2 Issues relating to education

Sub-theme	*Indicator – statistics on:*
Alternative Education	Students Attending Alternative Educational Institutions such as Montessori; Rudolf Steiner; 'Free' and Democratic Education Schools

Table 10.3   Issues relating to births and childrearing (Added features appear in italics)

Sub-theme	Indicator – statistics on:
Births	Percentage of Natural Births
Breast-feeding	*Percentage of Mothers Breast-feeding Their Children; Time of Weaning* *Sale Figures on Milk Formula Per Infant*
Time Parents Spend with Their Children	*One-income and Two-income Households*

Table 10.4   Issues relating to relationships (added features appear in italics)

Sub-theme	Indicator – statistics on:
Conflict Resolution	Relationship Breakdowns Domestic Violence Children living with Foster Parents Perceived Happiness in Relationships

Table 10.5 Psychosocial sustainability testing questions

Psychosocial Sustainability - Please rate on a scale from one to six (circle the appropriate number, e.g., ②) your ability to:
• Identify and solve conflicts
• Create leisure time and opportunities to be creative
• Maintain a balance between work-life and private life
• Identify your needs and feelings and to find appropriate expressions for them
• Reclaim the feelings that at times you might project onto other people or the natural environment
• Accept your emotional and energetic limitations
• Feel and maintain a sense of nurturing connection with other people and the rest of the natural world
• Understand the psychological dynamics in your family and the roles people hold in it
• Live without having to resort to consuming goods and services to stabilise your self-esteem (retail therapy)
• Define yourself through "just being", i.e., through having a good sense of self without having to resort to social roles, status or wealth

Table 10.6 Physio-emotional sustainability testing questions

Physio-emotional Sustainability - Please rate on a scale from one to six (circle the appropriate number, e.g., ②) your ability to:
• Cope with life's demands without consuming alcohol or other drugs
• To practice "self-regulation" by means of yoga, Tai Chi, Kum Nye, meditation, body-psychotherapy, and the like
• Have a friendly and nurturing relationship with your body and to use its signals as a way of knowing about your needs and limits
• Identify environmental factors that might be contributing to stress and illness
• Identify emotional and social factors that might be contributing to stress and illness
• Experience a unity of body and mind, to which you feel what you think, and think what you feel
• Generate and maintain energetic streamings and pulsations in your body (these sensations appear naturally when people have learned to become comfortable with deep breathing and strong emotional charge, and when they have softened their muscular tensions)
• Maintain a felt sense of oneness with the creation, often also called person-planet unity or grace
• Sense the interrelationships between your personal self-regulation (physio-emotional sustainability), your relationships to other people, and your behaviour towards the natural environment

Table 10.7 Environmental sustainability testing questions

Environmental Sustainability - Please rate on a scale from one to six (circle the appropriate number, e.g., ②) the extent to which you:
• Feel that environmental destruction is a serious threat to our health and the health of future generations
• Believe that more needs to be done than recycling waste and promoting sustainable development (shallow versus deep environmentalism)
• Regard the present high level of consumption of goods as a threat to the natural environment
• Reject the notion that environmental destruction is the price we have to pay for our present living standard
• Believe that people have to change their consciousness in fundamental ways to avert an environmental catastrophe
• Regard the natural environment as a source of healing, inner peace and inspiration.
• Are actively involved in political and social actions to protect the natural environment

- Believe that to achieve a sustainable earth people have to profoundly improve their personal (psychosocial and physio-emotional) sustainability
- Engage in 'inner work' to improve your personal sustainability

Sustainable living through downshifting

Few people would have expected at the beginning of 2008 that by October of that year a number of major investment banks such as Bear & Stearns would have failed and that most of the world's economies would be on the verge of, or already in, recession, a recession that many economists believe could develop into a severe depression. The current economic downturn, apparently caused by the so-called subprime mortgage crisis in the United States of America, has so far led to a loss of paper value wealth of approximately five trillion US Dollars and dramatically altered the return on investment expectation of large-scale and small-scale investors alike. When in early 2008 it was the norm to expect at least a two-digit increase in returns, at present investors are grateful if they can find a bank where they can park their money without risking losing it.

In this last segment of Chapter 10 we will explore some of the scenarios that have led to the dramatic economic downturn (or downshift). Although not pretending that we have simple truths to these highly complex economic and psychological scenarios, we believe that this downshift provides us with a profound opportunity and challenge to reexamine the values and perceptions on which we have based our expectations for happiness and wellbeing.

One of the significant differences between shallow and deep ecology relates to economic growth. Proponents of shallow ecology paradigms believe that a sustainable society can be achieved while retaining economic growth. Deep and social ecologists, in contrast, believe that achieving profound sustainability requires a significant, if not dramatic, downshift in our economic activities. We are now faced with the situation that our past unsustainable economic activities, including the unfair distribution of wealth and income within and between nations, are producing this urgently needed downshift, albeit without the changes in consciousness that we believe should underpin this dramatic change for it to be sustainable.

It is too early to see whether many people will experience and value the current downturn as a challenge to reorient themselves and learn to live sustainably, or whether they will simply cut corners and lie low while waiting for a booming economy to return. Governments and most economists certainly want us to believe that a booming economy has now become the norm; and that reducing interest rates, spending money on public projects and protecting banks from failing) will suffice to overcome the current crisis. We doubt that these financial interventions will have the long-term desired effects. We also believe that from an ecological perspective such a reversion to a booming economy would be an ecological disaster, because it would mean that we would have successfully managed to burden the next generation with the whole debt that we have incurred by pursuing an unsustainable way of living over many decades.

Recognising that a comprehensive discussion of the background of the economic downturn is beyond the scope of this chapter, we present in the following 10 key reasons on why we believe the current downshift is hear to stay.

Fictitious losses

Much of the money that investors seemingly lost in the past months they actually never earned. Much wealth that they felt they owned was speculative wealth that existed only in Wall Street's parallel universe. It emerged because people were willing to invest in packaged debt, believing that they would be able to sell these 'values" with profit in the future, and because in the current economic system strong demand for a commodity increases its perceived value. This wealth never existed in the real economy in which most commodities constantly lose value because of ageing and decay, and in which the value of commodities is far less polarized than in the Wall Street economy. In the following sections we outline some of the economic key features of this real economy:

Exploitation

In his book *Economia,* Davies (2004) writes:

> In a dept-burdened monetary system the rich get richer and the poor get poorer. [...] Relative to their real contributions, the poor do not deserve such poverty and the rich do not deserve such wealth (pp. 361-362).

Exploited by an economic system that allows and encourages huge disparities between income and wealth, the poor seek to satisfy some of their needs and wants by taking out loans. This high level of debt, as expressed in mortgage stress, together with the economically irresponsible outsourcing of jobs, has started the so-called subprime mortgage crisis that finally broke the financial camel's back, and that is now exposing the structural weaknesses of the current economic system. The extreme disparity in income and wealth between the rich and poor inadvertently leads to shrinking consumption, because a healthy public economy cannot be maintained through the purchase of luxury goods. Experience shows that the wealthy tend to reinvest money to increase their wealth and influence, rather than purchase that third yacht or fourth lear-jet. Although it is important to acknowledge the value of philanthropic giving in terms of the jobs it generates, we believe that it would be preferable to distribute wealth more evenly in the first place.

Money volume

Money is a system designed to facilitate the exchange of goods and services; and to overcome the limitations of barter systems. It is a system in which the intrinsic value of the medium (e.g., pieces of printed paper) is far less than the face value assigned to the medium. Common sense would suggest that the face value in circulation has to represent the total value of available goods, useable infrastructure, productive workforce, and accessible resources. This means that when resources become less accessible, infrastructure loses its usability, or workers get sick and need a lot of health maintenance, the amount of money in circulation should be reduced to reflect the value of the real economy.

Yet, exactly the opposite is taking place. In the current system, banks are allowed to generate loans at a face value that exceeds many times the original available deposit. The fact that banks have to retain only a fractional reserve of the money they are lending has led to huge differences between the total amount of cash available and the total amount of money invested, including loans. In other words, money is being generated from nothing. Referring to this topic, Davies (2004) writes:

> This means that the money system is intrinsically unstable, just as it was in the early days of banking. If a bank has too many borrowers default on its loans and it goes bankrupt, it can trigger a contraction of the money supply (p. 320).

The guarantees developed by governments to protect depositors from losing their money simply shift the responsibility to the taxpayers. This is because governments do not actually own any of their own money. With the USA already being hopelessly indebted, one has to wonder how the American people will ever be able to repay their loans to the rest of the world.

Creative accounting

Booming economies can exist for a limited time under the following conditions: (a) the presence of money-generating facilities, (b) a big drawer to store invoices to be paid in the distant future or never, and (c) the ability to disconnect the phone. This sounds like a joke, because it is one. What we mean with this is that it is easy to generate double digit returns on investments and high trading volumes if we operate with borrowed money, do not pay for goods and services received, and do not have to listen to the people asking for the money owed to them. This way of running a company has even been referred to as 'creative accounting'.

The basic idea behind creative accounting is to generate maximum profit by finding ways to disguise, and not honor, their liabilities. This practice must, of course, sooner or later lead to the downfall of the companies using this kind of accounting. What happened to 'Enron' in 2002, and to other companies in more recently, is also likely to happen to the whole current economic system, because it also uses creative accounting as a key operating principle. Exploitation and the generation of money from nothing are integrated parts of this system, as is hiding the real ecological costs of production and consumption.

As we have described above, in Winter's (1994) example of the Hamburger, very few companies make serious attempts to find out the real and often hidden costs of producing a commodity. Rather, a lot of mind power and money is invested in disguising the real costs. Governments are usually complicit in allowing companies to deflect from the real ecological impacts of their activities by employing means of deception such as front groups (Beder, 2002) or misleading concepts such as the notion of 'Corporate Social Responsibility (Banerjee, 2007).

Decline in marginal returns

In his book *The Collapse of Complex Societies*, Tainter (1988) describes the pressure of declining marginal returns in complex societies as one of the key features of societal collapse and decline. Tainter argues that an increasing amount of energy has to be used to produce a certain quantum of energy. This scenario can be seen in the peak-oil phenomenon, in the increases in failed harvests resulting from draughts and floods, in the destruction of infrastructure through storms and landslides, and the increasing poisoning of people in modern societies (Ashton & Laura, 1998). With the amount of energy needed to produce energy moving towards the one-to-one ratio, communities and societies move towards survival modes of existence, and eventually starvation, and collapse.

In addition to this, failures of group decision-making, conflicts of interest among groups, and disco-ordinate group dynamics often prevent us from making important ecological decisions aimed at enhancing sustainability to be made (Diamond, 2005). On a national scale, this has, for example, led to the failure of the USA car industry to adapt to Peak-oil and other environmental pressures. On an international scale, this is manifest in the argument used by politicians and business leaders that we can only change our ways if other nations do it as well, since other nations and companies cannot be allowed to gain an unfair economic advantage. The current economic downturn is unlikely to lead to changes concerning this position. Partly because they do not understand the deeper ecological causes and implications of our current situation, many politicians are using the economic downturn as an argument to put ecological projects even further back on the backburner.

Re-examining the GDP

We conclude this section and chapter with a brief critical discussion of the GDP. We believe that one of the key flaws of the Western economic system is the practice of lumping all aspects of economic activities into one account. Does it make sense to count sales figures on alcohol consumption, building materials for dwellings, wages for prison attendants, expenses on the restoration of polluted soil, and advertising expenses into the same account? The author of the article entitled *Three Reasons to Scrap GDP* (http://www.condoroptions.com/index.php/more-to-life/three-reasons-to-scrap-gdp/) argue that the concept is flawed because:

- it fails to track domestic labour, volunteer work, and other forms of unpaid labour;
- it lopsidedly measures the wellbeing of a society in terms of production and consumption;
- it grows with the production of weapons and ; and
- promotes wastefulness and the production of goods with a short lifecycle.

As Robert F. Kennedy said at an address at the University of Kansas on 18 March, 1968:

The gross national product includes air pollution and advertising for cigarettes and ambulances to clear our highways of carnage. It counts special locks for our doors and jails for the people who break them. GNP (a slightly different but related measure) includes the destruction of the redwoods and the death of Lake Superior. It grows with the production of napalm, and missiles and nuclear warheads... it does not allow for the health of our families, the quality of their education, or the joy of their play. It is indifferent to the decency of our factories and the safety of our streets alike. It does not include the beauty of our poetry or the strength of our marriages, or the intelligence of our public debate or the integrity of our public officials. It measures everything, in short, except that which makes life worthwhile (http://www.mccombs.utexas.edu/faculty/michael.brandl/main%20page%20items/Kennedy%20on%20GNP.htm).

This suggests that we have to learn to differentiate between different classes of economic activities: ones that make a serious contribution towards a sustainable economy, and ones that promote harmful and unsustainable behaviours and practices. Van den Bergh in his Tinbergen Institute Discussion Paper entitled 'Abolishing GDP' writes:

Firms employ separate accounts for benefits (revenues) and costs (outlays). The GDP, however, adds benefits and costs together. A company that would function as such, would quickly go broke (countries, however, face another type of competitive environment than firms). According to Stiglitz (2005) "No one would look at just a firm's revenues to assess how well it was doing. Far more relevant is the balance sheet, which shows assets and liabilities. That is also true for a country." In addition, a decline in stocks that represent value or welfare is not taken into account (e.g. natural gas in the earth). An additional shortcoming is that GDP covers the costs of the provision of certain public goods, such as national defence, even though it is evident that the costs of public goods cannot serve as an adequate measure of the benefits associated with these goods (Van den Bergh, 2007, p3, http://www.tinbergen.nl).

What we have discussed in this chapter, and in the book as a whole, suggest that it will be necessary to strengthen people's ability to lead meaningful and satisfying lives with a small ecological footprint. In the next chapter we proceed with the formulation of an extended educational framework of ecological change and healing, a framework designed to enable people to enhance their wellbeing with simple, ecologically sustainable, and relationship-oriented means.

11 Learning for Sustainable Living (LfSL)

In Chapter 11, we endeavour to integrate the issues discussed so far into a practical framework that we can use to assist people in enhancing their physio-emotional, psychosocial, and ecological sustainability. By analogy to the existing notion of education for sustainable development (ESD), we call this framework Learning for Sustainable Living, or LfSL.

To place this educational approach to deep change and healing in a larger context, we will describe its defining features, objectives, and epistemological underpinnings. We will conclude the chapter with a brief description of key aspects of Werner's *'Learning for Sustainable Living'* project, which has emerged as an offshoot of this study. It consists of twelve one-day workshops. The courses integrate educational strategies, awareness-raising approaches, and body-mind practices into a system aimed at enhancing people's ability to lead more sustainable lives, both for their own benefit and for the benefit of the wider social and natural environment.

Ecological approaches underpinning LfSL

In this segment, we outline the existing knowledge and educational approaches that underpin LfSL.

Integration of the personal, social, and environmental (Social Ecology)

Many aspects of the thinking presented in this study are the results of studies pursued at the School of Social Ecology and Lifelong Learning (SELL) at the University of Western Sydney. My (Stuart's) views on the psychological background of our ecological crises have greatly contributed to this study (1991, 1992, 1999b, 2001, 2003a, 2003b).

We emphasise the importance of the integration of the individual with the social and the environmental and the importance of holistic learning and experiential knowing, which, despite some strong advocacy (e.g., Gough, 1987; Eisner, 1988; Elias, 1997; Van Matre, 1990; Heron, 1996; Kasl and Yorks, 2000), has so far only received relatively little attention. By insisting that we need to work at the personal (including 'spiritual'), social, and environmental levels at the same time, and by emphasising the strong interrelationships between these levels, we have developed a holistic understanding of sustainability. In this view, a sign of healthy living is the full expression of autonomy, mutualistic relationships, and sense of place, which, according to him, is still rare within industrialised societies (Hill, 2000, 2003a). We also go beyond the usual social critique by pointing out that people are extensively unconscious and largely unknowingly 'adapted' to unsustainable and addictive behaviours. I (Stuart) have written that:

> [w]e have adapted to living reactively to external stimuli and, because of the inability of these stimuli to provide any lasting satisfaction, we are addicted to the maintenance, or more often the growth, of such stimulation. This occurs through acts of consumption, domination and control over others, and a variety of assaults on our senses and the rest of our biology. Such compensatory stimulation, and its cultural acceptance as 'normal' keeps us from:
>
> - acknowledging our woundedness;
> - confronting our fears, our helplessness and our fundamental disconnectedness and isolation, not just from place, but from all others; and
> - deeply investigating and coming to know our own essential nature and biology (Hill, 2003a, 2005).

At the School of Social Ecology and Lifelong Learning we have been emphasising the strong links between childhood experiences and the emergent difficulties with experiencing autonomy, mutualism, and sense of place. Rather than using object-relations theory or psychoanalytic thinking as the primary basis for his conceptual framework, we refer wish to refer particularly to Lauer's (1983, 1999) *Roots of Knowing*, DeMause's (1982) overlapping psychosocial stages in the evolution of childhood, to Josselson's (1996) work on the development of relationship competencies, and to the groundbreaking work of Williamson and Pearse (1980; Stallibrass, 1989) on the 'causes of health and wellbeing' to inform his approach. Describing the notions of core self and of adapted selves as results of adaptive processes used by children to cope with emotionally oppressive experiences, we suggest that through these experiences we become increasingly expert at living responsively and, often, fearfully (from the outside in). In such a state, we are extremely vulnerable to manipulation, colonisation, and to violence, and we tend to do to others what has been done, and is being done, to us (see Hill, 2003a).

Learning ecology

An educational paradigm that promises to make an important contribution to ecological sustainability is 'Learning Ecology'. Formulated independently by Hill, Wilson, and Watson (2004) at the School of Social Ecology and Lifelong Learning at the University of Western Sydney, and similarly by Visser (1996, 1998), it describes an approach to education that:

- is based on enabling learners to clarify and implement their unique learning agendas, rather than having such agendas imposed on them, as is still the dominant practice;
- places learning within a holistic meta-framework that is both ecological and cosmological;
- provides a means for working with the complex and diverse ways in which teachers and students learn, change, expand their consciousness, and act on their values;
- acknowledges that for effective learning to take place, everybody involved needs to have an understanding of the others' learning ecology profile, which results from previous life experience, learning styles, and personalities;
- includes an awareness of the importance of personal development for the achievement of ecological sustainability; and
- is based on the beliefs that we have to transcend the needs of the individual and be enabled to construct mutualistic relationships between the various stakeholders.

By insisting on the importance of personal development, and by taking a deep approach to changing consciousness 'Learning Ecology' integrates the more advanced stages of eco-self consciousness described in this present study.

Sustainable communities and ecoliteracy

The educational and transformative approach described in this chapter is a response to the growing recognition that one of the great challenges of our time is:

> to build and nurture sustainable communities – social, cultural, and physical environments in which we can satisfy our needs and aspirations without diminishing the chances of future generations (Capra, 1999, p. 1).

What, then, might be the goals of such communities, as viewed by Capra and other futurists? How might the notions of ecoliteracy and sustainable communities relate to the views put forward in this study? And what might sustainability mean in such communities?

There is growing agreement among those concerned with ecological and social sustainability that it is not economic growth and development, market share or competitive advantage (Capra 1999, p. 1), but what Capra calls 'the entire web of life' that needs to be sustained. According to Capra, to achieve sustainability, we need to attain 'ecoliteracy', which includes an acknowledgment that all species are interdependent. This view also acknowledges that one species' waste comprises other species' food, and it highlights the necessity of being able to embody such an understanding in our daily lives.

A key question, then, is how to attain such an embodied understanding of the interdependency of all species, and how to integrate it in our thinking and behaviour. The most widespread assumption is that ecoliteracy can be learned, for example, by enabling people to work in gardens (horticultural therapy) attached to schools (Capra, 1999), and by engaging in ecotherapies such as wilderness therapy, animal-assisted therapy, and sustainable lifestyle therapy (Ecotherapy Newsletter, October 2004). Yet, the question arises whether being closer to nature will suffice to enable people to significantly extend the limitations imposed by their character structures and woundedness. To achieve such deep change, many of us may also have to find additional ways to enhance such 'emotional literacy'.

Several projects have been undertaken in the past to enable wellbeing and emotional literacy, and to promote sustainable living. These include Reich's establishment of sexual hygiene centres in Vienna in the 1920s, an initiative that had the goal to lower the number of neuroses by meeting people's needs for information on sexual physiology, contraception, and family planning (cf. Cattier, 1969).

An important initiative that may serve as a model for our present efforts to enable wellbeing and sustainable living became known as the Peckham Experiment. It was conducted at the Pioneer Health Centre, in a part of London called Peckham, between 1926 and 1950. Initiated by Dr Scott Williamson and his wife Dr Pearse (Williamson and Pearse, 1965; Pearse, 1979; Stallibrass, 1989) the project was designed to discover the 'causes of health' by providing families with a place where they could, under minimal supervision, access facilities such as a pool and gyms, engage in creative activities, consume wholesome foods, and share their experiences. The experiment demonstrated that health and wellbeing of individuals and social cohesion are the predictable outcomes of an emotionally and psychosocially supportive environment. Hill (2000, p. 2) summarises the positive outcomes of the experiment by noting:

> All of its numerous important discoveries coalesced around the central concept that health is a process (not a product) that requires freedom and opportunity to experience being in a relationship of mutual synthesis with the environment. Health is thus emergent from acts of spontaneity. What the Centre provided was a context and an approach to activity enablement that supported and facilitated such freedom, experience and spontaneity. Indeed, in such an environment, they found that health became 'contagious'. Of particular importance was the preparation for and subsequent caring for an addition to a family.

A more current approach to promoting sustainable behaviour has been devised by McKenzie-Mohr and outlined in his (1999) book *Fostering Sustainable Behaviour: An introduction to Community-Based Social Marketing*. His approach called *Community-Based Social Marketing* is designed to assist workshop participants in identifying barriers to behaviour change and in applying his social marketing approach to overcome these barriers. According to the authors of the *Social Change Media* website (http://media.socialchange.net.au/strategy/), "Social change marketing looks beyond advertising and PR techniques. It extends to things like community development, recruitment, training, infrastructure planning and more."

Emotional literacy and alexithymia

The psychological perspectives used to inform this study suggest that the ecoliteracy described above also needs to be grounded in emotional literacy and emotional intelligence – the ability to identify, name, and appropriately express one's full range of feelings and emotions. According to the unspecified author of the paper entitled *Emotional Literacy* (eqi.org/elit.htm), we are emotionally literate when we are able to:

- name our feelings;
- consciously observe our non-verbal communication;
- replace indirect with direct communication (i.e., avoiding the masking and overusing of feelings); and
- adequately communicate the intensity of our feelings.

Although not explicitly stated in the text, two additional important aspects of emotional literacy need to be added to this list, they are the ability to firstly identify and secondly express our feelings in the right context, both in terms of past and present experiences.

Whereas the views explored in this present study correspond with these key factors of emotional literacy, they do not resonate with the view expressed by the abovementioned author(s) that feelings simply need to be labelled as negative or positive feelings. This view, which is dominant in modern (non-holistic) psychology, often leads people to disown feelings and emotions perceived as negative and undesirable, rather than as feelings appropriate in relation to certain events in the environment. The continuing decline of psychosocial and environmental sustainability in large parts of this planet appropriately lead to feelings of pessimism, frustration, anguish, hopelessness, and annoyance – feelings that many would judge as negative.

Emotional illiteracy is similar to alexithymia, a term created by Sifneos (1964) to denote the difficulties many of us experience with identifying and distinguishing between our diverse feelings. Typical of the condition of alexithymia are difficulties with:

- identifying and distinguishing between diverse qualities of feelings (emotional illiteracy);
- verbalising feelings and needs;
- referring to oneself as 'I' and 'myself' rather than as 'one' and 'oneself' in conversations involving feelings and emotions (or as 'the author' in academic literature!);
- creating fantasies and thinking in abstract terms;
- viewing others as different from themselves;
- forming deep relationships with other people (and the other-than-human environment); and
- maintaining a bond with an object that is not physically present.

Transformative education

A form of learning and pedagogy that has been developed over the past 25 years, and that informs LfSL, is transformative education. Based particularly on the work of Freire (1970), Mezirow (1991), Cranton (1994) and Daloz (1986), "transformative learning represents a heroic struggle to wrest consciousness and knowledge from the forces of unconsciousness and ignorance" (Kovan and Dirkx, 2003, p. 99).

Mezirow's theory on transformative learning, which he first introduced in 1978 (primarily in relation to adult learning), conceptualises how learners construe, validate, and reformulate the meaning of their experiences (cf. Cranton, 1994, p. 22). Whereas Mezirow's work revolves around the notions of critical reflection of experience and rational discourse, and is thus broadly similar to Kolb's (1984) approach to learning, some educators feel that Mezirow's work has overemphasised conscious processes and rationality at the expense of intuition and emotional and unconscious processes (Boyd and Myers 1988; Grabov, 1997; Scott, 1997; Taylor, 1998; O'Sullivan, 1999, 2003). In contrast, Boyd and Myers (1988) have developed an approach to transformative learning and education based on psychoanalytic theory and Jungian psychology. For these authors, transformation is the fundamental change of personality emerging from the expansion of consciousness and personal integration. The process of discernment, an integral part of transformative education, is assumed to use images and archetypes in the creation of visions of what it might mean to be human (cf. Cranton, 1994). Emphasising the importance of insights, judgments, and decisions, but also of symbols, images, and feelings, Boyd and Myers view the process of discernment as involving particularly the activities of receptivity, recognition, and grieving (Scott, 1997). In this three-pronged approach to deep change, receptivity denotes the ability to engage with alternative expressions of meaning, recognition allows people to validate the expression's authenticity, and grieving allows them to let go of superseded meanings and feelings. In its educational practice, transformative education aims to foster deep change by:

- emphasising the teacher's role in establishing a safe environment for the development of sensitive relationships among learners (Imel, 1998; Taylor, 1998);
- creating a community of knowers (Loughlin, 1993) united by their need to make meaning of their life experiences;
- committing teachers to serve as role models who are willing to share and learn; and
- assisting learners in embracing both the rational, cognitive and objective, but also the intuitive, imaginative, and subjective aspects of learning (Grabov, 1997).

Dirkx (2000) notes that Boyd's approach to transformative education is based on a soul-centered psychology (Dirkx, 1997; Moore, 1992; Scott, 1997). By referring to Sells (2000), Dirkx holds that "what matters most in learning is what matters to the deep ground of our being, the psyche or soul, what is primary, original, basic and necessary" (2000, p.1). He calls this approach the mytho-poetic perspective of transformative learning, a form of learning that leads to the experience of soul by working with images that represent "deep-seated emotional or spiritual issues and concerns" (Dirkx, 2000). In *Learning for Sustainable Living*, even illnesses, addictions, and the various symptoms of ecological deterioration may be interpreted as such expressions of soul (see Chapter 8 of this present study). In other words, the symptoms of ecological degradation are both features that threaten the integrity of the web of life, but they are also guides that we may employ to deepen our understanding of our unconscious struggles.

Shamanism

The psychological conditions underlying our continuing ecological deterioration and the resistances to change associated with these conditions suggest that behaviourist, cognitive, and participative learning will not suffice to bring about the deep transformation needed to achieve personal and planetary healing. An approach to change and healing that may be employed to enhance sustainability is shamanism. It is, according to Metzner (1986, p. 101):

> a set of practices in which altered states of consciousness are induced by various means, including chanting, drumming, dancing, and use of hallucinogenic plants. Such an altered state is experienced by the shamanic initiate as an inner journey in which she or he enters another world for the purpose of connecting with a source of power, obtaining a vision, or bringing about a healing.

A metaphor often used for the shaman is the one of the wounded healer (Deikman, 1982). In contrast to the 'health technician', who has acquired techniques and skills in a formal training program, this healer has learnt from engagements with his or her personal psychological wounds. This intimate engagement heals the person and enables them to become a healer able to assist others during their healing journeys. Such healing may entail the acknowledgment of one's 'wrongdoing' and guilt, and may lead to a reaching out for forgiveness and help, and a willingness to entertain deep changes in behaviour.

The experience of being wounded may be accepted as a challenge for positive transformation, or it may be experienced as a punishment, in which case the level of guilt and emotional burden is likely to be increased. A situation in which punishment was chosen was the 9/11 event that provided the American people with an historic chance to reflect on their worldviews and foreign policies. Although many citizens might have chosen the healing path, the US Administration used the event as a welcome excuse to expand their colonial and hegemonic agendas.

Objectives of Learning for Sustainable Living

Having outlined the epistemological basis for LfSL in the previous segment, we will now describe the goals and key features of this approach, an approach that applies transformative education to the notions of sustainability and sustainable living. LfSL has manifested in the creation of courses and processes, some of which we have successfully presented at recent conferences.

At present, five key features of this interdisciplinary and depth psychological approach to sustainability 'education' are conceptualised. Education is placed in inverted commas to indicate that learning is conceptualised here as processes that enable the development of emotional and psychosocial capabilities.

(1) Facilitating emotional and ecological literacy

A key goal of Learning for Sustainable Living is the deepening of emotional literacy. Work with alexithymia assists people in enhancing their emotional literacy by providing opportunities for practising communication skills, the identification of disowned and projected feelings, the sharing of feelings towards other people, and for considering natural environment and social and political issues. Structured exercises are used to enhance people's literacy in all of these fields.

(2) Facilitating awareness of personal sustainability issues

As an approach to healing based on depth psychology, psychosomatics, and transpersonal psychology, LfSL suggests that to create a sustainable world we need to assist people in:

- enhancing their understanding of the varied aspects of personal sustainability;
- identifying their conflicts with other people and finding creative solutions for them;
- identifying with their feelings, and with finding adequate expressions for them in our relationships;
- enhancing their respect for other humans, for their social boundaries, and for their otherness;

- enhancing their ability to enjoy committed relationships and connections with other people without the need to use 'retail therapy' or mood-altering substances such as alcohol and recreational drugs; and
- improving their 'sustainable living' skills that respect cultural and ethnic diversity.

The Sustainability Mapping Process

As part of this research project we have developed a process designed to enable course participants to enhance their understanding of the complex and interrelated features of their personal and environmental sustainability. The process aims to enable people to:

- visually document different key aspects of their lives;
- better understand the areas in which they need to seek balance between giving and taking;
- identify areas of their lives that have become "black holes", and that draw precious emotional energy without providing any nurturing;
- experience deep insight into their key conflicts;
- visually identify links between the diverse aspects of their lives
- rate the extent of their involvement in particular important areas of their lives;
- identify where changes might improve their personal and ecological sustainability; and
- enhance their understanding of the interrelationships and analogies between personal and environmental sustainability.

A blueprint for the sustainability mapping process is provided in Fig. 11.1 on page 262. There are of course many alternatives to this model, and some people who have worked with this process have produced stunningly creative representations of their personal sustainability patterns. Discrepancies in the flow of energy, attention, and meaning, graphically indicated by the thickness of the arrows in the graphic representation below, are intended to show the significance of a relationship's level of sustainability.

(3) Facilitating awareness of environmental sustainability issues

In relation to the natural environment, LfSL aims to foster:

- a caring interest for the non-human beings on this planet ;

- a need to preserve the Earth's resources and to keep air, water, and soil 'healthy' for the benefit of all beings, both in the present and future;
- the experience of a strong sense of self without habits of harming the environment through compensatory self-support mechanisms, such as consuming non-essential goods and services and holding racist or anthropocentric values and attitudes;
- a deep understanding of the psychological conditions that lead to ecological crises, and to ecological wellbeing; and
- the exploration of opportunities that might contribute towards ecological sustainability, personally, in one's community, at work, and generally.

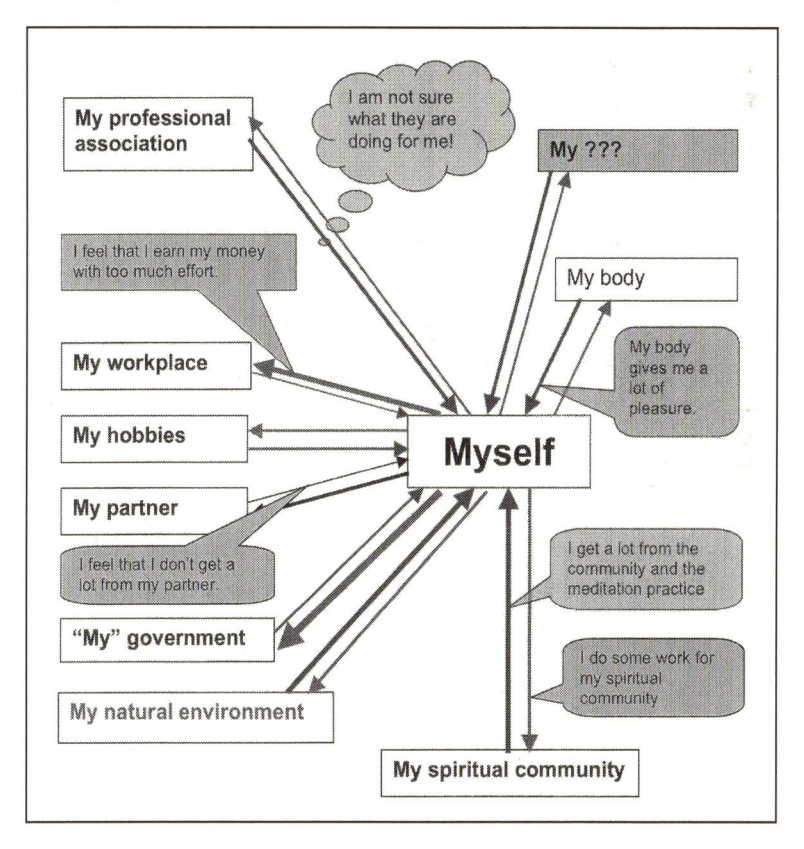

Figure 11.1 Sustainability Mapping Process

(4) Facilitating the experience of body-mind unity

The depth psychology perspectives of our ecological crises explored in this study suggest that our ability to live sustainably is, to a large degree, dependent on our capacity to experience a felt sense of body-mind unity. LfSL addresses this issue by enabling people to enhance their:

- self-experience of a felt sense of body-mind unity;
- capacity to identify and 'make friends with' their body's needs and limitations;
- understanding of the meaning of their body's signals, which they may then consciously use as important guides and self-regulation mechanisms;
- understanding of the meaning and purpose of physical illnesses
- capacity to handle life's demands without having to stabilise their selves through the consumption of excessive food, alcohol, nicotine, or other drugs; and their
- capacity to generate and regulate physical and emotional aliveness.

(5) Facilitating the experience of person-planet unity

Acknowledging that our ability to experience a love for nature, a phenomenon Wilson (1986) has called biophilia, is highly dependent upon our capacity to feel energetically connected to the biosphere, LfSL can assist people in:

- enhancing their felt sense of person-planet unity through meditation and energy harmonisation exercises;
- enhancing their ability to trust in the value of their transpersonal experiences; and in
- deepening their awareness of the ways in which they might have compensated their natural need for love, emotional identity, and belongingness through unsustainable coping mechanisms.

Features of LfSL

Focusing on educating adults

Unlike most conventional approaches to environmental education (EE, EFS, ESD), LfSL exclusively focuses on educating and enabling the people who are likely to be most active in actually harming the environment, which are in most cases adults. The choice of this focus emerges from the recognition that learning sustainability is as much an emotional issue as it is an issue of learning, and that such emotional learning is largely influenced by the modelling of parents' attitudes and behaviours. 'Educating' adults is essential since educating children without healing their home environment has the potential of increasing conflicts within families – an issue not sufficiently considered by most environmental educators.

Working in community settings

Although sessions with individual clients undoubtedly represent a useful way of working towards deep sustainability and healing, it nevertheless is not a sustainable way of using available resources, both in terms of available practitioners and in terms of stories and experiences to learn from. A more efficient and thus sustainable way of working is to facilitate learning and growth in small groups that allow participants to learn from one another and to practice with each other. These may also provide a context for learning and practising conflict resolution and provide a space that can fulfill our need to belong to a group of people.

Starting with personal sustainability

Although LfSL has the objective of assisting people in deepening their understanding of the interrelationships and analogies between physio-emotional, psychosocial, environmental, and institutional sustainability, all undertakings start with a focus on self-healing and on emotional and physical wellness. This focus addresses the perception held by many that caring for the environment is an additional demand and an issue isolated from their personal wellbeing. By starting the journey towards ecological sustainability through identifying pressing issues of personal sustainability, participants experience personal healing and an increase of wellness at the same time as they learn to understand their sustainability issues in a larger societal and environmental context. It is acknowledged, however, that planetary recovery will require us to work at all possible levels.

Working with energy awareness

To facilitate a deepening of people's felt sense of body-mind and person-planet unity, LfSL provides techniques and processes synthesised from existing body-mind healing systems such as Biodynamic Psychology (G. Boyesen 1976, 1985) Reiki (Baginski and Sharamon, 1988), Kum Nye (Tulku, 1977, 1981), Aikido, and Yoga.

Working with the somatic dialogue

Based on Gestalt psychology and Psychodrama techniques, the psychosomatic dialogue is a therapeutic technique that I (Werner) have been using for the last 15 years to assists clients in deepening their understanding of the meaning of illness through identification with the symptoms. By asking people to give their illness a voice, or other physical expression, it is possible to invite deeper meanings and connections to emerge in their consciousness. The technique may be used in an extended manner by inviting people to identify with a symptom of ecological degradation and by assisting them in making connections between analogous experiences within their family life, their community, and their bodies (and their 'god').

Using 'total' transference interpretations in counselling and group processes

Influenced by my social ecology studies, I (Werner) have been seeking ways to 'ecologise' my work as a bodyoriented psychotherapist. Trying to conceptualise this modified way of working, I have come to propose the notion of 'total transference interpretation'. This notion constitutes an extension to the concept of 'full transference interpretation', a term often used for the practice of interpreting the stories of clients in terms of past feelings and experiences, present feelings and experiences in the outside world, and projections onto their therapists. A full transference interpretation is accomplished when therapists are able to refer to feelings and stories at all these levels of self-experience.

Yet, when viewed from an ecopsychology perspective, such full transference interpretations may still be still lacking appropriate and meaningful interpretations of the roles of clients' natural environments at the time of their upbringing. They may also lack an awareness of the often -unconscious choices of their present environments and of the circumstances surrounding particular therapy sessions. Furthermore, it is reasonable to suggest that the integration of the influences covered by this 'total' transference interpretation would also influence people's beliefs about the state of the world, and about what might be done to improve both personal and ecological sustainability.

Sustainability policies and 'sustainology'

If the knowledge attained in this study is to have a positive effect on society and the other-than-human environment, it needs to be translated into policies, educational curricula, and possibly a new science of sustainable living. Diesendorf (1999, p. 9) writes about policy:

> Policy is a means of coordinating collective action for change. It is made by governments, businesses, trade unions, professional organisations, and community organisations. [...] Sustainability policy must foster environmental protection and social equity; identify barriers to sustainability and ways of overcoming them (and so have a research component); and involve both the power structure and ordinary people.

In applying Diesendorf's concepts to the approach to change and healing promoted in this present study, we are confronted with the following questions:

- How might sustainable living and *Learning for Sustainable Living* best be communicated and presented to the public?
- How might people be motivated to engage with courses and workshops designed to enable personal and ecological sustainability?
- How might stakeholders such as government agencies, non-government organisations, and other organisations be encouraged to adopt SL and LfSL principles as extensions to their existing ESD and EFS programs?
- How might society develop the infrastructure needed (e.g., ecologically and psychosomatically literate educators and group facilitators) to provide large numbers of people with opportunities to attend such courses and workshops?

Currently, in most Western countries, the public continues to elect politicians who favour band-aid solutions to ecological problems over long-term and deep-change initiatives. Influenced by a powerful media apparatus that has widely replaced honest journalism with rhetoric biased towards the economic interest of the ruling elite, and that skilfully uses fear and self-esteem issues as means of manipulation, most people in modern societies significantly lack the emotional and psychosocial ability to elect parties and politicians that hold ecological long-term visions. This results in the continuing decline of the various ecological issues described in this study.

The shift from sustainable development towards sustainable living requires a profound redesign of many policies, regulations, and programs.

Since in the current political climate it is unlikely that politicians in government will focus significantly on deep sustainability goals, the onus will be on the public, on NGOs, and on progressive academics and writers to look through the rhetoric and other manipulative strategies, and to promote sustainable living agendas. An educated and more eco-self aware public would, then, more likely be enabled to elect politicians willing to address our ecological problems on a deep level.

The considerations outlined in this study also suggest a radical reorientation of our scientific approaches to sustainability. As modern science has divided knowledge into horizontal discipline categories such as medicine, psychology, religion, biology, physiology, and philosophy, the knowledge and taxonomies that we have generated in particular over the last four centuries seem to have made it impossible to hold all this knowledge together. As knowledge has become increasingly specialised, few fields of inquiry are currently enabled to question this trend and to insist on generating a transdisciplinary and holistic view of doing science in general, and on sustainability issues in particular.

Studying issues of deep sustainability enables us to move across a range of diverse fields of inquiry, such as ecology, ecophilosophy, ecopsychology, and educational studies, and to use a fragmented terminology – one that distinguishes, for instance, between sustainability and self-regulation. A solution to this problem might be to formulate a transdisciplinary discipline, a 'sustainology' that could focus on the many analogical and interrelated aspects of sustainable and unsustainable living, and that would aim to develop an all-encompassing interdisciplinary lexicology for this purpose. A key task of those involved in such a discipline would be to create an awareness of how we construct and maintain unsustainable structures as manifestations of our unhealed ego-consciousness. Examples of these structures across a range of epistemological disciplines are provided in Table 11.1 on the following page. Although the items in each column are not structured along specific levels of sustainability, they vividly demonstrate the two opposing paradigms.

The overarching science of sustainable living envisioned here would include disciplines such as:

- Social Ecology;
- Education for Transformation;
- a psychology concerned with personal and planetary healing rather than with supporting the modern paradigm (Winter, 1996);

- an "Eco-Psychosomatics", exploring the synergies between body-mind and person-planet unity;
- an 'eco-psychosomatic' medicine focusing on the complex issues of wellness and illness in relation to emotional, psychosocial, and environmental factors;
- an anthropology and archaeology focusing on the processes that have led to our current ego-self consciousness; and
- a spirituality concerned with issues of person-planet unity, meaning and purpose, and sense of place.

Table 11.1 Examples of sustainable and unsustainable structures

Unsustainable structures	Sustainable structures
The neurotic (egocentric) state of being in the world.	The non-neurotic state of being in the world.
Possessing a fragmented sense of self that is in a constant need of external stabilisation	Possessing a stable yet transcendent sense of self
Chemical fertilisers	Thick layer of topsoil
Notion of change/short-term help	Healing
Isolated sex – platonic love	Love and sex integration
Buzzing resulting from caffeine, dangerous sports, etc.	Aliveness from natural energetic streamings and pulsations
Modern and deconstructionist linguistic concepts	Emotional and psychosomatic language
Darwinism	Lamarckism
Mechanistic–progress-orientated–disembodied philosophies that justify fragmentation and discontinuation	Holistic, psychosomatic, and transpersonal "philosophies"
The notion of chance occurrence	The notions of meaning and purpose
The notion of sense of place is reduced to the notion of location.	Strong awareness of our sense of place, our connectedness with the place we call home
Body and mind are unrelated entities; self-experiences of fragmentation	Body and mind are experienced as a unit
God is projected into heaven and disconnected from everyday experiences	God takes multiple forms and is integral to all areas of life

An overview and summary of key distinctions between ESD and LfSL is provided in Tables 11.2 to 11.7 on the following pages.

Table 11.2 Knowledges underpinning ESD and LfSL

Knowledge underpinning ESD:	Knowledge underpinning LfSL:
• Behaviourism • Cognitive psychology • Critical thinking • Natural sciences • Social sciences • Humanities	• Depth psychology • Psychosomatics • Transpersonal psychology • Perennial philosophy • Systems thinking • Transformative education

Table 11.3 Objectives of ESD and LfSL

Objectives of ESD:	Objectives of LfSL:
• to foster development that meets the needs of the present without compromising the ability of future generations to meet their own needs.	• to facilitate the creation of self-aware citizens able to live in harmony with their inner world and outer environment without having to bolster themselves through consuming non-essential goods and services or holding power over others.

Table 11.4 Means to achieve ESD and LfSL

Means to achieve ESD:	Means to achieve LfSL:
• improving basic education; • reorienting existing education; • expanding public understanding and awareness of sustainability issues.	• assisting people in strengthening their embodied sense of self; • facilitating the ability to sense the interrelationships between the personal, psychosocial, and ecological aspects of sustainability.

Table 11.5 Foci of ESD and LfSL

ESD focuses on:	LfSL focuses on:
• educating adults and young people usually in formal settings; • development (economic, social, ecological, political); and • respect for ethics and values (cognitive approach).	• educating adults (the people who actually harm the environment); • issues of sustainable living, (emotional, psychosocial, ecological); and • a deep understanding of the psychological conditions that lead to ecological crises.

Table 11.6 Issues facilitated by ESD and LfSL

ESD facilitates:	LfSL:
• the increase of general levels of education and critical-thinking skills; • the ability to analyse issues that confront communities; • the ability to identify unsustainable and destructive values, attitudes and behaviour, and to work towards sustainable ones; and • the motivation to engage in public debates and decision-making processes.	• assists people in identifying the areas in which their lives lack personal sustainability and in which they need healing; • assists people in developing strategies to achieve emotional, psychosocial, economic, and ecological sustainability; • facilitates integration of any disowned feelings that may lead to conflicts and unsustainable values, attitudes and behaviour; • facilitates a deep understanding of the interrelationships between emotional, psychosocial and ecological sustainability; and • explores opportunities to contribute towards ecological sustainability in the community.

Table 11.7 Issues promoted by ESD and LfSL

ESD promotes:	LfSL promotes:
• engaging in training to become literate and environmentally aware citizens; and • the view that peace, development and environmental protection are interdependent and indivisible.	• sustainable living skills that respect cultural and ethnic diversity; • self-healing processes that foster emotional autonomy and wellness; and • an interest in protecting nature for the benefit of all living beings.

Our aim in these 11 chapters has been to examine key manifestations of our ecological crises from the perspectives of depth psychology, holism, and transpersonal psychology. We believe that the views and experiences of the research participants and the subsequent discussion based on my own experiences and a literature review have enabled a deepening of our perceptions of our ecological crises and of appropriate effective actions.

In the following concluding chapter, we will summarise the key issues discussed, and share some thoughts on possible futures. These thoughts describe a possible story of the future as a projection of our present situation.

12 Summary and Conclusion

In the introduction to this study, we noted that whereas we may have 'solved' most of our ecological problems in theory, we still lack a deep understanding of the psychological underpinnings of our perception of, and behaviour towards, the other-than-human environment. We also suggested that we have accumulated plentiful knowledge of the factors leading to environmental deterioration and that the challenge ahead is to enable people in the Western world to do what many of them, deep down, know they must do. By employing depth psychology, holism, and transpersonal psychology as frames of reference, we have endeavoured to explain why the psychosocial and environmental living conditions of most people are still deteriorating, despite the efforts of millions of people to make the world a better place to live. The issues examined are summarised under the following eight points.

1) Expanding research methodology and epistemology

Our present understanding of the complexity of our ecological crises is still limited because of our almost exclusive reliance on an epistemology and research methodology based on natural science and cognitive and behaviourist psychology. The findings outlined here provide reasons to conclude that we must re-examine and expand the dominant conventional scientific paradigm to enable it to embrace the complex scenarios of sustainable living. This paradigm, we consider, will have to include an understanding of our ecological crises based on depth psychology, holism, psychosomatics, and transpersonal psychology.

2) Shifting towards a more inclusive view of our ecological crises

Our present perception of what constitutes ecological crises predominantly revolves around the degradation of the natural environment and, most progressively, around a decline of social equity and cohesion. It fails to include an understanding of the ecological functions of issues such as psychosomatic and environment-induced illnesses, addictions, terrorism, and violent and exploitative attitudes and behaviours towards humans and the other-than-human environment. The issues discussed here in this regard suggest that we have to make concerted efforts to broaden our understanding of what constitutes ecological crises and examine the meaningful synergies and synchronicities between its various manifestations.

3) Ego-self consciousness

The issues examined in this study have led me to conclude that many key aspects of our ecological crises are predictable manifestations of neurotic living, a form of consciousness that we have called here ego-self consciousness; also that the main features of our ecological crises are likely to remain part of human functioning until we have recovered from this emotional and psychosocial condition. The fact that egocentric consciousness is still firmly entrenched in Western societies requires us to take urgent action to pursue a widespread recovery from this condition.

4) Eco-self development as a six-stage process

The shift from this ego-self consciousness towards an experience of deep forms of eco-self consciousness can be described as a six-stage process. We have labelled these six stages: (1) manipulated, (2) learned, (3) participative, (4) deep, (5) holistic, and (6) experiential eco-self consciousness; and we have argued that most environmentalists presently base their theorising and behaviour-change practices on the first three of these six stages, and thus continue to neglect the deep psychological roots of our ecological crises.

Acknowledging the crucial role of environmentalists and educators in the creation of an ecologically sustainable world, this study leads to the conclusion that those concerned with ecological and social change will need to expand their perception from an ecology based on environmental ethics and behaviour change towards one based on a transformation to more advanced levels of eco-self consciousness. This will require them to both model personally environmentally sustainable behaviours and to enable the adoption of practices designed to foster eco-consciousness at all of the levels discussed in this study.

5) Self-development and disconnection from nature

Ego-self consciousness is the result of the failure of modern people to develop both a mature personal and a transpersonal sense of self. This failure in personal development recreates and maintains in modern societies at the ontogenetic level a process of societal development that has led to a widespread loss of the experiences of body-mind and person-planet unity, a loss that predictably also manifests in modern people's experience of disconnection from nature.

6) A character-analytical view of ecological crises

In this study, we have endeavoured to show that a deep understanding of our ecological crises may be gained from a characterological interpretation of their influencing factors. This interpretation has demonstrated that our ecological crises may be framed as predictable outcomes of the three prevailing emotional conditions referred to here as the schizoid-terrorising, oral-exploiting, and narcissistic-shaming conditions. We have also suggested that to achieve deep planetary recovery we need to address these conditions within the framework of a 'psycho-ecological education'. For this purpose, a number of practices designed to enable deep experiences of eco-self consciousness have been described, and others have been developed in conjunction with this study.

7) Extending our framework on sustainability

Many key aspects of sustainability may be framed in terms of the four interrelated and mutually influencing categories: (a) physio-emotional, (b) psychosocial, (c) environmental, and (d) institutional sustainability. This study has led me to conclude that our ability to live sustainably on this planet will be greatly improved by expanding the presently dominant triple bottom line scenario towards an understanding of the interrelationships and synergies between these four aspects of sustainability.

8) From ESD to LfSL

We have argued in this study that the notions of sustainable development (SD) and Education for Sustainable Development (ESD) so far have failed to address the deep roots of our ecological crises. Acknowledging that we already have formulated the notion of sustainable living, it makes sense to use this concept and to broaden it by including the four categories of sustainability proposed in this study. The notion of Education for Sustainable Living may be employed as a basis for a 'psychologised' version of Education for Sustainable Development.

The way ahead

What, then, can we conclude from this study? What visions might we realistically maintain of possible ways ahead, of possible futures? Struggling to find answers to these questions, we are wondering whether or not large numbers of people in the Western countries will embark soon enough on the personal healing journeys that are likely needed to stop the currently continuing ecological and psychosocial degradation. Particularly, we are wondering whether or not the people with access to wealth and power – the ones who are in modern societies in positions to make far-reaching decisions on the ecological future of this planet – will continue to rely on their wealth and power to bolster their false selves, which also means that they will continue to contribute to the exploitation and abuse of large segments of the population with all its dire consequences.

Although an increasing number of people are engaging in physio-emotional, psychosocial, and ecological change and healing, so far politicians and business leaders have done very little to reduce the output on greenhouse gas emissions and to promote leaner and meaner production. While at the grassroots level people are working hard to create positive change, many corporate companies continue to set up front groups and conservative think tanks to manipulate the public to and sponsor confusion about global warming (Beder, 2002).

Paradoxically, it will probably be the economic downturn in 2008, which by the end of the year had wiped about five trillion dollars off the balance sheets of both wealthy and small-scale investors, that will teach us the important lessons about sustainable living that we would otherwise not have considered. During the last few months of 2008 the world has indeed started to change. Whereas at the beginning of 2008 our unsustainable debt-financed and speculation-driven economy was still 'booming', by the end of the year most Western economies had come close to, or were already in, a recession that may have the potential to turn into a prolonged depression.

We are already, however, well into the realm of what I call depression economics. By that I mean a state of affairs like that of the 1930s in which the usual tools of economic policy — above all, the Federal Reserve's ability to pump up the economy by cutting interest rates — have lost all traction. When depression economics prevails, the usual rules of economic policy no longer apply: virtue becomes vice, caution is risky and prudence is folly. - Paul Krugmann: Depression Economics Returns, The New York Times, November 14, 2008 - www.nytimes.com/2008/11/14/opinion/ 14 krugman.html?_r=1&oref=slogin

---

As in the Great Depression of the 1930s, most politicians and economists have not yet been able or willing to recognize the deep, root-level causes of our current crisis. Rather than acknowledging that the current recession may partly be a result of the structural inequalities in the distribution of wealth and income (Eccles, 1951), most continue to believe that a Keynesian approach to this crisis, in particular deficit spending by governments, will be able to get the Western economies back on track. Deficit spending, of course, is done mainly with the money of those taxpayers that have already missed out on their fair share of wealth in the first place. It cannot replace the needed deep structural changes, such as those employed during the Great Depression as part of the so-called New Deal. At that time, besides stimulating demand through increased government spending, the US Government set minimum wages and prices, strengthened the unions, and forced businesses to cooperate with government is setting price codes.

Eccles laid the blame for the Crash of '29 and the resulting Great Depression on the moneyed class.
"Had there been a better distribution of the current income from the national product - in other words, had there been less savings by business and the higher-income groups and more income in the lower groups - we would have had far greater stability in the economy". http://www.sltrib.com/news/ci_10997754

A key issue to challenge is the belief in a trickle-down economy, in which tax cuts and other benefits to businesses and rich individuals are provided in the belief that by supporting the financial elite - Bush's base - the wider population will be indirectly benefited.

Although a fairer distribution of wealth within societies, and between societies, will be an important cornerstone of an ecologically, psychosocially, and economically sustainable future, it cannot be achieved by reverting back to the so-called boom economy that we are just leaving behind. Rather it will be a sign of positive progress to conceptualise the emerging recession or depression as an ecologically necessary economic downturn; as an opportunity to pave the way for a more sustainable society, one that must have a much smaller ecological footprint. This shift in consciousness is unlikely to be a simple process, considering that the current downturn is not the result of orchestrated political and social efforts, but of the effects of unsustainable economic and other societal structures reaching crisis thresholds.

With the focus of attention still shifting from concerns for the environment to the ill-conceived war on terror and the costly protection of national security, and with managerial and technological solutions to ecological problems now under threat, the environmental movement could lose credibility if it does not reform itself into an ecological movement equipped to address the larger ecological and political issues outlined in this study. On our shared journey towards a sustainable society it will not suffice to rely on new clever technologies, to seek more efficient ways for manipulating people's behaviour, and to include ecological topics in school curricula; rather, we must be willing to ask some very challenging questions, such as:

- To what extent will the USA Administration be allowed by its people, by other countries, and by the UN to continue on its path (towards creating the most powerful dictatorship that this planet has ever seen)?
- To what extent will Barack Obama, the new President-Elect, be able to follow through on his agenda for deep change?
- When, and to what extent, might the USA fall apart under the weight of its debts, and under the increasing loss of good standing among the League of Nations; and, if so, how will this affect the global economy, world peace, and the natural environment?
- What roles might illnesses and environmental catastrophes play in the future of humanity?

Without pondering such global ecological questions, it will become increasingly difficult to believe in the value of eradicating noxious weeds in one part of the world, at the same time as some Western governments turn whole countries into ecological minefields and make once protected wilderness areas available for economic exploitation.

The psychological background of the ecological crises examined here suggests that without radical action the future looks indeed grim. If we acknowledge the validity of the psychological scenarios outlined in this study, then, generally speaking, we seem currently to be psychologically ill-equipped to address the psychological factors underpinning our ecological crises. The greed, hatred, and ignorance maintained by the majority of people in Western countries, paired with an increasing economic, emotional, and psychosomatic vulnerability of large parts of the public, may continue to create an environment that continues to accelerate physio-emotional, psychosocial, and ecological deterioration.

Tragically, the psychological scenarios explored in this study have predictably led to the dynamic scenario that Krieger (2001) aptly described in his short paper entitled 'The Frog's Malaise: Nuclear Weapons and Human Survival'. Krieger refers to the well-known phenomenon in which a frog dropped into a pot with hot water will immediately jump out, whereas when dropped into a pot of tepid water, it will remain there and succumb when the water temperature reaches a lethal threshold. Written five months before the 9/11 events, Krieger lists the psychological scenarios that keep us 'human frogs' trapped in a political, psychosocial, and emotional landscape that continues to heat up. His key factors are:

- Ignorance
- Complacency
- Deference to authority
- Sense of powerlessness
- Fear
- Economic advantage
- Conformity
- Marginalisation
- Technological optimism
- Tyranny of experts

Whereas Krieger regards the nuclear threat to humanity as the main problem, his considerations can be extended to our continuing ecological degradation, the emerging neocolonialism in the USA and some other Western countries, and the continuing loss of trust in the values of the Western world. Mesmerised by rhetoric that uses the ten factors mentioned by Krieger, most people in the Western countries hardly notice that the dynamic processes arising from egocentric consciousness are currently taking the whole planet to an increasingly dangerous political and ecological position. Bache (2000, p. 233) writes thus:

> Our best environmental estimates are that current industrial and social trends are driving humanity towards a devastating ecological and economic collapse that will take place probably within the next several decades. As we show no signs of pulling back from our suicidal policy of perpetual economic expansion, the only uncertainty seems to be how severe the ecological overshoot will be and how catastrophic the period or periods of recovery after the collapse takes place.

Bache's prediction has now truly caught up with us. Considering that, as Krieger (ibid.) suggests, those who put the frog into the pot are not likely to be the same ones who will take the frog out, we need, as Einstein warned, 'a new way of thinking'. Without such a way of thinking and perceiving the world in a holistic and interdisciplinary manner, the fate of humankind is likely to continue to be to a large extent determined by our unconscious motivations, by addictive compensatory pseudo self-support mechanisms, and by Gaia's inherent self-regulation forces, such as psychosomatic illnesses and natural disasters. The current acceleration of rollbacks of environmental achievements at all levels of administration, and the continuing increase of polarisation between the rich and poor suggests that humans are presently not consciously able to make the far-reaching conscious efforts needed to instigate the urgently needed planetary recovery.

On the positive side, it is important to acknowledge that an increasing number of people are motivated to examine their problems with emotional and psychosocial sustainability. These people seek assistance in facing their disowned feelings and conflicts in order to heal themselves and become sustainable human beings. These are people, who, like most of the research participants that have contributed to this book, have learned that an increased sense of self also increases their capacity to care for others and the other-than-human environment, and that deep change and healing require consistent work.

In the USA, hundreds of cities, counties, colleges, and businesses have decided to ignore federal policies and push ahead with efforts to meet the guidelines set out by the Kyoto Climate Change Accord. The Californian Governor Arnold Schwarzenegger even wants to go beyond these targets. With some delay, the first American newspapers are now publishing editorials on the so-called Downing Street memos – texts that indicate that Congress and the American public were deceived about the reasons for starting Gulf War II. The leaked memos prove that intelligence had been fixed to achieve regime change in Iraq. As we are preparing this book for publication, the support for the Bush Administration is dwindling and the first black person is only months away from moving into the Oval Office.

In Germany, to use another example, the so-called Giessen-Study on the Germans' sense of self at the turn of the millennium revealed that an increasing number of German adults (cited in Richter, 2002):

- have shifted their focus from competition towards a sense of mutuality;
- seek other conflict solutions than arguments;
- find it easier to commit themselves to long-term relationships;
- care more for others;
- seek meaningful associations with other people;
- want to become more honest in relationships; and
- make bigger efforts to achieve set goals.

Richter concludes that many Germans are making strong efforts to grow emotionally and to shift from a narcissistic self-experience towards an experience of mutuality.

The above examples of positive self-development and environmentally sustainable actions indicate that an increasing number of people in the Western world reject the new economic world order and the unsustainable tenets of hypermodernism. Although the present development suggests that we may not yet have reached the low point of decadence, and that the situation will get worse for many people and the more-than-human environment, there can be no doubt that a process of consciousness transformation is now under way. This process is carried by millions of people who have learned that a sustainable natural environment has to be based on a high level of personal sustainability. During this painful process of healing and growth, our task as ecological educators and growth facilitators (sustainability workers) will be to assist our fellow human beings in becoming personally and environmentally sustainable people for a sustainable world. We are now called upon to create the political structures, courses, and processes needed to assist people in healing themselves and the Earth.

Appendix A – Summary of Research Findings

The following topics were explored:

- Views on the environment;
- Behaviours and feelings towards the environment;
- Connections between people's feelings, emotions, and behaviours towards the natural environment;
- Learning about environmental deterioration and influences affecting behaviour changes; and
- Views on sustainability and sustainable living.

Question 1: What do people associate with the notion of environment?

Comments on findings

A significant number of research participants define 'environment' in ways that extend the boundaries beyond the academic notion of the natural and built environment into relational, emotional, and energetic spheres. This expanded understanding of 'environment' will be further examined in Chapter 7 under the topic, Holistic Eco-self Consciousness.

Question 2: What do people associate with the notion of harming the environment?

Comments on findings

Similar to the responses to the previous question, some research participants have extended their views on what constitutes the environment and on what it means to harm this environment by including their relationships towards their bodies and to other people. Harming the environment for these participants not only relates to burning coal fires and throwing out recyclable garbage, but also denotes behaviours such as meeting people with a lack of empathy, a failure to resolve conflicts, and the uncritical transposing of our values to indigenous people, and possibly to other people in a more general sense.

Remarkable in the responses to the question is that some research participants emphasise the destructive effects of emotional and psychosocial factors, such as greed, lack of self-esteem, lack of self-care, negative thinking about self, and the projection of image. By holding these views, they point at the emotional underpinnings of our ecological crises.

The research participants have in general a high level of awareness of the mechanisms contributing to the degradation of the natural environment. Whereas a number of participants are aware that they can choose to engage with the world in different and more sustainable ways, others acknowledge that in some areas our choices are limited (for example, in relation to packaged goods).

The responses to the question relating to the justification of harmful behaviour shows a wide variety of feelings, ranging from a sense of powerlessness, to the admission of being addicted, and to the blaming of others for their irresponsible behaviour. A psychological interpretation of these responses suggests conceptualising these feelings as emotional defence mechanisms against the experience of conflict and anxiety.

Question 3: *What are the connections betweens people's feelings, emotions, and their behaviour towards the environment?*

Comments on findings

Research participants provided a wide variety of responses to this question. What stands out is that a number of participants experience that being tense, tired (stressed) and busy reduces their capacity to care for the environment. These responses confirm my [WHO????] own observations and the views expressed to me in talks with clients and with students in training programs.

The logical consequence of these findings suggests that there is perceived to be a significant link between personal and ecological unsustainability, that personal and ecological sustainability inform one another, and that these are integrated parts of circular processes.

The research participants most commonly expressed that they know what it is that harms the environment, and that they love the environment, but that nevertheless they still choose to pursue a lifestyle that has detrimental effects on the environment. Responses to earlier questions suggest that this lifestyle is particularly associated with the perceived necessity of driving cars.

Research participants responded to this question by reporting feelings of irritation, frustration, anger, and powerlessness and by mentioning some strategies that they use to deal with these feelings. The ways in which people respond to these feelings and emotions are varied. Whereas some participants appear to take direct action by talking to the perpetrator, usually in a non-confronting manner, others appear to choose to lead by example and by using their workplace to create change. Some people share their grievances with the relevant political bodies. It appears, however, that these bodies are not always responsive.

The research indicates that most people take action where they can identify a safe way of doing this. Some are concerned with ensuring that their approach is adequate to the situation in size and quality.

Question 4: How have people learned about the deterioration of the environment and what has influenced them to change their perception of and behaviour towards the environment?

Comments on findings

Although acknowledging that the number of research participants was too small to allow statistical interpretations and rigorous comparisons of data, the above responses do suggest that the research participants learned more about the environment from courses and their own observation than from books, magazines, radio, and television. This finding is supported by the fact that many research participants stated that they learned about the environment and changed their behaviour through self-maintenance processes, including yoga, self-esteem courses, psychotherapy, meditation, witchcraft, and bodywork. The findings support the notion held by deep ecologists, social ecologists, and many ecofeminists that the personal is political, and that working for increased personal sustainability also benefits society and the other-than-human environment.

Although acknowledging that the small number of research participants does not allow generalising claims about the significance of different choices, it is nevertheless interesting, and worth further examination, that the participants chose holistic counselling and psychotherapy approaches rather than behaviourist and cognitive ones. This can be read as indicating that deep changes in awareness of, and improvement in, behaviour towards the environment appear to be based on an expansion and stabilisation of people's self concept rather than on cognitive learning and superficial behaviour modification. The responses to the previous questions suggest that people's learning about the environment is deeper where their personal healing process is involved, that is, where they have an opportunity to deepen both their personal and their environmental sustainability at the same time.

The environmental educator among the research participants clearly has good reason to be proud of his work when he sees people in industry making changes to their systems. The health practitioners and therapists among the participants without exception report that the increased wellbeing of their clients has an impact on the clients' surrounding environment, which reaches from the immediate family to the "community and world, and beyond to the cosmos/creation".

Question 5: *What do people associate with the notions of sustainability and sustainable living, and which experiences, if any, have enhanced their ability to live sustainably?*

Comments on findings

A number of participants believe that the notion of sustainability not only refers to the preservation of precious resources, but also to issues related to feelings, belonging, and the ability to have a stable self without the need to consume drugs. Some of the data obtained from the research participants, in this sense, suggest that conventional environmentalism has a narrow perception of what constitutes the environment, sustainability, and sustainable living.

The responses show that there is no clearly defined understanding of what it means to live sustainably or to be a sustainable human being. At the same time, almost all research participants indicate that living sustainably relates to deeper issues than the ones concerned with keeping our natural environment free from pollution and waste. By talking about balance and longevity, a healthy inner and outer world, a spiritual appreciation, and feelings and emotions, they point to an understanding of sustainable living that stretches across the emotional, social, and environmental/ecological spheres.

Apart from one participant, who seems to feel that he or she does not have much influence in shaping his or her fate and sustainability, and who appears quite resigned about a possible early death due to human ignorance, arrogance and greed, most participants appear to be actively engaged in making their lives more emotionally, socially and ecologically sustainable. Having identified systems to assist them in staying fit, flexible, and emotionally balanced, they point to the results of these activities by emphasising their increased awareness of their bodies, small signals, issues they marginalise, and people's struggles. An important outcome that we believe deserves further examination is the degree to which our ecological predicament may be linked to greed, hatred, and ignorance.

Research participants also responded to this question by mentioning that their increased personal sustainability has led to effects such as an increased:

- emotional availability;

- ability to communicate;
- ability to feel an interconnectedness between 'all that is';
- understanding of their impact on the natural environment;
- need to eat seasonal food;
- need to contribute towards environmental and social change; and a
- commitment to their profession.

One of the participants also reports that he has become aware that deep change requires us to model sustainable behaviour.

Additional Comments

Re: Views on the environment

Most of the interviewed research participants, who consisted of naturopaths, counsellors, psychotherapists, and one environmental educator, demonstrated an expanded understanding of the notion of environment by including aspects such as parent's love, emotional and energetic phenomena, and the importance of community and relationships. These findings suggest that the dominant, generally quite narrow, approaches to environmental education need to be broadened. This also implies that the notions of ecology and sustainability need to be re-examined and reframed in broader contexts. Although these findings are meaningful as personal accounts of lived experience, they need to be placed in a larger theoretical context, both to deepen our understanding of where the research participants are coming from and to develop more appropriate strategies for effective action.

Re: Behaviours and feelings towards the environment

Research participants responded to the questions by listing the commonly acknowledged aspects of our ecological crises, such as overconsumption, water wastage, and the effects of greenhouse gases. Whereas most environmentalists and environmental educators remain within this framework of understanding, most of the research participants went well beyond this by including self-related and internal factors, such as negative thinking about self, self-esteem, image, lack of self-care, ignorance, and greed. By mentioning such contributing factors, they revealed that they had employed, knowingly or unknowingly, the sort of perspectives common in depth psychology and holism in developing their understanding of ecological crises.

The question regarding possible justifications for environmentally destructive behaviour tended to generate responses that could serve as defence mechanisms against anxiety and an awareness of conflict. Within the context of depth psychology and other holistic perspectives, the ignorance, powerlessness, carelessness, and addictions mentioned can be regarded as symptoms and manifestations of our struggles with maintaining at least some superficial self-stability in the face of the deterioration of environmental and psychosocial living conditions.

Re: Connections between people's feelings, emotions, and behaviours towards the natural environment

Responses to this question were diverse. Whereas some people experience their anger about witnessing destructive acts against the environment as disempowering, others are motivated to take action exactly because of their awareness of these aggressive acts. Remarkable is the repeatedly mentioned experience that being busy significantly reduces ability and motivation to care for the environment. In other words, even people who are concerned about the environment reduce their active caring under time constraints. This suggests that time management, which can be regarded as an important aspect of self-care, is obviously not only important for people's personal wellbeing, but also for the integrity of our biosphere. However, more important will be a cultural change that prioritises wellbeing over busyness.

Re: Learning about environmental deterioration and influences affecting behaviour changes

As the listed responses to the questionnaire indicate, the research participants learned about the state of the environment and were influenced to change by an amazing array of information channels, processes, and techniques relating to a diverse range of social and spiritual worldviews. However, as indicated above in my comments on the findings, the number of research participants was too small to allow for a statistically useful interpretation of these data. At the same time, it was to be expected that naturopaths, counsellors and psychotherapists, as for professionals in other fields, would perceive environmental issues from a biased perspective – one that is shaped by the worldviews underpinning their training, and by the constraints of their working conditions. In this sense, the only thing that could be concluded is that people do indeed make meaning of our ecological crises through the lenses shaped by the contexts in which they were socialised and trained.

It seems, however, that what enabled the naturopaths, counsellors and psychotherapists interviewed for this study to change their behaviours challenges the assumptions of most environmental educators concerning how to facilitate change.

Re: Associations and experiences regarding sustainability and sustainable living

In addition to the typical characteristics of sustainability usually mentioned by many environmentalists, most of the participants chosen for this study demonstrate a wide-ranging and inclusive understanding of the notion of sustainability. They associate sustainability with industry and business, relationships, the actions and potential of individuals, a sense of belongingness, and even with life as a whole. Similarly, they associate the notion of sustainable living not only with issues relating to resource conservation and the health of the natural environment, but also with concerns such as:

- the internal world of feelings and emotions;
- an ability to maintain inner health;
- longevity;
- an interest in self-analysis;
- an awareness of what they marginalise;
- an empathy for people's struggles; and
- a tolerance for 'otherness'.

Appendix B - Learning for Sustainable Living Programme

Learning for Sustainable Living

learning psychosocial and ecological living skills for a sustainable earth

There is a growing recognition that community development, population health, ecosystem health, and social justice are highly interrelated and influenced by a wide range of factors. These factors include:

- lifestyle-related and psychosomatic causes of physical and mental illnesses;
- our sense of embodiment and connectedness;
- pollution of water, soil and air;
- the availability, quality, and purity of foods and drinks;
- appropriate amounts of mental stimulation and physical exercise;
- our ability to develop and maintain a coherent sense of self within an emotionally supportive family and wider community;
- our ability to form and maintain harmonious and nurturing relationships with one another and with nature;
- opportunities to engage in meaningful careers and to receive adequate remuneration for one's efforts;
- our ability to deal with life's demands and challenges without having to engage in addictive compensatory practices such as 'retail therapy' and the use of alcohol, smoking, and illicit drugs;
- our ability to lead a happy and sustainable life on a small ecological footprint;
- the availability of well-supported and adequate health and community support systems; and
- political and educational institutions that foster participation in political processes and equality between the genders and ethnic groups.

Currently, a growing number of psychologically oriented ecologists observe that many of the worthwhile advancements in technology and education are being undermined by the need for many of us to stabilise our sense of self and to find meaning through the consumption of non-essential goods and services. These scholars consequently emphasise the necessity to employ a complementary ecopsychological and interdisciplinary approach to research and Sustainability Education. Such a 'Learning for Sustainable Living' will address the deep emotional and psychosocial roots of our ecological crises by enabling us to:

- form and maintain nurturing relationships and to find creative solutions for conflicts;
- enhance their communication skills;
- find opportunities to be creative and to develop sustainable and satisfying personal agendas;
- experience a strong sense of self without the use of alcohol, nicotine, drugs, or 'retail therapy' (the compensatory consumption of non-essential goods and services);
- find inner peace and time to experience a deep connection with nature;
- actively contribute to ecological sustainability;
- engage with appropriate 'green' technologies; and to
- understand the complex interdependencies between emotional, psychosocial, and environmental sustainability.

The 13 units of the *Learning for Sustainable Living Programme* described below have been designed to provide professionals with the competencies required to facilitate emotional, psychosocial, psychosomatic, and environmental literacy and wellbeing in the community.

1 - Social Ecology and Aspects of Unsustainable Living

Using social ecology thinking, this unit provides an overview of the complex and interrelated aspects of our ecological crises, and of sustainable and unsustainable living. Emphasising that our ecological predicament is far broader and deeper than is currently acknowledged, it includes an examination of the psychological background of terrorism, racism, and of practices that continue to waste precious resources and threaten wellbeing, equity, social cohesion and environmental health.

2 – Sustainability Mapping and Education for Transformation

Participants in this unit will have opportunities to map their lives in terms of emotional, social and environmental sustainability. Drawing on paper the complex web of relationships with people, workplaces, organisations, spiritual affiliations, assets, and other factors, will enable participants to recognise more clearly which aspects of their lives are most sustainable and which are less sustainable and in need of change. This process will be followed by discussions that will enable participants to envisage possibilities for change and the 'redesigning' of relationships to enhance sustainability and quality of life.

3 - Sustainable Embodiment, Wellbeing, and Health

In this unit we will share insights and 'infeels' into key aspects of what it means to be sustainably embodied. Research has demonstrated that the current dominance of narcissistic and functional values on embodiment, the lack of psychosomatic literacy, and our struggles with body-mind unity experiences are at the core of our ecological predicament.

4 - The Sustainability Revolution

A comprehensive overview of practices such as recycling, green investing, composting, and the many ways in which we can tread more lightly on the planet, will be discussed in this unit. We will also focus on ecological strategies and principles, such as Deep Ecology's Basic Principles, the Precautionary Principle, Permaculture, the Five Principles of Ecological Design, and others. Participants will have opportunities to share their experiences in applying these sustainability principles.

5 – Depression, Decadence and the Collapse of Complex Societies

In this unit we explore key aspects of economic depression and decadence. We will also explore how unsustainable economic practices and decadent perceptions can lead to the collapse of complex societies. Using the Great Depression as an example, learners will engage with literature on the causes and effects of this recurring economic and social phenomenon.

Decadence in the Roman Empire was characterised by:

- a breakdown of faith and morality;
- unchecked power;
- overcentralised governments;
- lethargic bureaucracies;
- a decline in self-reliance;

- a shrinking of the middle class;
- an increased use of cheap labour to increase profits for the wealthy;
- an increased appetite for violence, drugs, distraction, perversity, cruelty and sensation;
- an erosion of civil society;
- a loss of higher purpose in human life;
- the trivialisation of art; and
- the breakdown of the family as an institution.

Many of these features can be identified in our hypermodern era, an era that Swimme and Berry call the 'terminal cenozoic'. In the last part of this unit you explore features of a possible collapse of western societies. You will in particular engage with the views of Toynbee, Tainter, and Diamond.

6 – Meditation and Sustainable Living

This unit emphasises the importance of our connection with nature, and how the loss of this connection is contributing to our ecological crises. We will examine how people in modern societies, often unconsciously, commonly try to satisfy their natural needs to be part of nature through memberships in clubs, sects, or through the use of drugs. Practical meditation exercises will assist course participants in enhancing their felt connection with nature.

7 – Aspects of Ecological Consciousness

Here we will review key aspects of social psychology, cognitive psychology and behaviourist psychology, and how these approaches are presently used in environmental education to influence people's behaviour to enhance sustainability. The advantages and disadvantages of each of these will be discussed and compared with the possibilities offered by depth psychological, and holistic and transpersonal approaches to ecological change, healing and wellbeing.

8 - Ecological Counselling and Eco-psychotherapy
This unit offers insights into the emerging fields of eco-counselling and eco-psychotherapy, ways of working with people that consider the role of the natural environment as provider of healing and nurturing. Effective

approaches will be discussed, and opportunities provided to practice key elements of these approaches.

9 – Psychosomatic Medicine, Cancer, and Earth Cancer

In this unit we will discuss key aspects of psychosomatic and environmental medicine. Illness is here regarded as a conflict solution, a response to environmental health hazards, an overflow-valve for physio-emotional charge, and as a mirror image of our inner unhealed world. These understandings are then applied to the phenomenon of cancer and the view held by some scholars that in many ways modern cultures are behaving like 'cancers' on the Earth.

10 - Lifestyle Choices, ADD, and ADHD

Here we will provide a holistic understanding of two increasingly common manifestations of unsustainable living: ADD (Attention Deficit Disorder) and ADHD (Attention Deficit Hyperactivity Disorder). These disorders defy a clear categorisation as psychosomatic or an environment-induced illnesses, and are probably best understood as predictable outcomes of our modern consumer lifestyles. Current psychosocial research links ADD and ADHD with issues such as excessive sugar and caffeine consumption, over-stimulation through TV and computer games, and excessive pressure to perform at school. On the other hand, the conditions are also often associated with a chronic lack of the following: sleep, physical activity, calm and conscious parental attention, support in conflicts, and access to nature.

11 - Psychosocially Sustainable Corporate Practices

Creating a sustainable social and environmental environment will be dependent on the willingness of politicians and business leaders to consider the impact of their activities on all stakeholders and to implement ecologically sustainable production and marketing practices. In this unit we will focus on key issues of corporate sustainable responsibility and business ethics, discuss their possibilities and limitations, and explore ways of helping responsible business leaders resist short-sighted, unrealistic, and unsustainable expectations of returns on investment.

12 – Young People – Future Leaders

Currently young people struggling with the confusing complexity of growing up in an unsustainable social and environmental environment are mainly met with a management-style approach to addressing their difficulties. Social ecology thinking suggests that these attempts to make the perceptions and behaviours fit neatly into a world with unsustainable values will in the long term only exacerbate the problems and perpetuate them into the future. In this unit we will explore ways of addressing youth issues based on the promotion and development of age-appropriate life skills. This exploration acknowledges that the struggles of young people pose challenges to learn and grow for all of us.

13 – Social Ecology Approaches to Population Health

A holistic and social ecology approach to population health recognises that our current understanding of illness and wellness is socially constructed and thus reflects our modern individualistic, mechanistic, technology-driven, and economy-oriented worldview. In this course we will consider key features of an approach to medicine that acknowledges the importance and ecological usefulness of all aspects of nature, including the existence of micro-organisms and of our often unconscious choices of places and lifestyles.

References

Abram, D 1995, 'The Ecology of Magic', in T Roszak, ME Gomes, AD Kanner (eds.) *Ecopsychology*, Sierra Club Books, San Francisco, pp. 301–15.

Abram, D 1997, *The Spell of the Sensuous*, Random House, New York.

Ahmad, EA 2000 *Confronting Empire*, South End Press, Cambridge, MA, USA.

Aitken, R 1982, *Taking the Path of Zen*, North Pot Press / Farrar, Strauss & Giroux, New York.

Alexander, F 1950, *Psychosomatic Medicine: Its Principles and Applications*, Norton, New York.

Ali, T 2003, *Bush in Babylon*, Verso, London.

Almaas, AH 1996, *The Point of Existence: Transformation of Narcissism into Self-realization*, Diamond Books, Berkeley, CA, USA.

Alterman, E 'Bush's War on the Press', *The Nation*, viewed 16 January 2006, <www.thenation.com/doc20050509/alterman>

Anderson, JR 1983, *The Architecture of Cognition*, Harvard University Press, Cambridge, MA, USA.

Anthony, C 1995, 'Ecopsychology and the Deconstruction of Whiteness', in T Roszak, ME Gomes, AD Kanner (eds.) *Ecopsychology*, Sierra Club Books, San Francisco, pp. 263–78.

Aronson, E. & O'Leary, M 1983, 'The Relative Effectiveness of Models and Prompts on Energy Conservation: A Field Experiment in a Shower Room', *Journal of Environmental Systems*, no. 12, pp. 219–24.

Ashton, J & Laura, R 1998, *Perils of Progress*, UNSW Press, Sydney.

Australian Bureau of Statistics, *Australian Yearbook of Statistics*, viewed 5 July 2005, http://www.abs.gov.au/Ausstats/abs@.nsf/0/C67A858BA00CB846CA 2568A9001393C6 ?Open

Bache, CM 2000, *Dark Night, Early Dawn*, SUNY Press, Albany, NY, USA.

Baginski, B & Sharamon, S 1988, *Reiki: Universal Life Energy*, Life Rhythm Publication, Mendocino, CA, USA.

Bahne-Bahnson, C 1982, 'Psychosomatic Issues in Cancer', in RL Gallon (ed.) *The Psychosomatic Approach to Illness,* Elsevier North Holland, New York.

Banerjee, SB, 2007, *Corporate Social Responsibility: The Good, the Bad, the Ugly*, Edward Elgar, Cheltenham, UK.

Barrows, A 1995, 'The Ecopsychology of Child Development', in T Roszak, ME Gomes & AD Kanner (eds.) *Ecopsychology*, Sierra Club Books, San Francisco, pp. 101–10.

Basch, MF 1980, *Doing Psychotherapy*, Basic Books, New York.

Basch, MF 1988, *Understanding Psychotherapy: The Science behind the Art*, Basic Books, New York.

BBC News, 'Mobile Phone "Brain Risk"', 6 November 1999, viewed 21 March 2005, <http://news.bbc.co.uk/1/hi/health/507112.stm>.

Bechtel, RB & Churchman, A (eds.) 2002, *Handbook of Environmental Psychology*, John Wiley & Sons, Hoboken, NJ, USA.
Beck, DE & Cowan, CC 1996, *Spiral Dynamics: Mastering Values, Leadership and Change: Exploring the New Science of Mimetics*, Blackwell, Cambridge, MA, USA.
Beck, U 1992, *Risk Society: Towards a New Modernity*, Sage, London.
Beck, U 2000, *The Brave New World of Work*, Polity, Cambridge, UK.
Beder, S 2002, *Global Spin*, Green Books, Foxhole, Dartington, Totness, UK.
Behaviourism, Stanford Encyclopedia of Philosophy, viewed 30 December 2005, <www.plato.stanford.edu/entries / behaviourism>
Bell, S & Morse, S 1999, *Sustainability Indicators: Measuring the Immeasurable*, Earthscan, London.
Berger, A 1999a, *Earth Requiem*, Association for Experimental Education, Individual monograph, # 300198, Boulder, CO, USA.
Berger, A 1999b, 'On Adventure Therapy and Earth Healing', *Australian Journal of Outdoor Education*, vol. 4, no. 1, pp. 33–9.
Berkowitz, L 1972, 'Frustrations, comparisons, and other sources of emotion aroused as contributors to social unrest', *Journal of Social Issues*, no. 28, pp. 77–92.
Berkowitz, L 1973, 'The case for bottling up rage', *Psychology Today*, vol. 7, no. 2, pp. 24 ff.
Berry, T 1988, *The Dream of the Earth*, Random House, New York.
Bertalanffy von, L. 1949, 'Zu einer allgemeinen Systemlehre', *Biologia Generalis*, no. 195, pp. 114–29.
Bertalanffy von, L 1955, 'An Essay on the Relativity of Categories', *Philosophy of Science*, no. 225, pp. 243–63.
Bertalanffy von, L 1960 'General System Theory and the Behavioral Sciences', in JM Tanner & B Inhelder (eds.) *Discussions on Child Development*, vol. 4/1960 London.
Bertalanffy von, L 1966, 'Mind and Body Re-examined', *Journal of Humanistic Psychology*, no. 6, pp. 113–38.
Bertalanffy von, L. 1976, *General Systems Theory: Foundations, Development, Applications*, George Braziller Publishing, New York.
Biography of Thomas Hobbes, viewed 2 June 2005, <http://www.bookrags.com/biography-thomas-hobbes/>.
Blackburn, S 1994, *Oxford Dictionary of Philosophy*, Oxford.
Blum, W 2003, *Rogue State: A Guide to the World's Only Superpower*, Zed Books, London.
Boadella, D (ed.) 1976, *In the Wake of Reich*, Coventure, London.
Boadella, D 1987, *Lifestreams*, Routledge & Kegan Paul, New York.
Bookchin, M 1980, *Towards an Ecological Society*, Black Rose Books, Montreal, Canada.
Bossel, H 1997, 'Finding a Comprehensive Set of Indicators of Sustainable Development by Application of Orientation Theory', in B Moldan & S

Billharz (eds.) *Sustainability Indicators*, John Wiley & Sons, New York, pp. 101–09.

Boyd, RD & Myers, GJ 1988, 'Transformative Education', *International Journal of Lifelong Education*, vol. 7, no. 4, pp. 261–84.

Boyesen, ML 1974, 'Emotional Repression as a Somatic Compromise: Stages in the Physiology of Neurosis', *Energy and Character*, vol. 5, no, 2.

Boyesen, G 1976, 'The Primary Personality and its Relationship to the Streamings', in D Boadella (ed.) *In the Wake of Reich*, Coventure, London.

Boyesen, G 1985, *Entre Psyche et Soma*, Payot, Paris.

Bowlby, J 1997, *Attachment*, Random House UK, London.

Bradley, I 1990, *God is Green*, Dorton, Londman & Todd, London.

Braeutigam, W & Christian, P 1986, *Psychosomatische Medizin*, Georg Thieme Verlag, Stuttgart, Germany.

Braud, W & Anderson, R 1998, *Transpersonal Research Methods for the Social Sciences: Honoring Human Experiences*, Sage, Thousand Oaks, CA, USA.

British Government Sustainability Indicators, viewed 14 February 2005, <http://www.sustainable-development.gov.uk/uk_strategy/quality/life/03.htm>.

Bregg, P. 1991, *Toxic Psychiatry*, St. Martin's, New York.

Bucke, RM 1991, *Cosmic Consciousness*, E.P. Dutton, New York.

BushGreenwatch, viewed 3 June 2005, info@ bushgreenwatch.org.

Cahalan, W 1995, 'Ecological Groundedness in Gestalt Therapy', in T Roszak, ME Gomes, AD Kanner (eds.) *Ecopsychology*, Sierra Club Books, San Francisco, pp. 216–23.

Cameron, JI (ed.) 2003, *Changing Places: Re-imaging Australia*, Longueville Books, Double Bay, NSW, Australia.

Campbell, C 1981, *The Schizoid*, Unpublished Paper on Character Structures, Vedam Training Program, Munich, Germany.

Capra, F 1999, 'Ecoliteracy: The Challenge for Education in the Next Century', *Liverpool Schumacher Lectures*, March 20, 1999.

Carey, A & Lohrey A (eds.) 1996, 'Taking the Risk out of Democracy: Corporate Propaganda versus Freedom and Liberty', in *History of Communication*, University of Illinois Press, Champaign, IL, USA.

Carson, R 1962, *Silent Spring*, Houghton Mifflin, Boston, MA, USA.

Cattier, M 1969, *The Life and Work of Wilhelm Reich*, 1st English translation 1971, Avon Books, New York.

Chaplin, JP 1985, *Dictionary of Psychology*, Bantam Doubleday Dell, New York.

Chomsky, N 1957, *Syntactic Structures*, Mouton, The Hague, The Netherlands.

Chomsky, N 1959, 'Review of B. F. Skinner's Verbal Behavior', *Language*, vol. 35 no. 1, pp. 26–58.

Chomsky, N 2002, 'September 11 Aftermath: Where is the World Heading?' in P Scraton (ed.) *Beyond September 11: An Anthology of Dissent*, Pluto Press, London, pp. 66–70.

Chomsky, N 2003, *Pirates and Emperors, Old and New: International Terrorism in the Real World*, South End Press, Cambridge, MA, USA.

Clayton, AM & Ratcliffe, NJ 1996, *Sustainability: A Systems Approach*, Earthscan Publications, London.

Clinebell, H 1996, *Ecotherapy*, Fortress Press, Minneapolis, MN, USA.

Cohen, MJ 2003, *The Web of Life Imperative: Regenerative Ecopsychology Techniques That Help People Think in Balance with Natural Systems*, Institute of Global Education & Trafford Publications, Victoria, BC, Canada.

Conger, JP 1994, *The Body in Recovery*, Frog, Berkeley, CA, USA.

Conn, SA 1995, 'When the Earth Hurts – Who Responds?' in T Roszak, ME Gomes & AD Kanner (eds.) *Ecopsychology*, Sierra Club Books, San Francisco, pp. 156–71.

Cox, E 2000, 'Creating a More Civil Society: Community Level Indicators of Social Capital', *Just Policy: A Journal of Australian Policy*, vol. 19 no. 20, pp. 100–07.

Cranton, P 1994, *Understanding and Promoting Transformative Learning: A guide for Educators of Adults*, Jossey-Bass, San Francisco.

Cranton, P (ed.) 1997, 'Transformative Learning Action: Sights from Practice', *New Directions for Adult and Continuing Education*, no. 74, Jossey-Bass, San Francisco.

Crayton, JW 1983, 'Terrorism and the Psychology of the Self', in LZ Freedman & Y Alexander (eds.) *Perspectives on Terrorism*, Scholarly Resources, Wilmington, DE, USA, pp. 33–41.

Csikszentmihalyi, M 1992, *Flow: The Psychology of Happiness*, Rider, Sydney.

Cunningham, I 1988, 'Interactive Holistic Research: Researching Self-managed Learning', in P Reason, *Human Inquiry in Action: Developments in New Paradigm Research*, Chapter 8, pp. 144 – 162, Sage Publications, London.

Cushman, P 1990, 'Why the Self Is Empty: Towards a Historically Situated Psychology', *American Psychologist*, vol. 45, no. 5, pp. 599–611.

Daloz, L 1986, *Effective Teaching and Mentoring: Realizing the Transformational Power of Adult Learning Experiences*, Jossey-Bass, San Francisco.

Dahlke, R & Klein, N 1986, *Das senkrechte Weltbild*, Hugendubel, Munich, Germany.

Davies, G 2004, *Economia*, ABC Books, Sydney.

Davis, J 1999, *An Outline of Environmental Psychology*, viewed 20 April 2005, <http://www.clem.mscd.edu/ ~davisj/ep/ envpsy.html>.

Davies, TR 1973, 'Aggression, Violence, Revolution and War', in JN Knutson (ed.) *Handbook of Political Psychology*, Jossey-Bass, San Francisco, pp. 234–60.

Dean, SR 1974, 'The Ultraconscious Mind', in J White (ed.) *Frontiers of Consciousness*, Avon Books, New York.

De Gobineau, A 1986, The Equality of the Races, The Noontide Press, original 1854, Los Angeles, USA.

Deikman, AJ 1982, *The Observing Self*, Beacon Press, Boston, USA.

DeMause, L 1982, *Foundations of Psychohistory*, Creative Roots, New York.

DeMause, L 2002, *The Emotional Life of Nations*, Other Press, New York.
Derrida, J 1978, *Writing and Difference*, translated by Alan Bass, University of Chicago Press, Chicago, IL, USA.
De Saussure, F 1965, *Course in General Linguistics*, McGraw-Hill, New York.
Dethlefsen, T 1984, *The Challenge of Fate*, Coventure, London.
Dethlefsen, T & Dahlke, R 1990, *The Healing Power of Illness*, Element, Brisbane, QLD, Australia.
Devall, B 1990, *Simple in Means, Rich in Ends: Practicing Deep Ecology*, Green Print, London.
Devall, B & Sessions, G 1985, *Deep Ecology*, Peregrine Books, Salt Lake City, UT, USA.
De Young, R 1999, 'Environmental Psychology', in DE Alexander & RW Fairbridge (eds.) *Encyclopedia of Environmental Science*, Kluwer Academic Publishers, Hingham, MA, USA.
Diamond, J 2005, *Collapse: How Societies Choose to Fail or Survive*, Allen Lane – Penguin, London.
Diamond, N 1986, 'The Copernican Revolution: Social Foundations of Conceptualizations in Science', in L Levidov (ed.) *Science as Politics*, Free Association Books, London.
Diekmann, A & Preisendoerfer, P 1991, 'Umweltbewusstsein, ökonomische Anreize, und Umweltbefragung', *Schweizerische Zeitschrift für Soziologie*, no. 2 / 91.
Diesendorf, M 1997, 'Ecologically Sustainable Development Principles', in M Diesendorf & C Hamilton (eds.) *Human Ecology, Human Economy: Ideas for an Ecologically Sustainable Future*, Allen & Unwin, Sydney, pp. 64–97.
Diesendorf, M 2000, 'Sustainability and Sustainable Development', in D Dunphy, J Benveniste, A Griffiths & P Sutton (eds.) *Sustainability: The Corporate Challenge of the 21st Century*, Allen & Unwin, Sydney, pp 19–37.
Dilthey, W 2002, *Selected Works, Volume III: The Formation of the Historical World in the Human Sciences*, Princeton University Press, NJ, USA.
Dirkx, JM 1997,'Nurturing Soul in Adult Learning', in P Cranton, (ed.) *Transformative Learning in Action: Insights from Practice, New Directions for Adult and Continuing Education*, no. 74, Jossey-Bass, San Francisco, pp. 79–88.
Dirkx, JM 1998, 'Knowing the Self through Fantasy: Toward a Mytho-poetic View of Transformative Learning', in JC Kimmel, (ed.) *Proceedings of the 39th Annual Adult Education Conference*, University of Incarnate Word and Texas A&M University, San Antonio, TX, USA, pp. 137–42.
Dirkx, JM 2000, 'Transformative Learning and the Journey of Individuation', *ERIC Digest*, no. 223, viewed 11 March 2004, <http://www.cete.org/acve/docgen.asp?tbl=digest&id=108>.
Doerner, K, Plog, U, Teller, C, & Wendt, F 1984, İrren ist menschlich: Lehrbuch der Psychiatrie und Psychotherapie, Psychiatrie Verlag, Rehburg-Loccum, Germany.

Durning, AT 1992, *How Much is Enough? The Consumer Society and the Future of the Earth*, Norton, New York.
Durning, AT 1995, 'Are We Happy Yet?', in T Roszak, ME Gomes & AD Kanner (eds.) Ecopsychology, Sierra Club Books, San Francisco, pp. 68-76.
Dychtwald, K 1986, *Bodymind*, J.P. Tarcher, Los Angeles.
Eagly, AH & Kulesa, P 1997, 'Attitudes, Attitude Structure, and Resistance to Change', in MH Bazerman, DM Messick, AE Tenbrunsel & KA Wade-Benzoni (eds.) *Environment, Ethics and Behaviour: The Psychology of Environmental Valuation and Degradation*, The New Lexington Press, San Francisco.
Eccles, M 1951, *Beckoning Frontiers*, Alfred A. Knopf, New York.
Ecotherapy Newsletter, October 2004, lbuzzell@aol.com.
Ehrenfels von, C & Smith, B 1988, *Foundations of Gestalt Theory*, Philosophia Resources Library, Philosophia Verlag, Munich, Germany.
Eisner, EW 1993, 'Forms of Understanding and the Future of Educational Research' *Educational Researcher*, vol. 22, no. 7, pp. 5-11.
Ekins, PH 1992, *The Gaia Atlas of Green Economics*, Anchor Books, Toronto.
Eliade, M 1959, *Cosmos and History: The Myth of the Eternal Return*, Harper Torchbooks, New York.
Eliade, M 1989, *Shamanism: Archaic Techniques of Ecstasy*, Arkana, London.
Elias, D 1997, 'It's Time to Change Our Minds: An Introduction to Transformative Learning', *Revision*, 20 (1), pp. 2-6.
Elliot, J 1991, *Developing Community-focused Environmental Education through Action Research*, Mimeograph, Centre for Applied Research Education, School of Education, University of East Anglia, Norwich, UK.
Ellner, M & Cort, A 1997, 'Programmed to Die: Cultural Hypothesis and AIDS', in J Lauritsen & I Young (eds.) *The AIDS Cult: Essays on the Gay Health Crisis*, Asklepios, Provincetown, MA, USA.
Ellul, J 1964, *The Technological Society*, Vintage/Random House, New York.
Ely, M, Anzul, M, Friedman, T, Garner, D, & Steinmetz, A 1991, *Doing Qualitative Research: Circles within Circles*, Falmer Press, London.
Emery, F 1981, 'Educational Paradigms', *Human Futures*, Spring 1981, pp. 1-17.
Engelmann, B & Wallraff, G 1976, *Ihr da oben, wir da unten*, Rowohlt Taschenbuch Verlag, Reinbek, Germany.
Enzensberger, HM 1974, *The Consciousness Industry*, Seabury Press, New York.
Erikson, EH 1968, *Identity*, Norton, New York.
Evernden, N 1992, *The Social Creation of Nature*, Johns Hopkins University Press, Baltimore, MD, USA.
Evernden, N 1993, *The Natural Alien: Humankind and Environment*, University of Toronto Press, Toronto.
Fairbairn, WRD 1994, *From Instinct to Self*, Aronson, Northvale, NJ, USA.
Fairfax Digital, July 1, 2005, viewed 1 July 2005, <http://www.smh.com.au/articles/2005/ 06/30/1119724757442.html?oneclick -true>.
Fanon, FA 1967, *Dying Colonialism*, Grove Press, New York.

Fanon, F 1969, *Black Skin, White Masks*, Grove Press, New York.
Fanon, F 1986, *The Wretched of the Earth*, Grove Press, New York.
Feigenbaum, EA 1970, 'Information Processing and Memory', in DA Norman (ed.) *Models of Human Learning*, Academic Press, New York.
Ferster, CB & Skinner, BF 1957, *Schedules of Reinforcement*, Appleton-Century-Crofts, New York.
Fien, J 1992, *Education for the Environment: A Critical Ethnography*, University of Brisbane, Brisbane, QLD, Australia.
Fien, J 1993, *Education for the Environment: Critical Curriculum Theorising and Environmental Education*, Deakin University, Geelong, VIC, Australia.
Fien, J & Greenall Gough, A 1996,'Environmental Education', in R Gilbert (ed.) *Studying Society and Environment: A Handbook for Teachers*, MacMillan Education Australia, Sydney.
Finger, M 1993, 'Politics of the UNCED Process', in W Sachs (ed.) *Global ecology*, ZED Books/Fernwood Publishing, London.
Finger, M 1994, 'From Knowledge to Action? Exploring the Relationships between Environmental Experiences, Learning and Behaviour', *Journal of Social Issues, vol.* 50, no. 3, pp. 179–97.
Fisher, A 2002, *Radical Ecopsychology*, SUNY Press, Albany, NY, USA.
Flew, A 1979, *A Dictionary of Philosophy*, Pan Books, London.
Fox, W 1990, *Toward a Transpersonal Ecology*, Shambhala, Boston, MA, USA.
Freire, P 1970, *Pedagogy of the Oppressed*, Herder & Herder, New York.
Freud, A 1937, *The Ego and the Mechanisms of Defence*, Hogarth Press, London.
Freud, S 1910, 'The origin and development of psychoanalysis', *American Journal of Psychology,* no. 21, pp. 181–218.
Freud, S 1920, *Beyond the Pleasure Principle,* Standard Edition vol. 18, 1955, Hogarth Press, London.
Freud, S 1923, *The Ego and the Id*, Standard Edition, vol. 19, 1961, Hogarth Press, London.
Freud, S 1926, *Inhibitions, Symptoms and Anxiety*, Standard Edition, vol. 20, 1959, Hogarth Press, London.
Freud, S 1935, *A General Introduction to Psychoanalysis*, Washington Square Press, New York.
Freud, S 1940, *An Outline of Psychoanalysis,* Standard Edition, vol. 23, 1964, Hogarth Press, London.
Freud, S 1961, *The Future of an Illusion*, W.W. Norton, New York.
Freud, S 1964, 'Splitting of the Ego in the Process of Defence', in J Strachey, & A Freud (eds.) *Standard Edition*, vol., Hogarth Press, London.
Friend, AM & Rappaport DJ 1989, 'Environmental Information Systems for Sustainable Development', Proceedings of 7th Annual Meeting of the International Association for Impact Assessment, Montreal. 24-28 June, 1989, Institute for Research on Environment and Economy, University of Ottawa, Ottawa, Canada.
Fromm, E 1955, *The Sane Society*, Fawcett World Library, New York.

Fromm, E Suzuki, DT de Martino, R 1971, *Zen Buddhismus und Psychoanalyse*, Suhrkamp Verlag, Frankfurt/Main.
Fromm, E 1973, *The Anatomy of Human Destructiveness*, Pimlico/Random House, London.
Fromm, E 1979, *To Have or to Be*, Abacus, London.
Gaard, G 1993, 'Living Interconnections with Animals and Nature', in *Ecofeminism*: *Women, Animals, Nature*, Temple University Press, Philadelphia, PA, USA, pp. 1-12.
Gallop, CG 1997, 'Indicators and Their Use: Information for Decision-making', in B Moldan & S Billharz (eds.) *Sustainability Indicators*, John Wiley & Sons, New York, pp. 13–27.
Gebser, J 1986, *The Ever-present Origin*, Ohio University Press, Athens, OH, USA.
Geller, ES Scott, E, Winnett, RA. & Everett PB 1982, *Preserving the Environment: New Strategies for Behavior Change*, Pergamon Press, New York.
Gerald Heard, <http://home.wxs.nl/~brouw724/GeraldHeard/html>, viewed 20 May 2005
Gergen, KJ 1991, *The Saturated Self*, Basic Books, Harper Collins Publishers, New York.
Gergen, K.J 1997, 'The Place of the Psyche in a Constructed World', *Theory and Psychology*, no. 7, pp. 723–46.
Giesecke, H 2004, *Einführung in die Pädagogik*, Juventa, Weinheim, Germany.
Glaser, BG & Strauss, AL 1967, *The Discovery of Grounded Theory*, Aldine, Chicago, IL, USA.
Glendinning, C 1995, 'Technology, Trauma, and the Wild', in T Roszak, ME Gomes, & AD Kanner (eds.) *Ecopsychology*, Sierra Club Books, San Francisco, pp. 41–54.
Goerlitz, G. 1998, *Körper und Gefühl in der Psychotherapie – Basisübungen*, J. Pfeiffer Verlag, Munich, Germany.
Gomes, ME & Kanner, AD 1995, 'The Rape of the Well-maidens: Feminist Psychology and the Environmental Crisis', in T Roszak, ME Gomes & AD Kanner (eds.) *Ecopsychology*, Sierra Club, San Francisco, pp. 111 - 21.
Goodman, F 1990, *Where the Spirits Ride in the Wind: Trance Journeys and Other Ecstatic Experiences*, Indiana University Press, Bloomington, IN, USA.
Goodman, P 1964, *Compulsory Miseducation and the Community of Scholars*, Vintage Books, New York.
Gosselink, L *Creativity and Mental Illness*, viewed 6 January 2006, <serendip.brynmawr.edu/bb/neuro/neuro99/web2/Gosselink.html>
Gough, A 1997, *Education and the Environment: Policy, Trends and the Problems of Margalisation,* Australian Council for Educational Research, Melbourne, VIC, Australia.

Gough, A 2002, 'Mutualism: A different Agenda for Environmental and Science Education', *International Journal of Science Education*, vol. 24, no 11, pp. 1201–15.
Gough, N 1987, 'Learning with Environments', in I Robottom (ed.) *Environmental Education: Practice and Possibility*, Deakin University Press, Geelong, Victoria, Australia.
Grabov, V 1997, 'The Many Facets of Transformative Learning Theory and Practice', in P Cranton (ed.) *Transformative Learning Action: Insights from Practice, New Directions for Adult and Continuing Education*, no. 74, Jossey-Bass, San Francisco, pp. 89–96.
Graves, C 1974, 'Human Nature Prepares for a Momentous Leap', *The Futurist*, April 1974, pp. 72–87.
Gray, L 1995, 'Shamanic Counselling and Ecopsychology', in T Roszak, ME Gomes & AD Kanner (eds.) *Ecopsychology*, Sierra Club Books, San Francisco, pp. 172–82.
Greenway, R 1995, 'The Wilderness Effect and Ecopsychology', in T Roszak, ME Gomes & AD Kanner. (eds.) *Ecopsychology*, Sierra Club Books, San Francisco, pp. 122–35.
Gugerli-Dolder, B 2000, 'Denken wie eine Spinne: Tiefenökologie – ein neuer Impuls für die Umweltbildung?' paper presented at *Ecokultur: Umwelterziehung an der Schwelle zum 3. Jahrtausend*, 20 and 21, Oktober 2000, HOB Schule, Bozen, Switzerland.
Guntrip, H 1980, *Schizoid Phenomena, Object Relations and the Self*, The Hogarth Press, London.
Gurr, TR 1970, *Why Men Rebel*, Princeton University Press, Princeton, NJ, USA.
Hamilton, C 2003 *Growth Fetish*, Allen & Unwin, Crows Nest, NSW, Australia.
Hamilton, C & Barbato, C 2005, *Who Drives 4WDs?* Australia Institute Webpaper, September 2005, p. 1).
Hammond, LJ 2004, *Decadence and Renaissance*, viewed 11 December 2004, <http:// www.ljhammond.com/cwgt/14.htm>.
Harms, V *Our planet, Our Selves*, viewed 6 May 2005, <http://ecopsychology.athabascau.ca/0197/tro.htm>.
Harner, J 1973, *Hallucinogens and Shamanism*, Oxford University Press, Oxford.
Heisterkamp, G 1993, *Heilsame Berührungen: Praxis leibfundierter analytischer Psychotherapie*, J. Pfeiffer Verlag, Munich, Germany
Henschel, G & Vester, F 1977, *Krebs – fehlgesteuertes Leben*, Deutscher Taschenbuch Verlag, Munich, Germany.
Hern, WM 1990, 'Why Are There So Many of Us? Description and Diagnosis of a Planetary Ecopathological Process', *Population and Environment*, vol. 12, no 1, pp. 9-39.
Herman, ES 1982, *The Real Terror Network: Terrorism, Fact and Propaganda*, South End Press, Cambridge, MA, USA.
Heron, J 1996, *Cooperative Inquiry*, Sage, Thousand Oaks, CA, USA.
Hill, SB 1991, 'Ecological and Psychological Pre-requisites for the Establishment of Sustainable Prairie Agricultural Communities', in J

Mart (ed.) *Alternative Futures for Prairie Agricultural Communities*, Faculty of Extension, University of Alberta, Edmonton, AB, Canada, pp. 197–229.

Hill, SB 1992, *Ethics, sustainability and healing: ecological agriculture projects*, viewed 10 November 2004, <http://eap.mcgill.ca/Publications/eap_foot.htm>.

Hill, SB 1999a 'Conservation Challenges and Opportunities for the Future', paper based on the presentation for the Nature Conservation Council of NSW, Sydney University, March 4–5, 1999 entitled: *New Solutions for Sustainability: Integrated Natural Resources Management Conference*.

Hill, SB 1999b 'From Shallow to Deep Environmental Communication: Ecological Sustainability and Co-evolutionary Change', Notes from a presentation at the Australian and New Zealand Communication Association Annual conference entitled *Stirred Not shaken? Communication Challenges and Change*, Sydney, July 5–7, 1999.

Hill, SB 1999c 'Social Ecology as Future Stories', *A Social Ecology Journal*, vol. 1, pp. 197–208.

Hill, SB. *What is Social Ecology?* viewed 13 July 2004, <http://www.zulenet.com/ see/ chair.html>.

Hill, B 2000 *The Peckham Experiment to Health Ecology: An Old Study with Modern Implications*, paper, University of Western Sydney, Sydney.

Hill, SB 2001, 'Transformative Outdoor Education for Healthy Communities with Sustainable Environments', in *Education Outdoors – Our Sense of Place*, *Proceedings* of the 12th *National Outdoor Education Conference*, Victorian Outdoor Education Association, Carlton, Victoria, Australia.

Hill, SB 2001 'Working with Processes of Change, Particularly Psychological Processes, When Implementing Sustainable Agriculture', in H Haidn (ed.) *The best of... Exploring Sustainable Alternatives: An Introduction to Sustainable Agriculture*, Canadian Centre for Sustainable Agriculture, Saskatoon, SK, Canada, pp. 125–34.

Hill, SB 2003a, 'Autonomy, Mutualistic Relationships, Sense of Place, and Conscious Caring: A Hopeful View of the Present and Future', in JI Cameron, (ed.) 2003, *Changing Places: Re-imaging Australia*, Longueville, NSW, Australia, pp 180–96.

Hill, SB 2003b, *Research Needs for 'Wise Policy' Regarding Population and Environment in Australia*, Population and Environment Research Fund Committee of the Australian Academy of Science. Canberra, ACT, Australia, viewed 10 July 2005, http://www.conference.science.org.au/papers/ StuartHillResponse.pdf.

Hill, SB Wilson, S & Watson, K 2004, 'Learning Ecology: A New Approach to Learning and Transforming Ecological Consciousness: Experiences from Social Ecology in Australia', in EV O'Sullivan & M Taylor (eds.) *Learning Toward an Ecological Consciousness: Selected Transformative Practices*, Palgrave Macmillan, New York, pp. 47–64.

Hill, SB 2005, 'Social Ecology as a Framework for Understanding and Working with Social Capital and Sustainability within Rural Communities', in A Dale & J Onyx (eds.), *A Dynamic Balance: Social Capital and Sustainable Community Development,* University of British Columbia, Vancouver, BC, Canada, pp. 48-68.

Hill, SB in prep, *Enabling Learning for Life: the Partnership Challenge for the 21st Century.*

Hill, SB in press a, 'Enabling Redesign for Deep Industrial Ecology and Personal Values Transformation', in K Green & S Randles (eds.) *Industrial Ecology and Spaces of Innovation,* Edward Elgar, London, chapter 12.

Hill, SB in press b, 'Redesign as Deep Industrial Ecology: Lessons from Ecological Agriculture and Social Ecology', in R. Cote, J Tansey & A Dale (eds.) *Industrial Ecology: A Question of Design?* University of British Columbia, Vancouver, BC, Canada.

Hill, SB *Social Ecology for a Sustainable Future,* viewed 20 April 2004, <http://www.zulenet.com/ see/chair.html>.

Hillman, J & Ventura, M 1993, *We've Had a Hundred Years of Psychotherapy and the World's Getting Worse,* Harper, San Francisco.

Holdgate, M 1996, *From Care to Action,* Earthscan, London.

Holland, J 1988, 'A Postmodern Vision of Spirituality and Society', in DR Griffin (ed.) *Spirituality and Society: Postmodern Visions,* SUNY Press, New York.

Holling, CS 1973, 'Resilience and Stability of Ecological Systems', *Annual Review of Ecology and Systems* no. 4, pp. 1–23.

Hubbard, DG 1983, 'The Psychodynamics of Terrorism', in Y Alexander, T Adeniran, & RA Kilmarx, (eds.) *International Violence,* Praeger, New York, pp. 45–53.

Huckle, J 1983, 'Environmental Education', in J Huckle (ed.) *Geographical Education, Reflection and Action,* Oxford University Press, Oxford, pp. 99–111

Huckle, J 1990, 'Environmental Education: Teaching for a Sustainable Future', in B Dufour (ed.) *The New Social Curriculum,* Cambridge University Press, Cambridge.

Huckle, J 1996, 'Realising Sustainability in Changing Times', in J Huckle & S Sterling (eds.) *Education for Sustainability,* Earthscan Publications, London, pp. 3–17.

Huckle, J & Sterling, S (eds.) 1996, *Education for Sustainability,* Earthscan Publications, London.

Hudson, RA 1999, *The Sociology and Psychology of Terrorism: Who Becomes a Terrorist and Why?* A report prepared under an interagency agreement by the Federal Research Division, Library of Congress, Washington DC, USA

Hunnicutt, B 1988, *Work without End: Abandoning Shorter Hours for the Right to Work,* Temple University Press, Philadelphia, PA, USA.

Husserl, E 1970, *Crisis of European Sciences and Transcendental Phenomenology: An Introduction to Phenomenological Philosophy*, Northwestern University Press, Evanston, IL, USA.

Huxley, J 1992, *Evolutionary Humanism*, Prometheus Books, Loughton, UK.

Hyam, R. 1992, *Empire and Sexuality*, Manchester University Press, Manchester, UK.

International Institute for Sustainable Development, *Measurement and Assessment*, viewed 1 April 2005, <http://www.iisd.org/measure/principles/bp_full.asp>.

Illich, I 1972, *De-schooling Society*, Harper & Row, New York.

Imel, S 1998 *Transformative Learning in Adulthood*, viewed 20 May 2005, <http://www.calpro-onle.org/eric/docs/dig200.pdf>.

Insecurity and the Corrosion of Character: Richard Sennett on the Personal Consequences of Work in the New economy', *The Jobs Letter*, no. 102, 30 June 1999, viewed 2 June 2005, <http://www.jobsletter.org.nz/jbl10210.htm>.

IUCN 1980, *World Conservation Strategy: Living Resource Conservation for Sustainable Development*, International Union for the Conservation of Nature and Natural Resources, IUCN, Gland, Switzerland.

IUCN/UNEP/WWF, 1991, *Caring for the Earth: A Strategy for Sustainable Living*, Gland, Switzerland.

JanMohamed, AR 1986, 'The Economy of Manichean Allegory: The Function of Radical Difference in Colonialist Literature', in HL Gates Jr, (ed.) *Race, Writing and Difference*, University of Illinois Press, Chicago, IL, USA.

Jason, LA Zolik, ES. & Matese, F 1979, 'Prompting Dog Owners to Pick-up Dog Droppings', *American Journal of Community Psychology*, vol. 7, no. 33, pp. 339–51.

Jaynes, J 1976, *The Origin of Consciousness and the Breakdown of the Bicameral Mind*, Penguin Books, London.

Johnson, D 1994, *Body, Spirit and Democracy*, North Atlantic Books, Berkeley, CA, USA.

Johnson, RA1989, *Ecstasy*, Harper & Row, San Francisco.

Johnson, SM 1985, *Characterological Transformation*, W.W. Norton, New York.

Johnson, SM 1994, *Character Styles*, WW Norton, New York.

Jones, K 1993, *Beyond Optimism*, Jon Carpenter Publishing, Oxford.

Jordan, T 2000, *Dimensions of Consciousness Development: A Preliminary Framework*, Version 1.0, January 2000, viewed 28 April 2005, <http://www. lightmd.com/library/essays/Jordan-01.html>.

Josselson, R 1996, *The Space Between Us: Exploring the Dimensions of Human Relationships*, Sage, Thousand Oaks, CA, USA.

Jung, CG 1958, *The Undiscovered Self*, Routledge & Kegan Paul, London.

Jung, CG 1971, *The Portable Jung*, J Campbell (ed.) Penguin Books, New York.

Kagan, R & Asmus, RD 2002, 'Commit for the Long Run', *The Washington Post*, 29 January 2002.

Kals, E 1996, *Verantwortliches Umweltverhalten*, Beltz Psychologie Verlags Union, Weinheim, Germany.

Kalweit, H 1992, *Shamans, Healers, and Medicine Men*, Shambhala, Boston, MA, USA.

Kanner, AD & Gomes, ME 1995, 'The All-consuming Self', in T Roszak, ME Gomes & AD Kanner (eds.) *Ecopsychology*, Sierra Club, San Francisco, pp. 77 - 91.

Kaplan, LJ 1978, *Oneness and Separateness*, Simon & Schuster, New York.

Kasl, E & Yorks, L 2000, 'An Extended Epistemology for Transformative Learning Theory and its Application through Collaborative Inquiry', in *Challenges of Practice: Transformative Learning in Action*, Columbia University, 3rd International Transformative Learning Conference, paper, New York, pp. 175-180.

Keating, M 1993, *The Earth Summit's Agenda for Change: A Plain Language Version of Agenda 21 and the Other Rio Agreements*, Centre for Our Common Future, Geneva, Switzerland.

Keleman, S 1975, *Your Body Speaks its Mind*, Center Press, Berkeley, CA, USA.

Kernberg, OF 1985, *Borderline Conditions and Pathological Narcissism*, Rowman & Littlefield Publishers, Lanham, MD, USA.

Kidner, D 2001, Nature and Psyche: Radical Environmentalism and the Politics of Subjectivity, SUNY Press, Albany, NY, USA.

Kirk, R 1988, 'A Culture's Road to Avernus', *Essays on Our Times*, vol. 4 July 1988, p. 4.

Kirkman, R 2002, *Skeptical Environmentalism*, Indiana University Press, Indianapolis, IN, USA.

Klemm, U 1984, *Die liebertäre Reformpädagogik Tolstois*, Trotzdem Verlagsgenossenschaft, Grafenau, Germany.

Knutson, JN (ed.) 1973, *Handbook of Political Psychology*, Jossey-Bass, San Francisco.

Knutson, JN 1973, 'Personality in the Study of Politics', in J Knutson (ed.) *Handbook of Political Psychology*, Jossey-Bass, San Francisco, pp. 28–56.

Koestler, A 1990, *The Act of Creation*, Reissue Edition, Penguin Books, London.

Kohler, W 1975, *Gestalt Psychology: An Introduction to New Concepts in Modern Psychology*, New American Library, New York.

Kohut, H 1971, *The Analysis of the Self*, International Universities Press, New York.

Kohut, H 1977, *The Restoration of the Self*, International Universities Press, New York.

Kohut, H 1984, *How Does Analysis Cure?* University of Chicago Press, Chicago, IL, USA.

Kolb, DA 1984, *Learning Style Inventory*, Prentice Hall, Englewood Cliffs, NJ, USA.

Kovan, JT & John M. Dirkx, JM 2003, 'Being Called Awake: The Role of Transformative Learning in the Lives of Environmental Activists' *Adult Education Quarterly*, 2003, no. 53, pp. 99-118.

Kovel, J 1976, *A Complete Guide to Therapy*, Penguin, New York.

Kovel, J 1981, *The Age of Desire: Case histories of a Radical Psychoanalyst*, Pantheon, New York.

Kovel, J 1984, *White Racism: A Psychohistory*, Columbia University Press, New York.

Krieger, D 2001, *The Frog's Malaise: Nuclear Weapons and Human Survival*, viewed 5 May 2005, <http://www.wagpeace.org/articles/2001/04/00_krieger_frogs-malaise.htm>.

Kubzansky, LD Sparrow, D Vokonas, P & Kawachi, I 2001, 'Is the Glass Half Empty or Half Full? A Prospective Study of Optimism and Coronary Heart Disease in the Normative Ageing Study', *Psychosomatic Medicine,* no. 63, pp. 910-16.

Kuhn, T.S 1970, *The Structure of Scientific Revolutions*, 2nd edition, University of Chicago Press, Chicago, IL, USA.

Kurtz, R 1990, *Body-centered Psychotherapy: The Hakomi Method: The Integrated Use of Mindfulness, Nonviolence and the Body*, LifeRhythm Books, Mendocino, CA, USA.

Kvale, S 1992, 'Postmodern Psychology: A Contradiction in Terms?' in S Kvale (ed.) *Psychology and Postmodernism*, Sage Publications, London, pp. 31–57.

Lamarck, JB 1914, *Zoological Philosophy: An Exposition with Regard to the Natural History of Animals*, Macmillan, London.

Lasch, C 1980, *The Culture of Narcissism*, Abacus Sphere Books, London.

Laszlo, E 2006, *Science and the Reenchantment of the Cosmos*, Inner Traditions, Rochester, VT, USA.

Lauer, RM 1983, 'An Introduction to the Theory of Adult Learning or after Piaget What?' in M Levy (ed.) *Research and theory in developmental psychology*, N.Y. State Psychological Assoc., Lovington, NY, pp. 195-219.

Lauer, RM 1999, *Learners of the World Unite!* Unpublished manuscript, Columbia University, New York.

Lauritsen, J 1997, 'Psychological and Toxicological Causes of AIDS', in J Lauritsen, & I Young (eds.) *The AIDS Cult: Essays on the Gay Health Crisis*, Asklepios, Provincetown, MA, USA.

Leweson-Gower, H. 1997, 'Trade and the Environment', M Diesendorf, & C Hamilton (eds.) *Human Ecology, Human Economy*, Allen & Unwin, St. Leonards, NSW, Australia.

Liedloff, J 1976, *The Continuum Concept*, Futura Publications, London.

Livingston, J 1981, *The Fallacy of Wildlife Conservation*, McClelland & Stewart, Toronto.

Logan, R & Meuse, C 2001, *The Nurture of Nature: Healing Ourselves through Applied Ecopsychology*, viewed 5 October 2004, <www.consciouschoice.com/culture/nurtureofnature1401.html>.

Lopez, TJ Regier, PR & Holder-Webb, L 2001, '*Do Restructurings Improve Operating Performance?* Department of Accounting, Lowry Mays College and Graduate School of Business, Texas A& M University, College Station, TX & School of Accountancy and Information Management, College of Business, Arizona State University, Tempe, AZ, <http://www2.owen.vanderbilt.edu/fmrc/Activity/paper/HolderWebPaper.pdf>.

Loughlin, KA 1993, *Women's Perceptions of Transformative Learning Experiences with Consciousness-raising*, Mellen Research University Press, San Francisco.

Lovelock, J 1989, *The Ages of Gaia*, Oxford University Press, Oxford.

Lowen, A 1958, *Physical Dynamics of Character Structure*, Grune & Stratton, reprinted as *Language of the Body*, 1969, Macmillan, London.

Lowen, A 1972, *Depression and the Body*, Collier Macmillan, New York.

Lowen, A 1975, *Bioenergetics*, Penguin Books, New York.

Lowen, A 1980, *Fear of Life*, Collier Macmillan Publishers, New York.

Lowen, A 1985, *Narcissism*, Collier Books, Macmillan, New York.

Lubell, M 2002,'Environmental Activism As Collective Action' *Environment and Behaviour* vol. 34, no. 4, pp. 431–54.

Ludwig, D, Walker, B & Holling, CS 1997, 'Sustainability, Stability, and Resilience', *Conservation Ecology* vol.1, no.1, p. 7, viewed 28 May 2005, <http://www.consecol.org/vol1/iss1/art7>.

Lundberg, J 'Alternative to Oil: Technofix, or Lifestyle Change? *Culture Change*, viewed 3 June 2005, <http://www.culturechange.org/issue10/alternative-to-oil.htm>.

Lundberg, J 2005, 'End-time for U.S.A. upon Oil Collapse: A Scenario for a Sustainable Future', *Energy Bulletin, Culture Change*, 27 June, viewed 1 July 2005, <http://www.energybullet.net/prt.php?id=6933>.

Mack, JE 2005, "The Politics of Species Arrogance', in T Roszak, ME Gomes & AD Kanner (eds.) *Ecopsychology*, Sierra Club Books, San Francisco, pp. 279-87.

Macy, J 1985, *Dharma and Development*, Kumarian Press, Bloomfield, CT, USA.

Macy, J 1991, *World as Lover, World as Self,* Parallax Press, Berkeley, CA, USA.

Macy, J 1991, Mutual Causality in Buddhism and General Systems Theory, SUNY Press, New York.

Macy , J 1995, 'Working through Environmental Despair', in T Roszak, ME Gomes & AD Kanner (eds.) *Ecopsychology*, Sierra Club Books, San Francisco, pp. 240–59.

Madsen, D 1995, *Postmodernism: A Bibliography, 1926 – 1994*, Rodopi Bv Editions, Amsterdam.

Mahler, M 1975, *The Psychological Birth of the Human Infant*, Basic Books, New York.

Manfield, P 1992, *Split Self - Split Object*, Jason Aronson, Northvale, London.

Mann, WE 1973, *Orgone, Reich and Eros: Wilhelm Reich's Theory of Life Energy*, Simon & Schuster, New York.

Margulis, L 1998, *The Symbiotic Planet*, Weidenfeld & Nicolson, London.

Maslow, AH 1964, *Religions, Values, and Peak-experiences*, Ohio State University Press, Columbus, OH, USA.

Mathiesen, T 2002, 'Expanding the Concept of Terrorism', in P Scraton (ed.) *Beyond September 11: An Anthology of Dissent*, Pluto Press, London.

Matthews, F 1994, *The Ecological Self*, Taylor & Francis, London.

McKenzie-Mohr, D & Smith, W 1999, *Fostering Sustainable Behavior: An introduction to Community-based Social Marketing (Education for Sustainability Series)*, New Society Publishers, Gabriola Island, BC, Canada.

McMichael, A J 2001, *Human Frontiers, Environments, and Disease: Past Patterns, Uncertain Futures*, Cambridge University Press, Cambridge, UK.

Meadows, D 1998, *Indicators and information systems for sustainable development*, The Sustainability Institute, Hartland, VT, USA.

Memmi, A 1991, *Colonizer and the colonized*, Beacon Press, Boston, MA, USA.

Merleau-Ponty, M & Smith, C 2002, *Phenomenology of perception*, 2nd edition, Routledge, New York.

Metzner, R 1986, *The unfolding self*, Origin Press, Novato, CA, USA.

Metzner, R 1999, *Green psychology*, Park Street Press, Rochester, VT, USA.

Metzner, R *Expanding Consciousness in a Living Systems Universe*, viewed 5 May 2005, <http://www.greenearthfound.org/expanding.html>.

Meyer, H 1986, *Astrologie und Psychologie*, Rowohlt Taschenbuch Verlag, Reinbek, Germany.

Mezirow, J 1991, *Transformative Dimensions of Adult Learning*, Jossey-Bass, San Francisco.

Milbrath, L 1989, *Envisioning a Sustainable Society*, SUNY, New York.

Miller A 1997, *Breaking Down the Wall of Silence: The Liberating Experience of Facing Painful Truth*, revised edition, Plume Books / Penguin, New York.

Mindell, A 1984, *Dreambody*, Routledge & Kegan Paul, London.

Mindell, A 2002, *Working on Yourself Alone: Inner Dreambody Work*, Lao-Tse Press, Portland, OR, USA.

Minelli, MJ. & Schroll, MA 2003, *The Art of Living: Discovering the Transcendent and the Transpersonal in Our Lives*, Stipes Publishing, Champaign, IL, USA.

Moehring, M 1996, Von der Umwelterziehung zu ganzheitlicher Bildung als Ausdruck integralen Bewusstseins, Dissertation, University of Bremen, Germany.

Moffat, I Hanley, N Wilson, M & Faichney, R 2000, *ESRC Global Environmental Change Programme*, viewed 14 February 2005, <http://www.sussex.ac.uk/Units/ gec/pubs/briefg/brief-26.htm>.

Monbiot, G 'Bottom of the Barrel', *The Guardian Weekly*, 2 December, 2003, viewed 22 July, 2005, <http://www.coldtype.net/Assets/pdfs/GM.41.pdf>.

Moore, T 1992, *Care of the Soul: A Guide for Cultivating Depth and Sacredness in Everyday Life*, HarperCollins, New York.

Moore, T 1996, *Re-enchantment of Everyday Life*, Hodder & Stoughton, Rydalmere, NSW, Australia.

Muck, O 1983, *Alles ueber Atlantis*, Econ Verlag, Munich, Germany.

Mulligan, M & Hill, SB 2001, *Ecological Pioneers: A Social History of Australian Ecological Thought and Action*, Cambridge University Press, Melbourne, VIC, Australia.

Mumford, L 1963, *Technics and Civilisation*, Harvest / HBJ Book, New York.

Mumford, L 1968, *The City in History: Its Origins, Its Transformations, and Its Prospects*, Harvest Books, Harcourt Trade Publishers, New York.

Mumford, L 1973, *The Condition of Man*, new edition, Harcourt Trade Publishers, New York.

Murphy, M 1992, *The Future of the Body: Explorations to the Further Evolution of Human Nature*, Jeremy P. Tarcher / Putnam, New York.

Naess, A 1973, 'The Shallow and the Deep, Long-range Ecology Movements: a Summary', *Inquiry*, no. 16, pp. 95–100.

Naess, A & Rothenberg D 1990, *Ecology, Community and Lifestyle: Outline of an Ecosophy*, Cambridge University Press, Cambridge, UK.

Neill, AS 1984, *Summerhill: A Radical Approach to Childrearing*, Hart Publishing, Oxford.

Neill, AS 1991, 'The Self-regulated Child', in D Boadella (ed.) *In the Wake of Reich*, 2nd edition, Coventure, London.

Neisser, U 1967, *Cognitive Psychology*, Appleton-Century-Crofts, New York.

Nemiah, JC 1977, 'Alexithymia: Theoretical Considerations', *Psychother. Psychosom.*, vol. 28, no.1–4, pp. 199–206

Norgaard, R 1995, 'Beyond Materialism: A Coevolutionary Reinterpretation of the Environmental Crisis' *Review of Social Economy* LIII, pp. 475-92.

Nozick, M 1992, *No Place Like Home*, Canadian Council of Social Development, Ottawa, Canada.

Noyes, R Jr. 1974, 'Dying and Mystical Consciousness', in J White (ed.) *Frontiers of Consciousness,* Avon Books, New York.

O'Connor, T 1995, 'Therapy for a Dying Planet', in T Roszak, ME Gomes & AD Kanner (eds.) *Ecopsychology,* Sierra Club Books, San Francisco, pp. 149–155.

Oelschlaeger, M (ed.) 1995, *Postmodern Environmental Ethics,* State University of New York Press, Albany, NY, USA.

Orbach, S 2004, 'The John Bowlby Memorial Lecture 2003: The Body in Clinical Practice', in K White, *Touch, Attachment and the Body,* Karnac Books, London, pp. 17 – 34.

O'Riordan, T 1981, *Environmentalism,* 2nd edition, Pion, London.

O'Riordan, T 1989, 'The Challenge for Environmentalism', in R Peet, & N Thrift (eds.) *New Models in Geography,* Unwin Hyman, London, pp. 77–102.

Orr, DW 1992, *Ecological Literacy: Education and the Transition to a Postmodern World,* State University of New York, Albany, NY, USA.

Orr, DW 1994, *Earth in Mind: On Education, Environment and the Human Prospect,* Island Press, Washington, DC, USA.

Oschmann, J 1995, *Somatic Recall I and II: Readings on the Scientific Basis of Bodywork.* Vol. II, viewed 5 November 2004, <http://www.somatics.de/Bishop_Ray_Maps.htm>.

O'Sullivan, E 1999, *Transformative Learning: Educational Vision for the 21st Century,* University of Toronto, Toronto.

O'Sullivan, E 2003, 'Bringing a Perspective of Transformative Learning to Globalized Consumption', *International Journal of Consumer Studies,* vol. 27, no. 4, pp. 326–30.

Overbeck, G 1984, *Krankheit als Anpassung,* Suhrkamp Verlag, Frankfurt/Main, Germany.

Palmer J 1998, Environmental Education in the 21st Century: Theory, Practice, Progress and Promise, Routledge, London.

Parenti, M 1995, *Against Empire,* City Lights Publishers, San Francisco, USA.

Pearlstein, RM 1991, 'The Mind of the Political Terrorist', *Scholarly Resources,* Wilmington, DE, USA, p. 9.

Pearse, IH 1979, *The Quality of Life: The Peckham Approach to Human Ethology,* Scottish Academic Press, Edinburgh, UK.

Peat, DF 1989, *Synchronizitaet: Die verborgene Ordnung,* Goldmann Verlag, Munich, Germany.

Pelletier, K 1979, *Toward a Science of Consciousness,* Delta, New York.

Pepper, DM 1996, *Modern Environmentalism: An Introduction,* Routledge, London.

Perls, FS 1973, *The Gestalt Approach and Eye Witness to Therapy,* Science & Behaviour Books, Palo Alto, CA, USA.

Perls, FS 1992, *Gestalt Therapy Verbatim,* Gestalt Journal Press, Highland, NY. USA.

Pestalozzi, JH 1894, *How Gertrude Teaches Her Children*, translated by LE Holland & FC Turner, Swan Sonnenschein, London.
Piaget, J 1959, *Language and Thought of the Child*, Routledge & Kegan Paul, London.
Pierrakos, J 1990, *Core energetics: developing the capacity to love and heal*, Life Rhythm, Mendocino, CA, USA.
Pilger, J 2005, 'Let's Face It – the State Has Lost Its Mind', *New Statesman*, viewed 14 May 2005, <http://www.newstatesman.com/nscoverstory.htm>.
Platt, J 1973, 'Social Traps', *American Psychologist*, vol. 28, pp. 641–51.
Plumwood, V 2000, 'Nature, Self, and Gender: Feminism, Environmental Philosophy and the Critique of Rationalism', in J Benson (ed.) *Environmental Ethics: An Introduction with Readings*, Routledge, London.
Polkinghorne, DE 1992, 'Postmodern Epistemology of Practice', in S Kvale (ed.) *Psychology and Postmodernism*, Sage Publications, London.
Pollmann, W 1982, *Viren – Botschafter lebender Systeme*, R. Piper & Co. Verlag, Munich, Germany.
Pope, C & Rauber, P 2004, *Strategic Ignorance: Why the Bush Administration Is Recklessly Destroying a Century of Environmental Progress*, Sierra Club Books, San Francisco.
Porsch, U 1997, *Der Körper als Selbst und Objekt*, Vandenhoek & Ruprecht, Göttingen, Germany.
Post, JM 1984, 'Notes on a Psychodynamic Theory of Terrorist Behavior', *Terrorism: An International Journal*, vol. 7, no. 3, 242–56.
Post, JM 1985, 'Individual and Group Dynamics of Terrorist Behavior', World Congress of Psychiatry, *Psychiatry: The State of the Art*, 6. Plenum, New York.
Post, JM 1987, 'Rewarding Fire with Fire? Effects of Retaliation on Terrorist Group Dynamics', in A Kurz (ed.) *Contemporary Trends in World Terrorism*, Praeger, New York, pp. 103–15.
Post, JM 1990a, 'Current Understanding of Terrorist Motivation and Psychology: Implications for a Differentiated Antiterrorist Policy', *Terrorism*, vol. 13, no. 1, pp. 65–71.
Post, JM 1990b, 'Terrorist Psycho-logic: Terrorist Behavior as a Product of Psychological Forces', in W Reich (ed.) *Origins of Terrorism: Psychologies, Ideologies, Theologies, States of Mind*. Cambridge University Press, Cambridge, pp. 25–40.
Preisendoerfer, P 1999, 'Umwelteinstellungen und Umweltverhalten in Deutschland: Empirische Befunde und Analysen auf der Grundlage der Bevölkerungsumfragen', in Umweltbundesamt, *Umweltbewusstsein in Deutschland 1991–1998*, Leske und Budrich, Opladen, Germany.
Prochaska, JO 1984, *Systems of Psychotherapy*, The Dorsey Press, Homewood, IL, USA.
Putnam, D 2000, 'The Strange Disappearance of Civic America' *American Prospect*, May–June 2000, pp. 34–48.

Ralston Saul, J 2005, *The Collapse of Globalism and the Reinvention of the World*, Viking / Penguin, Camberwell, VIC, Australia.

Reason, P 2002, *Justice, Sustainability and Participation*, paper presented at the inaugural lecture, Centre for Action Research in Professional Practice *(CARRP)*, University of Bath, January 2002.

Reich, W 1933, *Character Analysis*, reprinted 1969, Farrar, Strauss & Giroux, New York.

Reich, W 1942, *The Function of the Body*, Orgone Institute Press, Rangeley, ME, USA.

Reich, W 1946, *Mass Psychology of Fascism*, 3rd ed., Orgone Institute Press, Rangeley, ME, USA.

Reich, W 1968, *The Function of the Orgasm*, Panther Books, London.

Reps, P 1971, Zen Flesh, Zen Bones, Pelican / Arkana, London.

Richter, HE 1972, Patient Familie, Rowohlt, Reinbek, Germany.

Robottom, IM 1988, *Science Education: Exploring the Tension*, Hyperion Books, New York.

Robottom, IM & Andrew-Gannon, J 1995, *Environmental Education across Australia: Study Guide*, Deakin University Press, Geelong, VIC, Australia.

Robottom, IM & Hart, P 1995, *Research in Environmental Education: Engaging the Debate, Research in Environmental Education*, Hyperion Books, New York.

Roderick, K *Cry for your heart's sake*, viewed 22 February 2005, <http://www.thirdage.com/news/ archive/ALT02010206-01.html>.

Rousseau, JJ 1979, *Emile: Or, on Education*, Basic Books, New York.

Roszak, T 1973, *Where the Wasteland Ends*, Bantam, Doubleday, Dell, New York.

Roszak, T 1975, *Unfinished Animal*, Harper & Row Publishers, New York.

Roszak, T 1981, *Person/Planet*, Granada Publishing, London.

Roszak, T 1995 'Where Psyche Meets Gaia', in T Roszak, ME Gomes & AD Kanner (eds.) *Ecopsychology*, Sierra Club, San Francisco, pp. 1–17.

Roszak, T Gomes, ME & Kanner AD (eds.) 1995, *Ecopsychology*, Sierra Club, San Francisco.

Roszak, T 2001, *The Voice of the Earth: An Exploration of Ecopsychology*, Phanes Press, York Beach, ME, USA

Rycroft, C 1972, *A Critical Dictionary of Psychoanalysis*, Penguin, New York.

Russell, CA & Miller, BH 1978, 'Profile of a Terrorist', in JD Elliott & LK Gibson (eds.) *Contemporary Terrorism: Selected Readings*, International Association of Chiefs of Police, Gaithersburg, MD, USA, pp. 81–95.

Russell, D 2003, 'A Psychological Perspective on Place' in JI Cameron, *Changing Places*, Longueville Books, Double Bay, NSW, pp. 149-58.

Sachs, W 1993, *Global Ecology and the Shadow of Development*, ZED Books / Fernwood Publishing, London.

Sardar, Z & Davies, MW 2002, *Why Do People Hate America?* Icon Books, Cambridge, UK.

Sattmann-Frese, WJ 1992, 'A Holistic View of AIDS', Southern Crossings Magazine, January/February 1992.

Schrauth, N 2001, *Körperpsychotherapie und Psychoanalyse*, Ulrich Leutner Verlag, Berlin.

Schroll, MA 2000, 'Gaia Consciousness: A Review of Ralph Metzner's Green Psychology: Transforming Our Relationships to the Earth', *Resurgence*, 200, May/June 2000, pp. 60–61.

Schroll, MA 2005, Remembering Ecopsychology's Origins: A Chronicle of Meetings, Conversations, and Significant Publications, viewed 5 May 2005, <http://www.ecopsychology.org/journal/eze/ep_origs.html>.

Schumacher, EF 1974, *Small is Beautiful*, Abacus / Sphere, London.

Schumacher, EF 1978, *A Guide for the Perplexed*, HarperCollins/ Perennial, New York.

Schur, M 1974, 'Zur Metapsychologie der Somatisierung', in K Brede (ed.) *Einführung in die Psychosomatische Medizin*, Fischer, Frankfurt / Main, Germany.

Scott, SM 1997, 'The Grieving Soul in the Transformation Process', in P Cranton (ed.) *Transformative Learning Action: Insights from Practice, New Directions for Adult and Continuing Education*, no. 74, Jossey-Bass, San Francisco, pp. 41–50.

Scull, J 1999, *Ecopsychology: Where Does It Fit in Psychology?* viewed 5 October 2004, <http://members.shaw.ca/jscull/ECOINTRO.pdf>.

Sells, B (ed.) 2000, *Working with Images: The Theoretical Base of Archetypal Psychology*, Spring Publications, Woodstock, CT, USA.

Sennett, R 1998, *Corrosion of Character: The Personal Consequences of Work in the New Capitalism*, WW Norton, New York.

Sessions, G 1985, 'Ecological Consciousness and Paradigm Change', in M Tobias (ed.) *Deep Ecology*, Avant Books, San Diego, CA, USA.

Sessions, G 1995, *Deep Ecology for the 21st Century*, Shambhala, Boston, MA, USA.

Sewall, L 1995, 'The Skill of Ecological Perception', in T Roszak, ME Gomes & AD Kanner (eds.) *Ecopsychology*, Sierra Club, San Francisco, pp. 201–215.

Shapiro, E 1995, 'Restoring Habitats, Communities, and Souls', in T Roszak, ME Gomes & AD Kanner (eds.) *Ecopsychology*, Sierra Club Books, San Francisco, pp. 224 –39.

Shem, S & Surrey, J 1998, *We Have to Talk: Healing Dialogues between Women and Men*, Basic Books, New York.

Shepard, P 1982, *Nature and Madness*, Sierra Club Books, San Francisco.

Shields, K 1993, *In the Tiger's Mouth: An Empowerment Guide for Social Action*, New Society Publishers, Gabliola Island, BC, Canada.

Siegelman, E 1990, *Metaphor and Meaning in Psychotherapy*, Guilford Press, New York.

Sifneos, PE 1972, *Short-term Psychotherapy and Emotional Crisis*, Harvard University Press, Cambridge, MA, USA.

Sifneos, PE 1996, 'Alexithymia: Past and Present', *American Journal of Psychiatry*, vol. 153, no. 7, pp.137–142.

Simmons, D 2002, *Black Sheep, Rudyard Kipling's Narcissistic Imperialism*, *PSYART – Online Journal for Psychological Studies of the Arts*, Article Number: 020529, viewed 22 January 2004, <http://www.clas.ufl.edu/ipsa/journal/2002_simmons01.shtml>.

Simon, HA & Newell, A 1964, 'Information Processing in Computer and Man', *American Scientist*, vol. 52, pp. 281–300.

Skinner, BF 1948, *Walden Two*, Macmillan, New York.

Skinner, BF 1953, *Science and Human Behaviour*, Free Press, New York.

Skinner, BF 1971, *Beyond Freedom and Dignity*, Alfred A. Knopf, New York.

Skolimowski, H 1996, *The Participatory Mind: A New Theory of Knowledge and of the Universe*, Penguin Arkana, New York.

Smith, H 1992, *Beyond the Post-modern Mind*, Quest / Theosophical Publishing House, Wheaton, IL, USA.

Smith, RA 1974, 'Our Passport to Ecological Awareness', in J White, (ed.) *Frontiers of Consciousness*, Avon Books, New York.

Smuts, J 1936, *Holism and Evolution*, 3rd edition, MacMillan, Oxford.

Solter, A 1989, *Helping Young Children Flourish*. Shining Star, Goleta, CA, USA.

Spada, H 1990, 'Umweltbewusstsein: Einstellung und Verhalten', in L Kruse, CF Graumann & ED Lantermann (eds.) *Ökologische Psychologie: Ein Handbuch in Schlüsselbegriffen*, Beltz Psychologie Verlags Union, Weinheim, Germany, pp. 623–31.

Spretnak, C 1991, *States of Grace*, Harper Collins Publishers, New York.

Spretnak, C 1997, *The Resurgence of the Real*, Addison-Wesley Publishing, New York.

Stallibrass, A 1989, *Being Me and Also Us: Lessons from the Peckham Experiment*, Scottish Academic Press, Edinburgh, UK.

Staunton, T 2002, *Body Psychotherapy*, Brunner-Routledge, Hove, East Sussex, UK.

Steele, EJ Lindley, RA & Blanden, RV 1998, *Lamarck's Signature*, Allen & Unwin, Sydney.

Steiner, R 1987, *Die Erziehung des Kindes vom Gesichtspunkte der Geisteswissenschaft*, Rudolf Steiner Verlag, Dornach, Switzerland.

Sterling, S & EDET Group, 1992, *Good Earth-keeping: Education, Training and Awareness for a Sustainable Future*, Environment Development Education Training Group, UNEP-UK, London.

Sterling, S 1996, 'Education in Change', in J Huckle & S Sterling (eds.) *Education for Sustainability*, Earthscan Publications, London.

Sterling, S 2001, *Sustainable Education: Re-visioning Learning and Change*, Green Books, Totnes, UK.

Stettbacher, JK 1991, *Making Sense of Suffering: The Healing Confrontation with Your Past*, Dutton, New York.

Stevenson, RB 1987, 'Schooling and Environmental Education: Contradictions in Purpose and Practice', in I Robottom (ed.) *Environmental Education: Practice and Possibility*, Deakin University Press, Melbourne, VIC, Australia.

Strauss, AL & Corbin, JA 1980, *Basics of Qualitative Research: Grounded Theory Procedures and Techniques*, Sage, Newbury Park, CA, USA.

Strub, J 2001, *USA: the FTAA and the AIDS Crisis in the Global South*, ACT-UP Philadelphia, viewed 2 June 2003, <http://www.corpwatch.org/article.php?id=478>.

Suzuki, D & McConnell, A 1997, *The Sacred Balance: Rediscovering Our Place in Nature*, Allen & Unwin, St. Leonards, NSW, Australia.

Swimme, B & Berry, T 1992, *The Universe Story: An Autobiography of Planet Earth*, Harper & Row, San Francisco.

Tainter, J A 1988, *The Collapse of Complex Societies*, Cambridge University Press, New York.

Tanner, RT 1974, *Ecology, Environment, and Education*, Professional Educators Publications, Lincoln, NE, USA.

Taylor, EW 1998, 'The Theory and Practice of Transformative Learning: A Critical Review', in *Information Series no 374, Columbus: ERIC Clearinghouse on Adult, Career, and Vocational Education*, Center on Education and Training for Employment, College of Education, Ohio State University, OH, USA.

Taylor, MM 2003, *Learning Toward an Ecological Consciousness*, Palgrave Macmillan, Basingstoke, UK.

Tilbury, D 1993, *Environmental Education: Developing a Model for Initial Teacher Education*, PhD thesis, University of Cambridge, Cambridge, UK.

Tilbury D 1995, 'Environmental Education for Sustainability: Defining the New Focus of Environmental Education in the 1990s', *Environmental Education Research*, vol. 1, no. 2, pp. 195–212.

Tilbury, D & Stevenson RB 2002, *Education and Sustainability: Responding to the Global Challenge*, Island Press, Washington DC, USA.

Tilbury, D & Wortman, D 2004, *Engaging People in Sustainability*, IUCN, Gland Switzerland.

Tolstoy, L 1861, *On Popular Education, Yasnaya Polyana: A project for a General Plan for Elementary Schools*, viewed 12 July, 2005, <http://www.linguadex.com/tolstoy/works.htm>.

Tolstoy, L 1872, *Progress and the Definition of Instruction, Yasnaya Polyana: A project for a General Plan for Elementary Schools*, viewed 12 July, 2005, <http://www.linguadex.com/tolstoy/works.htm>.

Tolstoy, L 1874, *On Popular Instruction, Yasnaya Polyana: A project for a General Plan for Elementary Schools*, viewed 12 July, 2005, <http://www.linguadex.com/tolstoy/works.htm.

Trainer, T 1995, *The Conserver Society*, Zed Books, London.

Tulku, T 1977, *Gesture of Balance*, Dharma Publishing, Berkeley, CA, USA.

Tulku, T 1981, *Hidden Mind of Freedom: Meditation for Compassion and Self-healing,* Nyingma Psychology Series, Dharma Publishing, Berkeley, CA, USA

UK Defra, *Quality of Life Counts 2004: List of Objectives and Indicators within the framework of the Sustainable Development Strategy,* viewed 27 January 2005, <http://www.sustainable-development.gov.uk/sustainable/quality04/annexa.htm>.

UNESCO-UNEP, 1977, *Tbilisi Declaration and Final Report,* Intergovernmental Conference on Environmental Education, Tbilisi, 14-26 October 1977.

UN Department of Economic and Social Affairs – Division for Sustainable Development, *Table 4: CSD Indicator Framework,* viewed 27 January 2005, <http://www.un.org/ esa/sustdev/natlfo/ indicators/ isdms2001/ table_4.htm>.

Van den Bergh, 2007, *Abolishing GDP,* viewed 5 December 2008, <http://www.tinbergen.nl>.

Van Houten, R Nau, P & Mari, Z 1980, 'An Analysis of Public Posting in Reducing Speeding Behaviour on an Urban Highway', *Journal of Applied Behaviour Analysis,* no. 13, pp. 383 – 95.

Van Matre, S 1990, *Earth Education: A New Beginning,* Institute of Earth Education, Warrenville, IL, USA.

Verny, T 1981, *The Secret Life of the Unborn Child,* Summit Books, New York.

Visser, J 1996, *Facilitating the Evolution of Cultures of Learning: Implications at the Global and National Level,* keynote address presented at the Second Global Conference on Lifelong Learning, Ottawa, ON, Canada, March 23 – 26, 1996.

Visser, J 1998, *Cities that Learn, Cities that Care,* keynote address presented at the European Conference on Learning Cities, Southampton, UK, June 20 – 23, 1998.

von Uexkuell, T 1963, *Grundfragen der psychosomatischen Medizin,* Rowohlt Taschenbuch Verlag, Reinbek, Germany.

von Uexkuell, T von Adler, Herrmann, JM Köhle, K Schonecke, OW Wesiack, W (eds.) 1979, *Psychosomatische Medizin, Urban & Schwarzenberg,* Munich, Germany.

Volk, TL Hungerford, HR & Tomera, AN 1984, 'A National Study of Curriculum Needs as Perceived by Professional Environmental Educators', *Journal of Environmental Education,* vol. 16, no. 1, pp. 10–19.

Wachtel, P 1989, *The Poverty of Affluence,* New Society Publishers, Philadelphia, PA, USA.

Walker, B 1979, *Body Magic: An Encyclopedia of Esoteric Man,* Paladin Books / Granada Publishing, London.

Walker, B Holling, CS Carpenter, SR & Kinzig, A 2004, 'Resilience, Adaptability and Transformability in Social–ecological Systems', *Ecology and Society,* vol. 9, no 2, Art 5, viewed 22 April 2005, http://www.ecologyandsociety.org.

Washington, H 2002, *A Sense of Wonder*, Ecosolution Consulting / Nullo Books, Rylstone, NSW, Australia.

Watkins, M 2002, *Waking up: Terrorism and Depth Psychology*, viewed 30 June, 2005, <http://www.online.pacifica.edu/alumni/watkins 2002 address>.

Watson, JB 1914, *Behavior: A Textbook of Comparative Psychology*, Henry Holt, New York.

Watson, JB 1925, *Behaviorism*, People's Institute, New York.

Watson, JB 1928, *The Psychological Care of Infant and Child*, Allen, London.

Watts, A 1951, *The Wisdom of Insecurity*, Vintage Books, New York.

Watts, A 1958, *Nature, Man and Woman*, Vintage Books, New York.

Watts, A 1961, *Psychotherapy East and West*, Ballantyne, New York.

Watts, A 1962, *The Book: On the Taboo against Knowing Who We Are*, Vintage Books, New York.

WCED, 1987, *Our Common Future, Brundtland Report*, World Commission on Environment and Development.

Weigel, VB 1995, *Earth Cancer*, Praeger, Westport, CT, USA.

Werner, CM 1999, 'Psychological Perspectives on Sustainability', in E Becker, & T Jahn (eds.) *Sustainability and the Social Sciences*, Zed Books, London, pp. 233–42.

White, J (ed.) 1974, *Frontiers of Consciousness*, Avon Books, New York.

White, L 1967, 'The Historic Roots of Our Ecologic Crisis', *Science*, no. 155, pp. 1203–07.

Whitehead, AN 1997, *Science and the Modern World*, reissue edition, Free Press / Simon and Schuster, London.

Whitney, G 1997, 'Russell Kirk's Conception of Decadence', *The Freeman: Ideas on Liberty*, July 1997.

Wilber, K 1983, *Up from Eden*, Shambhala, Boulder, CO, USA.

Wilber, K 1995, *Sex, Ecology, Spirituality: The Spirit of Evolution*, Shambhala, Boston, MA, USA.

Wilber, K 1996, *A Brief History of Everything*, Hill of Content Publishing, Melbourne, VIC, Australia.

Wilber, K 1997, 'An Integral Theory of Consciousness', *Journal of Consciousness Studies* vol. 4 no. 1, pp. 71–92.

Wilber, K 2000a, *Integral Psychology: Consciousness, Spirit, Psychology, Therapy*, Shambhala, Boston, MA, USA.

Wilber, K 2000b, *A Theory of Everything: An Integral Vision for Business, Politics, Science and Spirituality*, Shambhala, Boston, MA, USA.

Wilkinson, P 1974, *Political Terrorism*, Macmillan, London.

Wilkinson, P 1986, 'Terrorism: International Dimensions', in *Contemporary Terrorism*, Facts on File, New York, pp. 29–56.

Williamson, GS & Pearse IH 1980, *Science, Synthesis and Sanity*, Scottish Academic Press, Edinburgh, UK.

Wilson, EO 1986, *Biophilia*, Harvard University Press, Cambridge, MA, USA.

Winn, W & Snyder, D 1996, 'Cognitive Perspectives in Psychology', in DH Jonassen (ed.) *Handbook of Research for Educational Communications and Technology*, Simon & Schuster, New York, pp. 112–42.

Winnicott, DW 1960, Ego Distortions in Terms of True and False Self, in *The Maturational Processes and the Facilitating Environment*, International Universities Press, New York.

Winnicott, DW 1969, *Child, the Family and the Outside World*, Penguin Books, New York.

Winter, DD 1996, *Ecological Psychology: Healing the Split between Planet and Self*, Harper Collins Publishers, New York.

Woltmann, L 1936, *Politische Anthropologie*, Domer Verlag, Leipzig, Germany.

Yale Center for Environmental Law and Policy, *Environmental Sustainability Index*, viewed 10 April 2005, <http://www.cies. org/dicators/ESI.html>.

Ymparistoministerio Ministry of the Environment, 2000, *Sustainable Development Indicators for Finland*, viewed 10 April 2005, <http://www.ymparisto.fi/eng/ envirosustdev/dicat/ds2000.htm>.

Yirmemahu, SCAM.COM, 15 June 2005, viewed 1 July 2005, <http://www.scam.com/ showthread.php?t=3389>.

Zander, W 1989, *Neurotische Körpersymptomatik*, Springer Verlag, Berlin.

Zimmerman, ME 1994, *Contesting Earth's Future*, University of California Press, Berkeley, CA, USA.

Index

9

9/11 · 3, 11, 259, 276

A

Abram · 48, 159, 293
Abu Ghraib prison · 102, 113, 173
abuse of animal rights · 16
academic research · 48
ADD/ADHD · 147
addictions · 88, 108, 125, 133, 190, 215, 242, 259, 271, 285
  reduced levels of · 190
addictive behaviour · 149, 209, 253
adult learning · 257, 296, 297, 306, 308
advertising industry · 25
Agenda 21 · 229, 230, 235, 305
Ahmad · 178, 293
AIDS · 15, 21, 148, 149, 150, 151, 152, 157, 210, 298, 306, 313, 315
Aikido · 264
Aitken · 57, 293
alcohol · 1, 118, 133, 150, 184, 203, 244, 261, 263
Alexander · 25, 126, 127, 143, 293, 296, 297, 303
alexithymia · 142, 256, 257, 260
Ali · 91, 179, 293
Allen · xvii, 297, 301, 306, 314, 315, 317
Almaas · 114, 293
Alterman · 12, 293
alternative states of consciousness · 32
American Way of Life · 102
analogical thinking · 129
Anderson · 31, 32, 72, 293, 295
Anna Freud · 93
Anthony · 48, 293
anthropocentrism · 42, 94, 120, 121, 140, 207
Anzul · 298
Aronson · 68, 293, 298, 308

arteriosclerosis · 137
Ashton and Laura · 141
Asmus · 304
atomism · 15, 105, 168
Australian Aborigines · 168
Australian Yearbook of Statistics · 145, 293
Averroes · 165
Axis of Evil · 100, 139

B

Baader-Meinhof group · 177
Bache · 277, 293
Baginski · 264, 293
Bahne-Bahnson · 145, 293
Balaton Group · 235
Banerjee · 293
Barbato · 17, 301
Barrows · 161, 169, 293
Basch · 90, 293
Bazerman · 298
BBC News · 141, 293
Bechtel · 48, 113, 294
Beck · 50, 51, 54, 174, 185, 294
Beder · 274
behaviour towards the environment · 69, 94, 106, 203, 204, 281, 282
Behavioural technologies · 200
behaviourism · 10, 44, 66, 71, 129, 199, 200, 294
  criticism of · 200
behaviourist and cognitive psychology · 203
behaviourist psychology · 7, 15, 43, 65, 66, 67, 198, 271
Bell · 294
Berger · 294
Bergquist · 129
Beringer · 143
Berkowitz · 176, 294
Berry · 14, 122, 164, 186, 187, 294, 315
Bertalanffy · 19, 38, 92, 126, 200, 294
biology · 34, 38, 253, 267
Blackburn · 40, 57, 294

Blanden · 314
Blum · 178, 294
Boadella · 59, 88, 106, 155, 158, 160, 166, 294, 295, 309
Bodhisattva · 57
body contact · 9, 88, 95, 103, 107, 109, 148
bodyoriented psychotherapists · 88
bodyoriented psychotherapy · 141
bodywork · 118, 157, 160, 167, 217, 282, 310
Bookchin · 40, 294
Bossel · 238, 239, 240, 294
Bowlby · 158, 169, 295, 310
Boyd · 258, 295
Boyd and Myers · 258
Boyesen · 25, 88, 94, 135, 141, 157, 158, 166, 209, 264, 295
Bradley · 122, 295
Braeutigam · 150, 295
Braud · 31, 32, 295
breastfeeding · 109, 242
breathing · 32, 88, 94, 108, 128, 148, 152, 154, 155, 156, 161, 167, 171, 244
Breggin · 85, 88, 295
Brookhiser · 180
Bucke · 163, 295
built-in obsolescence · 18
Bush · 2, 12, 173, 278, 293, 295, 311
Bush AdministrationA · 173

C

Cahalan · 220, 295
Cameron · xvii, 120, 137, 295, 302, 312
Campbell · 171, 295, 304
Capra · 254, 255, 295
Carey · 40, 295
Carpenter and Kinzig · 190
carrying capacity · 119, 149, 234
Carson · 1, 13, 295
Catholicism · 55, 163
Cattier · 255, 295
cause-and-effect thinking · 21
Center for Psychology and Social Change · 47
Chaplin · 57, 295
Chomsky · 72, 79, 178, 179, 295

Christian · 121, 122, 150, 164, 295
Christian belief · 122
Christian faith · 121
Christian worldview · 122
Churchman · 48, 294
Clayton · 38, 296
Clinebell · 48, 103, 220, 222, 223, 296
cognitive psychology · 7, 8, 38, 43, 45, 72, 76, 203, 212
cognitivism · 45
Cohen · 143, 296
Coleridge · 220
colonialism · 46, 123, 183, 298
community development · 34, 256, 303
Community-Based Social Marketing · 256
comparative physiology · 38
compensatory self-stabilising activities · 190
complexity theory · 21
computer-related terminology · 45
Conger · 166, 296
Conn · xvii, 5, 48, 60, 61, 103, 183, 220, 221, 296
consciousness · 50, 52, 53, 62, 94, 126, 131, 163, 165
   and spiritual, physical, and ethnic roots · 160
   archaic stage of · 53
   based on body-mind and person-planet unity · 161
   Buddhist notion of · 59
   communitarian · 52
   expansion of · 134, 189
   four expressions of · 56
   magic stage of · 53
   magical animistic · 52
   mental stage of · 54
   mythical stage of · 53
   relevants notions on · 50
consciousness development
   five stages of · 53
consciousness paradigms · 30
consciousness transformation · 55
constructionism · 76
consumerism · 95, 110, 137, 145, 152, 177, 186, 210, 213, 229, 231, 233
   as creative process · 186
   unbridled · 145
Corbin · 34, 315
Cort · 151, 298

cosmic consciousness · 129, 163, 165
cosmic purpose ethics · 43
cosmic streamings · 160
Cowan · 50, 51, 54, 185, 294
Cranton · 257, 258, 296, 297, 301, 313
Crayton . 178, 296
critical theory · 34, 79
critical thinking · 73
Csikszentmihalyi · 296
cultivation of ecological consciousness · 216
culture-nature dichotomy · 27, 47
Cunningham · 296
Cushman · 85, 296

D

Dahlke · 25, 126, 129, 146, 150, 296, 297
Daloz · 257, 296
Dark Ages · 162
Darwin · 20, 162
Davies · 176, 177, 180, 296, 312
Davis · 45, 296
de Martino · 300
De Saussure · 297
De Young · 45, 297
Dean · 55, 296
decadence · 185, 279, 317
deconstructionist thinking · 82, 207
deep breathing · 244
Deep Ecology · 41, 42, 185, 205, 216, 217, 218, 297, 313
Deep Ecology Platform · 42
deep eco-self consciousness · 192, 197
defence mechanisms · 24, 25, 35, 83, 85, 89, 92, 93, 94, 101, 106, 209, 212, 281, 285
deforestation · 3, 99, 132
Deikman · 59, 134, 259, 296
demands of our modern society · 142
DeMause · 87, 92, 97, 115, 176, 177, 253, 296, 297
denial of limitations · 116
depersonalisation · 136
depression · iii, xiv, 5, 137, 150, 151, 245, 274, 275, 289
Depth psychology · 46, 89, 207, 211, 213, 217, 269

Derrida · 79, 212, 297
de-schooling · 204
desertification · 3, 132
desktop research · 32, 34
destructive behaviour towards the natural environmen · 19
destructive behaviour towards the natural environment · 43
Dethlefsen · 25, 126, 127, 129, 130, 134, 143, 144, 146, 150, 215, 297
Devall · 42, 166, 218, 297
development · 9, 83
development aid · 227, 228
development of the self · 214
Diamond · 20, 61, 187, 290, 293, 297
Diekmann · 203, 297
Diesenberg · 100
Diesendorf · 100, 266, 297, 306
Dilthey · 297
Dirkx · 258, 297, 306
disowned feelings · 136
Doerner · 88, 297
dog defecation · 202
dualistic worldview · 138
Durning · 25, 111, 114, 149, 298
Dychtwald · 25, 94, 102, 128, 134, 167, 298

E

Eagly · 66, 67, 201, 298
Eccles · 274
ecoalienation · 222, 223
ecofeminism · 41, 42, 43, 185, 216, 218, 300
ecological consciousness · 42, 60, 203, 216, 302, 315
and sustainable behaviour · 203
ecological footprint · 146, 149
ecological philosophy · 7, 34
ecological psychotherapy · 34
ecological thinking · 28, 76, 226
economic exploitation · 16, 149, 176, 227, 276
ecopsychology · 47, 293, 295, 296, 298, 299, 300, 301, 305, 307, 310, 312, 313

eco-self · 6, 8, 34, 40, 56, 57, 61, 62, 65, 66, 67, 71, 72, 76, 83, 126, 145, 154, 155, 159, 161, 169, 173, 184
  higher levels of · 154
eco-self consciousness · 6, 8, 56, 66, 67, 72, 76, 154, 161, 187, 190, 192, 193, 218, 224, 254, 272, 273
  first level of · 190
  higher levels of · 196
  manipulative · 67
  sixth level of · 154
eco-self XE "eco-self" development · 34
eco-self experience · 40
eco-self transformation · 71, 126, 186
eco-self-development · 73, 155, 169, 204
Ecotherapy Newsletter · 255, 298
ecstasy · 155, 160, 162, 163, 165, 298
education for sustainability · 9, 48, 73, 76, 77, 78, 81, 210, 226, 315
education for sustainable development · 8, 15, 73, 75, 76, 80, 81, 252, 273
Education for Sustainable Living · 11, 196, 252, 260, 273
effects of electromagnetic fields · 36
effects of homelessness · 45
egocentric consciousness · 9, 23, 30, 31, 65, 86, 125, 126, 137, 139, 191, 221, 272, 277
  creation of · 199
  deep roots of · 200
ego-directed world · 136
ego-self consciousness · 8, 29, 50, 62, 63, 64, 133, 190, 195, 197, 268, 272
  currently dominant · 190, 195
Ehrenfels · 39, 47, 298
Eisner · 252, 298
Ekins · 227, 298
electrosmog · 1, 141
Eliade · 187, 188, 298
Elias · 252, 298
Ellner · 151, 298
Ely · 298
embodied feelings · 118
Emery · 77, 79, 212, 298
emotional and psychosocial sustainability · 22, 242, 278
emotional literacy · 255, 256, 257, 260
emotional underpinnings · 280
Encyclopedia Britannica · 122, 176

Endangered Species Act · 2
energetic streamings · 158, 160, 244
Engelmann · 113, 298
Enlightenment · 162
environmental catastrophe · 244, 276
environmental destruction · 45, 94, 103
environmental education · xvii, 6, 8, 9, 14, 34, 48, 59, 72, 73, 74, 75, 76, 77, 78, 80, 81, 82, 188, 197, 203, 204, 205, 206, 207, 210, 211, 218, 226, 263, 284, 298, 299, 301, 303, 310, 312, 315
  and cognition · 8
  and co-operation between teachers · 207
  and ecological education · 218
  and eco-self consciousness · 72
  and educating young people · 77
  and ESD · 75
  and knowledge · 203
  and radical ecopsychology · 34
  and sustainability · 48, 226
  based on cognition and conventional science · 74
  based on natural science · 76
  conventional approaches to · 78, 263
  deconstructionist approach to · 76
  empowering attitudes · 9
  in schools · 8
  inclusive approach to · 77
  limited effectiveness of · 206
  narrow approaches to · 284
  postmodern approach to · 9, 207
  present approaches to · 205
  progressive approaches to · 197
  term first used · 73
  various approaches · 34
Environmental Footprint Index · 237
environmental psychology · 7, 43, 45, 48, 294, 296
environmental stimuli · 45
Environmental Sustainability Index · 237, 241
environmentalists · 34, 73, 175
environmentally damaging behaviour · 206
Enzensberger · 76, 298
epistemology · 7, 11, 38, 48, 127, 155, 183, 210, 271, 305, 311
Erikson · 146, 177, 298
ESD indicator framework · 11

esoteric thinking · 7, 34, 128
European Union · 148
Everett · 300
Evernden · 39, 43, 159, 298
evolutionary thinking · 21
exoteric thinking · 131
experiential eco-self consciousness · 193, 194, 196, 272
exploitation of the natural environment · 125

F

Fairbairn · 199, 298
Fairbridge · 297
Fanon · 178, 298, 299
fate · 62, 297
feedback loops · 39, 86
feelings · 28, 31, 59, 84, 98, 103, 160, 212, 222, 223, 257
  and addictive habits · 56
  defences against unconscious · 56
feelings towards the environment · 280, 284
Feigenbaum · 72, 299
feminism · 42, 43, 311
feminist research methods · 32
Ferster · 68, 299
Fien · 78, 79, 212, 299
Finger · 5, 229, 299
Fisher · 5, 39, 47, 48, 85, 103, 114, 136, 162, 220, 299
Flew · 57, 299
Fox · 5, 48, 58, 160, 164, 299
free will · 91
Freire · 204, 257, 299
Freud · 55, 58, 83, 86, 87, 93, 95, 97, 128, 160, 166, 168, 172, 212, 219, 299
Friedman · 298
Friend · 299
Frodeman · 27
Fromm · 63, 64, 84, 136, 139, 175, 299, 300
Full Transference Interpretation · 265

G

Gaard · 42, 43, 300
Gaia theory · 39
Gallopin · 237
Garner · xvii, 298
Gates · 304
GDP · 131, 236, 241, 316
Gebser · 50, 53, 54, 57, 145, 185, 300
Geller · 66, 69, 202, 300
gender inequality · 16
gene-mediated · 36
General Systems Theory · 38, 92, 223
genetic defects · 27
genetics · 34
Gergen · 35, 76, 77, 80, 144, 208, 209, 213, 300
Gestalt philosophy · 39
Gestalt psychology · 39, 44, 47, 265, 305
Giesecke · 204, 300
Gilbert · 299
Glaser · 34, 300
Glendinning · 183, 300
global sustainability · 196
globalisation · 3, 81, 112, 148, 153, 178, 186, 230
Gnostic tradition · 160
Goethe · 219, 220
Gomes · 5, 39, 42, 48, 57, 110, 111, 143, 149, 293, 295, 296, 298, 300, 301, 305, 307, 310, 312, 313
Goodlad · 74
Goodman · 188, 204, 300
Gough · 77, 78, 79, 210, 212, 252, 299, 300, 301
Grabov · 258
Great Depression · 274, 275, 289
Greenall Gough · 78, 299
Greenway · 47, 220, 301
Grof · 160
Grounded Theory · 34
Gugerli-Dolder · 206, 301
Guntrip · 170, 301
Gurr · 176, 177, 301

H

habitat loss · 45
Haeckel · 129
Hakomi · 59, 306
Hamilton · 111, 297, 301, 306
Hammond · 185, 301
Hardin · 70
Harms · 47, 301
Harner · 188, 301
Hart · 77, 79, 210, 212, 309, 312
Harvard Medical School · 47
healing · 205, 211
   practice of susbsituting · 143
healing journeys · 22, 31, 159, 202, 259, 273
healing process · 138
Heard · 187, 300
Hegel · 40
Heinze · 188
Heisterkamp · 88, 301
Henschel · 146, 301
Herman · 178, 301
hermeneutics · 7, 34, 37
Hern · 146, 301
Heron · 252, 301
Hil
   and outward-oriented beings · 204
Hill · 1, 2, 5, 14, 40, 41, 48, 63, 84, 87, 89, 90, 104, 105, 214, 301, 302, 303, 309, 317
   and adapted self · 199
   and aspects of sustainable living · 214
   and body and mind · 41
   and childhood experiences · 253
   and child-rearing · 87, 105
   and compensatory mechanisms · 89
   and core self · 90
   and domination of humans by humans
      and active participatory democracy · 87, 303, 309, 317
   and emotionally and psychosocially supportive environments · 256
   and environmental influences · 105
   and external stimuli · 63
   and human self-development · 168
   and inadequate parenting · 104
   and inner and outer-oriented living · 131
   and knowing our essential nature · 253
   and mutualistic versus individualised experiences · 63
   and psychosocial catastrophe · 14
   and social change · 41
   and Social Ecology · 40
   and superficial change · 234
   and terminology · 41
   and the School of Social Ecology and Lifelong Learning · 254
   and University of Western Sydney · 40
   monitoring our extinction · 2
   on emablement · 197
   onnurturing and emotional holding · 233
Hillman · 29, 221, 303
Hitler · 97, 123
HIV-virus · 21
Hobbes · 294
Holdgate · 172, 303
holistic eco-self consciousness · 192, 193
holistic epistemology · 38
holistic nature of perception · 39, 47
Holistic thinking · 37, 38, 39, 172
Holland · 193, 293, 303, 311
Holling · 190, 303, 307, 316
Hopkins · 298
Hubbard · 177, 303
Huckle · 76, 77, 79, 80, 207, 210, 212, 213, 226, 303, 314
Hudson · 176, 178, 303
Hunnicutt · 143, 303
Husserl · 40, 304
Huxley · 200, 304
Hyam · 124, 304
hypnoidal states · 32

I

Illich · 204, 304
Imel · 258, 304
imperialism · 12, 125, 176, 178, 227, 314
indigenous peoples · 138

individual healing journeys · 202
industrial production · 140
industry · 2, 4, 25, 35, 97, 99, 282, 286
   and sustainability · 286
   changes to systems · 282
instrumental value theory · 43
interdisciplinary approach · 78
internal streamings · 128
interpretations
   of religious texts · 37
intrinsic value theory · 43, 58
IUCN · 73, 74, 228, 232, 304, 315
IUCN/UNEP/WWF · 74, 228, 232, 304

J

James · xvii
JanMohamed · 123, 304
Jason · 202, 304, 308
Jaynes · 162, 304
Johnson · 83, 88, 106, 107, 108, 114, 115, 165, 170, 172, 181, 212, 304
Jones · 21, 30, 89, 132, 197, 200, 304
Jordan · 50, 304
Josselson · 105, 106, 168, 253, 304
Jung · 20, 22, 53, 126, 159, 188, 212, 304

K

Kagan · 304
Kals · 4, 66, 305
Kalweit · 188, 305
Kanner · xvii, 5, 39, 42, 48, 57, 110, 111, 143, 149, 293, 295, 296, 298, 300, 301, 305, 307, 310, 312, 313
Kaplan · 155, 305
Kaposi sarcomas · 157
Kasl · 305
Kasl and Yorks · 252
Keating · 230, 305
Keleman · 106, 305
Kennedy · 250
kerbside recycling · 74
Kernberg · 114, 305
Kirk · 185, 186, 305, 317
Kirkman · 18, 305
Klein · 129, 296

Knutson · 176, 177, 296, 305
Koestler · 129, 305
Kohler · 47, 305
Kohut · 59, 90, 104, 105, 115, 145, 305
Kolb · 188, 189, 258, 305
Kovan · 306
Kovan and Dirkx · 257
Kovel · 85, 92, 306
Krieger · 276, 277, 306
Kubzansky · 137, 306
Kuhn · 29, 306
Kulesa · 66, 67, 201, 298
Kum Nye · 156, 160, 244, 264
Kurtz · 59, 306
Kvale · 28, 77, 306, 311
Kyoto Climate Change Accord · 278
Kyoto Protocol on global warming · 2

L

lack of freedom · 16
Lake · 297
Lamarck · 17, 306, 314
language · 179
language of the body · 128
language-mediated social and formal learning · 36
Lasch · 85, 114, 116, 143, 306
Lauer · 253, 306
Lauritsen · 150, 298, 306
learned eco-self consciousness · 191
Learning ecology · 254, 302
Learning for Sustainable Living · i, ii, viii, 194, 196, 214, 252, 259, 260, 266, 287, 288
Leveson-Gower · 228
Leweson-Gower · 306
Liedloff · 108, 306
limits of language · 28
Lindley · 314
Livingston · 39, 164, 306
Logan · 143, 307
Lopez · 174, 307
Loughlin · 258, 307
Lovelock · 39, 307
love-power conflicts · 30
Lowen · 25, 83, 88, 94, 106, 114, 117, 118, 119, 120, 136, 167, 209, 307

Ludwig · 28, 190, 307

M

Mack · 47, 307
Macy · 15, 48, 59, 103, 220, 223, 224, 307
Madsen · 207, 215, 308
Mahler · 103, 104, 169, 308
Mahood · 53
Manfield · 93, 116, 308
manipulated eco-self · 191
manipulated eco-self consciousness · 197
manipulation at symptom level · 202
Mann · 165, 308
Margulis · 17, 39, 308
Marini · 316
Martin · 295, 302
Maslow · 160, 308
materialistic disorder · 220
Matese · 202, 304
Mathiesen · 179, 308
Matthews · 61, 84, 308
May · 204, 239, 300, 301, 304, 306, 307, 308, 311, 313
McDougall · 25
McKenzie-Mohr · 256, 308
McMichael · 150, 308
MDMA · 165
Meadow · 38
Meadows · 238, 241, 308
meditative states · 32
Merleau-Ponty · 39, 40, 308
Mesmer · 166
Metzner · 5, 48, 55, 57, 121, 122, 129, 138, 193, 206, 224, 259, 308, 313
Meuse · 143, 307
Meyer · 124, 308
Mezirow · 257, 308
Middle Ages · 29
Milbrath · 79, 212, 308
Miller · 105, 308, 312
Mindell · 130, 308
Moehring · 204, 206, 309
Moldan and Billharz · 238
Monbiot · 119, 309
Montessori · 220, 242
Moore · 64, 95, 155, 159, 165, 258, 309

more-than-human environment · 279
Morse · 294
Muck · 187, 309
Mulligan · 309
Multiple Sclerosis · 21, 27
Mumford · 19, 309
Murphy · 88, 309
muscular armour · 25, 128, 136
muscular armouring · 128
Muslim countries · 178
Myers · 258, 295

N

Naess · 4, 101, 119, 166, 205, 309
narcissistic condition · 114, 116, 118, 120, 152, 180
natural desomatisation · 166
natural sciences · 23, 37, 138, 208
Nau · 316
Neill · 204, 309
Neisser · 79, 309
Nemiah · 309
neoteny of human beings · 164
New-Ageism · 216
Newshour · 150
nicotine · 35, 203, 263
non-exploitative science · 42
non-linear thermodynamics · 21
North Korea · 91, 100
Noyes · 164, 310

O

O'Connor · 310
O'Riordan · 310
O'Sullivan · 310
Object relations theory · 103, 104, 105, 167, 168, 172, 183
objective truth · 63, 192
occupation of Iraq · 102
oceanic streamings · 183
Oelschlaeger · 22, 207, 208, 215, 310
operant conditioning · 44, 68, 199, 200
Orbach · 199, 310
Orr · 78, 106, 310
O'Sullivan · 310

other-than-human environment · 62, 69, 70, 83, 137, 159, 278
Overbeck · 126, 127, 310

P

paganism · 217
painful childhood memories · 93
Palmer · 73, 232, 310
Paracelsus · 166
paradigm of economic growth · 8, 73
Parenti · 178, 310
participative eco-self consciousness · 190, 191, 192, 194, 197
Paul · 294, 304, 308, 311
Pavlov · 44
Pearlstein · 178, 310
Peckham Experiment · 255
Pelletier · 187, 310
Pepper · 19, 310
Perls · 39, 310
personal healing · 61, 202, 205, 264, 273, 282
personal healing process · 202
personal self-regulation · 107, 244
personal sustainability · 132, 245, 260, 261, 264, 270, 279, 282, 283
perspectivism · 7, 34, 35, 36, 37
Pestalozzi · 204, 220, 311
phenomenology · 7, 34, 39, 40, 304, 308
physio-emotional cycles · 140, 141, 142, 153
physio-emotional self-regulation · 36, 93, 149, 156
physio-emotional streamings · 160, 162, 205
physio-emotional sustainability · 32, 233, 244
physio-emotionally sustainable lives · 202
Piaget · 72, 79, 306, 311
Pierrakos · 88, 311
Pilger · 40, 311
planetary healing process · 22
Platt · 70, 311
Plog · 88, 297
Plumwood · 217, 311
Polkinghorne · 221, 311
Pollmann · 17, 28, 36, 85, 139, 311

pooper-scooper modelling · 202
Pope and Rauber · 2, 240
positive reinforcement · 44
positivist paradigm · 19
Post · 176, 178, 304, 311
postmodern psychology · 7, 44, 48, 76, 78
postmodernism · 214
  and social discourses · 28
  constructionist · 215
  constructive · 216
  critique of constructive · 216
  deconstructionist · 36
  variety of · 28
    and social discourses · 28, 36, 207, 208, 214, 215, 216, 306, 311
Preisendoerfer · 203, 297, 311
Prochaska · 86, 311
pseudo self-esteem · 26
Psychodrama · 265
psychological underpinnings of worldviews · 29
psychosocial separation · 138
psychosomatic illness · 10, 15, 87, 88, 149, 210, 215, 242, 278
Psychosomatic medicine · 26, 127, 293
psychosomatic thinking · 127, 128
psychotherapy · 303, 311, 314, 317
  alternative · 217
  and counselling · 282
  and nature · 222
  and neurosis · 89
  and object relations · 105
  based on individualistic pathology · 221
  healing aspect of · 220
  healing from traumatic experiences · 153
  modern · 221
  theory and practice in · 220
  traumatic experiences in · 6, 31, 34, 56, 59, 89, 105, 141, 153, 157, 167, 188, 197, 220, 221, 222, 241, 282, 293, 303, 306, 311, 313, 314
psychotropic drugs · 178, 184

Q

qualitative research · 298, 315

R

radical ecopsychology · 34
Ramakrishna · 166
Rappaport · 299
Ratcliffe · 38, 296
Reason · 17, 29, 296, 312
recreational drugs · 150, 261
Regier · 174, 307
Reich · 25, 83, 87, 88, 92, 93, 94, 106, 136, 158, 160, 167, 199, 209, 212, 219, 255, 294, 295, 308, 309, 311, 312
Reiki · 264, 293
Renaissance · 29
Reps · 112, 312
Resilience Alliance · 190
Richter · 278, 279, 312
Robottom · 77, 79, 210, 212, 301, 312, 315
Roderick · 137, 312
Rolland · 166
Roman Empire · 185, 186
Roszak · 5, 47, 137, 146, 164, 204, 217, 220, 221, 293, 295, 296, 298, 300, 301, 305, 307, 310, 312, 313
Rothenberg · 101, 119, 205, 309
Rousseau · 204, 220, 312
Rove · 12
Russell · 312, 317
Rycroft · 87, 92, 95, 101, 312

S

Sachs · 152, 227, 229, 230, 299, 312
Sardar · 180, 312
Sattmann-Frese · 150, 313
scarcity metaphor · 148
schizoid-terrorising condition · 10, 107, 159, 170, 171, 172, 173, 175, 176, 182, 183, 184
Schrauth · xvii, 88, 313
Schroll · 47, 48, 197, 309, 313

Schumacher · 14, 19, 295, 313
Schur · 155, 166, 167, 313
Schwarzenegger · 278
Scott · 255, 258, 300, 313
Scull · 45, 48, 313
seasonal food · 284
seed production · 3
self-knowledge · 204
Sells · 258, 313
Sennett · 173, 304, 313
separation of body and mind · 136
Sessions · 4, 42, 101, 119, 218, 297, 313
Shamanism · 259, 298
Shapiro · 48, 85, 220, 222, 313
Sharamon · 264, 293
Shem and Surrey · 233
Shepard . 5, 164, 187, 313
Shields · 17, 240, 313
Siegelman · 134, 135, 313
Sifneos · 142, 257, 313, 314
Simmons · 123, 314
Simon · 79, 230, 305, 308, 314, 317, 318
Sinclair · 183
Skinner · 44, 66, 68, 70, 198, 199, 200, 295, 299, 314
Skolimowski · 19, 314
Smart and Waldfogel · 174
Smith · 39, 40, 216, 298, 308, 314
Smuts · 38, 314
social and economic inequality · 16
Social Change Media · 256
social Darwinism · 2, 148
social ecology · 7, 15, 18, 27, 34, 35, 185, 216, 218, 265, 302, 303
  and interrelated fields · 34
  and sustainability · 18
  and viewson our ecological crises · 27
Social ecology thinking · 15
social psychology · 44
social sciences · 138, 161, 295, 317
social-reformist approach to ecological change · 8
Socrates · 54
soil erosion · 148
solar panels · 232
Solter · 233, 314
somatic psychotherapy · 34
somatic channels of communication · 28

somatic psychotherapy · 59, 167, 222
Sonoma State University · 47
Spada · 203, 314
Spiral Dynamics · 50, 51, 52
Spretnak · 30, 37, 38, 96, 122, 162, 186, 214, 215, 218, 219, 314
stable sense of self · 164
   importance of · 28, 161, 164, 207
Stallibrass · 253, 255, 314
Staunton · 88, 314
Steele · 17, 86, 314
Steiner · 204, 242, 314
Steinmetz · 298
Sterling · 77, 78, 79, 210, 211, 212, 226, 303, 314
Stettbacher · 234, 314
Stevenson · 74, 77, 210, 315
Stoddard · 123
Strauss · 34, 293, 300, 312, 315
streamings · 156, 160, 161, 167, 268, 295
Strub · 150, 315
subject-object dichotomy · 168
substance abuse · 47
subtle streamings · 120
Sufi tradition · 160
Suskind · 12
sustainability indicators · 1, 2, 3, 235, 236, 237, 238, 239, 241, 242, 295
Sustainology · 11, 226
Suzuki · 47, 300, 315
Swimme · 186, 187, 315
symptoms as symbolic expressions · 26
system of production · 36
systems thinking · 38, 39, 126, 154

T

Tai Chi · 244
Tanner · 77, 294, 315
Taoism · 112, 131, 187
target audience · 201
Taylor · 258, 302, 308, 315
Teller · 88, 297
terrorism · 3, 10, 101, 113, 175, 176, 178, 186, 271, 295, 296, 301, 303, 308, 311, 312, 317
   acts of · 181
   analyzing the causes of · 177
   and colonialisation · 179
   and lack of empathy · 179
   and primary narcissism · 178
   and USA's arrogance · 179
   committed by the West · 179
   decontextuialising · 178
   definitions of · 179
   depth psychology interpretation of · 10
   fight against · 184
   global battle of · 177
   multiple causal factors of · 178
   nations supporting · 123
   objectives of · 176
   phenomenon of · 175
   psychological explorations of · 177
   reactive · 180
   root causes of · 176
   socio-psychological aspects of · 176
   state and reactive · 181
   understanding of · 182
   Western state · 182
terrorism and imperialism · 125
theory of human existence · 37
theory of indeterminacy · 21
thinking · 28, 213, 214
Tilbury · xvii, 77, 210, 232, 315
Time Magazine · 137
tissue armouring · 25, 94, 142, 167
tobacco industry · 35
Tolstoi · 204
total transference interpretation · 265
toxic substances · 142
Trainer · 4, 75, 315
transgressing duality consciousness · 30
transpersonal consciousness · 59
transpersonal psychology · 5, 7, 15, 18, 27, 31, 34, 35, 41, 44, 158, 159, 160, 205, 215, 260, 270, 271
Transpersonal research methods · 31, 295
tuberculosis · 148, 149
Tulku · 156, 160, 264, 315, 316

U

Uexkuell · 25, 126, 143, 316
UNCED · 228, 230, 299

unconscious compensatory behaviour · 18
unconscious feelings · 20, 23, 25, 46, 48, 56, 83, 85, 96, 128, 188
unconscious feelings and motivations · 20, 23, 25, 46, 84, 188
unconscious motives and feelings · 142
UNESCO · 15, 73
uniformitarianism · 219
unio mystica · 55, 129, 163
United Nations Development Program · 14
United Nations Environment Program · 14, 228
University of Western Sydney · xvii, 41, 252, 254, 302
unmanageable emotional pressure · 93
unmanageable feelings · 167
unsustainable lifestyle · 150

V

Van den Bergh · 250, 316
Van Matre · 252, 316
VanHouten · 69, 316
Ventura · 29, 221, 303
Verny · 168, 316
Vertical learning · 188, 189
Vester · 146, 301
visceral sensations · 134
Volk · 77, 316
von Helmholtz · 162
Von Uexkuell · 143

W

Wachtel · 110, 316
Walker · 64, 165, 190, 307, 316
Wallraff · 113, 298
Washington · 157, 299, 303, 304, 310, 315, 317
Watkins · 179, 317
Watson · 44, 68, 233, 254, 302, 317
Watts · 15, 60, 64, 135, 136, 155, 159, 163, 317

WCED · 228, 317
Weigel · 126, 146, 317
Wendt · 88, 297
Werner · 200, 201, 317
Western societies · 10, 41, 50, 56, 59, 62, 83, 204
White · 121, 296, 299, 306, 310, 314, 317
Whitehead · 19, 317
Whitney · 185, 186, 317
whole-person learning · 41
Wilber · 5, 50, 51, 54, 59, 164, 185, 216, 317
Wilkinson · 178, 317
Willamson and Pearse · 253
Wilson · 233, 254, 263, 302, 309, 317
Winn · 79, 318
Winnett · 300
Winnicott · 104, 199, 223, 318
Winter · xvii, 5, 39, 44, 45, 46, 47, 48, 56, 61, 70, 83, 92, 94, 98, 101, 102, 103, 110, 114, 116, 117, 136, 209, 220, 230, 267, 318
wise use of resources · 8, 73
Wissenschaft Unzensiert · 141
Wittgenstein · 28
Woltmann · 123, 318
Wordsworth · 220
World Bank · 14, 64, 227, 241
World Conservation Strategy · 74, 232
World War II · 113, 150
worldviews · 29, 34
Wuppertal Institute · 235

Y

Yoga · 55, 70, 160, 163, 264, 282
Yorks · 305
Young · 45, 74, 297, 298, 306

Z

Zen · 112, 113, 160, 163, 300, 312
Zimmerman · 216, 217, 318
Zolik · 202, 304

Made in the USA
Lexington, KY
12 October 2012